GET BACK

The Beatles' *Let It Be* Disaster

by

Doug Sulpy and Ray Schweighardt

Helter
Skelter
publishing

This edition published in 1998 by Helter Skelter Publishing
4 Denmark Street, London WC2H 8LL

Published in 1997 by St. Martin's Press, incorporated under the title *Get Back: The Unauthorised Chronicle of the Beatles "Let It Be" Disaster*.

First published in the United States of America by *The 910 Magazine* as *Drugs, Divorce and a Slipping Image*.

A CIP catalogue record for this book is available from the British Library.
ISBN 0 900924 12 9

Cover and book design by Mick Fish and Dave Hallbery at SAF Publishing.

Front cover photograph Corbis, copyright © 1970, United Artists Corporation.

Printed in England by Redwood Books, Trowbridge, Wiltshire.

The author would like to thank the following for knowingly or unknowingly contributing in some way to this project:

Glen Banks, Anne Bergsma, Tom Brennan, Andrea Bucchieri, Eric Clark, Bob Clements, U.K. Dave, Al Fontana, Mario Gianella, Ted Greenwald, Arno Guzek, Jim Hilgenberg, Rich Hochadel, Melissa Hunter, Hiroshi Kawauchi, Adrian Last, Mark Lewisohn, Chip Madinger, Massimo Mere-galli, Rodney Morgan, Steven G. Nordhougen, Bob Purse, Randy Remote, Pierpaolo Rizzo, Richard Royston, Steve Shorten, Lynn Sulpy, Takashi Watanabe, Thom Whetston, Dave White, Andrew F. Wilson

And the various people we've invariably forgot

Introduction

January, 1969, the month of The Beatles' "Get Back" sessions, is the most misunderstood and misrepresented period of their career. In interviews for their *Anthology* project even the three surviving Beatles showed that they have an inaccurate memory of events that took place during this time. Ironically, this was the most well-documented month of the group's existence, with virtually every moment of their time together captured on audio tape which now, nearly thirty years later, allows us a fly-on-the-wall perspective of this key period in Beatles' history. Granted, not all of the moments described in this book are revelatory, but buried amongst the light chat and sometimes tedious rehearsals lie the answers to the question "why did The Beatles break up?"

Before we begin, though, let's introduce the cast of characters.

The years of playing second-class Beatle had created a very deep, bitter resentment in George Harrison. The respect he received from fellow musicians such as Bob Dylan and Eric Clapton could not be found within his own band. His new compositions were routinely derogated and rejected by John Lennon and Paul McCartney, even though some were far better than their own. In addition, by January, 1969, George found yet another person ahead of him in the Beatle pecking order, as Yoko Ono involved herself (with John's blessing) in the group's affairs. This would contribute to George's abrupt departure midway through these sessions.

Ringo Starr had temporarily left the band himself during the sessions for *The Beatles*. He arrives at most of the sessions sounding tired and miserable. Apart from expressing his aversion to performing outside of England, Ringo expresses virtually no opinion on any of the important issues facing the band.

Despite any revisionist claims to the contrary, John's all-consuming relationship with Yoko had a huge detrimental effect on his relationship with the rest of The Beatles. 'Heightened awareness,' one of the many concepts that John shared with Yoko, drove a deep wedge into the band, as John was now convinced that verbal communication was not necessary for people as tuned-in as themselves. John and Yoko's heavy drug use during this period further alienated them from everyone else as John vacillated between silent boredom and bubbling nervous energy depending on the time of his last fix. His creativity at a career low and his ability (or desire) to rationally communicate nearly gone, John spends most of the "Get Back" sessions hiding behind the facade of 'the witty Beatle.'

John's unspoken abdication as leader of the group (which had evolved over time and was now complete), coupled with the death of manager Brian Epstein, had forced Paul to assume the uncomfortable role of decision-maker for the band. Even so, Paul was the only one truly *happy* to be a Beatle, and is willing to go to great extremes to save the group. The common portrayal of Paul as an excessively bossy, egocentric bully during this period is simply erroneous and unfair. It's only the moribund behaviour of the other Beatles that makes Paul's assertiveness stand out.

Despite their unhappiness and bitterness, George, John and Ringo all desire to keep the band alive, but destiny seems to be working against them, and as the sessions wear on the end becomes more and more inevitable. What drove the most popular and prolific rock and roll band in history to its disintegration? What happened? How did it fall apart?

Welcome to the "Get Back" sessions.

In large part, the "Get Back" project was doomed from the start. It had been conceived by Paul in late 1968 as a reaction to the in-fighting that the group had experienced throughout the sessions for their album *The Beatles*. Apparently, Paul felt that a return to live performances would refocus and invigorate the band. He envisioned the band playing three December shows at The Roundhouse in London. When these plans failed to materialise, he decided that the group should perform a single concert in January (at an undetermined site) for a live, worldwide television broadcast. He also decided that the rehearsals for the concert should be filmed to be used in a documentary that would precede (and therefore promote) the live broadcast. Consequently, The Beatles found themselves rehearsing on a huge soundstage at London's Twickenham Studios - the same place they had filmed *A Hard Day's Night* five years earlier.

Most of the crew hired to film and record these sessions had recently worked together on another television extravaganza, The Rolling Stones' *Rock and Roll Circus*. Michael Lindsay-Hogg, an American with an impressive resumé, was taken on as director. Michael had previously worked with The Beatles on various promotional films, most recently those for "Hey Jude" and "Revolution." Although Michael's ideas for the documentary do not match Paul's, he does have a very keen awareness of the importance of the events that were unfolding before his cameras, and thankfully strove to record far more audio material than could ever be used in the documentary.

Glyn Johns, whose initial role was to oversee the sound of the television broadcast, found himself acting as the Beatles' personal sound engineer, recording their rehearsals for playback and appraisal. Once serious recording commenced at Apple, George Martin (whose earlier role would have only been to work with the multi-track tapes of the live broadcast) resumed his familiar role as Beatles' producer (although this was occasionally assumed by Glyn).

Tony Richmond and Ethan Russell, two more members of the *Rock and Roll Circus* alumni, serve as head cameraman and still photographer, respectively. Denis O'Dell, the project's producer, occasionally stops by the sessions as do Neil Aspinall and Derek Taylor, long time employees and friends. Almost always present is Mal Evans, who has been the group's stage manager almost since their beginning. Mal is more of a flunkie than a friend, performing any number of menial tasks whenever a Beatle calls his name. Kevin Harrington has the unenviable position of assistant flunkie.

Yoko is consistently present at John's side. Ringo's wife, Maureen, stops by on several days, as does Paul's girlfriend and eventual wife, Linda Eastman. Linda's daughter, Heather, is also brought to one of the sessions at Apple.

Finally, we have Billy Preston, an American keyboard player who sits in with the band during most of the later sessions.

Unfortunately, we did not have access to every recorded moment of the "Get Back" sessions. In addition, some days are very well represented on the available tapes while others are not. Rest assured, however, that each of the performances logged in this book has actually been *heard* and studied by the authors.

The material in this book is divided into 20 chapters, each representing a day of the "Get Back" sessions. Performances and discussions concerning the dialogue are presented chronologically within each chapter, with each performance receiving a number, the prefix of which represents the date. Each performance is timed, and in the case of performances only available in truncated form, a '>' or '<' symbol is used in place of the parenthesis on either side of the time, indicating that one or both sides of the performance is incomplete.

Timings should be considered approximate due to speed fluctuations in the available source tapes. Stop-and-go rehearsals have been placed under one listing. Titles that appear in quotation marks (or with a generic indicator) are unidentified (and in a majority of instances unidentifiable).

Thursday January 2nd, 1969

The sessions begin on a large, open soundstage at Twickenham Film Studios, London. It is important to remember that at this time The Beatles view these sessions as rehearsals for a television concert, and not as preparation for a new album. Consequently, their performances are both unstructured and informal.

All of the recorded material from this particular day has come to light. "Don't Let Me Down," "Two Of Us" and "I've Got a Feeling" were all introduced and rehearsed during this session, and these songs dominate the day's work. Other original compositions included "Sun King," (later recorded for *Abbey Road*) "On The Road To Marrakesh," (recorded with a different set of lyrics as "Jealous Guy" on John's 1971 release *Imagine*) and early versions of "Dig a Pony," "Let it Down" and "All Things Must Pass" (the latter two recorded by George for his 1970 solo album *All Things Must Pass*), with the exception of "Don't Let Me Down" John is apparently unhappy with his current crop of unrecorded songs and hopes that The Beatles can come up with some rock and roll numbers.

The main topic of discussion on this day is the embryonic plan for a live performance (or performances). Paul, perhaps thinking of the promotional films for "Hey Jude" and "Revolution" which had been filmed there several months earlier, prefers to have the show take place at Twickenham, although he muses at one point that they might hold it outdoors. John feels that rehearsing in the middle of a monstrous soundstage doesn't make much sense, and suggests that a smaller room would be more appropriate. George seems lukewarm to the entire project, and complains about the acoustics in the large, open space. Despite these discussions, there is no attempt to make any firm decisions regarding the date or venue of the show.

2.1 DON'T LET ME DOWN (0.22<

A brief instrumental performance from John, more to warm up than anything else. Although technically not the beginning of the "Get Back" project (that honour goes to shots of assistants Mal Evans and Kelvin Harringion setting up The Beatles' equipment on the empty Twickenham soundstage about an hour earlier), this is the first recorded performance, captured on tape about 10:30 a.m.. John and George have probably just sat down (undoubtedly with Yoko Ono nearby), and are in the process of tuning their guitars. Paul and Ringo have not yet arrived. In this performance and for the following few minutes, George and John will informally play a number of their unrecorded compositions which were possibly seen at this point as candidates for more serious rehearsal.

2.2 ALL THINGS MUST PASS >0:26<

George plays a rough version of one of his recent compositions as John tries to follow along. George is singing, but his voice is nearly inaudible since the vocal microphones are not yet set up.

"All Things Must Pass," a beautiful song, is clear evidence how George's songwriting skills had progressed by this point. Although the song will be given extensive rehearsal during the Twickenham sessions, it will never be properly recorded by The Beatles. Instead, George will use it as the title track on his first post-Beatles release.

2.3 DONT LET ME DOWN >3:00)

Considering the informal nature of the performances at this point, this version of "Don't Let Me Down" hangs together relatively well, although the song is far from finished. John gives a spirited vocal performance, and George sings along on the chorus (their vocals are now miked). Midway through the song, Ringo (who's just arrived) joins in on drums and does a credible job. The performance stumbles near the end because George doesn't know what to play. Consequently, John makes a brief attempt to teach him an ending.

"Don't Let Me Down" will be rehearsed quite a bit throughout this first day. Early demo tapes of the song which predate the "Get Back" sessions indicate that it was, like many Beatles songs, composed in stages. In the 1968 tapes, all of the various elements of the song are present *except* the title hook.

It should be noted that "Don't Let Me Down" is John's first choice for serious rehearsal, rather than other unfinished numbers from the previous year, such as "On The Road to Marrakesh," "A Case of The Blues," "Across The Universe" or "Dig a Pony." Perhaps John preferred to work on a song which referred to his relationship with Yoko Ono rather than his waning interest in spirituality.

Following the performance, George and John wish Ringo a happy new year and John asks Yoko if she's given George a copy of his fictitious diary (for a detailed discussion of this see entry 8.1). Ringo leaves his drums to join the others for their morning tea. George notices that a member of the "Hare Krishna" religious sect is present, and he and John greet him. John briefly mentions that he'd prefer a smaller rehearsal space (he'll return to this topic a bit later - see entry 2.22) and George complains about the acoustics.

2.4   DIG A PONY (2:21)

In order to give the others a taste of another one of his new numbers, John plays a solo version of "Dig a Pony." George interrupts at one point to ask what the title is, which suggests that he has never heard the song before. This loses something as a performance when John stops singing in order to illustrate the chords, but it is still passable.

The three Beatles then discuss Eric Burdon's reunion concert with The Animals which had occurred the previous month. John mentions that he likes the new Animals' recent single "Ring of Fire."

2.5   "EVERYBODY GOT SONG" (0:39)

John improvises five lines of this brief number before turning back to "Don't Let Me Down."

2.6   DON'T LET ME DOWN (3:10)

As he begins another perfunctory run-through of "Don't Let Me Down," John jokes that all of his songs use the same chords. As he continues to play, George half-jokes that the film crew should wait until the afternoon to film them, after they've spent the morning becoming acquainted with the songs.

2.7   LET IT DOWN (1:59)

An excellent performance from George, playing an abbreviated version of his own composition, which is seriously marred by John's distracting accompaniment on guitar. John jokes about the complexity of the "Let It Down" chords, prompting George to attempt to teach him a few. In the course of John's comment, he mentions a time frame of three weeks for the rehearsals. This is an approximation. In November of 1968, The Beatles had announced a series of three concerts to be held in mid-December at London's Roundhouse Theatre.

Shortly thereafter, the date was moved to January, 1969. As the year began, January 15th or 18th were announced as tentative dates, and the venue announced as undecided.

"Let it Down," a Harrison original, was written the previous year. Although it's a fine song, it was never properly recorded by The Beatles. It did, however appear on George's 1970 solo album *All Things Must Pass*, in much the same arrangement as here.

2.8   LET IT DOWN   (0:31)

George plays a few more chords from "Let It Down," while singing out the title of "Don't Let Me Down." George is unhappy with his guitar and requests a screwdriver, presumably to adjust its intonation.

2.9   (IMPROVISATION)   (0:47)

A repetitive instrumental guitar riff from John.

2.10   BROWN-EYED HANDSOME MAN   (0:32)

John performs two verses of this lively Chuck Berry number, with George singing along at several points. Both John and George have moved away from their mikes. This performance is preceded and followed by more tuning and riffs.

Like many musicians, The Beatles often began their sessions by running through a series of familiar tunes, in this case a cover version of Chuck Berry's 1956 classic.

Ringo, who's sitting around listening to John and George play, decides he wants a cigarette. George loans him a lighter.

2.11   I'VE GOT A FEELING   (0:59)

This performance has a pleasant, gentle breeziness which is generally lacking in later arrangements. John is still singing off-mike, and there are quite a few discordant notes throughout the song because George doesn't know what to play. Less than half way through the song, John suddenly stops.

This brief performance is interesting because John has evidently reverted to his conception of the song before Paul began to work on it with him (prior to these sessions). In its final arrangement, "I've Got a Feeling" features two distinct parts, sung (and, in fact, composed) by Paul and John respectively. John deviates from the familiar arrangement and begins this performance with his own lyrics, using a variant of Paul's part as a chorus. When The Beatles actually begin rehearsing the number about a half hour later, Paul incorporates his part, and the song is substantially as we know it.

2.12   A CASE OF THE BLUES   (0:40)

This is almost an instrumental performance, with only one audible line from John. It dissolves towards the end into tuning.

"A Case of the Blues" is a Lennon composition which was never properly rehearsed or recorded, perhaps because it bears a distinct resemblance to the Lennon/McCartney song "Drive My Car."

2.13   (IMPROVISATION)   (0:32)

John plays a variation on the chord pattern for "I've Got a Feeling." This improvisation is not really a song, but merely some repetitious rhythmic picking.

2.14   (IMPROVISATION)   (0:32)

John and George break into a brief blues instrumental.

Although we've classified this as a song, it's such a common blues progression that it would be impossible to pin a definitive title on it.

2.15   ON THE ROAD TO MARRAKESH (1:50)

John and George run through this Lennon original, which they obviously know quite well. John sings two verses, with George joining in for several lines and the chorus. Both of their vocals are slightly off-mike. The song almost breaks down before the second verse, as John takes a few seconds out to tune.

This song would later be re-recorded under the title "Jealous Guy" for John's 1971 album *Imagine*, with lyrics completely different from those that we have here. It was originally composed for the album *The Beatles* during the group's 1968 sojourn in India, but was never professionally recorded by them. Despite the fact that John called this song "I'm Just a Child of Nature" in his 1980 *Playboy* interview, we've chosen to title it "On the Road to Marrakesh" based on his reference to it during the January 3rd session.

John's eventual abandonment of this lovely tune in favour of less melodic compositions such as "Dig a Pony" and "Dig It" falls into line with his continuing preference during the "Get Back" sessions to work on harder-edged material. It's also possible that he abandoned the song because the lyrics reminded him too much of The Beatles' experiences in India the previous year, which he had publicly disavowed by this time. This last theory is supported by an alteration in the first line of the song between this performance and an existing 1968 demo, where the place name has been changed from Rishikesh (India) to Marrakesh (Morocco).

As the performance winds down, George notes the absence of familiar recording studio equipment.

2.16   REVOLUTION (0:07)

A brief, loping guitar riff from John's 1968 composition. John suggests that they write some up-tempo numbers (most of his unrecorded compositions at this point were not really rockers). He supports his suggestion by playing a riff from "Revolution."

2.17   I SHALL BE RELEASED (1:51)

John's comment about writing rock and roll songs interrupts George in the process of singing the first line of this song. He begins again, however, with John occasionally joining in. Once again, most of the singing is done slightly off-mike. Although George has difficulty remembering the verses, this is still an enjoyable performance.

George would have known this Dylan composition from its inclusion on The Band's *Music From Big Pink* album, or Dylan's own demo which circulated as part of the "Basement Tapes" (for commentary on these, see 3.6). It was also a contemporary U.K. hit for The Tremeloes.

Following the performance, George reads out several song titles from the setlist of songs for The Beatles' last concert (at San Francisco's Candlestick Park, in August, 1966) which was (and still is) taped to the side of Paul's Hofner bass guitar.

2.18   SUN KING (2:20<

This competent performance is primarily a solo instrumental from John although someone (presumably Ringo) is tapping along through much of it. John softly sings over the music a couple of times.

Although it was never a serious candidate for rehearsal during these sessions, "Sun King" would be recorded later in the year for *Abbey Road*.

It's 11:00 am. George has probably just noticed the heat being generated by the film lights, and remarks upon this to John.

At this point we have a gap of 30-60 seconds while the film's soundman changes tape reels.

When the available tapes resume, Ringo is discussing the placement of his drum kit in relation to the other Beatles (a topic which will be returned to shortly). George laughingly blames the unsatisfactory arrangement on the roadies because they're now working during the day (like The Beatles, the assistants would have been used to attending late night recording sessions. These daylight rehearsals were necessitated by the requirements of the film crew). He also chats with long-time Beatles producer George Martin who was slated to oversee the multi-track recording of the live broadcast.

2.19   medley SUN KING / DON'T LET ME DOWN (3:39)

John (with George on harmony vocal) begins singing the words to "Don't Let Me Down" over a variation of the "Sun King" backing, which evolves into the recognisable melody of "Don't Let Me Down." Ringo goes back on drums during this performance. This performance consists primarily of the title "Don't Let Me Down" sung over and over, although John attempts the bridge several times as well. Paul arrives during this performance, and George wishes him a happy new year.

As the song concludes, George once again reads out the playlist for The Beatles' 1966 Candlestick Park concert which is taped to Paul's bass guitar. Ringo bashes his drums, and Paul remarks that the guitar is right handed, a reference to the fact that his early guitars were actually right handed models, strung backwards to allow him to play them (Paul is left handed). His Hofner bass was no longer used for studio recordings at this time, and was probably brought out of mothballs to rehearse for the live show because it was nostalgically considered his 'live' bass.

At this point, the sound was recorded by overhead boom mikes. These picked up extraneous dialogue 'live,' while the sounds of the instruments were picked up from The Beatles' amplifiers. Director Michael Lindsay-Hogg indicates that he'd like the band to turn down their amps so that his microphones can pick up their dialogue on tape. This somewhat surprises George, who hadn't realised their conversations were being recorded, and prompts Paul into a light-hearted warning as to what the tapes will contain.

2.20   DON'T LET ME DOWN (3:23)

John, impatient with conversation, begins to sing "Don't Let Me Down" as someone claps out the rhythm. The song comes near to breaking down as John works on the lyrics. As John and George continue to rehearse, Paul plugs in his bass guitar, and plays a few tentative notes. Then, perhaps to test his mike, he sings a few variant lyrics of his own changing the word 'me' in the title to 'him.' John picks up on this, and he and Paul sing a few bars this way, before John good-naturedly restores the original. Paul asks John what key the song is in, and he and George express concern because they're not in tune, John disagrees, and believes they're pretty near to concert pitch.

2.21   "THE TEACHER WAS A-LOOKIN'" (0:39)

This brief rock 'n' roll improvisation seems to have been inspired simply by the band's need to tune their guitars. The performance features a pulsating bass guitar line with bass drum accompaniment and even has backing vocals for a few bars. George paraphrases a few lines from Chuck Berry's "Johnny B. Goode" as a chorus.

John points out their visitor from the "Hare Krishna" sect and he and Paul reprise one of the jokes from their film *A Hard Day's Night* at his expense.

2.22   DON'T LET ME DOWN (0:14)

A brief instrumental reprise, played during conversation. This still has heavy undertones of "Sun King."

During this and the following two performances The Beatles have the day's first real discussion, conducted, it should be noted, in the breakneck, not quite articulate fashion which is their typical method of communication. The general topic is: why are we here, what are we doing, and who will be watching us? John is dissatisfied both with Ringo's physical distance from the other Beatles and the open soundstage at Twickenham, claiming that it's unnecessary for the film crew to rehearse the camera angles they'd be using for the planned television performance for a full three weeks (see entry 2.7 for discussion of John's three weeks time frame). Paul begins to defend the choice of an open sound-stage (which had evidently been his) and explains the benefit of rehearsing in a performance-like environment, although he indicates that he thought they would have had at least a couple of days without people watching them. He then suggests that they might get rid of the onlookers for a few days, or keep the open atmosphere as it is, if the others are agreeable. He follows up on this by indicating that it was his original intention to rehearse without an audience, until he realised that it would be good for the group to play in front of others. John observes that visitors will show up wherever The Beatles choose to rehearse, and suggests again that they consider a smaller rehearsal space, sizing off a portion of the soundstage to illustrate his point. George agrees, at least until they have a few songs under their belt, and John reiterates his desire that Ringo should be moved closer, so that the others can communicate with him. The topic of the conversation then changes from *here and now* to *what if*. John says that when they do open up the rehearsals for an audience, they can get a P.A. system. Paul's response to this indicates that his plan at the moment is for the television show to be broadcast from Twickenham. George enthuses about the possibility of obtaining a Binson echo unit, which the Beatles had used early on when they played at Germany's Top Ten Club. Both George and Paul worry about the acoustic side-effects of playing in a large, open area, and Paul suggests that there might be a smaller venue around somewhere which might be more suitable. The group then begins rehearsing, and little actually results from the various actions discussed here, except that Ringo's drum kit is moved closer to the other Beatles.

2.23   DON'T LET ME DOWN (0:06)

A continuation of the 'performance' begun in 2.22, timed separately here because of the intervening dialogue. Like the other, this is not a serious attempt.

2.24   SUN KING (0:19)

A short instrumental version with conversation over it.

2.25   MAILMAN, BRING ME NO MORE BLUES (0:17)

Paul plays the bass line from this 1957 Buddy Holly song during the discussion about P.A. systems, at one point managing to blend his conversation with a line from the song. As the performance ends, John asks Paul if he would like

to do a few of his numbers. When Paul politely demurs, John initiates a rehearsal of "I've Got a Feeling," in which Paul takes the lead.

2.26   I'VE GOT A FEELING (3:37<

After a rough start, Paul leads a relatively sincere rehearsal. John begins to
sing "I've Got a Feeling" much as he had earlier (see entry 2.11) but stops -
evidently having remembered that this is not the latest arrangement. In order
to illustrate the correct structure of the song, Paul sings the first verse, calling
out the chords to John and George at various points. The rehearsal breaks
down several times.

Even at this early stage, the light-hearted vocal call-and-response between
Paul and John which would characterise this song is evident.

2.27   I'VE GOT A FEELING >1:14<

A variety of guitar riffs and stray vocal lines which occur as John and Paul
loosely rehearse the descending guitar riff which occurs during the song's
bridge.

George asks an assistant for a copy of an unidentified mono mixdown tape,
presumably of tracks from Jackie Lomax's album *Is This What You Want?*
(see commentary following entry 2.32 for details).

2.28   I'VE GOT A FEELING >0:03<

A few guitar notes from the descending guitar break.

2.29   I'VE GOT A FEELING >0:05<

A bit of vocal harmony from John and Paul. Rehearsals of "I've Got a Feeling"
have now begun in earnest.

2.30   I'VE GOT A FEELING >12:23<

A continuation of 2.29 as the band continues a series of early rehearsals. Following a fairly coherent run-through, Paul works on an ending for the song.
John suggests that George play lead and Paul briefly switches to acoustic guitar to illustrate the middle eight and descending guitar riff. He then leads them
into another loose run-through starting at the middle eight. George asks about
the chords and they try again, this time instrumentally running through the
number. After this disintegrates, they turn in a more successful performance,
as Paul puts a bit more effort into his vocal. This falls apart at the end. Consequently, John restarts at the beginning of his verse, and they once again practice an ending for the song.

After they've finished, Paul asks if the film tape can be played back over the
P.A.. It can't (since a P.A. is not present), but it *can* be stopped so that Paul
can listen back on headphones. Obviously they take a few minutes out for him
to do this, since the recording cuts off at this point.

2.31   I'VE GOT A FEELING (0:47)

John, George and Ringo bash out this loose version of "I've Got a Feeling" as
Paul, Michael, George Martin and the project's producer Denis O'Dell discuss
the advantages of playing in a smaller space.

2.32   (UNKNOWN) (2:00)

As Paul and the others continue their discussion, the remaining Beatles run
through this disorganised, unidentified number. George is singing, but his
voice is barely audible.

Michael tries to steer the discussion into the possible venue for the live
show, but the others seem more interested in making plans for lunch.

At some point in the day - perhaps here - The Beatles took a significant amount of time off, possibly to scout for a better location.

The next available tape offers us a conversation in progress, as George asks the others if they like Jackie Lomax's album *Is This What You Want?* which he had produced and which featured instrumental accompaniment from himself, Paul and Ringo (among others). Although it wouldn't be released by Apple Records until the following March, the basic tracks had been completed by this time, and acetates given to individual members of The Beatles. John obviously hasn't spent much time with his copy, and admits to only having half-listened to one side of it.

2.33   SPEAK TO ME   (1:49<

Less cohesive than the timing might indicate, George performs a loose cover version of the lead off song from Jackie Lomax's album. Ringo accompanies him on drums.

2.34   I'VE GOT A FEELING   >0:28)

The available tape begins in progress. This seems to have part of a loose run-through which Paul interrupts. The miking here is significantly different from the earlier rehearsals. George's guitar is far too loud. John's vocal microphone is set too low, and Ringo's drums are less pronounced than earlier.

2.35   I'VE GOT A FEELING   (4:51)

The first three minutes of this constitute a relatively complete (though sloppy) performance. Significant progress has been made on the song, and The Beatles are now attempting to play it straight through. The alternating vocals between Paul and John are in place, as is the final contrapuntal verse. The performance finally breaks down because they don't have a proper ending for the song worked out. Paul suggests a temporary arrangement, of which they play a brief, improvisational variation.

Following this, George asks what the name of the song is. George might have been confused because "I've Got a Feeling" was assembled from separate Lennon/McCartney components, each bearing different titles. John suggests Paul's title ("I've Got a Feeling," corrupted to "I've Got a Hard On"), and Paul suggests John's ("Everybody Had a Hard Year" parodied as "Everybody Had a Hard On"). Paul jokingly adds "Except For Me And My Monkey" to the title (a reference to John's 1968 composition "Everybody's Got Something To Hide Except Me and My Monkey"), and George picks up on that reference by singing the first line of Bob Dylan's "Mighty Quinn (Quinn the Eskimo)" (see entry 2.37), which is similar.

2.36   I'VE GOT A FEELING   (0:06)

This brief parody of "I've Got a Feeling" is sung by John during the conversation above.

2.37   MIGHTY QUINN (QUINN THE ESKIMO)   (1:00)

A line from "I've Got a Feeling" reminds George of Bob Dylan's composition "Mighty Quinn (Quinn the Eskimo)" George sings the verse, and Paul takes over for a single chorus while John attempts to follow along on guitar, leading the performance to a tattered end.

"Mighty Quinn (Quinn the Eskimo)" was recorded by Bob Dylan in 1967 as part of a series of home recordings known as "The Basement Tapes," dubs of which were in The Beatles' possession. They were also undoubtedly familiar with Manfred Mann's hit cover version from 1968.

2.38   I'VE GOT A FEELING   (3:22)

This is another loose attempt to perform the song all the way through, which breaks down near the end. George not-so-tactfully suggests that part of "I've Got a Feeling" is a note-for-note copy of Otis Redding's "Hard to Handle." John and Paul agree, but don't place much importance on that fact, since the lifted material only constitutes a small part of the song.

Paul begins to sing again and the performance limps to an end. George's guitar is horribly out of tune. Paul and John then discuss the arrangement of the song's various elements.

2.39   I'VE GOT A FEELING   (1:55)

The Beatles begin the song at John's verse and follow with a ragged run-through of the polyphonic verse. As the performance slowly dies out, George repeatedly plays one of the song's riffs.

2.40   I'VE GOT A FEELING   (1:20<

A hard-edged blues jam on "I've Got a Feeling." John offers a repetitive riff (quite similar to what he would play towards the end of the January 7th session) while George punctuates the song with "I've Got a Feeling" riffs, Paul occasionally vocalises, and Ringo bashes out a steady rhythm on drums.

As the next available recordings begin, Paul is discussing the project with Michael and sound engineer Glyn Johns. The other Beatles are not involved although John can be heard in the background near the end of the dialogue

This would appear to be Paul's first opportunity to discuss the sound recording for these rehearsals with Glyn. As the tape begins, they're discussing the acquisition of further sound recording equipment, presumably to record the proposed live concert on multi-track tape. Glyn admits to not knowing the technical side of things and says that George Martin will be in charge of procuring the additional equipment. Michael asks Glyn where they acquired the sound equipment to record *Rock and Roll Circus* which they (and John and Yoko) had worked on the previous month. Paul expresses his reservations about the sound quality of the television show, and Glyn laughingly reminds him that the sound will only be as good as one's television set is able to produce. Paul persists, and relates his memory of the inferior sound on the British program *Cool For Cats*. Glyn and Michael have more good things to say about the sound quality of *Rock and Roll Circus*, and Glyn invites Paul to Olympic Studios to hear The Rolling Stones' tapes for himself. Paul backs off, preferring to stay at Twickenham, claiming that they can't really judge the sound there until all the equipment is set up and functional. To prove his point, he relates an interesting anecdote about the recording of John's 1968 composition "Yer Blues," which was recorded in a small room (actually an annex to studio two at E.M.I.). In that unlikely environment they were able to get an acceptable stereo recording. Michael is willing to go along with whatever the others want, and his ostentatious verbiage in expressing this amuses Paul and Glyn, who laugh and poke gentle fun at him. Annoyed, perhaps, he responds by making fun of Paul's board. This dialogue segment ends as Glyn enthuses about the prospects of recording outdoors.

The next tape fragment begins with Glyn and Michael enthusing about the prospect of The Beatles playing in a torchlit amphitheatre in front of 2000 Arabs. Paul quickly kills *that* idea by quite firmly stating that playing overseas is out of the question because Ringo refuses (although he does joke that they'll get around this by using Jimmy Nicol, who understudied Ringo for part of The Beatles' 1964 tour). Michael cautions Paul about making a decision so early in the game and suggests that they wait a few days before deciding. Paul reiterates Ringo's disinclination to travel overseas, and once again says no to the idea. The discussion then turns to the possibility of playing out of doors. Michael worries that it's too cold out (a reasonable concern, given that it's the dead of winter). Paul believes that the right arrangement of heaters can solve that problem. Michael responds that, even so, they have the rain to deal with (again, reasonable - this is England), but Paul doesn't mind playing in the rain - in fact, he seems taken with the idea, except for the fact that a few people would probably die from electric shocks.

Denis O'Dell, producer of the documentary-in-progress joins Ringo at the side of the stage to discuss the shooting schedule for *The Magic Christian*, which he is also producing. Ringo, who will co-star in the film, is under the impression that filming will begin on January 17th. Denis informs him that the start date has been pushed back to the 24th, apparently in part to accommodate Ringo's involvement in the project at hand. Ringo foresees spending only two weeks on the rehearsals and live performance, but Denis isn't so sure that things can be wrapped up that quickly. It's interesting to note that Ringo hasn't read any of the three *Magic Christian* script revisions that have been given to him. As Ringo and Denis converse, Michael speaks to Paul about the difficulty of acquiring good cigars. Paul points out that he has difficulty obtaining *his* vice - Scotch. Denis updates Ringo on the progress of the *Magic Christian* sets (which are being constructed at Twickenham). John can be heard in the background readying his guitar, so Ringo excuses himself to return to work.

2.41   I'VE GOT A FEELING (1:26<
A loose rehearsal of the middle eight, apparently performed just to get everyone re-acclimatised to their instruments. Just as they begin another performance the available tape cuts off.

2.42   I'VE GOT A FEELING (0:32<
After a break for tuning (with the inevitable stray riffs), George leads the band into a loose run-through. The available tape cuts off during the first verse.

2.43   I'VE GOT A FEELING >0:08<
A brief fragment captured on tape as a new slate is announced.

2.44   I'VE GOT A FEELING >1:23<
The band rehearses John's verse, but John's microphone is set too low. Paul calls for Mal so that the song's lyrics can be transcribed and distributed to the other Beatles.

2.45   I'VE GOT A FEELING (2:12<
Paul suggests some embellishments for George's guitar part and George responds with a series of riffs which builds into an instrumental performance. They then return to rehearsing John's verse.

Perhaps in response to Paul's direction of the rehearsal, George states that he would like to have the band get a basic knowledge of each of the songs rather than perfecting them one at a time. Paul agrees, but John would like another couple of attempts at "I've Got A Feeling" before moving on.

2.46   I'VE GOT A FEELING (4:02)

After some riffing and stray vocal lines, they take the song again from the top. This complete performance definitely reveals some progress and that the song's structure, still nebulous earlier in the afternoon, is now firmly in place.

2.47   I'VE GOT A FEELING (0:50<

A discussion of the various elements of the song (and their merit) spurs on this bass-heavy performance, led by Paul.

2.48   I'VE GOT A FEELING >3:54)

A continuation of the previous performance which breaks down into a long series of riffs. Mal returns with the transcribed lyrics, but The Beatles' interest in the rehearsal is waning and they offer only a loose instrumental perform-ance.

Paul's had enough and wants to move on, but John asks for one final at-tempt. George prefers taking home a cassette of the song and Paul suggests making a dub of the film tape. George questions the quality of a tape made from a single overhead boom mike, but Paul assures him that it's passable (in fact, the quality of the Nagra recordings are quite good).

2.49   medley SUN KING / DON'T LET ME DOWN (1:11)

With "I've Got a Feeling" set aside, John plays an instrumental bit of "Sun King," but begins singing "Don't Let Me Down" instead. George halts the performance to ask what his vocal role in the song will be.

2.50   DON'T LET ME DOWN (4:15<

John, Paul and George discuss the vocal arrangement of the song. Their brief discussion resolves very little, but leads into a performance (in which Paul and Ringo don't participate). John complains of not having an order for the song's various components. The performance starts again, and John once again begins interjecting "Sun King" elements shortly before the available tape cuts off.

2.51   DON'T LET ME DOWN (2:13)

The Beatles perform the chorus and then stop to discuss the instrumentation for the song. Both John and Paul would like to have a piano part, but are faced with a shortage of guitarists if Paul shifts from bass. Paul doesn't see this as a problem, and reminds John that one guitarist sufficed for the 1968 recording of "Julia." John responds that he desires a heavier sound than that for "Don't Let Me Down."

2.52   medley SUN KING / DON'T LET ME DOWN (1:18)

Once again a series of instrumental riffs underscores the conversation. This follows closely on the preceding fragment.

John and Paul decide the question of instrumentation by choosing to leave things as they are for the time being. They then begin to work on the structure of the song.

2.53   DON'T LET ME DOWN (6:41<

John is still unsure how the song's various parts should be ordered. Paul is ir-ritated and urges him to solve the problem so that rehearsals can continue. John and George continue to perform the song loosely as they brainstorm, and Paul envisions a counter melody for piano. Although a keyboard part would not be added to the arrangement for another three weeks, the idea of a counter melody (for voice, rather than piano) would resurface during the rehearsals on the 6th.

Although they've apparently agreed to give up the idea, The Beatles continue to discuss the possibility of a piano part for "Don't Let Me Down." George grudgingly volunteers to play bass in order to free Paul to play piano, but Paul decides that his ideas can be achieved with the current band configuration. They still consider adding someone for the show, and keyboard player Nicky Hopkins (who had played on their recording of "Revolution") is considered. George even suggests adding a stand-up bass player, but John and Paul don't like the idea.

The "Don't Let Me Down" rehearsal resumes and Paul (who hasn't been participating) joins in on tambourine. He then suggests that John drop a line he has been using as a tag for the chorus and that they sing the title twice to start the song off. As John dictates the lyrics to Mal (admitting their lack of meaning), Paul arranges the song's pieces into a logical order. These items offer a fascinating insight into Paul's contribution to a song that has long been considered one that John wrote on his own.

John admits that he didn't worry about the lyrics' meaning when he was composing them.

2.54   DON'T LET ME DOWN >0:21)
Nothing more than some instrumental riffs.

2.55   (IMPROVISATION) (0:39)
John plays this simplistic guitar instrumental as George, Ringo and Mal engage in conversation.

2.56   (UNKNOWN) (0:18<
Everyone contributes to this fairly cohesive performance. George offers a very brief and indecipherable vocal.

2.57   DON'T LET ME DOWN >3:04)
Unlike the previous "Don't Let Me Down" rehearsals, Ringo and Paul fully contribute here. Progress is evident, but uncertainty over the insertion of a short break before the verse causes the performance to break down.

2.58   DON'T LET ME DOWN (0:02<
A brief instrumental fragment.

Following this, we have a less-than-exciting exchange as The Beatles eat sandwiches and dry buns. John equates dry buns with rock cakes, and Yoko wonders if John wants some grapefruit (which is perhaps an attempt at humour, since *Grapefruit* is the name of a book she had written).

2.59   WELL...ALRIGHT (0:05<
George plays the first few notes of this 1958 Buddy Holly song before the available tape cuts off.

2.60   WELL...ALRIGHT >0:59)
A few more bars (obviously a continuation of the above) sung by George with heavy electric backing. George knows the chorus of the song, but little more.

It's 6:35 p.m. John offers to teach the others a new song, but this isn't acted on.

2.61   (UNKNOWN) (0:17<
A guitar riff from John coupled with a brief, indecipherable vocal from Paul.

2.62   ALL THINGS MUST PASS >1:24<
This is basically a solo performance from George, with only brief guitar accompaniment from John. After the first two verses the available tape cuts off.

Perhaps George was playing this in order to suggest it as the next song for rehearsal but evidently the group bypassed it and began work on "Two Of Us" instead.

2.63   TWO OF US (6:58)
Part of the first rehearsal session for Paul's song. After improvising a few lines to set the tempo, he leads the others through a preliminary run-through. This disintegrates into a long, rambling, stop and go rehearsal. Paul, playing acoustic guitar, is teaching the song to the other three. In certain spots he's calling out the chords and time changes, or vocalising the rhythm parts for Ringo. George is trying to follow Paul on electric guitar, with varying degrees of success.

2.64   "WE'RE GOIN' HOME" (0:17)
This brief bit of clowning is sandwiched between two extensive rehearsals of "Two Of Us." It's probable that this is nothing more than an improvised variation of "Two Of Us" which they're singing because they're about to go home.

2.65   TWO OF US (4:14<
After a short digression, the stop and go rehearsal continues. John makes his first attempt to harmonise with Paul.

2.66   TWO OF US >0:37<
The stop and go rehearsal continues.

2.67   TWO OF US >3:30)
The available tape begins at the first middle eight. Paul and George make some cursory attempts at harmonising, and Paul sings a number of joking references to Henry Cooper. Paul introduces the idea of performing the second middle eight in near double-time and they take the song from the top again, but it quickly breaks down.

2.68   TWO OF US >0:32<
A further rehearsal fragment. George's guitar is more prominent here, as he becomes more familiar with the song.

2.69   TWO OF US >0:05<
A brief fragment captured as a new slate is announced.

2.70   TWO OF US >0:55<
Paul is still singing but has stopped playing guitar, allowing John and George to carry the song. He observes that it's difficult to determine when the song's beat changes.

2.71   TWO OF US >4:36)
This rehearsal segment shows that the double-time middle eight will not fit into the song (indeed, the idea would be dropped from subsequent rehearsals). When the group performance breaks down, John sings a verse on his own, accompanying himself on guitar. Paul picks up his bass and leads the group through another run-through.

2.72   "IT'S GOOD TO SEE THE FOLKS BACK HOME" (0:16)
A brief number, evidently improvised by Paul, who backs himself on bass.

2.73   TWO OF US (4:44<
Paul mentions that he can't envision a bassline in the song, but despite this he continues to play. The song is coming together, but it's clear that the band members are becoming bored with rehearsing it. Paul proposes increasing the tempo, but no one is inclined to act on this since the session is about to end.

This is the final extant performance of the day, and it can be assumed that The Beatles went home shortly hereafter.

Friday , January 3rd 1969

On the second day of rehearsals things become a bit more structured. The Beatles organise their works-in-progress into what is jokingly referred to as a schedule (in actuality a collection of individual song lyrics attached to a clipboard) which at this point included George's "All Things Must Pass," John's "Don't Let Me Down" and Paul's "Maxwell's Silver Hammer" and "She Came In Through the Bathroom Window" (although no performance of the latter has surfaced from this day). Despite Paul's attempts to co-ordinate the rehearsals, The Beatles often ignore the new material in favour of oldies, ranging from old standards ("What's The Use of Getting Sober," "What Do You Want To Make Those Eyes At Me For", to '50's rock 'n' roll classics ("Blue Suede Shoes," "Crackin' Up," "All Shook Up"), performances of semi-contemporary songs by Bob Dylan ("Please Mrs Henry," "I Want You," "Blowin' In The Wind") and versions of their own songs ("Ob-La-Di, Ob-La-Da," "I'm So Tired"). Most interesting of all, perhaps, are a number of performances of Lennon/McCartney compositions from the dawn of their song-writing partnership. One of these, "One After 909," will be rehearsed throughout the "Get Back" sessions and included in the film and album *Let It Be*.

When The Beatles finally get serious, they attempt the first group performances of George's "All Things Must Pass" and Paul's "Maxwell's Silver Hammer." "Don't Let Me Down" and "Two of Us" are also rehearsed. Although they get along fine while they're jamming or playing oldies, they quickly get on each other's nerves when they attempt to seriously rehearse.

Some time is also spent discussing topics related to the live show, such as whether to include older songs or not, what type of audience it will have, and where it will take place.

3.1 ADAGIO FOR STRINGS >3:21<

A solo piano performance by Paul, who attempts to play Samuel Barber's 1938 "Adagio For Strings" on piano. Paul will return to this again briefly on January 8th and 10th.

It's 10:55 a.m.. Paul and Ringo are the only Beatles present as filming begins. As he would on several other occasions during these sessions, Paul takes advantage of the others' absence by getting in some early morning piano practice as the cameras roll. Despite the fact that the bass guitar is his primary instrument, Paul is very fond of playing the piano, and seizes the opportunity to play it whenever he can.

An edited version of this can be heard at the beginning of the film *Let it Be - heard*, not seen, since the sound and image do not correspond.

3.2 ADAGIO FOR STRINGS >0:45)

The conclusion of the previous performance. Although tapes have not become available, we do know that Paul also ran through "The Long and Winding Road," "Maxwell's Silver Hammer" and "Oh! Darling" during this early morning piano session.

3.3 TEA FOR TWO CHA-CHA (1:05)

Paul plays this upbeat little number on the piano while Ringo 'tap dances' by slapping his knees and provides percussion by tapping on his tea cup.

"Tea For Two" was originally composed in 1924 by Irving Caesar and Vincent Youmans. It's likely that Paul is remembering the U.K. pop hit that Tommy Dorsey had with a cha-cha rearrangement of the song in late 1958. Of course, the very title "Tea For Two" is also a topical reference.

3.4   TEA FOR TWO CHA-CHA (0:34)

Paul laughingly plays a bit of the same tune in an exaggerated fast tempo.

3.5   CHOPSTICKS (0:24)

A brief instrumental run-through of this standard piano novelty. Paul plays a poor rendition of this very simple tune.

The original title of this 1877 piece was "The Celebrated Chop Waltz," Composed by Euphemia Allen.

3.6   (UNKNOWN) (0:39)

A quiet piano number from Paul on which he vocalises softly.

3.7   "TODGY, TODGY, THE BATTERY BOY" (0:59)

Paul plays this simple, childlike little tune. Near the end, Ringo starts singing out the name Todgy in time with the music, and Paul sings out the title (twice) following up with a few lines of lyric.

Obviously, both Paul and Ringo are remembering the same song here. Since it's unidentified, though, we don't know if Paul has been playing the same song throughout.

3.8   WHOLE LOTTA SHAKIN' GOIN' ON (0:49)

Ringo joins Paul behind the keyboard, and the two perform a piano arrangement of Jerry Lee Lewis' 1957 classic. Paul's vocal can barely be heard. This runs right into the next performance.

3.9   (UNKNOWN) (0:35)

Another slow, solo piano performance from Paul.

3.10   LET IT BE (1:10)

Without hesitation Paul rolls into this unfinished composition. He sings the first verse and a bit of the chorus.

This brief performance is the earliest version of "Let It Be" to have become available. Its appearance here, without fanfare and amid some aimless piano tinkering, comes as a surprise.

3.11   (IMPROVISATION) (1:12)

Paul follows "Let It Be" with this repetitive piano instrumental. During the performance George arrives and apologises for having overslept. Paul and Ringo are unconcerned because John hasn't shown up yet either.

Paul resumes munching on the half-eaten apple that has been placed atop the piano (perhaps as a bit of symbolist humour for Michael's cameras) and apologises to Michael for not performing anything worthwhile during this extended piano session. Michael is unconcerned and says that he's happy just to have footage that he can lay any moody piano performance over. This is interesting, since Michael will in fact match the audio of 3.1 with the image of this performance when putting together the *Let It Be* film. The conversation then turns to *The Beatles Book*, a monthly publication for fans that Ringo has been leafing through. George complains that their age is beginning to show in the photographs.

3.12   TAKING A TRIP TO CAROLINA (0:34)

As Paul leaves the piano, Ringo takes over and sings a few lines from this work-in-progress. He'll return to it in a few minutes. In the background, George continues to talk to Paul about *The Beatles Book*.

3.13   (UNKNOWN)   (0:16)

Ringo takes over on piano and improvises a few seconds of this unknown number, mumbling a few lyrics in the process. He then evidently decides that plunking random piano notes is more interesting.

3.14   PLEASE MRS. HENRY   (1:07)

As Ringo meanders tunelessly on the piano, George plays guitar and sings a bit of this Dylan song, mumbling his way through a single half-remembered verse and chorus.

"Please Mrs. Henry" comes from Bob Dylan's "Basement Tapes" demos, which Dylan had recorded in 1967 (and which remained commercially unreleased until 1975). George had spent the previous Thanksgiving with Dylan, and probably acquired the material then, subsequently passing copies along to Ringo and (one presumes) the rest of the group. Ringo, at least, obviously hasn't spent much time listening to them, since he doesn't recognise "Please Mrs. Henry" as a Dylan song (he asks George if it's a blues number). George, a great admirer of Dylan, expresses his admiration for the tapes and enthuses about Dylan's lyrics.

3.15   "RAMBLIN' WOMAN"   (1:33)

Another solo acoustic song featuring George on vocal. Paul harmonises a bit in the background, and Ringo continues to plunk away tunelessly on the piano.

George's admiration for Dylan manifests in this gentle folk tune, reflecting Dylan's own early fondness for the adjective "rambling." The song's romanticism is decidedly un-Dylanesque, however, and the fact that, with some variations in the lyrics, it reappears at the session of the 9th suggests that George is the author.

3.16   "IS IT DISCOVERED?"   (0:37)

George continues to play acoustic guitar and sings this unfinished (or half-remembered) song. Virtually all of the lyrics are mumbled. It is possible that this is an early attempt at a middle eight for "Ramblin' Woman," but equally likely that it is a separate unfinished composition. In any case, this is the only known performance.

Paul, George and Ringo continue to discuss *The Beatles Book*, joking about how that publication retains a positive attitude about the band no matter what, and how they would do so even if one of The Beatles should land in jail.

3.17   (IMPROVISATION)   (0:16)

Another simple piano workout from Ringo, who is accompanied briefly by George on acoustic guitar. This resembles Cream's "As You Said" (from their 1968 *Wheels of Fire* album) but it's not played well enough to really be identified as *anything*.

In late 1968, Paul had begun to grow a beard. George and Ringo both compliment him on it, and Ringo jokingly addresses him as a sea captain. Paul is a little uncomfortable with this change of appearance however, but admits that this is characteristic of him. George has a more aggressive attitude about it, and firmly suggests to Paul that he keeps the beard until he makes up his mind about it. The conversation then turns back to a subject which had evidently been raised before the start of the available tape - namely, the live show. Someone has once again suggested the possibility of doing the show abroad, and George flatly rejects this idea. The previous day Paul had emphatically stated that Ringo refused to go abroad, effectively killing *that* idea (see 2.40). Since George, Paul and Ringo agree, there's not much point in further discussion, and George turns to another subject - the contemporary group The Band. He mentions that the members of The Band had lived together while recording their album *Music From Big Pink*, and expresses his great admiration for drummer Levon Helm (particularly his smile and profusion of whiskers) He then flatters Ringo by telling him that The Band's favourite track on The Beatles' latest album was Ringo's country and western tune "Don't Pass Me By" (playing a brief, illustrative riff in the process). Paul unthinkingly asks Ringo when he'll write another song, but quickly regrets his question (it took Ringo four years to write "Don't Pass Me By"). George says that *he* plans to write a song the following Sunday (as, in fact, he will), but the topic remains on Ringo's compositional skills (or lack thereof). Ringo expresses his frustration at songwriting. Paul empathises, understanding how hard it would be to write songs without much knowledge of chords. Both George and Paul then speak enthusiastically of one of Ringo's unfinished compositions which Paul would like to see rehearsed because it's an up-tempo number. Ringo chuckles at his own lack of musical prowess and, in response to Paul's request, begins to play.

3.18   PICASSO   (0:33)

This unusual performance and the one that follows are Starkey works-in-progress. As one would expect, they are extraordinarily simplistic both lyrically and musically, and, not surprisingly, they both went unused and unpublished. Ringo's still on piano, with Paul joining in on vocals at times, and George provides a loose guitar accompaniment. Ringo begins to sing the song in too high of a key. Paul corrects him, and Ringo starts the song over.

The lyrics of "Picasso" perfectly reflect Ringo's 'common man' public persona - someone unable to comprehend modern art. During an improvised piano duet between Paul and Ringo on January 14th Paul will recall these few moments by referencing a line from "Picasso." Other than that, this is the only available performance.

As Ringo introduces the next composition ("Taking a Trip to Carolina"), George asks him what key the song is in. When Ringo replies that it's in the same key as "Picasso," Paul jokes about Ringo having Carolina on his mind - a pun based on the title of the James Taylor song "Carolina In My Mind," which had been released by Apple Records a month before, and on which Paul had played bass.

3.19   TAKING A TRIP TO CAROLINA   (0:22)

Musically, this one's even simpler than "Picasso." Ringo can only remember two lines of the lyric, but mentions that he possesses a more complete demo recording. Coincidentally, one of the lines here mentions an ocean voyage. Five days later The Beatles will have serious discussions on this subject.

George is the only Beatle to appear uncomfortable in front of the cameras. The previous day he had expressed concern that Michael was recording their conversations. Now, he wonders aloud why anyone would bother to preserve The Beatles early morning tea and chat for posterity. Paul responds that it's good to have every aspect of the rehearsals filmed so that the documentary can follow the progression of the numbers from the earliest rehearsals to a finished product, comparing this to an artwork taking shape upon a blank canvas. The down side, which he also points out, is that the filmmakers will have recorded many hours of tedious rehearsal. He doesn't seem too concerned, though.

Also on the previous day, John had complained about a lack of up-tempo songs to rehearse. Now it's George and Paul's turn, as George explains that many of his songs are slow and Paul agrees that most of his are too. George recalls one of his songs, which he calls "Taxman Revisited" (i.e., equates it to his 1966 composition "Taxman"). Taking into account his description of the song, this would appear to be a reference to "Isn't It a Pity," which (as we'll learn through a conversation on January 26th) was also written in 1966. He then pokes gentle fun at the sombre nature of his work by playing a few illustrative chords as he facetiously sings an upbeat bit of lyric for Paul. But George's numbers aren't just slow. He also feels they'll be better off performed solo. Paul and Ringo enthusiastically agree, but at the very end of the conversation George backs off, and suggests that it would work as well with the others playing. There could have been a number of reasons for him to say this, but the bottom line is that George is still too insecure at this point to step out as a solo act, even within the context of The Beatles.

3.20   HEY JUDE (0:09)
George begins playing a song on acoustic guitar, but is interrupted as Paul sings out the title of "Hey Jude."

Paul asks if anyone has heard Wilson Pickett's cover version of that song. George hasn't, but is anxious to hear it, as well as Arthur Conley's cover of "Ob-La-Di, Ob-La-Da" (a record which, ironically, will be played on the set during George's self-imposed absence later in the month). Paul and George both express their happiness with the fact that Beatle songs are now being covered by artists that The Beatles themselves admire.

3.21   ALL THINGS MUST PASS (1:29)
John's absence allows George to present one of *his* candidates for rehearsal, as Paul takes over on Ringo's drum kit. George begins singing the song in too high of a key (much as Ringo had on "Picasso"), stops, curses at himself, and starts over again in a lower key as Paul offers a bit of harmony. The performance ends after one verse and a chorus, although Paul hardly seems to notice as he cheerfully bangs away on the drums.

3.22   DON'T LET ME DOWN (2:02)
As Paul continues to pound the drums, George moves to electric guitar and begins to play this loose instrumental version of "Don't Let Me Down."

3.23   CRACKIN' UP (0:24)
Paul and George perform a brief duet of the 1959 Bo Diddley song.

There's an obvious gap between this and the previous song, during which John has arrived. The Beatles have reclaimed their familiar instruments and filming has shifted to the 'group set' on the soundstage. Although tapes aren't available, we do know that The Beatles played an unidentified jam and instrumental version of "Crackin' Up" before the available tape begins.

Paul makes a comment about having more rehearsal space. Presumably this refers to the differences between the two sets, one of which had evidently not been used the previous day. John, perhaps because he's having his morning's tea, is notably quiet through the next few performances. Also present, in addition to the film crew, are George Martin (once again visiting the session), Mal and Yoko

3.24   ALL SHOOK UP (1:08)

George leads the band into another oldie. He and Paul share vocals, remembering about half of the 1957 Elvis Presley classic. Part way through the song Ringo decides to join in. George replaces the official second line of the song by extemporising a line about tea - an obvious topical reference. This performance segues into the next.

3.25   YOUR TRUE LOVE (1:40)

Paul and George continue as the primary vocalists, this time for a 1937 Carl Perkins tune. Like "All Shook Up," the performance is a bit loose but spirited, and everyone sounds like they're having great deal of fun. At times George's vocal is difficult to hear, probably because he's moving off mike.

3.26   BLUE SUEDE SHOES (1:30)

A slightly disjointed, but quite enjoyable performance, with distant vocals from John, Paul and George.

An interesting (and probably unintentional) juxtaposition of influences occurs in this and the previous two performances. "All Shook Up" is an Elvis Presley hit, "Your True Love" is a Carl Perkins tune, and this one is a song associated with them both, though the first recorded version was by Perkins in 1955.

3.27   THREE COOL CATS (2:07)

Paul starts off this cover of The Coasters 1959 novelty song. George sings lead vocal (as he had on the early Beatle performances) with help from John and Paul, but no one's paying much attention to staying on mike. The full performance is followed by a very brief reprise. Following this, John 'reads out' a series of mock requests from imaginary individuals and organisations for The Beatles to play "Walk Don't Run."

As will be shown on the 7th, The Beatles intended to preface their performances on the live show with dedications to public figures or fans, much as they had done in their early club appearances. 'The Bulldog Gang' and 'The Cement Mixer's Guild' (two of the clubs that John mentions) were actual early fan clubs. There is no known Beatles performance of The Ventures' "Walk Don't Run," from the "Get Back" sessions or elsewhere.

Both this and the following group of songs can only be described as silly - obviously The Beatles are not ready to get down to business yet.

3.28   BLOWIN' IN THE WIND (0:32<

An extremely off-the-cuff cover of Bob Dylan's 1963 classic, mercifully cut short by an edit in the available tape immediately after the start of the second verse. George and Paul share the lead vocal.

3.29   LUCILLE >2:24)

A fairly complete cover of Little Richard's 1957 hit. Paul is quite free with his vocal: his imitation of Little Richard's characteristic howl leads him into a series of dog noises, and during the instrumental break he vocalises the sax part. Nonetheless, the musicianship on everyone's part is reasonably competent.

3.30   I'M SO TIRED (2:14)

Paul takes the lead vocal on this Lennon composition. The lyrics are similar to those in the version released on *The Beatles*, except that Paul laughingly interjects a line about abstaining from alcohol (possibly a topical reference). George sings back-up. Again, despite the fact that Paul isn't taking his vocal seriously, the musicianship is competent. Inspired, perhaps, by the 'state of wakefulness' topic raised in "I'm So Tired," Paul lapses into a comic representation of someone (named Del) hooked on various drugs to control their state of consciousness. For the record, he mentions 'Emma' (a contemporary term for morphine) and 'seggy' (slang for Seconal, a barbiturate). By alternating the two, the drug-user would he caught in a vicious cycle of up-and-down. Paul ends this nonsense by quoting from The Beatles' song "Ob-La-Di, Ob-La-Da" which was currently number one on the British singles charts, performed by the group Marmalade.

3.31   OB-LA-DI, OB-LA-DA   (1:19)

Paul's Jamaican influenced bass line leads off this slightly off-colour (and substantially different) version of a song which originally appeared on *The Beatles*. John does most of the singing here, perhaps as a response to Paul's having taken the lead vocal on *his* song "I'm So Tired" a few moments earlier. Someone (perhaps George Martin) pounds out the rhythm on a tambourine throughout. Everyone is obviously having a great time, and John and Paul laugh their way through the performance.

It's interesting that John and Paul sing the same parody lyric simultaneously at one point; presumably they'd done this sort of thing before. It's also interesting to note that John's enthusiasm for this number is in marked contrast to his post-Beatle opinion of it, which was consistently negative. As the performance ends, Paul utters some bitter words about entertainer Jimmy Scott who publicly claimed that Paul 'stole' "ob-la-di, ob-la-da" from him (the phrase, not the song). The final line of the performance is a direct reference to Marmalade's recording which added a reference to jam to the song as a pun on their name.

3.32   "GET ON THE PHONE"   (0:46)

Paul begins to play a soul groove on bass, while pounding out the rhythm on the body of his guitar. Somewhere in the background a telephone rings, prompting John and Paul to extemporise lyrics (with Paul continuing to affect a Jamaican accent). John begins to play, but his amp no longer works, so he stops. Mal is called upon to help. Acting under explicit directions from George, he manages to track down the problem and fix it. It's worth noting the condescending tone George uses in speaking to Mal, their long-time associate and go-fer. When Paul begins to question the way their equipment is hooked up, George responds with a quote from Bob Dylan's "All Along The Watchtower."

3.33   OB-LA-DI, OB-LA-DA   (0:06)

This is nothing more than a brief bass riff, reprising 3.31.

3.34   DONT LET ME DOWN   (0:19)

Paul suggests that they rehearse "Don't Let Me Down," and sings a few lines from the song (again, with a lingering Jamaican accent) as John provides a loose accompaniment on guitar.

John asks Mal to retrieve the lyrics for "Don't Let Me Down." Meanwhile, Paul has been singing the song in a manner which reminds George of Fats

Domino's Creole accent. Paul admires the purple light being used as a back-drop behind the group, and jokingly refers to it as "Purple Haze" - the title, of course, of a seminal Jimi Hendrix number. John mutters about having to shave that night (as, indeed, he will) and he and Paul test their microphones. John makes a comment (inspired, it seems, by the silly accent he uses for his mike test) about the previous week's *New Musical Express* gossip column *Tail-Pieces By The Alley Cat*, which had asked: "have you heard John Lennon's amusing impression of Harold Wilson?"

3.35   THE THIRD MAN THEME   (1:47)

After a few tentative bars, The Beatles play an almost perfect rendition of this instrumental favourite.

"The Third Man Theme" (popularised in a film of the same name) was a hit in 1950 for Anton Karas. This was one of the songs in The Beatles' early live repertoire. John dedicates the performance to Ray Coleman, a journalist who worked for the British music publication *Disc and Music Echo*.

3.36   (IMPROVISATION)   (0:17)

Barely qualifying as a song, this starts out as a guitar riff, which Paul echoes on bass.

3.37   "MY WORDS ARE IN MY HEART"   (0:08)

A brief, four line a capella performance from John, leading directly into 3.38.

John pokes gentle fun at his inability to remember the lyrics to his own songs. Immediately thereafter, both Paul and George request the "Don't Let Me Down" lyrics as well. John improvises a nonsense song based around this subject, but Paul does him one better by introducing a fully-fledged nonsense number.

3.38   "NEGRO IN RESERVE"   (0:45)

John and Paul laughingly share vocals on this unusual up-tempo number which is possibly a parody of a real song. While it's tempting to read some kind of social meaning into this number, we must not lose sight of the fact that the lyrics here are basically meaningless, inspired in large part by the mention of holes (by George) and heart (by John), with the spectre of Jimmy Scott (who is black) still in the air. More than anything else, it sounds like a song parody - possibly a continuation of a trend begun a few minutes earlier with "Ob-La-Di, Ob-La-Da." The vocal styling here bears a distinct resemblance to Elvis Presley.

Some of the lyrical references in the song bear further examination - the use of the name Ted, for example. This could be short for 'Teddy boy,' British slang for an early '60's tough. Paul had written a song the previous year entitled "Teddy Boy" (which, like "Negro in Reserve," is *also* about a boy named Ted and his mother) which will be performed several times during these sessions. Then again, it could simply have been the first thing that came to John's mind that rhymed with head. The phrase "hole in the head" is also suggestive. In addition to being the catch phrase for a number of rock and roll songs from the 1950's, it brings to mind the topical interest in trepanning. This dangerous procedure involved drilling a hole in one's skull in order to attain a permanent high. This was of interest among the British counter-culture of the time, and would certainly have attracted someone with John's temperament.

3.39   DON'T LET ME DOWN   (1:44<

A relatively sincere effort on John's part. Paul vocalises a countermelody in the middle eight (an idea which he'll return to during the session on January 6th) although it's not clear whether this was meant for backing vocals, or to represent a potential guitar part. Ringo doesn't begin playing until the song is well under way.

It's around noon, and after a lengthy stretch of oldies and parodies to warm up, The Beatles finally begin to rehearse. They had worked the previous day in integrating the various elements of "Don't Let Me Down," and it's clear from this performance that quite a lot of progress had taken place. A day earlier, John had mentioned his desire to have a P.A. system. Someone acted fast and got one, but the speaker system isn't functioning. This (and the following entry) begin about a half hour of "Don't Let Me Down" rehearsals, most of which are not yet available.

3.40   DON'T LET ME DOWN >1:02)
This and 3.39 are part of the same performance (there's a gap between them in the available tape during which the tape can be heard spooling forward). Paul continues to vocalise, and John improvises a spoken interlude parodying his song "Happiness Is A Warm Gun," the original recording of which appeared on *The Beatles*.

John mentions that he'd like to emulate the peculiar guitar sound that George achieved in his song "Long, Long, Long" which appeared on *The Beatles*. John wasn't present for the "Long, Long, Long" recording session and assumes that George had used a fretless guitar. George informs him that he used his Gibson on that number, but that really doesn't matter - it isn't the specific kind of guitar that interests John, but the tone that it produced.

3.41   DON'T LET ME DOWN (0:03)
Paul sings part of a single line.

3.42   OB-LA-DI, OB-LA-DA (0:03)
John sings a single line of parody lyric.

3.43   GOING UP THE COUNTRY (0:06)
A one line version from Paul with a single note backing. George, Paul and Michael then discuss the American blues/rock group Canned Heat (who they may have seen on the previous evening's television program *Top of the Pops*), with particular praise for "Going Up The Country," their latest single.

3.44   ON THE ROAD AGAIN (0:05)
A one line performance from George with a loose guitar backing of this 1968 Canned Heat song.

3.45   ONE AFTER 909 >3:01)
Paul and John share vocals on a substantially complete but sloppy performance of this old Lennon/McCartney number. This is the first available performance of this song from these sessions.

"One After 909" was originally written around 1957, possibly under the influence of Lonnie Donegan's 1956 "Rock Island Line" which shares the same rhythm and theme. There are a number of unreleased early Beatles recordings of "One After 909" - two takes from early 1960, two from 1962, and an E.M.I. recording session from 1963. A comparison of these shows a progressive slowing down of the tempo, and a replacement of the simple skiffle-based beat with a full rock and roll arrangement. Interestingly enough, all of the 1969 performances of this song are closer to the 1960 arrangement than the 1963 studio session.

  Someone has obviously suggested prior to the beginning of this performance that "One After 909" could be the up-tempo number that they've been needing for the show. At the song's conclusion, both George and Paul express their enthusiasm and Paul nostalgically relates the history of the song. John appears slightly embarrassed about its lyrical shortcomings, however, and apologetically states that he'd always meant to rewrite the lyrics. Paul and George think it's fine as it is, and Paul in particular gushes on and on with boyish enthusiasm, enjoying this relic from the earliest days of the band. George shares this feeling, in his own way, as he first suggests that they practice it, but then warns that over-rehearsal will ruin it - a subtle indication of how he views the current rehearsals. This said, they work up to another runthrough, which is delayed when John leads them into another oldie.

3.46   "BECAUSE I KNOW YOU LOVE ME SO"   (2:27<

John leads them into this pleasant, country influenced number. John and Paul duet on this song, although John is a bit off mike. After the first verse, Paul stops for a moment and practices the title line a few times. He and John repeat the verse, after which George plays a Carl Perkins-style instrumental break. Paul then repeats the verse again by himself (with the exception of one line, which is shared by John). The song appears to be winding to a close as the available tape runs out. It's clear that "One After 909" has inspired John to recall this other unpublished early Lennon/McCartney song.

3.47   ONE AFTER 909   >0:31)

The end of a performance, joined in progress on the available tape. It has very much the same feel as the previous performance of this song (3.45), and is followed by a further discussion of the lyrics and background of "One After 909" which John, Paul and George continue to heap praise upon. George makes the somewhat disarming observation that listeners don't care about the words of a song as long as the tune is catchy. Several people are mentioned during the course of this discussion. Paul refers to his brother, Mike McCartney, and mentions Pete Shotton, an old friend and early member of John's group The Quarrymen, who would certainly have been around when this group of songs was composed.

3.48   "I'LL WAIT 'TIL TOMORROW"   (0:58)

Paul and John share vocals on another unpublished Lennon/McCartney original, which is even more country influenced than "Because I Know You Love Me So." They can only remember two verses, but perhaps that's all there ever were. Following the performance, George reflects that many of their early songs were influenced by country music. Paul agrees.

3.49   A PRETTY GIRL IS LIKE A MELODY   (0:06)

John sings a garbled version of the title of this 1919 Irving Berlin standard.

3.50   "I'VE BEEN THINKING THAT YOU LOVE ME"   (0:15)

George and Paul simultaneously sing this single line and then stop. This is probably another early Lennon/McCartney composition. Paul seems to lose interest in doing this one, or perhaps he can't remember the words.

3.51   "WON'T YOU PLEASE SAY GOODBYE"   (0:50)

Another early Lennon/McCartney tune. John and Paul sing what they can re-member from this one. After the performance, John admits to having lifted the song off of Sam Cooke's "Bring It On Home To Me."

3.52   BRING IT ON HOME TO ME (1:51)

Reminded by John of "Bring It On Home" George begins to sing it, and Paul and John join in. Even though none of them quite remember the lyrics to this 1962 Sam Cooke song, they obviously enjoy performing it.

3.53   HITCH HIKE (1:57)

George handles the lead vocal on this lively performance. John and Paul both go to falsetto for the chorus in emulation of the female backup singers found on Marvin Gaye's original 1963 recording.

3.54   YOU CAN'T DO THAT (2:14)

John, Paul and George share vocals on this version of a song from their 1964 LP *A Hard Day's Night*. At one point, George calls out the title to "Hitch Hike," perhaps in an unsuccessful attempt to lead the band back into that song.

When one listens to "Hitch Hike" followed by "You Can't Do That" one can easily hear the musical similarity between the two. Presumably The Beatles were thinking the same thing, and this is, perhaps, the continuation of a trend 'our songs and their influences' begun with "Won't You Please Say Good-bye" and "Bring it On Home."

3.55   HIPPY HIPPY SHAKE (2:27)

Paul recalls their attempts to remember a certain song, and settles on "Hippy Hippy Shake." This prompts a complete performance of this 1959 Chan Romero number. Paul is very enthusiastic, but has trouble remembering how the song goes, and actually stops the performance at one point to correct him-self. The Beatles performed the song extensively during 1962 and 1963.

Following the performance, George suggests that they have an attempt at "Two Of Us" before breaking for lunch. Paul is already displeased with the way that "Two Of Us" is progressing, but George encourages him. In this dia-logue exchange, we learn that during the previous day's rehearsal Glyn Johns had suggested that they perform the song with two acoustic guitars. We also get an insight into how Paul and John envision the planned live performance. Paul makes a reference to doing some forced on-stage patter (such as they had early in their career), but John feels they can be more natural with their audi-ence, as they were in their early days playing the Cavern Club. Paul agrees.

3.56   TWO OF US (1:15<

After tuning up with a series of "Two Of Us" riffs, Paul attempts to begin the rehearsal by playing the song straight through. Unfortunately, he doesn't have the words in front of him, and remembers nothing from the first verse. John isn't much better. The available tape cuts off during the middle eight.

Once again, only the beginning of the rehearsal is available. In this case, however, they only play the song for a short time before breaking for lunch.

3.57   SUN KING >0:17)

George laughs his way through a few bars of this very ragged instrumental, as Paul tunes up on bass.

It's now mid-afternoon, and John greets the others upon their return from lunch. Once again, Paul is impressed with the purple light being used as a backdrop behind the group. John has evidently been discussing the live show with Michael, and continues this topic as he makes the ludicrous suggestion that they have an audience of one, or at most one family, for the show.

3.58   (IMPROVISATION)   (0:24<

As John speaks, Paul plays a rock and roll bass line and someone bangs out a rhythm. This is a bit more focused than the usual stray riffs that occur during conversations, but is too generic to identify as a specific number.

3.59   (IMPROVISATION)   (0:37)

As the available tape begins, a second or two of music can be heard as George laughingly states how fine the (unknown) performance was. Immediately following this, John and Ringo launch into a repetitious jam. Towards the end, George begins whistling, which leads the band into the next performance. Paul suggests that they learn a new song, but no one responds.

3.60   SHORT FAT FANNIE   (2:48)

This cover of Larry Williams' 1957 novelty tune is one of the better performances of this session. George handles the lead vocal, with occasional help from Paul, and seems to remember almost all of the words.

Once again, Paul asks the others what they'd like to rehearse next. It's obvious he's trying to get the group off the oldies track, and back into serious rehearsal - not too forcefully, though, since he enthusiastically joins in on the next group of cover versions.

3.61   MIDNIGHT SPECIAL   (2:02)

John leads the band into this traditional folk tune. Paul sings along and they have a great time even though they remember hardly anything but the chorus.

"Midnight Special" is a traditional East Texas prison work song, popularised in America by Huddie 'Leadbelly' Ledbetter, and later interpreted in England by Lonnie Donegan, who is the influential artist here. John mixes up the words, but at least he's consistent, repeating the same mangled verse twice.

3.62   WHEN YOU'RE DRUNK YOU THINK OF ME   (0:12)

George starts this one off, and sings a few garbled lines. Paul laughs and he and John jump in, but George stops performing because he can't remember the song. This is reportedly a cover of a song originally performed by The Dubliners.

3.63   WHAT'S THE USE OF GETTING SOBER (WHEN YOU GONNA GET DRUNK AGAIN)   (0:07)

Spurred on by the subject of George's last 'performance,' John sings a drunk song of his own - in this case a bit of "What's The Use of Getting Sober," a number recorded in 1942 by Louis Jordan.

3.64   WHAT DO YOU WANT TO MAKE THOSE EYES AT ME FOR (WHEN THEY DON'T MEAN WHAT THEY SAY!)   (1:02)

John, Paul and George all hop gleefully into this one. George (who leads off the song) seems to know all the words but Paul has them a bit scrambled. After a single verse and chorus, they vamp to a blues ending.

"What Do You Want To Make Those Eyes At Me For" was a number one hit in England for Emile Ford and The Checkmates in 1959. The Beatles would certainly have been familiar with this popular 1914 composition through Ford's recording.

Inspired, it seems, by their instrumental finale for "What Do You Want To Make Those Eyes At Me For" George invokes the name of legendary bluesman B.B. King, and tells a brief, humorous anecdote about him and Albert King.

3.65   MONEY (THAT'S WHAT I WANT) (0:36)
Paul begins noodling on the bass, which develops into a short instrumental of Barrett Strong's 1959 classic (covered by The Beatles in 1963). This continues over dialogue.

Having played around for a while after lunch, The Beatles are ready to get back to rehearsal. The trouble is, they don't quite know what to rehearse. George offers to do one of his slower songs, and Paul, consulting his clipboard of lyrics, suggests "All Things Must Pass." George notes that there aren't many numbers available, and, leafing through his own clipboard, mentions "She Came In Through The Bathroom Window" and "Maxwell's Silver Hammer," two of Paul's songs. This leaves John unrepresented, and Paul asks him if he's written any new songs yet. In response, John offers an unfinished tune called "Give Me Some Truth," which he and Paul perform while George requests the appropriate instruments for "All Things Must Pass."

It might be noted that none of the songs mentioned during this discussion were seriously recorded during the 'Get Back' sessions, although all were subsequently released either on *Abbey Road* or post-Beatle solo projects.

3.66   GIVE ME SOME TRUTH (1:21)
After Paul recites the lyrics, he and John begin a loose performance of John's song. They start out tentatively, reaching to remember what key the song is in. This is more of a preliminary run-through of the song to see if they remember it than a serious attempt to rehearse it.

"Give Me Some Truth," although never recorded by The Beatles, would be resurrected for John's 1971 solo album *Imagine*.

3.67   ALL THINGS MUST PASS (1:06)
A few hours earlier George had performed a solo rendition of this number (see 3.21). Now the time has come for the full band to have a go at it. Unlike the earlier rehearsals of "Don't Let Me Down" and "Two Of Us," quite a bit of this lengthy "All Things Must Pass" session has become available for study (albeit in fragments). In this particular performance George is warming up by playing a rough draft of the introductory guitar part, while Paul is noodling aimlessly as George explains the chords. Since "All Things Must Pass" was originally conceived as a solo acoustic number, George is not quite sure what John's instrumental role should be, and suggests that he play a Lowrey organ equipped with a rotating Leslie speaker for special effects. As Mal prepares this, George jokingly remarks how they're like The Band, which prominently featured an organ.

3.68   ALL THINGS MUST PASS (0:45<
After being told the chord sequence, The Beatles attempt the first real group performance of the song. George, as its author, knows it fairly well while Paul's first attempt at following him is little more than an extension of the bass noodling he was doing during 3.67. Ringo does little more than pound out the beat, and John does nothing, since the organ is not set up yet. The available tape cuts off at the end of the first verse.

3.69   ALL THINGS MUST PASS (2:47)
The first minute of this is a very disjointed collection of riffs and stray vocal lines. Obviously, a few minutes of the rehearsal are missing, since the organ can now be heard. Paul is playing around with his harmony vocal, attempting to find the right register for it. The performance peters out as George decides

he wants to play "All Things Must Pass" on acoustic guitar, but worries how that would come off on the live show when amplified through loudspeakers. Paul defers the question to Peter Sutton (one of the sound men on the film crew). John attempts to help by reminding them that The Beatles' recording engineers had solved that problem at one time (although he's not quite sure how). But John is talking about a process involved with recording, not a live performance, and Paul points out that George's guitar needs to come through to the audience as well. Peter solves the problem (at least temporarily) by taking a mike from Paul, and putting it on George's acoustic guitar.

3.70   THE WEIGHT (0:06)
John sings a few parody lines as Ringo pounds out a beat on his bass drum.

"The Weight" appeared on The Band's 1968 *Music From Big Pink* LP. This performance was undoubtedly suggested by George's mention of The Band a few minutes earlier.

3.71   I'M A TIGER (0:30)
Taking advantage of a few free moments while George's guitar is being miked, Paul plays a few bars of this Lulu song which was currently number 12 in the British Charts.

3.72   ALL THINGS MUST PASS (0:06<
The very beginning of a performance as The Beatles have another attempt at the song. Unfortunately, the available tape cuts off after only a few seconds.

3.73   ALL THINGS MUST PASS >0:24)
The available tape contains only this fragmented end of a performance (possibly the end of 3.72). Clearly The Beatles have yet to work out an ending for the song.

The mike on George's acoustic guitar is in place, but when he touches that and his vocal mike together he gets shocked. Paul jokes to the technicians that they'll be held accountable if George dies, but George, none too happy at his experience warns that they'll *all* suffer. Paul and Michael continue to make jokes at George's expense as he attempts to show Peter Sutton how he got shocked. He claims that it must have been caused by the filmmakers' use of two mikes taped together, but Peter denies this. George calls on Mal to solve the problem, but is told that Mal is off with producer Denis O'Dell. Finally, to everyone's great joy, George manages to shock himself again. Oddly enough, the obvious solution to the problem (not to touch the mikes) doesn't seem to have occurred to anyone. This incident was documented in the *Let It Be* film, although the footage there was substantially edited and rearranged.

3.74   (IMPROVISATION) >0:23)
John plays a few organ chords behind a mock-sermon from Father McCartney. This has no doubt been suggested by the presence of an organ, a common instrument in church music.

3.75   ALL THINGS MUST PASS (1:05<
This begins as a collection of disjointed riffs leading to a loose, messy rehearsal with George going over the chords.

3.76   ALL THINGS MUST PASS >4:41<
A continuation of the above, which very quickly turns into a full performance. As George reaches the middle of the song he once again stops to give the others the chords and then suggests that they rehearse the middle. The performance, however, continues without major interruption.

The nadir of "All Things Must Pass" rehearsals. The band is a shambles, Paul is playing off key, and John can barely play at all. It must have been quite dispiriting to George to have his song treated in such a nonchalant manner.

3.77   ALL THINGS MUST PASS   >1:05)

The organ is slightly louder in this fragment, making it even more painfully evident that John has little idea what to play. This is the end of a performance.

3.78   ALL THINGS MUST PASS   >1:12<

The end of another performance, followed by a sequence of guitar riffs and a few lines sung by George. Once again he expresses his desire that "All Things Must Pass" be performed with the kind of feeling that The Band would have given it, offering particular praise to bassist Rick Danko. In order to show John what he means, George plays a few bars on acoustic guitar. This and the following acoustic renditions are a welcome relief from the dismal band rehearsals that have been going on.

3.79   ALL THINGS MUST PASS   (2:37)

Another collection of riffs and stray vocal lines, as George illustrates several points about the song. Paul and John provide subtle instrumental accompaniment.

George suggests that a chorus of background singers might be appropriate. John, however, wants to learn how to play the song before he worries about things like that. George feels the details are important and speaks positively of doing a solo performance because the subtleties get lost in a full band arrangement. He then delves into the history of the song, and mentions having been inspired by a line from one of counter-culture visionary Timothy Leary's poems. The subject then turns to achieving a bent-note effect using the foot pedal for the Leslie speaker. John is genuinely surprised when this is pointed out to him, and asks Paul if *he* knew about it. Once again George invokes The Band by pointing out that this is an effect that their organist Garth Hudson often uses. Finally, George expresses his preference for Lowrey over Hammond organs

3.80   ALL THINGS MUST PASS   (3:45)

Following John's experiments with the foot pedal, The Beatles launch into a complete performance of the song. They struggle a bit when they reach the middle eight, and also have difficulty at the finish, but this is still a great improvement over their previous attempts. As the song winds up, George leads them through the ending that he has in mind, and they play it a few times. Throughout this performance John can be heard experimenting with the bent-note sounds.

George then returns to the subject of backing vocals, indicating that he wants to get a sound like The Raylettes (Ray Charles' back-up singers) for the chorus. At Paul's prompting they launch into an attempt to see how the song would sound with backing vocals.

3.81   ALL THINGS MUST PASS   (1:02<

George picks up the song at the end of the first verse with Paul offering falsetto accompaniment during the chorus. George stops them to offer more instructions, and picks up near the chorus once again. John is not participating, despite prompting from Paul. Paul seems bored, too, since halfway through George's instructions he yawns.

3.82   (IMPROVISATION)   (0:22<

Paul offers an instrumental bass performance, tapping out the rhythm on his fretboard. Once again, George brings up The Band, explaining how each member can sing in harmony without competing with the others. Obviously, he wishes that The Beatles could do the same.

3.83   ALL THINGS MUST PASS   >0:08<

A brief fragment capturing a bit of tight harmony between Paul and George on the chorus.

3.84   ALL THINGS MUST PASS   (0:31)

Paul and George continue to practice their vocal harmony. As they engage in discussion about the song, George utters a few lines of mock-psychology. He then explains that the lines are from an avant-garde play named *The Beard* that he has seen, and relates the unconventional plot.

3.85   ALL THINGS MUST PASS   (1:05<

After a brief pause for George's anecdote about *The Beard*, The Beatles return to rehearsal. After a few bars George remarks that they've all gone out of tune. Regardless, he starts the song from the top. Both John and Paul provide vocal harmony for the chorus, but the performance seems to break down as John tests his vocal microphone.

3.86   ALL THINGS MUST PASS   (2:03<

Their energy level seems to be getting low as The Beatles attempt another performance. John experiments with his backing vocals by echoing each of George's lines during the verse. This doesn't work out very well. The available tape cuts off right before the song reaches the middle eight.

3.87   ALL THINGS MUST PASS   >0:30)

This fragment captures the end of a run-through (very likely the one started in 3.86). John continues to play the song on organ after everyone else has stopped and offers a brief parody line about how he feels *he'll* pass away. The gospel overtones of "All Things Must Pass" then inspire John to break into a few lines of Biblical parody. Obviously, John and Paul's tolerance for "All Things Must Pass" rehearsal is reaching its limit.

3.88   (UNKNOWN)   (0:06)

George begins to play a song on guitar before he changes his mind and opts for "Back In The U.S.S.R.." He doesn't play enough of this to identify it.

3.89   BACK IN THE U.S.S.R.   (0:11)

Just a short instrumental bit of the leadoff song from *The Beatles*, played by George on guitar.

  This performance spurs George to ask if they should include some older Beatles songs in the live show. When Paul offers nothing more than a muttered non-answer, George makes a reasonable point by suggesting that the audience for the projected live show might be turned off by hearing nothing but new, unfamiliar tunes and suggests that they either begin or end the show with some older songs. However, Paul is barely listening to him (he's trying to get milk for his tea), and Michael is more interested in trying to appear witty. Only John seems genuinely supportive, and wants to give the songs new arrangements as Joe Cocker had done with his cover of the Lennon/McCartney tune "With a Little Help From My Friends."

3.90   EVERY LITTLE THING   (0:24)

George and Paul play a bit of this song as they try to remember it.

The inclusion of "Every Little Thing" or any other Beatle oldie in the live show would certainly have called for more rehearsal. It had apparently been over four years since The Beatles played this particular song, having recorded it in 1964 for *Beatles For Sale*.

Michael asks if they intend to play any rock and roll numbers, and reminisces about The Beatles' warm-up performances given on September 4, 1968 as they filmed promotional clips for "Hey Jude" and "Revolution," which he directed. The performances he mentions ("Good Golly Miss Molly," "Lucille," Long Tall Sally" and "Jenny, Jenny, Jenny" - all of which are Little Richard numbers, by the way) have never seen the light of day and were possibly never recorded. John replies that they might consider doing some oldies.

3.91   PIECE OF MY HEART   (0:32)

A short performance from George amid conversation. He accompanies himself on guitar as he sings a bit of the chorus.

"Piece of My Heart" had been released by Janis Joplin a few months earlier.

John then makes the suggestion that The Beatles use their new numbers for their next album, intimating that it would be foolish to rehearse the songs and then take a break before coming back to record the album. Paul and George, however, interpret his remark to mean he wants to break up the band. With this in mind they carefully steer his mind away from that line of thought by pointing out optimistic prospects for the group. George stresses that he would like to continue the rehearsals until everyone can play every number on demand. As soon as John hears talk about the future of the band he characteristically tunes out and begins noodling on the organ.

3.92   SABRE DANCE   (0:10)

John plays a few bars on organ underneath the conversation discussed above.

"Sabre Dance" is a classical piece by Khachaturian. An instrumental adaptation of it by Love Sculpture was currently in the British Top Ten.

The conversation continues. In another very revealing piece of dialogue, George states that he resists putting a lot of work into the group and into Apple, but then adds that hard work is necessary if they are to enjoy the benefits of their labours. He then states his belief that what The Beatles need to achieve harmony is for each member to treat everyone else's songs as if they had written them themselves. This would almost certainly have been directed at John, since Paul can be seen throughout the sessions working enthusiastically on the other's songs. Whatever his feelings, though, George sees no better outlet for his songs than The Beatles.

3.93   PIECE OF MY HEART   (0.12)

George performs the same part of the song as a few moments earlier (3.91)

Enough serious discussion - The Beatles want drinks. George requests another guitar.

3.94   "OVER AND OVER AGAIN"   (1:15)

Paul interrupts some of John's monotonous and amateurish ramblings on the organ by singing this Little Richard style number while accompanying himself on bass. Ringo backs him on drums but George barely plays at all since he continues to talk with Kevin. John offers only some sporadic unrelated accompaniment on the organ. The lyrics consist of little more than repetitions of the title phrase. Paul makes an attempt at a verse, but nothing coherent results.

This is very likely an improvisation, based around a reference to the lengthy "All Things Must Pass" rehearsal which has just been concluded.

The Beatles then discuss what song they should rehearse next. John half-heartedly suggests "On The Road To Marrakesh." Although George is agreeable to this suggestion, John himself isn't too keen on rehearsing it because it's slow. Paul adds that he's got a few unrehearsed slow numbers as well, and George complains that *all* of his numbers are slow, but begins to suggest that an album (or show) built around slow numbers might not be bad, citing Ella Fitzgerald as an example of an artist who has made this work. Perhaps poking gentle fun at George's reference to music for an older generation, Paul equates The Beatles' next album to Frank Sinatra's *Songs For Swingin' Lovers* LP. John brusquely claims that singing anything except the rough-and-tumble chorus of "Don't Let Me Down" is too much work for him. George, remarkably adaptable, replies that though he'd prefer to do his slow numbers, he's willing to make a straight rock and roll album like Chuck Berry's *After School Session* if that's what the others want. Paul and John then decide that, instead of rehearsing a new number, they'll return to the numbers they've already done. Bringing the conversation full circle, George once again asks which number they'd like to rehearse, and Paul pulls "One After 909" out of his hat. John isn't too pleased with the prospect of repeatedly rehearsing a song they've already done, but George and Paul both realise that they don't have the song down well enough yet.

After John briefly reiterates his desire to do a fast number, George launches into a comparison between himself, John and Eric Clapton, obviously continuing a topic which had begun before the start of the available tape. He reasons that Clapton can be such a showman because he's the only guitarist in Cream. George respects Clapton's ability to improvise solos. John however feels that being a good lead guitarist means nothing more than figuring out the solo or playing faster than the next guy. Paul compares Clapton's improvisational style to jazz and mentions a television program he'd seen which featured various musicians. This leads The Beatles and Michael into a discussion on jazz. Both John and Paul had watched the previous evening's television program *Jazz at the Maltings from Aldedurgh Festival Concert Hall*, which had aired on BBC 2 at 9:30, and describe it to the others with particular praise for Buddy Rich and Errol Garner (whom they all refer to as Errol Gardner). Michael initially turns up his nose at jazz but after failing to get uniform agreement from The Beatles, modifies this by claiming that he *used* to hate that kind of music when he was young. George expresses a strong distaste for most jazz and Paul says he's not too keen on it either. John mentions he hates trad jazz (i.e. Dixieland as compared to modern jazz) and George offers his positive opinion of Ray Charles' band with particular praise for their organist, a fellow named Billy Preston.

In the next available dialogue segment, George relays his opinion that recording without overdubs will cause The Beatles to seize each moment and perform at their best. Underlying this is an admission that the band has grown lax in their studio procedures of late.

3.95   ALL THINGS MUST PASS (0:31)

Paul sings a single line. George follows by singing about the macrobiotic pills he's been expecting. Paul offers to run through the song once more (with a noticeable lack of enthusiasm in his voice) but they forego another pass at "All Things Must Pass" as John offers some suggestions for the lyric. As John jokes around with the lyric, George makes a disparaging remark about Mal's handwriting on their lyric sheets.

Despite all the discussion of moving on to another song that preceded the dialogue about jazz, The Beatles *still* don't know what to play.

3.96   I'VE BEEN GOOD TO YOU   (1:21)

George, with help from John and Paul, sings a bit more than a verse of this until his struggle to remember the lyrics ends it. Paul enjoys singing background vocals.

"I've Been Good To You" was originally performed by The Miracles. This is the only performance to have surfaced from a half hour or more of rehearsals which occurred at this point.

3.97   MAXWELL'S SILVER HAMMER   (0:37<

This is the first real attempt during these sessions to rehearse Paul's 1968 composition. Paul calls out the chords instead of singing any of the words and is playing bass, although he would play piano on this song during the following week's performances.

The time is 5:45 p.m.. Although The Beatles would rehearse "Maxwell's Silver Hammer" for a half hour or more, only this and the following fragment have become available. A portion of this performance appeared in the film *Let It Be*.

3.98   MAXWELL'S SILVER HAMMER   >0:33<

A very loose performance as Paul sings part of the chorus and appears to be in the process of teaching Ringo his drum part.

Paul suggests that they get a hammer and anvil to use on the song. When they return to rehearsing it on January 7th, he'll get his wish.

3.99   I WANT YOU   (1.17)

A brief, poorly performed cover version of the 1966 Bob Dylan song from George and Paul. George's vocal is almost inaudible, and the song comes perilously close to breaking down into tuning at one point.

3.100   "I'M GONNA PAY FOR HIS RIDE"   (3:40)

This blues-based improvisation has a spirited (and almost inaudible) vocal from Paul amid distortion-laden guitar.

Towards the end of their sessions, it was typical of The Beatles to break into extended jam sessions such as this. It is very much in the style of heavy blues for which Cream was noted. Certainly, George's statement of his and John's musical inferiority to Eric Clapton is borne out here. The rather bizarre lyric might simply be a topical reference - it's time to go home.

3.101   DONT LET ME DOWN   (0:50<

This has the same distorted guitar sound as 3.100, and was probably just a brief return to the bit that John had previously claimed is the only thing he enjoys playing.

Everyone says good night and agrees to meet again Monday morning at 10 Although The Beatles had historically recorded over weekends, they have chosen to take weekends off for the Twickenham sessions.

Monday, January 6th, 1969

The rehearsals begin to come apart at the seams on the 6th. The unproductive session of January 3rd had dampened everyone's spirits, and shortly after George's arrival he half-jokingly states that they should drop the idea of doing a live show. Ringo arrives and quickly states that he's not feeling too well, and John sits silently through important discussions. Even the ever-optimistic Paul has doubts when the subject of the live show is brought up.

The Beatles spend most of the morning jamming aimlessly, performing oldies and chatting about the desired audience for the live show. Little or no productive rehearsals occur. The afternoon rehearsals of "Don't Let Me Down" are nothing short of disastrous, as The Beatles spend more than an hour working on ideas they'll quickly reject. With nothing accomplished and bickering among themselves, The Beatles move on to "Two Of Us." These rehearsals are unsuccessful as well, and Paul and George argue over the band's working method. Although the rehearsals continue without further incident, the live show and the band are clearly in trouble.

6.1   OH! DARLING   >0:27)

The available tape begins in progress as Paul sings for the film crew and Beatles personnel, accompanying himself on piano. The song is clearly unfinished.

As he did on January 3rd, Paul takes advantage of the others' absence by getting in some early morning piano practice as the cameras roll. Unfortunately, this 27 second fragment of "Oh! Darling" is the only performance from this piano session currently available to us. Paul and the crew then sit around and talk while the other Beatles filter in. Although it was performed a number of times throughout the "Get Back" sessions, "Oh! Darling" wouldn't be recorded and released until later in the year on *Abbey Road*.

This is followed by a dialogue exchange in which Paul seemingly begins to suggest that "Oh! Darling" is a song that could be considered for serious rehearsal, but is cut off by Michael, who enthuses about "Maxwell's Silver Hammer," another McCartney number which had been premiered during the previous session on January 3rd. Paul begins to discuss "Maxwell's Silver Hammer" by comparing it to the satirical work of Tom Lehrer, but Michael cuts him off again, this time by soliciting his opinion of Wilson Pickett's cover version of "Hey Jude." Everyone seems to be enthusiastic about this recording. Paul gives it a thumbs-up, and Michael expresses his surprise that he likes it despite being so hooked on The Beatles recording.

Paul then gives the others a lesson in Beatles history. He begins by discussing his pleasure with the rehearsals of "One After 909" which had taken place on the 3rd, and nostalgically reminisces about the early Lennon/McCartney catalog. He states that approximately a hundred compositions went unused, and recites several couplets from a song called "Just Fun" to illustrate the simplicity of the early lyrics. We then learn that, while Paul once disliked the lyrics to "One After 909," he now thinks they're terrific. Michael enthuses about hearing older songs on the radio, and mentions Fats Domino as an example. This leads Glyn to raise the subject of Fats' new album, *Fats Is Back*. Paul mentions that it was produced by Richard Perry (who would go on to produce several albums for Ringo in the 1970's)

In the next dialogue fragment, Michael discusses how he and cameraman Tony Richmond had driven to work together, and had discussed Coral Records' practice of mining its vaults for posthumous Buddy Holly releases. In light of this, Michael asks Paul if The Beatles have a lot of unreleased material in the can. Paul, although seemingly hesitant to discuss the matter, mentions the existence of The Beatles' Decca audition tape (presuming that Decca still retained a copy), and Capitol having recorded The Beatles live at the Hollywood Bowl in 1964 and 1965.

As the next available tape begins, Paul mentions that he'd listened to The Beatles' 1967 classic *Sgt. Pepper's Lonely Hearts Club Band* LP the night before. Michael asks him if he liked it, to which Paul, somewhat incredulous, replies in the affirmative, expressing particular delight at the sound effects of a live audience which George Martin had added to the mix. He tells Michael that the sounds of the live audience on the record reminded him of what a live show might be like, and, with this in mind, he asks when the professional sound recording equipment first discussed on January 2nd will arrive. Glyn indicates that the equipment should arrive shortly (as indeed some of it does). Paul says that he hasn't thought of the project in terms of making a record album yet, and Glyn tells hint he shouldn't, but should concentrate on working the songs into the live performance. The discussion then turns to the question of whether The Beatles' new Fender amplifiers will be used for the live show.

Paul defers to Glyn, who says the new amps are fine. He also expresses his preference to record from small amps (rather than multiple, or more powerful amps), and explains to Michael that this is because they can be overloaded slightly so they can get to the point where they're just beginning to distort.

Ringo arrives, is greeted, and admits that he's *not* having a good morning. This suggests that he is having trouble adjusting to the new daytime working schedule. Michael, probably as a continuation of the 'loudness' thread begun in the previous conversation, brings up the subject or hearing loss when one is subjected to music at high volume levels. Neither Paul, Ringo or Glyn seem particularly concerned. Paul jokes that musicians are *expected* to lose their hearing, and mentions British bandleader Ted Heath and Beethoven as two famous examples. He then tells Michael that he used to be asked often about loss of hearing, and once again indicates that this often discussed subject doesn't particularly interest him. Glyn, Michael and Ringo agree that one gets used to loud volume after a while, and Ringo adds that the only loud sound that bothers him is the feedback which occasionally came through the headphones during recording sessions at E.M.I.. Glyn raises the related subject of a bass frequency which can somehow kill (we can feel lucky that John hasn't arrived yet - he would have probably wanted to try it), but Paul is more worried about being done in by feedback, and very amusingly acts out his experience with it, including a mock chastisement of E.M.I. engineer Ken Scott.

John and Yoko arrive, and are greeted by Paul, Ringo and the others. Paul asks John about *his* health, and John's response indicates that he had not been feeling well either. With most of the group present now, Michael unsuccessfully tries to raise the subject of the live show. Paul's somewhat sarcastic response suggests that he's beginning to tire of Michael's company. The Beatles have a remarkably cavalier attitude towards a performance which had, at this point, been widely publicised and announced for a date now less than two weeks away. Michael suggests the Royal Albert Hall as a possible venue for the live show (which is ironic since it had been announced as a venue back in October, 1968, only to be withdrawn a week later due to "booking and other problems"), and this reminds Paul of the television special *Cream - Farewell Concert from the Royal Albert Hall, London* which had been aired the previous evening at 10:20 on the BBC-TV program *Omnibus*. Paul solicits the others' opinions of that program, and Michael offers some highly negative views of its editing (this is interesting in light of the similar editing which occurred under his direction for the film *Let It Be*). Paul has an even worse opinion of the Cream program, and joins the others in making fun of it. John indicates that he and Yoko watched neither the Cream documentary nor *Rowan and Martin's Laugh-In* (which aired at the same time), but a play entitled *All Things Being Equal* which was broadcast on London Weekend Television. Ringo flipped channels.

6.2   C'MON MARIANNE   (0:28)

John sings a brief snatch of this song as he enters the studio. Paul picks up on it and sings a single further line. "C'mon Marianne" was a minor U.K. hit in 1968 for Grapefruit.

The next available tape fragment documents George's arrival at the rehearsal. George had evidently fallen victim to insomnia the night before and discusses the experience as The Beatles are served breakfast. He relates how he had tried to telephone Paul to wake him up, but was only able to reach an answering machine. Paul received his message, but missed the actual call because his phone wasn't turned on. It should be noted that among his other duties Mal Evans was responsible for waking The Beatles up each morning. In the course of this discussion, Paul mentions "Cosmic Consciousness" - a popular book by Richard M. Bucke which dealt with the evolution of the human mind.

6.3   I'VE GOT A FEELING   (0:14)

This short a capella rendition from George and Paul occurs during the conversation above. Someone is banging along with the singing at the very end.

Michael, obviously anxious to resume filming now that his four stars have arrived, inquires peevishly about the delivery time of another camera (evidently one was out of commission). Tony Richmond's answer (thirty minutes) irks the director, who obviously wanted to be able to film as soon as The Beatles resumed playing, and perhaps felt that that moment wouldn't wait for his equipment to arrive.

George is aware of the unusually lackadaisical atmosphere and pointedly asks what they're all doing, to which he receives a number of facetious replies. Michael returns to the earlier topics of conversation, but gets no further than the Cream television program before George interrupts him and asks the others what they thought of it. Paul responds with some more highly negative remarks, but except for his dissatisfaction with the cutting, George has basically positive things to say. Michael, finding himself unable to agree with both Beatles at the same time, tosses in some positive comments as well, with particular praise for Ginger Baker (Cream's drummer). This leads George into a humorous imitation of Baker's interview from the program, and prompts him to ask Ringo if he and Baker had ever met. Ringo replies in the affirmative and explains that they had met at the opening night festivities for The Beatles' film *Yellow Submarine* and had immediately gotten on well because of their shared profession.

6.4   I'VE GOT A FEELING (0:07)

A few more seconds "I've Got a Feeling" sung by George and Paul during the previous conversations.

George announces that he has written a gospel song ("Hear Me Lord") during the weekend break. This announcement generates nothing more than a flip comment from John, and George seems unsure whether to be indignant or self-effacing in his reply. After a few moments of silence, the topic of George's new song is entirely dropped. Michael, sensing a lull in the conversation, once again attempts to bring up the topic of the live show, which he wants to be performed in front of a large audience. Michael mentions merchandising the project in several ways - the live show itself, and the documentary which he's shooting of the rehearsals. George, perhaps a bit put off by the lack of interest the others have shown towards "Hear Me Lord," suggests that they should give it all up and go home. Paul simply laughs and agrees with him.

6.5   HIGH SCHOOL CONFIDENTIAL (0:07)

A single line from Jerry Lee Lewis' 1958 classic, sung by George as he works at tuning his guitar.

The long awaited sound gear arrives. Michael, probably eyeing the IBC Studios insignia, compares the gear to an ambulance which has arrived to save his ailing documentary. As Michael instructs one of the cameramen to get a shot of the equipment, Paul pokes gentle fun at his directorial style and mentions the Bonzo Dog Band's single "I'm The Urban Spaceman," which he had produced (as Apollo C. Vermouth) and which had been released a few weeks earlier. He says he did the session as a favour to Vivian Stanshall (a member of the Bonzos, who had all appeared in The Beatles film *Magical Mystery Tour*) .

6.6   I'VE GOT A FEELING (0:50)

A brief but pleasant performance by George as the others hold the above conversation. Not surprisingly, he doesn't remember the lyrics.

6.7   HEAR ME LORD (0:17)

George immediately follows "I've Got A Feeling" with the premiere of his new song. He's working from memory and doesn't remember many of the words. The performance stops after a few lines, perhaps because no one seems to be paying any attention.

Michael mentions having been asked to film the Bongo Dog Band's warm-up set for Tiny Tim's concert at the Royal Albert Hall which had been held the previous October 30th (with The Beatles in the audience) and complains about too much activity on the stage. Paul changes the subject and suggests that rehearsals begin. George reflects on the session by remarking that it seems to be another off-day, and verbalises his idea of the bizarre (to him) exchange of dialogue that would have occurred between the crew and IBC Studios as they arrive to borrow a tape recorder. This leads Paul and George into a discussion of the merits at George's new Revox tape recorder. The discussion is abbreviated as the available tape cuts off.

6.8   HEAR ME LORD (0:31)
George plays another version of his new song over the beginning of the above conversation. This is very similar to his previous performance of "Hear Me Lord," and there's probably only a few moments of tape missing between the two. Once again, George cuts his performance short, this time to join the conversation.

6.9   CARRY THAT WEIGHT (1:28)
It's 11:00, and not yet time for serious rehearsals to begin. Paul plays organ as the others tune, and amid this clatter introduces a new composition that he has written for Ringo to sing. Paul sings the chorus and John sings along a bit as he tries to follow on guitar. Paul then follows with a loose approximation of a middle eight, one which would never make it into the finished song.

"Carry That Weight," though touched on briefly a few times during these sessions, would not be completed and seriously recorded until later in the year, when it appeared on *Abbey Road*.

As the performance dies down, George compliments John on his "1969 Diary" (a comical magazine piece he had written - see 8.1 for further discussion). Yoko adds her opinion at length (the first such instance in these sessions and a harbinger of things to come).

6.10   medley OCTOPUS'S GARDEN / CARRY THAT WEIGHT (0:56)
Ringo plays piano and shows Paul his newest composition. Paul quickly joins in on organ, but he's basically playing the same tune as the previous performance. Ringo sings one verse (which is all he had written at this point), and Paul caps off the performance by singing a few more lines from his new song. Ringo then briefly relates his inspiration for the song, a conversation he had with a sea captain in Sardinia in 1968.

This is the earliest performance of "Octopus's Garden" to come to light. It's another song that wouldn't be completed and properly recorded until the *Abbey Road* sessions later in the year.

6.11   CARRY THAT WEIGHT (1:46)
Ringo's new song apparently doesn't hold Paul's interest, so he returns to his own number. Paul shows off a half-finished verse, as well as some alternate lyrics for a chorus (both of which go unused on the final recording).

Ringo joins in on vocals, offering a brief but charming duet with Paul.

6.12   (INSTRUMENTAL) / (IMPROVISATION) (12.45)
Paul follows "Carry That Weight" with another original, this time an instrumental, struggling a bit on the organ (later piano performances of the same tune are much smoother). After two minutes or so, Ringo takes his spot behind the drums and joins in. Over time John, then George, join in as well as the performance mutates into a simplistic jam. The band then beats this riff to death, repeating it for more than nine minutes with minimal variation. Perhaps the sole point of interest in all of this is to hear Ringo improvising a drum part.

The improvisation aside, this is the earliest of four available performances of the tune listed here as "Instrumental." Although The Beatles would never record this song, Paul returned to it years later and properly recorded it for an unreleased "Rupert The Bear" children's album (where it was reportedly titled "Castle of The King of The Birds").

6.13   (IMPROVISATION) (0:06<

After Paul doodles on the organ for a while, he and Ringo begin another jam.

6.14   (IMPROVISATION) >1:53)

An obvious continuation of 6.13, separated only by a brief tape edit. Paul plays a riff that resembles (but isn't quite, The Kingsmen's "Louie, Louie" as Ringo drums and John joins in with some uninspired guitar work.

6.15   "MY IMAGINATION" >2:08<

A faster, more spirited improvisation. Paul, who has moved from organ to bass, improvises a few lines of lyric. Much of this jam has a blues feel to it, suggesting Elmore James' "One Way Out." The Beatles (minus George) would return to this particular riff, jamming on it again on January 10th.

6.16   DIZZY MISS LIZZY (3:08)

The Beatles return to their rock and roll roots with a loose cover version of Larry Williams' 1958 classic. George and Ringo are still the primary performers here, and Ringo's drumming is particularly enthusiastic. No vocals are audible. After a couple of minutes the performance turns into a loose jam, which John leads into a cover version of "Money."

The Beatles had previously recorded "Dizzy Miss Lizzy" for their 1965 album *Help!*.

6.17   MONEY (THAT'S WHAT I WANT) (2:16)

Except for an errant wah-wah pedal, this is a fairly straightforward cover version of Barrett Strong's 1959 recording. Once again, Ringo is furiously bashing his drums. Unfortunately, John's vocal is almost inaudible.

The Beatles recorded "Money" for their 1963 LP *With The Beatles*. In addition, both this and the previous song were recorded by the group during appearances on England's BBC radio that same year.

6.18   FOOLS LIKE ME (3:21)

This cover version of Jerry Lee Lewis' 1959 recording is as loose as a performance can be without completely falling apart. Ringo isn't participating, and John and Paul are performing a duet. George's wah-wah'd guitar is far too loud and, once again, the vocals are almost inaudible - at least until the very end of the song.

The group is reported to have performed this country song during early live performances. They'll perform it again on January 8th. As the performance ends, John tries to remember the title of a Carl Perkins song they used to play.

6.19   SURE TO FALL (2:38)

Once they remember the title of the Perkins song, they attempt to play it. In contrast to the previous tune, this performance is quite nice - John and Paul obviously enjoy harmonising on this pleasant country tune.

"Sure To Fall," although never professionally recorded by The Beatles, was performed by the group for BBC radio in 1963, as well as their 1962 Decca audition (which they had discussed earlier). "Sure To Fall" was originally released in 1956 by Carl Perkins, although the lead singer on the record was his brother Jay. All four Beatles were big Carl Perkins fans, and it's not surprising that the song receives a respectful rendition from the group.

6.20   RIGHT STRING, WRONG YO-YO (3:23<

Immediately after they finish "Sure To Fall," the band breaks into a cover version of another Perkins record. Paul takes the lead vocal here, but does not remember many of the words. After a brief jam, he offers a bluesy reprise as their performance winds down.

"Right String, Wrong Yo-Yo" was originally an R&B hit for its composer "Piano Red" Perryman. Carl Perkins recorded his version in 1956, which is obviously the one The Beatles are remembering here.

6.21   (IMPROVISATION) >0:22)
The tail end of a guitar instrumental from George. This bears a slight resemblance to Bob Dylan's "I Shall Be Released."

6.22   LEANING ON A LAMP-POST (1:26)
As a discussion of the live show's location continues, George jokingly asks if they'll perform this song on the show. This inspires Paul to offer a short version as George and John back him on guitar.

"Leaning On A Lamp-Post" was originally recorded in the 1930's by British music hall artist George Formby.

6.23   ANNIE (0:22)
John breaks into this dance hall style number that he says he wrote for Ringo. Paul sings along as they perform only one chorus.

This brief performance is the only one of this song to ever become available. It was never properly recorded by The Beatles (or anyone else, for that matter), although its existence had long been rumoured among Beatles fans.

6.24   "MAUREEN" (2:01)
Since Paul and John have both offered up numbers for Ringo, George joins in with this number that he claims Bob Dylan wrote, evidently named after Ringo's wife. He sings and accompanies himself on guitar as Paul occasionally joins in on vocal and John attempts to play along on guitar. George performs a single verse and chorus a number of times.

Despite George's claim as to its authorship, no Dylan performance of this song is known to exist, although George might have learned it from Dylan when he had visited him in America the previous Thanksgiving. No other performances of this song are known to exist.

6.25   I'M TALKING ABOUT YOU (0:45)
George gives a brief, but competent solo performance.

"I'm Talking About You" was written and recorded by Chuck Berry in 1961. It was part of their early live repertoire and was performed by them on BBC radio in 1963. The rehearsals were halted at this point so that the group could go scout locations as Paul had suggested. The morning's rehearsal session had produced *nothing*, and the scouting expedition was apparently just as unsuccessful, as the venue location remains undecided.

6.26   (IMPROVISATION) (1:25<
The Beatles return to the soundstage, but are *still* not prepared for serious rehearsals. Paul positions himself behind Ringo's drum kit and bangs out a rhythm. John tunes his guitar and joins in shortly before the available tape cuts off.

6.27   (IMPROVISATION) >0:09<
A continuation of the above, with George joining in.

6.28   (IMPROVISATION) >3:31)

Again, a continuation of the above. Once again The Beatles have chosen to jam rather than rehearse their new songs. George and John both play guitar, while Paul continues on drums and Ringo sits out.

6.29   (IMPROVISATION) / TRACKS OF MY TEARS   (2:56)

After a very brief rest, the jamming resumes. George makes a few attempts to lead the band into "Tracks of My Tears," and finally succeeds (although it's obvious he knows the song much better than the others). George sings but, characteristically, doesn't care whether he's on mike or not. George and Ringo play a cover version of this Miracles song which they obviously know quite well. George is singing, but he's far off mike.

"Tracks of My Tears" was originally recorded by Smokey Robinson and The Miracles in 1965.

6.30   (IMPROVISATION)   (0.23<

John seems to be attempting to play a certain riff, but can't get it right. George and Paul continue to play aimlessly.

The next available tape contains a fascinating and unique conversation (joined in progress) which evidently occurred right before lunch. In it, Yoko Ono exhibits a domineering personality that is rarely evidenced in most of the other tapes from these sessions. After several aborted tries earlier in the morning, the group has finally gotten around to discussing plans for the upcoming live show. Paul, George, Yoko and Michael are discussing the theoretical uses of an audience (John is present, but silent). Paul has suggested that something special is needed for the show - something to top The Beatles' own live performances at the height of Beatlemania. George Martin quite rightly reminds Paul that The Beatles themselves can get something from an audience. Paul realises this, since he had just talked about three possible purposes in having an audience (to please them, get money from them, or to experience the pleasure of direct feedback from them). George, on the other hand, worries that their audience might be nothing more than the usual screaming young females and Yoko suggests that they dispense with the audience altogether and play to 20,000 empty seats. This conceptual slant irritates Michael, who nervously jokes that it would look like no one wanted to come. Both Paul and Yoko take this little joke too seriously, and argue with him. Yoko makes the observation that it would be undesirable to limit their audience to young people, preferring to invite royalty instead. Paul's subsequent comments suggest that two different shows were envisioned, but it's possible that he's simply placating Yoko, (and by extension, John). In fact, he goes so far as to suggest a possible compromise - that they could perform one show to empty seats, and another to a paying audience. Again, the concept of playing to an empty auditorium worries Michael. This time, however, we find out why - he's afraid that without an audience his film will be no different than the rehearsals (i.e., dismal). Paul understands this point, but argues that they haven't played to the cameras yet. The topic switches back to the use of an audience as the available tape comes to an end.

It's instructive to take a closer look at what's really going on here. The most striking element of this conversation is Yoko Ono's usurpation of a role that one would expect to have been played by John. When Michael expresses his opinion that the band needs an audience, Yoko quite comfortably talks down to him. Her tone clearly indicates that, in her own mind, at least, she's as important as any of the Beatles. Yet the blame for this dysfunctional situation lies as much with John's passivity as Yoko's aggressiveness. Although he's present, John contributes *nothing* to the conversation - offering as proxy Yoko's generally unorthodox and self-aggrandising observations. Even if he had wanted to, Paul could not have stood up to her for fear of further alienating John. Michael cannot assert himself for fear of alienating *anyone*. George complains, but everyone seems to be used to that by now, and Ringo, as usual, offers no opinion.

The conversation continues as Yoko encourages the others to accept her idea to play to empty seats by foretelling a mob scene with Beatle fans queuing up to get tickets. Denis mentions the Royal Albert Hall, but Michael thinks that this is no longer a 'hip' venue, and suggests that the choice of a more unusual location would provide the element that they're looking for. Just such a location (not specifically mentioned) had been discussed just before the available tape begins. A seaside location is tentatively supported by Michael, but is unacceptable to Paul, who strongly indicates that an outdoor venue must be in England. Paul had been quite firm about this during the discussions on January 2nd, primarily because Ringo had refused to go abroad. Now he reiterates that decision, and one gets the impression that he's happy that *anything* can be said to have been definitely decided, or even decided *against*. Ringo jokes about having a riverboat shuffle, the descriptive name of a Liverpool boat excursion on which The Beatles played a number of times in their early days - his way, perhaps, of saying he'd like to stick close to shore. John's only contribution to the conversation is an observation that it would be chilly playing outdoors in the English winter.

Perhaps jokingly, Paul conjures up a vision of the band playing in the nude. George, however, would prefer that the *audience* be naked. Yoko, never big on jokes, returns to the topic of the "Hey Jude" film and calculates that if the public doesn't see a wild audience then they won't think of The Beatles as too important anymore. This, of course, is in direct contrast to her comments a couple of minutes earlier, where she complained that it would be bad for their current public image to be seen playing for young teenagers. George, surprisingly optimistic, replies that they should make themselves *another* public image, but he seems to be at a loss as to what that image might be.

Paul then suggests that they return to their roots by performing the show in a ballroom. Perhaps he envisions this unpredictable environment energising the moribund Beatles. Michael somewhat wistfully brings him back to earth - The Beatles are too big to play clubs. It's a pipe dream. Paul wouldn't forget the idea, however, and would perform small, impromptu gigs during his 1972 tour with Wings.

The discussions then return to the idea of filming the live performance at Twickenham in a controlled environment. Considering this, Paul suggests it would be silly to try and artificially duplicate a real place (like the Tower Ballroom, a New Brighton venue where they played many times in 1961-2), when the venue itself still exists and might be utilised. Yoko seems quite obstinately set against the idea of The Beatles returning to their past (a past in which, incidentally, she did not play a part), and presents the somewhat confused argument that people would rather see Richard Burton shaving than returning to his roots on the stage. Denis tosses out the suggestion that they have the show in the middle of one of England's prestigious art museums, with no audience except the pictures. As one would suspect, this idea appeals to Yoko, who seconds the motion. Paul remarks that if they don't play to human beings they can play to animals. Since the available tape breaks again at this point, we can't say if his idea was taken seriously.

Finally, Yoko continues to develop her suggestion that the The Beatles be filmed in their private homes rather than before an audience. Michael sees this as fitting quite nicely into the documentary he's making, and George compares it to a television program which featured Brigitte Bardot in various locales.

6.31   DON'T LET ME DOWN   >14:56<

An extended stop-and-start rehearsal, focusing on the middle eight. As before, George makes extensive use of his wah-wah pedal.

This and the following dozen entries are excerpted from more than an hour of rehearsals for "Don't Let Me Down" which are already in progress as the available tape begins. This rehearsal, which was probably the first thing done after lunch, offers an insightful (if occasionally tedious) look into the working methods of the band.

As we begin, The Beatles play the end of the middle eight and chorus (with enthusiastic vocals from John). This leads into an instrumental version of the chorus which finishes out the song. John then suggests that they work on the middle eight, which he considers the weakest part of the song. Paul works on his bass guitar part and improvises a wordless falsetto harmony vocal which answers each line of John's lyric.

After several more rehearsals of the call-and-response middle eight, George suggests they change the song's rhythm. John, as he had on January 2nd, raises the possibility of using a piano. As they continue to rehearse the middle eight Paul improvises some lyrics for his vocal part. He thinks that John's lyrics are too corny, and that the addition of further trite lyrics would make the song seem to be a purposeful send-up. Although John doesn't respond, we'll learn in a few moments that he, too, thinks the lyrics are weak. George still wants to alter the rhythm.

They continue to rehearse the middle eight for a few minutes, with Paul crooning his harmony part. He then suggests that he, John *and* George sing, but John (evidently thinking of the live performance) seems to think this is too complicated, and talks about how he'd seen the contemporary group The Move on television unsuccessfully using a three microphone set-up. Paul defers the question to some future session, counting on Glyn Johns to fill George Martin's role as vocal arranger.

More rehearsals of the middle eight occur with Paul's harmony vocal. Paul remarks upon the weakness of his improvised lyrics, suggesting that they work on it later. John, however, wants to retain Paul's lyrics because he doesn't see much merit in his own lines either.

6.32   DON'T LET ME DOWN   >0:19<

A fragment wherein George and Paul have another go at the harmony vocal in the middle eight.

6.33   DON'T LET ME DOWN   >0:02<

An even briefer fragment, inadvertently capturing a moment of rehearsal as the soundman cues up another roll of tape.

6.34   DON'T LET ME DOWN   >3:39)

The rehearsals continue. Paul once again attempts to work out the vocal harmony between George and himself, suggesting they just vocalise the notes rather than worrying about what the specific lyrics are.

Having spent at least the past half hour on serious rehearsal. John takes a moment to relax, improvising intentionally corny lyrics, as they perform the song at a slower tempo than usual. He then plays a bit of the song at *faster* tempo than usual, then corrects himself and gradually slows it down. Following this, he suggests that they have an instrumental introduction to the song, so that they know when to come in with the vocal. He plays this, and a full performance begins.

6.35   DON'T LET ME DOWN   (3:22)

This is a complete run-through of the song, which starts out with the introductory guitar passage discussed above. One gets the impression they're playing it straight through just to hear the entire song after an extended period of fragmented rehearsal. Paul sings the harmony vocal that he initiated earlier and the song hangs together rather well until the end. After the last chorus it's once again evident that they haven't put much work into an ending.

John, obviously unhappy with the arrangement, again suggests a piano part. Paul disagrees. John then suggests that George lay off the wah-wah pedal. George disagrees with this, and claims that it would be uncreative to play it John's way. John, obviously irritated, says that *he* wouldn't mind using the usual instrumental line up. It's interesting to observe that John will entertain any number of musical suggestions from Paul, but does not allow George to present his view as to how the song should be played. When working within the framework of the Lennon/McCartney partnership, George is viewed as a sideman.

6.36   DON'T LET ME DOWN   (3:11)

After some riffs, Paul sings a stray line, and John picks up on it to begin a second complete run-through. This has a harder edge than the previous performance, and is taken at a slightly faster tempo. When the middle eight is reached, John does a very obvious imitation of Bob Dylan for a few lines. Once again, the performance fizzles out as the song reaches its end.

An excerpt from this performance can be seen in the film *Let It Be*.

6.37   DON'T LET ME DOWN   (4:46<

Rehearsals resume as The Beatles attempt a number of different rhythms.

Paul vocalises a percussion break for Ringo's benefit, and they continue to rehearse the middle eight with a syncopated rhythm very much like that used by Arthur Alexander in his early 60's hits "Anna" and "You Better Move On."

Paul and John then discuss the difference in feel that they want to achieve between the middle eight and chorus. George thinks the middle eight might be tried heavier, but John quickly presents his viewpoint that it's already heavy, and that's not the effect he wants. Paul suggests the beats might be heavy, as opposed to the vocal or guitar parts and plays an example of how he thinks this should sound, vocalising cymbal crashes to accentuate certain beats. He sings a harmony part over the verse in order to suggest a new guitar line to George. George begins to play this as the available tape comes to an end.

6.38   DON'T LET ME DOWN   (0:59<

John and Paul are frustrated that the middle eight is not working out and seek to emulate a 1950's-style vocal arrangement over the instrumentation for the middle eight.

6.39 DON'T LET ME DOWN (1:20<

More rehearsal. After another run-through of the middle eight, George once again suggests a different rhythm. As he tries it, Paul follows him on bass.

6.40 DON'T LET ME DOWN (0:21<

The Beatles return to rehearsing the harmony backing vocals for the middle eight with George and Paul vocalising instead of singing the lyrics.

6.41 DON'T LET ME DOWN >0:33<

Another rehearsal fragment. As the available tape begins, they're still rehearsing the harmony backing vocals discussed above. John suggests they go back into their usual voices, and Paul and George test out some very simple backing harmonies, still singing Paul's counterpoint verse. George gets the words wrong, and Paul corrects him.

6.42 DON'T LET ME DOWN (6:18)

The rehearsals continue. George has evidently expressed his dissatisfaction with Paul's addition to the middle eight. Paul responds that he made up the new words because George didn't like the others, but George tells him it wasn't the words that he had a problem with, but the music. Paul is beginning to sound frustrated by the lack of progress on the song, and suggests that they'll figure out what's wrong once they've tried to play it. George correctly points out that they've been trying to play it for quite a while. This said, they begin to rehearse the middle eight *again*, but this very quickly breaks down

After another try, Paul drops his response lyrics, and echoes exactly what John sings, effectively bringing the rehearsal back to where it was an hour or so earlier.

George is still unhappy with the melody, first facetiously saying how good it is and then flatly stating that it's terrible. When John asks if George can think of anything better he suggests a simpler vocal part using whole notes, and illustrates this on his guitar. Paul thinks that's even worse, and that the harmonies are *already* too syrupy. George disagrees and they settle the dispute by trying out George's idea. Once again, however, they very quickly mess up as Paul begins to sing the alternate lyrics which he had abandoned a few minutes before.

At this point, they're all frustrated that the rehearsals have gone nowhere. John sides with Paul, and expresses his desire that they get the words down first and work the music around them. Paul complains that they've wasted an hour on nothing, and George points out that the rehearsal isn't getting anywhere because they've concentrated on the middle eight to the exclusion of everything else. John wants to hear any of the middle eight configurations played correctly all the way through. Even though they sound bored and frustrated, none of them are ready to move on to the next song and Paul interrupts the discussion to run through the middle eight yet another time.

In lieu of additional lyrics, and obviously unhappy with simply parroting John's lines in their harmony vocal, Paul then suggests that he and George alter the order of John's lines in their response vocal. John agrees, no doubt simply to get the rehearsal back under way. Not surprisingly, this experiment stops after a few moments in complete confusion. Paul then suggests that they change only on the final line. Before they can start this, however. the available tape cuts off.

6.43   medley DON'T LET ME DOWN / SEND ME SOME LOVIN' (2:48)

The rehearsals continue. George plays a short guitar intro and John leads them once again into the middle eight. Evidently they've already tried altering Paul and George's last line (as Paul suggests above), and are now seeing how it sounds with no response to John's final line. Paul and George finally seem to have their harmonies worked out for their backing vocals, and the middle eight actually works quite well with the fourth line left unechoed.

George seems to feel that less vocal harmony would benefit the song, and comments that if they could listen to a playback they'd quickly see his point. Paul gives in, and says they've done enough work on the song for the moment. John sums up the unsuccessful rehearsal by pointing out that they've spent their time working on the vocal parts, when the real problem with the song lies in the rhythm. When Paul points out that they'd known that all along, John sings a few bars of Little Richard's 1957 hit "Send Me Some Lovin'," equating its guitar part to "Don't Let Me Down." George begins to offer his opinion as to what needs to happen to the arrangement, but is interrupted by Glyn who, at Paul's urging, suggests that John, Paul and George take turns singing each line of the middle eight. They give this idea a quick try-out, but George chooses not to participate.

In the next fragment of the available tape, Paul compares the call-and-response arrangement of "Don't Let Me Down" to The Beatles' 1967 number "With a Little Help From My Friends."

6.44   DON'T LET ME DOWN (0:10)

George sings the middle eight as Paul and John talk to Glyn.

6.45   DON'T LET ME DOWN >0:37)

Now that the rehearsal is winding down, The Beatles relax a bit, and perform a blues arrangement of "Don't Let Me Down." John then suggests they move on to something new.

All in all, this rehearsal session for "Don't Let Me Down" was a dismal failure. The Beatles tested out various ideas for improving the song, most of which (like the harmony vocal part and various different rhythms) they discard. Only one idea, an introductory guitar phrase, will be incorporated into the final arrangement of the song. They realise they've basically wasted their time, and Paul in particular feels frustrated at their lack of progress. He might have also felt frustrated at John's continued indifference - Paul and George have been doing most of the songwriting on what is essentially John's number.

6.46   TWO OF US (1:21)

This 'performance' is nothing more than two false starts that break down surrounded by stray lines of vocal and guitar riffs.

Despite George's attempt to deflect him to another song by suggesting some piano-based numbers, Paul begins to play "Two Of Us." John flips through the lyric sheets on his clipboard, searching for the words, and reads out one of the lines from "She Came In Through The Bathroom Window." Paul begins playing the galloping riff which begins the up-tempo arrangement of "Two Of Us" in order to illustrate it to John. Since John says they played it that way in the last session we can assume that the up-tempo arrangement was rehearsed during the session of January 3rd, although none of the available tapes verifies this. Not only does John not remember the words, he doesn't even recall if he sings on the number or not. Paul impatiently reminds him that he has to learn the lyrics, and John meekly replies that he's almost got them down.

6.47   TWO OF US (1:10)

The rehearsal has begun. In this extraordinarily loose fragment, Paul vocalises the cymbal part that he wishes Ringo to play, as John complains about the difficulty of the chords.

6.48   TWO OF US (1:05)

After some riffs, the band attempts to perform the song straight through, but they only make it through two verses before Paul stops them.

Paul realises they're having the same problem they had during the "Don't Let Me Down" rehearsals - they keep working on details rather than the broad outlines of the song.

6.49   TWO OF US (8:11)

The above breakdown is followed by a few attempts from John to work out one of the lines. This is followed by an extensive discussion interspersed with "Two Of Us" riffs and stray lines of lyric.

The day's frustrations reach a boiling point. Although quite a bit of this "Two Of Us" rehearsal remains unavailable, it's obvious things haven't gone well. Paul, as he has several times earlier, expresses his desire that they work out the structure of the song before working on specifics. George disagrees, and believes that they should just play until things come together. The conflict revolves around the different working methods of George, Paul and John. George is dissatisfied simply laying down the groundwork for a song, particularly since John and Paul all but exclude him from the basic songwriting process of their songs. John is withdrawn and uncommunicative, and only offers suggestions when pressed, even for his own compositions. This leaves Paul, by nature a song craftsman, as the only Beatle able to propel the rehearsals forward. This isn't, however, a role that he wants to assume. He bluntly states that he wants to encourage them, but worries that this will mean taking over a leadership role within the group - which would inevitably lead to ruffled egos. He reiterates his belief that they're spending too much time perfecting bits of the songs and once again George disagrees with him, claiming that the rehearsals are not too difficult, but offering to play simpler if Paul likes. The two men, seated a few feet apart, lean towards one another. Both are obviously uncomfortable. They don't meet each other's gaze, and their fingers constantly pick out notes on their guitars. Paul remarks that he's aware of George's irritation whenever he brings up the subject of how complicated a rehearsal should be, but again, George disagrees. The discussion might have become more personal at this point, but Paul backs off, well aware that they're being filmed. John attempts to resume the rehearsal, but Paul, obviously a bit upset, reminds them that they've only got twelve days to get their act together (the amount of time remaining before the TV show) and makes another plea for an organised rehearsal. They then briefly return to working on a galloping guitar riff which kicks off the up-tempo arrangement of "Two Of Us." The riff is too difficult for John, however, and he complains that it's irritating and suggests a far simpler guitar part. Paul, still attempting to express his thoughts, returns to the subject of communication, and, as a gesture towards George, points out that he doesn't want *any* of them to embellish the song until they get the basics worked out. George indicates that he understands this, but once again their different working methods come up as he points out that only by actually playing them can they see if things work in the song or not. Paul attempts a compromise, allowing George to improvise during the solo, but not during the vocal parts, but handing out musical responsibilities once again makes him feel uncomfortable because he sees himself as the only one who's willing to take charge. This is as direct a criticism of George and John as Paul is able to make, as he bluntly complains that they don't support him in his decisions to lead the rehearsal. John admits his non-participation, but makes the excuse that he has no suggestions to make. George, aware that Paul's upset, offers to give in and wait for Paul to get his part down before working on his own, but admits that he would rather work simultaneously. Paul, still trying to mend fences, stresses again that there's nothing personal against George in his desire to tackle the simpler parts of the song first, but that he senses (and dislikes) George's hostility towards his suggestions. He indicates once again that his comments are directed towards all of them and assures George he's not singling him out. When George begins to discuss this, Paul brings up a similar dispute which took place during the July 30, 1968 session which produced "Hey Jude," where George wanted to play a guitar part which Paul felt was inappropriate for the song. George, obviously trying to bring this conversation to a quick end, capitulates completely, and proclaims that he'll play whatever Paul wants, or even not play at all. Paul doesn't want capitulation, however, but cooperation, and he's referring to their working methods when he stresses that they have to work things out. His concerns are based in practicality, since they've only rehearsed four songs and need to develop some sort of organisation in order to produce the number necessary for the upcoming live performance. He's particularly concerned that the rehearsals have to show signs of progress - and obviously that's not the case. George, evidently rubbed the wrong way by Paul's implied criticism of his working method and the reopening of old wounds (the "Hey Jude" anecdote), responds with some bluntness of his own, explaining that he's wasted his entire day. George wants to feel that what he's doing will actually mean something. Paul and George then directly address the difference in their working methods, with Paul claiming that George's way of working leaves him unable to work the way he needs to. George responds that he can't work any other way. Having reached an obvious impasse, Paul cuts the argument short and suggests they move on to a different song. George suggests "Maxwell's Silver Hammer," but John, of all people, wants to continue the "Two Of Us" rehearsals. Paul angrily responds that they've wasted too much time on the song already. This is as close to honest communication as these guys get.

John then suggests that each Beatle should direct the rehearsals of their own numbers. Paul once again expresses his worry that he's being too assertive towards the others and admits that he's been placed in this position for some time. The conversation here is almost drowned out by aimless guitar riffs.

Finally, Paul recapitulates his arguments for an uncomplicated approach to the rehearsals, and concedes that the problem they're having is due to their different working methods. In the course of this discussion he mentions The Red Norvo Quintet, a jazz group from the '50's.

6.50   TWO OF US (1:36)

As Paul continues to discuss the song's arrangement, John offers his approximation of what a Red Norvo Quintet version *might* have sounded like, singing about half the song. The other band members join in halfheartedly midway through the performance.

6.51   TWO OF US (0:44)

Another 'Red Norvo' rendition, with the rest of the band lazily playing along as John sings a verse and chorus.

Paul offers a potential solution to the problem of conflicting working methods: each Beatle will arrange their own songs, including the power to direct and indicate spots for improvisation. This goes over fine with George, but John fears it will mean more work for him, and suggests they play it by ear. Paul and George then get philosophic for a moment as Paul muses that these matters go beyond the simple playing of music. Before this discussion can develop, John begins to play.

The rehearsal has once again gone full circle, as Paul wants to return to the song as it was when they started.

6.52   TWO OF US (2:15)

A lazy attempt at work on the chorus, coupled with numerous riffs from the song as they discuss it.

6.53   FRERE JACQUES (0:38)

A short, poorly played instrumental performance. Halfway into this Paul sings a few lines from "Two Of Us."

"Frere Jacques" is a traditional French folk song learned by grade school children throughout the western world. Since the English lyric contains the line "are you sleeping, Brother John?" this performance may just be a commentary on John's energy level.

6.54   IT AIN'T ME BABE (0:20)

George and Paul each sing a couple of lines to this 1964 Bob Dylan classic, but neither seems very sure of the words. Ringo bangs his drumsticks together rather than join in on drums.

After this brief pause for a couple of off-the-cuff cover versions, The Beatles continue to rehearse "Two Of Us." Paul indicates that he'd like a medium tempo, and George notes that the song is developing a hard edge and asks Paul if he'd like to try it in a country style. Obviously, the conflicts of the past hour have been temporarily solved, as we find George being more receptive to Paul's ideas, and Paul being less demanding as he backs down and indicates that he'll just wait and see how the song develops.

6.55   TWO OF US (4:52)

George begins to perform a country-flavored arrangement as Paul talks to John. Paul stops him by counting out, and a 'proper' performance begins for once, relatively complete. As they near the end of the song they stop to work on the end harmonies. This is taken at a medium tempo, and is quite pleasant, despite the fact that John is slightly off mike.

6.56   TWO OF US (2:40)

They take it from the top yet again, and improvement is evident. This is a complete performance.

6.57   TWO OF US (1.09<

Once again they stop to work on the ending of the song. Paul suggests some very high harmonies, an idea which was thankfully quickly dropped. "Two Of Us" riffs begin to give way to a loose jam as the available tape cuts off.

6.58   TWO OF US   >0:16)

The available tape begins just as The Beatles are finishing another run-through. Perhaps because of an infusion of alcohol their mood has improved, and they end the song by singing in three part harmony.

6.59   TWO OF US   (2:35)

Paul plays a galloping riff on bass, and they begin an even more up-tempo rendition. The band is beginning to come together, and this performance is quite enjoyable, despite the fact that John isn't too sure of the words and George hasn't quite worked out his guitar part. Towards the ends Paul improvises some light-hearted banter.

6.60   TWO OF US   (1:14)

Immediately after the preceding performance, Paul leads them back into the song for another try at the end. Once again, he is stressing the new rhythm.

6.61   WHEN THE SAINTS GO MARCHING IN   (0:05)

The guitar line that Paul wants them to play in "Two Of Us" reminds him of "When The Saints Go Marching In" and he plays a few seconds. This 'performance' is only a mangled single line of that traditional tune.

"When The Saints Go Marching In" was the b-side of The Beatles' first single (backing singer Tony Sheridan) in 1961.

6.62   LOOP DE LOOP   (0:07)

Paul has it wrong. The "Two Of Us" guitar part doesn't quite sound like "When The Saints Go Marching In," but sounds very much like "Loop De Loop." George makes this clear by singing a bit of this song as Paul is singing "When The Saints Go Marching In," and afterwards by himself.

"Loop De Loop" was a hit for Johnny Thunder in 1963.

A comment from Paul suggests the cause of his irritable mood - he suffers from jock itch. Both George and John helpfully suggest that he wash his genitals. George then leads them back into rehearsing "Two Of Us."

6.63   TWO OF US   (2:28)

Led by George, the group rehearses the end of the song. George asks if they sing at the end and they try it out that way as well. Paul then vocalises his idea for a new guitar riff. John attempts to follow Paul's suggestion, but after failing miserably he turns his attention to "Across The Universe," thus ending the lengthy "Two Of Us" rehearsal session.

The Beatles had originally recorded "Across The Universe" on February 4th, 1968 and subsequently donated that recording to a various artists charity album being assembled by The World Wildlife Federation (which wouldn't be released until the end of the following year). Justifiably pleased with the song, John was unhappy with The Beatles' 1968 performance, and saw "Across The Universe" as a candidate for rehearsal at the current sessions. Unfortunately, he doesn't remember the words, and evidently hasn't even kept a copy of them for himself. Mal informs them that Apple assistant Peter Brown is calling the office of their publisher Dick James in order to get John the lyrics.

6.64   HEAR ME LORD   (0:08)

As John discusses the "Across The Universe" lyrics with Mal, George plays the first line of his new song - another candidate for the next song to rehearse.

6.65   ACROSS THE UNIVERSE (0:03<

Despite the lack of lyrics, John begins performing "Across The Universe." Before he has made it through the first line, however, the available tape cuts off.

Brief as this fragment is, it shows that John has, at least, managed to remember the first line of his song. By the next day he will have forgotten even that.

6.66   ACROSS THE UNIVERSE >0:38)

The attempts to perform "Across The Universe" continue, but it's obvious that the rehearsal is doomed. The tempo is slow and plodding, and no one sounds particularly interested. Of note here is John's painful attempt to play the song on organ. George asks John about the fate of their 1968 recording, but John is more interested in recording the song again and suggests several times that their earlier recording can be bettered (it never is, and a doctored version of it will be used for the album *Let It Be*). Until the end of his life John would express regret that The Beatles never re-recorded this number.

6.67   I WANT YOU (0:53<

This Dylan cover is just as poor as the one that occurred on January 3rd. It's led by George, who mumbles a few lyrics off mike as Ringo thrashes around on drums.

Following this, George, Paul and George Martin discuss the configuration of the recording equipment for the live show. Martin says that Alex Mardas (head of Apple electronics) had called him and conveyed a message that the band requested an eight track console, a request which would have brought The Beatles' studio in line with the most sophisticated equipment of the day. Martin says this can't be acquired and scoffs at Mardas' plan to build one himself. He then explains that by linking two four track consoles together the same results can be achieved. Paul agrees with this arrangement.

George Martin wants to know for certain if the live show will take place at Twickenham so he can begin construction of a control room on the set. It's clear that although Glyn's job is to oversee the sound for the television programs, George Martin is expected to produce the eight-track recordings for potential album release. Paul wants to build three structures on the set, one for the control room, one for the film crew, and one for the band to play on. George Martin is unimpressed with this idea and inquires what the alternatives are. George responds that he's willing to play anywhere if the acoustics are good (a comment in marked contrast to his earlier suggestion that they kill the show altogether). Paul and George consider searching out a smaller studio at Twickenham, and Paul suggests one theatre that would have the intimacy of The Cavern Club. Paul then asks what would make the current location better acoustically. John and Ringo, although present, do not participate in these discussions.

6.68   HEAR ME LORD (3:01)

Various loose riffs and stray vocal lines, performed by George throughout the previous conversation.

Paul and company continue to discuss the physical arrangement of the proposed set for the live performance. The promotional film for "Hey Jude" (which had been filmed a few months earlier in the same location) had featured a random sampling of Beatle fans in close proximity to their idols. Neither George Martin nor George Harrison wishes to repeat this, but Paul feels the fans can be controlled simply by making it a rule that they stay away from the stage. George Martin half jokingly claims that barbed-wire will do the trick. After a bit more discussion on the subject of The Beatles' physical relationship to their audience, Paul tosses out the suggestion that they build a set like the Roman Coliseum, and have The Beatles come in along with the lions. This is only slightly more ridiculous than Yoko's suggestion earlier in the day that they play to 20,000 empty seats, or John's (on the 3rd) that they play to an audience of 8. Fully into the spirit of things, George Martin even suggests that they include women in chains.

6.69   (IMPROVISATION) (0:23)

Rather than contribute to the conversation in a conventional manner, John sings his opinion to the rhythm of this brief rock and roll song. John prefers the smaller locale so that the sound will be better, but Glyn feels that the close miking will make up for any loss of fidelity in a larger venue.

6.70   HEAR ME LORD (0:35<

George plays another few guitar riffs following John's improvised performances.

6.71   HEAR ME LORD (1:43)

George has returned to using his wah-wah pedal, and this is basically a solo performance, except for a few tentative bars from the bass. The words are still incomplete at this stage. John would rather work on *All Things Must Pass*.

6.72   HEAR ME LORD >2:17)

Another tentative attempt by George to show the others his new song. John and Ringo. obviously unfamiliar with the tune, offer primitive accompaniment, with Ringo keeping a simple beat on his hi-hat. Paul is not playing.

6.73   ALL THINGS MUST PASS (5:29)

John's request to work on this song, rather than "Hear Me Lord," is finally granted. They get down to business quickly, as this is a serious and nearly complete run-through. Although there are a lot of loose ends musically, the performance moves along well until John begins the last chorus too early. They forge ahead anyway, but the performance breaks down at the very end. Rehearsals of the final chorus follow, but rather than seriously address the problem area of the song (and risk further bad feelings on an already difficult day), they mostly just play riffs.

6.74   ALL THINGS MUST PASS (3.22)

With nothing settled, they take the song from the top again anyway. Despite some sloppy musicianship (especially from John on organ), this is a good performance - in fact, the best available from this day. They make it all the way through the song, although it's clear that a more formal ending is still needed

6.75   LET'S DANCE (0:42)

As a quick break from "All Things Must Pass" rehearsals, John leads the band through this loose but sprightly rendition of a song originally recorded by Chris Montez in 1962. Towards the end, Paul calls out the title of "At The Hop," Danny and The Juniors' 1958 hit.

6.76   ALL THINGS MUST PASS (3:28)

With minimal discussion, George leads the band into yet another pass at this song. Their playing is a bit more precise (if less inspired) than before, but things nearly fall apart during the middle eight. They continue on, but the song breaks down completely during the troublesome final chorus. They resume at that point, and it limps to an end.

The extended rehearsals of "Two of Us," "All Things Must Pass" and "Don't Let Me Down" from the afternoon session offer an excellent chance to compare and contrast the working methods of the band's three main composers. Paul, the perfectionist, likes to work on a song bit by bit, honing each small riff and fill and then assembling them together to create a finished product. Only at the very end of the "Two Of Us" rehearsals does he allow the group to attempt the song all the way through. George, conversely, prefers to have his songs played all the way through multiple times, allowing each band member to work out the part as they go. John hardly asserts himself at all when his songs are being rehearsed, causing Paul and George to attempt to direct the rehearsals out of necessity. This leads to the bickering that is evident in the afternoon's "Don't Let Me Down" rehearsals.

6.77   ALL THINGS MUST PASS (1:25)
It's clear that the final chorus and ending are a problem. Paul makes a half-hearted attempt to rehearse them, but no one seems to have the energy for it.

6.78   ALL THINGS MUST PASS (0:21<
A vocal line from Paul leads off another sluggish bit of half-serious rehearsal.

6.79   ALL THINGS MUST PASS >2:22)
Another attempt to perform the song straight through, with the beginning clipped on the available tape. George turns in an excellent vocal performance and Paul and John provide acceptable backing. At the end, John adds Maurice Kinn to the list of things which must eventually pass away. Maurice Kinn was the executive director of *New Musical Express*, which frequently poked fun at John and Yoko's excesses.

6.80   SHE CAME IN THROUGH THE BATHROOM WINDOW (0:15)
The Beatles attempt to perform a serious run-through, but it breaks down quickly.

This is the first performance of this song to have become available for study. "She Came In Through The Bathroom Window" would never be properly finished or recorded during the "Get Back" sessions, but would appear later in the year on *Abbey Road*.

6.81   SHE CAME IN THROUGH THE BATHROOM WINDOW (3:14)
John comments that he's playing the same chords on his guitar that he was on piano (a clear indicator that there are earlier rehearsals of this song that have not came to light). George is using the wah-wah pedal on his guitar to full effect here - perhaps *too* full an effect. The performance is a bit sluggish, but it does show that a lot of work has been put into the song.

These two tracks are the first performances of "She Came In Through The Bathroom Window" to have become available, although they are clearly not part of the group's first attempt to rehearse it. Although more rehearsals would follow, the song would not be properly recorded or released until the *Abbey Road* sessions later in the year.

6.82   SHE CAME IN THROUGH THE BATHROOM WINDOW (1:54<
Another, more focused attempt to summarise the day's rehearsal of the song. Although the musicianship is a bit lax, it's clear that the song has been nearly perfected.

The rehearsal ends and The Beatles walk out, with Paul singing a snatch of "Carry That Weight" and John asking once again about the missing lyrics for "Across The Universe." An unconvincing schoolmaster, Michael reminds them to show up the next morning at 10. He then talks to the film crew about the possibility of getting a few rolls of film printed for colour rushes.

6.83   CARRY THAT WEIGHT (0:09)

Paul sings a few lines from this song as he exits the studio.

Tuesday, January 7th, 1969

The ill feelings that surfaced on the 6th don't go away on the 7th. In fact, they intensify. The live show project and, in fact, the entire future of the band come perilously close to falling to pieces. Despite the many 'performances' available from this day, The Beatles spend much of the morning and part of the early afternoon discussing the problems within the group. Paul and George argue back and forth while John and Ringo spend most of their time sitting silently by. It seems possible that they didn't realise these conversations were being recorded, since the film cameras weren't rolling at this time. In any event, all of the questions regarding the live show go unresolved and The Beatles spend the afternoon lethargically rehearsing for a show that they're not even sure they'll do.

Musically, the 7th features the first available performances of many songs, including Paul's "Get Back," "The Long And Winding Road" and "Golden Slumbers" and George's "For You Blue." The most extensive rehearsals are dedicated to "Maxwell's Silver Hammer" and "Across The Universe" although The Beatles also work on "I've Got a Feeling," "Don't Let Me Down" and "One After 909." Things progress slowly, and none of the numbers are finished yet.

7.1   THE LONG AND WINDING ROAD   (4:31)
A solo piano performance from Paul, who is once again playing for the cameras to pass the time until the other Beatles arrive. Although he's completed the tune, only one verse of the lyrics has been written, and the words to the middle eight are incomplete. Nonetheless, he runs through the verse a half dozen times, sometimes singing, sometimes just playing. His musicianship, though, is similarly uneven, and the whole thing almost breaks down during his first stab at the middle eight. This is the earliest performance of "The Long and Winding Road" to have become available for study. The fact that it's a piano-based ballad hinders serious consideration of its use in the live show.

7.2   medley GOLDEN SLUMBERS / CARRY THAT WEIGHT   (3:49)
Without pause, Paul launches into a medley of two more piano-based numbers. Both of these compositions have already been worked out, and the lyrics are as complete as they'll get (with the exception of one line in "Golden Slumbers"). In fact, Paul sounds a little bored with the first tune, and intentionally ruins the chorus by singing poorly. After his second go at this, he switches to "Carry That Weight," but there's not enough to that song to sustain him very long and he reverts to "Golden Slumbers.'' He stops for a moment to greet Ringo who harmonises with him briefly on one line.

Although "Golden Slumbers" and "Carry That Weight" were probably considered unfinished at this point, they are as complete here as they will be on *Abbey Road*, recorded later in the year. This performance indicates that the two songs were tied together long before the conception of the *Abbey Road* medley.

7.3   THE LONG AND WINDING ROAD   (1:33)
Again without pause, Paul turns to "The Long And Winding Road." He performs the verse twice, and stops briefly at one point, perhaps to acknowledge George's arrival. As Paul plays, George holds an indecipherable conversation with Ringo.

7.4   (INSTRUMENTAL) (1:01)

Evidently growing bored with "The Long And Winding Road," Paul launches
this piano instrumental. Paul makes no attempts to put words to it, although he
vocalises along at one point.

Paul had attempted this same tune the previous day on organ (see 6.12).

As Paul plays the piano, George, Ringo and one of their friends converse.
Oddly enough, this exchange mirrors many elements of the previous morning's conversation. George asks the others if they've seen the Cream television program (referring to *Cream - Farewell Concert from the Royal Albert
Hall, London* which had been aired on the BBC-TV program Omnibus two
days earlier - see 6.1), and Ringo describes once again how he flicked back
and forth between the Cream program and *Rowan And Martin's Laugh In*.
Complaining once again about the show's choppy editing, Ringo compares it
to the promo clip for Arthur Brown's song "Fire." He and George then joke
about the bizarre juxtaposition of images that can occur while engaged in
channel flipping (e.g., Laugh-In's Ruth Buzzi into Cream's Ginger Baker).
The discussion gets a bit more serious as the unidentified third party in this
conversation equates Ginger Baker's frenetic style to jazz drummers from a
previous era. The rest of the conversation revolves around Baker's comments
about drumming as heard on the Cream program. George expresses great admiration for the way Baker plays the various drums in his kit. Ringo defends
his own simpler style of drumming by saying that they're playing the same
thing, just on different drums.

7.5   (INSTRUMENTAL) (0:16)

This recurs during the conversation above. Paul is evidently at a bit of a loss
what to play, so he breaks into this apparent improvisation. What there is of it
is discordant and simplistic.

7.6   LADY MADONNA (2:04)

Paul plays a very nice, upbeat version of his song on piano (accompanied by
foot tap). Unfortunately his vocal is not on mike and is virtually lost. Towards
the end, he runs out of steam and plays a slower variation of the song.

"Lady Madonna" had been released by The Beatles the previous year.

Despite having received a load of recording equipment the previous day,
The Beatles' performances are still not being recorded (other than by the film
crew) because they are still missing the necessary equipment. Because of this,
they are not able to hear playbacks of their rehearsal. Ringo erroneously assumes that the new tape recorder will be working and, when he learns it's not
yet functional, suggests the situation may be remedied by plugging into the
console feeding George Martin's eight track recorder (which is not operational and probably not even present). It's explained to Ringo that a mono machine will be sufficient to produce the reference recordings the band desires.

7.7   (INSTRUMENTAL) >0:42<

Continuing to play song after song on piano, Paul vocalises another tune.
This appears to be a fragmentary idea for a potential song (in fact, its chord
structure reminds one a bit of "Let It Be"). As it winds down he begins to me-
ander rather aimlessly on the keys. George complains about the smell of
someone's cigar (most likely Michael's, who can be seen smoking cigars on
other sessions).

7.8   SHE CAME IN THROUGH THE BATHROOM WINDOW (0:39<

Paul continues to run through his songbook. Ringo joins in briefly with a parody lyric.

George asks, as he had on January 2nd, if The Beatles' conversations are being recorded. Perhaps because he doesn't want too appear secretive, he indicates that this is because he's worried about ruining a good piece of film with stray profanity. He's assured however, that they can just put a beep over the offending word or disguise it by editing. Ringo understands this process, and disparagingly calls it cheating. Interestingly, a profanity uttered by George during his introduction of "I Me Mine" (see 8.1) will be edited out of the *Let It Be* film in exactly the manner described here. The rest of this conversation revolves around the rushes that were viewed by the film crew earlier in the morning. Praise is given to the coloured lights used as a backdrop for shots of the group, and the imaginative camera angles used for overhead shots. No mention is made of The Beatles' performances.

As the next available tape begins, George and Ringo are poking fun at someone in the crew who persists in giving them sports updates on a daily basis. We learn that Ringo's favourite sport is draughts, and that George simply doesn't care. George changes the subject to a photograph which had been taken the previous summer of The Beatles with Maharishi Mahesh Yogi (along with Jane Asher, John's wife Cynthia, George's wife Patti and her sister Jenny Boyd). George frankly states that Paul, Jane and Cynthia didn't understand what the Maharishi's teachings were about. It's clear from this conversation that George and Ringo harbour no ill feelings towards the Maharishi despite John and Paul's public condemnation of him. This topic will be discussed more thoroughly on January 22nd.

7.9   (IMPROVISATION) (0:20)
Another simplistic piano improvisation from Paul which can be heard underneath conversation. Paul bangs out a few chords, and offers a few Little Richard-like whoops.

Paul sings out the title of "She Came In Through The Bathroom Window" as he approaches Ringo and George, perhaps his way of suggesting they make it the first on their schedule for rehearsal once John arrives. With little else to do, the three Beatles and crew sit around and kid each other. Paul jokes about firing Glyn because he hasn't arrived yet and Michael facetiously points out that it's Ringo's turn to be late (as Paul had been on January 2nd, John on the 3rd and George on the 6th). An inane conversation between Ringo and Michael ensues as Paul asks for a pick and retrieves his bass guitar.

George then sings a misremembered line from "She Came In Through The Bathroom Window" as Paul mentions that he's bruised himself by leaning into his bass. George says the same thing happened to him the previous day, and that he also injured himself by walking into a chair in the dark (probably during his sleepless night on January 5th).

7.10   (INSTRUMENTAL) (1:20)
Paul plays an energetic, galloping rock and roll instrumental, thumping out the rhythm on the body of his bass.

Since Paul was occupied when the topic was raised earlier, George lightheartedly warns him about the boom microphones recording The Beatles' conversations. He then asks Mal for his guitar (which he jokingly refers to as a trombone).

7.11   "MR EPSTEIN SAID IT WAS WHITE GOLD"   (0:57)

Paul begins a simple blues-based improvisation, borrowing a few lines about white gold from the on-going conversation. Ringo harmonises at one point, and Paul vocalises the sound of a slide guitar. Paul is still the only one playing an instrument.

   George asks for a guitar so he can join in. Paul asks soundman Peter Sutton for a Binson echo unit for the microphones (George had suggested acquiring one of these for the P.A. system back on the 2nd). Both George *and* Paul then suggest that Peter find them some better microphones (preferably Neumanns). Michael teases that better mikes will allow the filmmakers to better record The Beatles' conversations. Although George and Paul humour him, they're probably less than thrilled with that idea. Finally, Paul reciprocates Michael's teasing by pretending that John has just walked by.

   Michael jokingly hypothesises that Glyn is late because he hasn't recovered from being called by the name Sonny the previous day. Paul immediately calls Michael 'Sonny,' perhaps hoping it will get rid of *him* as well.

7.12   "LOWDOWN BLUES MACHINE"   >1:53)

As the available tape begins George recalls Paul's earlier performance of "Lady Madonna" by singing a few words. Paul is concentrating on his bass line, however, as he improvises this blues parody, leading off with a line from John's "Don't Let Me Down" and following up with a series of simple blues-based couplets. George joins in on guitar and plays a standard blues riff quite similar to that used in "For You Blue," a song he'll premiere within the hour. As on the previous two performances, Paul pounds out the rhythm on his bass and taps his foot as well, shouting out the name of Anita Harris (a contemporary British singer) at the break.

7.13   medley WHAT'D I SAY / CARRY THAT WEIGHT / SHOUT!   (0:56)

Paul begins another bass riff and George sings a line from "What'd I Say." As George joins in on guitar, Paul sings a few lines from "Carry That Weight." Michael comments about a medley of "What'd I Say" and "Shout!" and this prompts Paul into offering brief performances of both of these songs. He ends "Shout!" in a frenzied falsetto, remarking that that's how Lulu would do it. Lulu, a popular British singer, had a hit with "Shout!" in 1963. She was currently starring in a new TV show called *Happening for Lulu*. Paul and Ringo had both seen the January 4th broadcast.

   Both "What'd I Say" and "Shout!" were in The Beatles' early live repertoire, and they had played "Shout!" on their television program *Around The Beatles*. "What'd I Say" had been a hit for Ray Charles and "Shout!" was recorded by The Isley Brothers. Both were originally released in 1959.

7.14   GET BACK   (1:40<

Paul starts off with a brief bass riff reminiscent of his performance of Lulu's I'm a Tiger" on the 3rd. This transforms into a galloping bass riff similar to 7.10. As George tosses in a few discordant guitar riffs, Paul begins to vocalise a melody over his bass line. Hesitantly, he tests out a 'verse,' but his timing is off, and he's having trouble making up words. He tries again, and things hang together a bit more satisfactorily. On the third try, it comes together, and we have the first performance of a song that is identifiably "Get Back." When he comes to the point where the chorus will be, Paul vamps, stops, thumps out a few beats on his bass guitar, and starts over with the verse again. Just as George starts to join in the available tape cuts off.

Nestled amid an hour of inconsequential dialogue and half-performances, this unique fragment captures "Get Back" (or at least the melody for its verses) at the moment of creation. When it reappears on January 9th, Paul will have grafted on a chorus and thought up some tentative lyrics. For the time being, this was undoubtedly thought of as just another improvisation.

7.15   I'VE GOT RINGS ON MY FINGERS   >0:12<

A loose 'performance' in which Paul sings several lines from this show tune, corrupting the first to mirror a remark about blisters which had been shouted by Ringo at the end of Paul's song "Helter Skelter."

"I've Got Rings on My Fingers" is from 1909's musical-comedy *The Midnight Sons*.

7.16   FOR YOU BLUE   (1:18)

As the available tape begins, George has already premiered his new composition. He describes to Glyn how an electric group arrangement would be inappropriate for the song (making it unusable for the show) as Paul and John (who has recently arrived) engage in silly banter. George then offers this abbreviated solo performance, with Paul offering a few handclaps and nonsense lyrics (some of which echo "Lowdown Blues Machine").

After the performance, George asks if they should consider covering other artist's songs in the live show. Paul and John quickly offer negative responses, and John half-kiddingly adds that he can barely stand doing songs written by Paul and George.

7.17   FOR YOU BLUE   (2:35)

George takes it from the top, offering another solo, acoustic performance. No one is paying attention to him, as Paul rudely spouts nonsense throughout. As with "Hear Me Lord" on the 6th, George's new composition has fallen on deaf ears.

In marked contrast to the previous hour's frivolity, the conversation now turns quite serious as The Beatles try to address the question of their live show. Paul wants to go ahead with it, and points out that if the footage comes out to be unsatisfactory it can be scrapped. George complains about the cost, but Paul says that a good deal of money would have already been wasted even if the show were to be cancelled. Michael correctly observes that they'll still have a documentary even if the concert is cancelled, and because the documentary itself is a bankable project the money wouldn't have been entirely wasted. Realising that the last thing he needs to do is to talk The Beatles out of a show they don't want to do anyway, he quickly reaffirms his support for the show and expresses his dislike of staging the performances at Twickenham. When Paul starts to disagree with him, Michael cuts him off. This is a continuation of a topic which Paul had enthusiastically discussed the previous day.

It might be noted that throughout this conversation and those that follow John and Paul persist in playing riffs and half-snatches of melodies on their guitars. We have avoided the temptation to tag titles on these. Due to their generic and nebulous nature, we feel they're best classified as aimless noodling.

We come now to one of the most illuminating dialogue passages of the sessions. Paul optimistically defends the live show, and claims that the problem is not with the concept of a show, but with the lack of an effective way to present it. He feels that the best way to do a show is not to repeat the standard concert situation that they had had in the past. John, who has no idea what to do to make the concert special, mirrors Michael's observation that even if the show falls through they'll have a documentary about the making of their new LP. He has been thinking along these lines for the past few days, and had made a similar observation on the 3rd. Initiated by George's sombre reflection that things have changed for the worse since the death of their manager Brian Epstein, the discussion turns to the lack of leadership in the group, one of the reasons why The Beatles (and therefore the rehearsals) are so obviously disintegrating. Paul, with remarkable candour, remarks how pessimistic they've been since Epstein died, and that it's become an unpleasant chore to be a Beatle. He then explains that they have two choices - to work to improve things, or call the whole thing off. George agrees, and indicates that he, at least, knows that The Beatles are coming to an end, and does not want to see them finish up their career with inferior product (which, of course, is what ultimately happens). John (sounding very sleepy) raises the subject of incentive. Paul draws him out, and John explains that if they need to think of some reason to continue, communication is reason enough. This is an ironic sentiment indeed, since part of the group's problem is John's refusal to engage in interpersonal communication. Paul returns to the topic of discipline, and presents a lengthy (and wholly accurate) lecture on what the group is lacking. Once again referring to Brian Epstein's death, Paul points out that Epstein's role as father figure and disciplinarian (even if it was only symbolic) now falls upon themselves. He then points out that because they're now controlling themselves they foolishly do as little work as they can, and reminds them of the thought and care which had gone into making *Sgt. Pepper's Lonely Hearts Club Band* two years before. Paul feels that they can still produce something (perhaps even a live show) with that kind of quality, if they can only get their act together. Unfortunately, it seems that the other Beatles are unwilling or unable to do this.

Michael, presumably thinking back a few minutes to the discussion about scrapping the footage if it turned out badly, makes the point that if the project falls apart, the responsibility lies with the group for their substandard work rather than on the filmmakers. Paul disagrees to some extent, and complains that most directors would order them off the soundstage for having such bad attitudes. He contrasts the morale within the group to Jackie Lomax's productive attitude during the sessions for his album *Is This What You Want?* (which Paul had attended), and stresses how easy such a person makes things for everyone. George bitterly tells Paul to go find that person and play with *them*, a complete turnabout from the co-operative stance he had taken on the 3rd. This direct and destructive comment causes Paul to remind him that The Beatles *used to be* a co-operative, creative unit. Rather than respond George takes refuge in a quote from Bob Dylan's song "My Back Pages." Given the tone of this exchange, it's hard to believe The Beatles ever survived the morning of January 7th.

7.18   MY BACK PAGES   (0:04)

George sarcastically performs a single line from this 1964 Bob Dylan song.

Continuing the discussion, Paul points out that films of the early Beatles performing before an audience clearly show their degree of motivation.

However, he makes a mistake in reminding George of touring for George immediately pinpoints this as a reason for not wanting to be involved anymore. Paul responds that negative feelings based on such things as putting on make-up or going through stage routines are pointless, because to go back before a live audience doesn't mean they have to do any of those things. To illustrate his point, he brings their attention to John who, he says, doesn't adhere to any standard stage traditions, but simply shows up hidden with Yoko in a bag (this is a reference to John and Yoko's brand of conceptual art which involved making such appearances). Having trouble, perhaps, envisioning George Harrison in a white canvas bag, Michael asks directly if The Beatles ever expect to perform in front of an audience again. After a vaguely positive response from Paul (and no responses at all from the other three) he follows up with a reflection on how hard it must be to recapture the thrill of live performances. Paul recalls the discussion they had had the previous day about their relationship to their audience, and Michael optimistically comments that the audience has aged just as they have. Paul agrees, and uses this to explain to the others why they needn't play down to them. John isn't concerned. The discussion then reverts to the earlier topic of enthusiasm within the group and a positive working attitude. Paul points out that they've been rehearsing some quality material and worries that in their current state they're unable to do it justice. John agrees with Paul's next observation that on albums they'll occasionally turn in a bad performance simply because they're not in the right mood when recording, but Paul also lays blame on the fact that John won't actively participate in rehearsals. Unfortunately, Michael interrupts this potentially explosive topic by steering the conversation back to the live show, pointing out that they're not motivated because they have no real idea as to where and how they'll stage the performance. He claims that their enthusiasm for the project will manifest itself once they find something to get enthusiastic *about*. George can't be swayed from his pessimistic outlook, however, and now insists that he doesn't want to contribute any of his songs to the project, fearing that they wouldn't turn out as well as they would in a studio environment. This exasperates Paul, who confronts George with a statement that he had made the year before where he had expressed his opinion that there was no limit to creative expression. George's response, which questions why one would even *want* to create, tears away his earlier pretences that The Beatles' current problems lie rooted in the fact that Brian Epstein died or that touring was unpleasant. In fact, George's apathy within The Beatles is caused by a variety of reasons which have not yet been directly addressed in this discussion, and he's probably being more honest than he intends when he admits that he's not particularly *interested* in putting energy into the band. This attitude is 180° from Paul's, who steadfastly continues to offer a positive outlook. As Paul sees it, they can still make great records if they *want* to, and he sees no point at *all* in thinking otherwise. He suggests that George lets go of his negative thoughts by reminding him of the processes they're both familiar with through transcendental meditation, telling him that The Beatles can work together even when one or the other gets tired of playing. He then reiterates that he sees no reason at all to just give up on the band.

Michael expresses his opinion that doing the live show at Twickenham would be the easy way out. He feels that because The Beatles don't have to fight for anything anymore they've become lazy and torpid. He adds that doing the show abroad would give it the framework that it's currently lacking. Paul agrees and John, who has been relatively silent, remarks that that's why he liked the idea of doing the show in Tunisia (although he's acquiesced to Ringo's desire not to travel). Michael continues his pep talk, and points out that if they do a show it should be to the best of their ability, stressing the high expectations of their fans, and how they really don't want to embarrass themselves. Michael feels that they need an obstacle to overcome. Unfortunately the only thing he can come up with is to perform the show abroad - an idea which, as Paul points out, has been unanimously ruled out. George explains why he sees no advantage to going away, and Michael restates his case again, warning them that if they film the show at Twickenham it'll come out like the Cream documentary that they all dislike. Paul, however, insists that they stay in England. Michael changes the course of his argument and says how something *else* must be found to challenge them. Paul agrees, and uses The Beatles' fan club show at Wimbledon Palais on December 14, 1963 as an example of a show that had a special element to it (The Beatles played to their fans from a cage!). George mutters about how awful that concert was for them to play and Paul hastily agrees, backs off and brings up Michael's idea of having the show at a hospital. Michael compares the sentiment of seeing sick children treated to a personal appearance from The Beatles to the sentimental elements that he perceives in The Beatles' music. Paul, ever the public relations expert, sees this type of venue as a good chance to show The Beatles off in a charitable light.

Michael and Paul continue to dominate the conversation. Michael comments how the closeness in age between pop stars and their fans allows the fans to fantasise about being one of them. Paul then offers a lengthy recap of a recent television program named *Late Night Line Up*, which aired most nights on BBC-2. The broadcast he refers to featured art students being given free rein to do what whatever they wanted with the hour. The point he's making is that if the students are brave enough to seize the opportunity to use the media to make a statement, there's no reason why The Beatles shouldn't do it. George mentions that he thought the live broadcast of "All You Need Is Love" (on a 1967 program called *Our World*) was successful because it captured the feel of the moment and was similar to a political broadcast because it reflected the prevailing philosophy of 'the summer of love.' Paul tries to capitalise on George's brief positive display, likens the current project to the earlier broadcast, and once again asks George to wait until they *have* a show before rejecting it. George, still pessimistic, points out that times have changed, but suggests that a political slant to the program might not be bad. Paul seems to agree, but equates this with the other problems facing the project, and wants to make sure they don't say something foolish.

7.19   I'VE GOT A FEELING   (0:09)

John, who seems to have no desire to be involved in the conversation, takes break from his unstructured strumming to play this brief riff during conversation.

Michael and Paul discuss the political impact of the "Hey Jude" promotional film, which showed a wide range of people coming together to sing the chorus along with The Beatles. Paul tries to kill the idea of a straight political broadcast by stating how he doesn't like them, but Michael points out that anything The Beatles do, because of their public stature, is a political statement. George agrees that the political messages in their songs get obscured because of the music, with the possible exception of the "All You Need Is Love" broadcast, which he feels was very direct. Mal makes mention of the fact that performing an album's worth of songs will use up of most of the hour allotted for the show, leaving little time for political speeches, but Paul rightly sees this as irrelevant - if the broadcast is to be political, the messages will be relayed through the lyrics of the songs, as well as their choice of where to play and what audience to play to. He then asks Michael about the possibility of doing the show in the Houses of Parliament. Michael claims that he tried to get that very location for his last TV spectacular (*Rock And Roll Circus*) but was turned down. Paul comes up with the idea of trespassing to do the show, which would provoke a confrontation with authorities. His description of being physically removed from the concert site is an uncanny prediction of what will eventually take place.

7.20   SHE CAME IN THROUGH THE BATHROOM WINDOW   (0:07)
Paul, accompanying himself on bass, gives a one line example of trying to perform a song while being dragged off by the police.

Paul continues to speak enthusiastically about being hauled off by the police, but George and Michael come out against the idea. Michael jokes that if Paul wants to get beat up The Beatles could return to Manila (where they were roughed up following a 1966 concert). George mentions Memphis, the site of another unpleasant concert experience, and Paul reminds him of some bad experience in Houston as well. Michael enthuses at some length about his idea of having the show in an orphanage, but Paul shoots the idea down. Paul himself offers up the prospect of Liverpool Cathedral, but this is met with no response. Michael wants to find a balance between doing a show for paying customers and performing before a charity audience.

7.21   STUCK INSIDE OF MOBILE WITH THE MEMPHIS BLUES AGAIN   (0:28)
George and Paul offer a brief but amusing parody of Bob Dylan as they change the location in the lyric from Memphis to Twickenham. John joins in on guitar.

"Stuck Inside of Mobile With The Memphis Blues Again" appeared on Dylan's 1966 album *Blonde on Blonde*.

Michael raises the prospect of doing the show overseas, but is met with tired silence. George offers the alternative of having dedications to public figures (such as British politicians Enoch Powell and Harold Wilson) as a way of politicising the show. This draws upon an earlier idea which had looked to revive the practice of dedicating songs to individual audience members as The Beatles had done during their early club appearances. Paul, obviously aware of John's lack of input during these discussions asks him directly for his opinion. When John responds that he has no idea what to offer an opinion about, Paul reminds him what they've been talking about, only to be met by silence.

7.22   (IMPROVISATION) (0:35)
A dreadfully ragged jam, as Paul and George join along with John's incessant guitar riffing, vocalising along with the 'performance.'

The conversation continues. Michael, too, tries to get a straight answer from John, who finally states that he doesn't want to play in the types of places they've been discussing. George agrees and Paul offers the impractical suggestion that they send planes to Africa to rescue Biafran refugees and perform a concert for them as they arrive. As the discussion of charities continues, Michael mentions *The Magic Christian*, a fictional story (and soon-to-be film featuring Ringo) of a millionaire who randomly gives money away. He then offers the very bizarre viewpoint that the most charitable thing The Beatles could do would be to put on masks and commit certain judicious murders.

7.23   I SHALL BE RELEASED   (1:27)
George performs a loose, gentle version of this Dylan song over conversation as John joins in on guitar. After two verses he stops to have a conversation with Denis O'Dell.

Michael reminds the group to stay focused on the problem of a venue for the live show. In response to Paul's request for input, Denis offers the level-headed opinion that they hold the show at Twickenham, but Paul returns to the more abstract ideas that they've discussed, joking that the show in the hospital could be capped off with John healing the children and allowing them to walk again, a sly comment on the public's over-adulation of the group.

At this point, several conversations occur simultaneously. Obviously unwilling to participate in further discussions about the live show, George raises the topic of The Band and their relationship with Bob Dylan. Having just sung "I Shall Be Released," George asks Denis if he's heard Dylan's own performance of the song (which was unreleased but had circulated as part of the "Basement Tapes"). Denis says he has, and also has kind words for The Band's version (which appeared on their album *Music From Big Pink*). Once again George expresses his great admiration for that group, and thinks their informal approach to music making would work well for The Beatles in their live show. This said, he loses no time pointing out the difficulty of preparing themselves for the upcoming live show when they haven't played live in years. He then mentions how impressed he was with John Simon's production on The Band's album until he saw the group perform live and realised how little a part their producer played in shaping their sound.

Assuming for the moment that the live show will take place at Twickenham, Michael and Paul discuss possible sets. Michael opts for a minimalist approach. Paul thinks the acoustical drapes might be enough of a set, and wants to include shots of the control room so that their audience can get an idea of what it's like behind-the-scenes. Michael then stresses that he wants the show to be the best rock and roll program ever including his own work on *Rock and Roll Circus*.

Mal suggests doing the show in a theatre, but Michael seems to feel it should be something a bit more special because The Beatles may never do this kind of thing again. This is certainly a perceptive (and bravely expressed) observa-

tion on his part. Paul wants a serious reason to do the show because he sees
as the only way to motivate the group.

7.24   TO KINGDOM COME (1:00)

George offers another unobtrusive solo performance during the course of the
following conversation. He sings one verse, stops for a moment, and then
plays an instrumental passage.

"To Kingdom Come" is another song from The Band's *Music From Big
Pink* album.

The conversation continues. Paul perceives that The Beatles' return to the
stage will be a sociological event during which they'll have an unparalleled
opportunity to make a statement. He just doesn't know what to make a statement about. To Mal, entertainment is both reason and statement enough, but
Paul and Michael disagree. George mentions a discarded idea that would have
seen The Beatles performing with other acts on the bill, implying that pride
and rivalry might serve to excite the band. He then jokes that The Beatles
might be upstaged by one of their guests (as The Who had done to The Rolling Stones on *Rock and Roll Circus*). Personally, he's willing to accept the
challenge, but Michael states that The Beatles can surely carry the hour long
show by themselves.

7.25   FOR YOU BLUE (1:18<

As Paul and Michael converse, George returns to this song, first mumbling his
way through a verse and then singing a line or two. John offers surprisingly
passable accompaniment, most likely thanks to the song's generic blues
changes.

"For You Blue" would not be a serious contender for rehearsal during the
Twickenham sessions, although more serious work on it would take place after the sessions move to Apple.

Meanwhile, Paul tells Michael that he feels that if The Beatles are *forced* to
they can rally and put on an excellent performance. But once again he is at a
loss as to the motivation that would make them feel compelled to perform. As
the available tape runs out, Michael half-suggests an impromptu performance
at a public location.

7.26   FOR YOU BLUE >0:04)

A brief fragment, as George sings half a line and stops. He then succinctly
categorises the others' attitudes toward the show by quoting the old aphorism
'hear no evil' (Paul, the persistent optimist), 'speak no evil' (John, who contributes nothing to the conversation) and 'see no evil' (Ringo, who really
doesn't care what they do). Paul, obviously disgusted, attempts a bit of direct
communication and asks the other Beatles why they're even bothering to
show up if they don't want to do the show. Quite typically, no one responds.

7.27   (IMPROVISATION) (3:13)

John's endless guitar noodling becomes a bit more structured. Paul and
George contribute on and off instrumental accompaniment, and someone offers handclaps. This performance continues as the discussions about the motivation, format and venue for the live show continue. George Martin arrives,
presumably with some recording gear in tow, and we learn that Paul originally
envisioned the documentary of the rehearsals and the live show as part of the
same program (although he's now rejected that idea). The most important moment, however, occurs as Paul confronts John (who has sat silently strumming

his guitar for most of the past half hour) and describes how terrible he feels to be the only one interested in performing. John testily replies that he's said all he's going to say on the matter. Paul asks for additional input, but all he receives is a truculent put-off from John.

7.28   BO DIDDLEY (0:15)

A short solo performance from George, who plays guitar and mumbles half a line of lyric.

"Bo Diddley" was named after its author, who recorded the song in 1955.

Driven to the breaking point by John's obtuseness, Paul finally loses his patience and demands a decision about the live show from the other Beatles, angrily proclaiming that he's not going to waste his time sitting around waiting for them to decide what they want to do. We learn that this morning's discussion is an informal extension of a business meeting which had taken place the previous evening where Mal (of all people) fearfully broached the same subject. Now Paul is ready to lay down some ground rules. If they're going to do the show they'll have to make a studious effort to learn so many new songs each day. If they're going to show up with a negative attitude then Paul himself will refuse to take part. George, incredibly, has not even been paying attention, as he is engaged in a conversation with George Martin regarding the hiring of string players for final overdubs on Jackie Lomax's album *Is This What You Want?* Paul implies that he accepts an occasional period of apathy from the others, but worries out loud that this will cause him to lose interest, and brings up the sessions for the previous year's double album, which he states were even worse in terms of The Beatles' inability to communicate with one another. Paul wants them to clear the air. This comment irritates George, who responds that past attempts to do this have led to compromises that no one really wanted to make. Paul answers by saying that if the live show turns out to be a compromise of that type then they should just give up and let The Beatles die. Almost enthusiastically, George agrees. It's worthwhile to note that, with their decade-old relationship on the verge of disintegration, John *still* has nothing to say. Michael, however, reflects how sad it would be to see the end of the group, and Paul angrily responds how idiotic it would be to let that happen. George, obviously thinking of his lesser role within the group, says that the time could be better spent individually, where one could actually create. This is a direct slap in the face to Paul, who's been more than ready to create, but has been faced with the insurmountable task of motivating the other Beatles. Paul pleads that all he's looking for in the others is some kind of positive attitude, but no one responds except Mal, who offers a rather maudlin statement about The Beatles' importance to their audience. Paul then returns to the problems he has been facing as de facto leader of the group, admitting that most of the ideas are his. He challenges the others to work to improve or replace his ideas, but once again no one responds as Ringo sits silently by and John plays aimless guitar riffs. In terms of pure drama, none of the available tapes top *this*.

George ponders how philosophical this is all getting, and Michael proudly offers a pun based on the name of existentialist philosopher Jean-Paul Sartre. He then suggests that The Beatles play for a while before lunch.

7.29   WHAT THE WORLD NEEDS NOW IS LOVE (0:07)

George sings two lines from this Bacharach-David composition spurred on by a comment from Michael in the above conversation.

"What The World Needs Now is Love" was a U K. hit for Cilla Black in 1968.

7.30   (INSTRUMENTAL) (0:22)

John plays a guitar riff to get warmed up for the impending rehearsal, and this develops into a brief jam as Paul joins in on bass, and Ringo supplies a few thumps on drum.

They're not *quite* ready to play however and, in the spirit of having it out, George bitterly complains about the lack of attention given his compositions throughout the years. Paul optimistically says that the most important thing isn't what's wrong between the members of the group, but the fact that the four of them notice it (and presumably do something to correct it). This doesn't satisfy George, however, who emotionlessly suggests that The Beatles break up. Paul agrees that the end is getting nearer and John, unable to contribute constructively to the discussion, picks this moment to throw in one of his famed witticisms, asking which one of them would get possession of the children. Paul, obviously thinking of their songs, nominates Dick James, The Beatles' publisher.

7.31   FIRST CALL (0:09)

A guitar riff from John to signal the beginning of the rehearsals.

This familiar bugle call is played at horse races at post time as the horses approach the starting gate. It was first published by George W. Behn in 1842.

Paul has one last thought to express before playing. Amazed and baffled at the thought of breaking up The Beatles, and cognisant of the artistic and financial havoc such an act would cause, he incredulously reminds the others how stupid it would be for them to break up, and points out the lack of creative energy within the group. In recognising that John has deflected some measure of his creativity towards projects with Yoko, Paul allows a bit of resentment to surface as he first complains that John talks condescendingly to them and then observes that he doesn't talk at all. Having raised a sensitive subject but still gotten no reaction from John (in fact, John tries to block him out by playing an annoying guitar riff), Paul reminds him that he, too, can be condescending and counts in for "I've Got a Feeling" to begin the rehearsals. The nearly hour long series of discussions has ended with nothing being resolved in terms of the show or the group's future.

7.32   SHE CAME IN THROUGH THE BATHROOM WINDOW (0:24)

After Paul's count-in John begins playing the wrong song, much to everyone's delight. Confused, he stops briefly and then sings a line of the song in an attempt to differentiate it from "I've Got A Feeling."

7.33   I'VE GOT A FEELING (1:00<

John plays the song's introduction a bit slower than usual and Paul corrects him. The Beatles then launch into an unenthusiastic but workmanlike performance. The available tape cuts off during the second verse.

The next fifteen minutes or so of the session are not available, but The Beatles undoubtedly continue to rehearse "I've Got a Feeling."

7.34   I'VE GOT A FEELING >1:40)

The available tape features the second half of an obviously complete run-through. This sounds much the same as 7.33, except that during the missing minutes George has rigged up his wah-wah pedals

7.35   (IMPROVISATION) (0:16)

As the technicians adjust Paul's microphones, George strums his guitar and improvises this brief number.

7.36   MAXWELL'S SILVER HAMMER (0:30)

Suggesting that this is his choice for the next song to rehearse, Paul plays a basically solo piano version with vocalising in place of the lyrics. During the course of this performance George changes over to bass guitar.

7.37   "WOMAN WHERE YOU BEEN SO LONG" (2:16)

The band jams as Paul pounds out a boogie woogie rhythm on the piano and sings what is presumably an improvisation. This isn't bad for what it is, although it deteriorates into a simple repetitive riff before it ends.

7.38   "OH JULIE, JULIA" (2:08)

The '50's flavour continues as Paul leads them into this Little Richard-like number. As the band plays what is essentially an instrumental version of Little Richard's song "Lucille," Paul sings in falsetto about a girl named Julie/Julia. Paul seems taken by this number, and manages to repeat the verse and chorus three times by the song's end.

7.39   OH! DARLING (3.35)

Reminded of "Oh! Darling" by Paul's falsetto singing on the previous number, John asks him to play it and Paul obliges, stopping at various points to go over the chords. Although this is the earliest full-band performance of this song to surface, it's obvious that they've done some work on it before. At one point during the middle eight Paul and George are reminded of the song "One Night" (no doubt remembering Elvis Presley's recording), and sing a bit of that song, underscoring the similarity between the two. Shortly after Paul goes over the bass line with him, George requests that the rehearsals switch to "Maxwell's Silver Hammer."

7.40   THE LONG AND WINDING ROAD (0:31)

Paul performs this brief instrumental to pass time as George prepares to play "Maxwell's Silver Hammer." Ringo chimes in with some jazzy drumming towards the end.

7.41   MAXWELL'S SILVER HAMMER (1:58)

George has the bass turned up quite loud for this performance, perhaps in an effort to hear himself better because he is unsure of his playing. He runs through the bass part by himself before Paul joins in with piano and vocal about a minute into the performance. John and Ringo go into a waltz tempo during the middle eight, and the song immediately breaks down as Paul proclaims that he doesn't care for the waltz tempo. This had apparently been an integral part of the song during the previous group rehearsal (which is unavailable), but Paul quickly gets rid of it here.

7.42   MAXWELL'S SILVER HAMMER (0:56<

This begins as a more focused attempt at the song, but Paul quickly begins to fool around with his vocal as he complains of feedback from his microphone.

7.43   MAXWELL'S SILVER HAMMER >14:38<

This long segment captures a good portion of the group's rehearsal. As the available tape begins Paul can be heard trying out the end of the chorus. This leads into the unfinished third verse, which at this point consists of little more than a few words and a lot of vocalising. As this loose run-through nears its end he stops to go over the song's structure and chords for the others. Presumably thinking of contemporary singer Tiny Tim and his trademark instrument, Paul wants John's guitar to sound like a ukulele (certainly the way he's playing suggests this). As they rehearse Mal makes clopping sounds along with the song (a distinctive element in Tiny's hit cover of "Tip-Toe Thru' The Tulips With Me") Paul likes this and suggests they retain it for the live show - an idea which has suddenly come back to life. The Beatles then attempt the song from the top, but it breaks down after the beginning of the second verse. After pausing to work on getting out of the chorus and back into the verse, Paul asks Ringo to play something fancier on his cymbals and works on the bass part with George. As a performance develops he calls for John to play a solo. John obliges, but his guitar playing is embarrassingly poor. Perhaps to cover for this he attempts a bit of verbal levity, explaining to Paul that he lost his ability to play on the way to the studio that morning. As the rehearsal continues Paul and George make their first attempt at harmonising on the chorus. George is confused about where to play a certain bit, so Paul plays a double-time rendition of half the song in an attempt to illustrate the structure for him. Rehearsals proper resume as Paul begins to sing from the second verse, stopping and starting to work on various elements. Shortly before the available tape runs out he mentions that he would like to have them whistle more seriously in the solo.

7.44   MAXWELL'S SILVER HAMMER >0:28<
This fragment features Paul reminding John and George to whistle on the song. When they oblige, he praises them.

7.45   MAXWELL'S SILVER HAMMER >1:42<
The available tape begins during the chorus. This leads into a whistling solo which Paul interrupts, because a guitar solo belongs in this spot. After George plays a short doubletime verse Paul suggests that Mal should play a hammer and anvil on the song. A performance is then attempted from the top which quickly breaks down as George and Paul stop to work on the introduction and bass line.

7.46   MAXWELL'S SILVER HAMMER >0:52)
Paul leads John and George through a rehearsal of the whistling chorus, once again offering some encouragement. He then mugs for the camera and holds up the warranty card for the band's new Fender amplifiers. This shot was included in the *Let It Be* film.

7.47   RULE, BRITTANIA (0:12)
John plays a few off-key bars of this patriotic song on guitar as someone whistles and Ringo joins in on drums.
  The melody for "Rule, Brittania" was written ca. 1740 by Thomas Arne.

7.48   (IMPROVISATION) (0:13)
John plays another few chords on guitar and Paul joins in and improvises a few lines about being lost-at-sea. He then makes a joke about The Beatles' stage costumes as an assistant helps George disentangle himself from the bass guitar.

7.49   (IMPROVISATION) (0:08)

Another brief improvisation, as someone sings a few lines to the assistant (Jim Garrady) in an Irish accent.

It's nearly 1:30, and The Beatles clown around a bit as they head off for lunch.

7.50   MAXWELL'S SILVER HAMMER >1:33<
The Beatles return from lunch, and resume the "Maxwell's Silver Hammer" rehearsals. Ringo and Paul take turns singing the chorus (surprisingly, this unique bit of vocal from Ringo fits the song quite well), and Ringo plays the jazzy drum part quite well. Paul makes a mock stage announcement during the song.

7.51   (IMPROVISATION) >0:24)
This performance sounds like the end of a jam that may have grown out of "Maxwell's Silver Hammer." Paul vocalises along with the tune which then dies down into a series of piano trills. Afterwards, George can then be heard fumbling about on bass, which he has set once again to a high volume.

7.52   SPEAK TO ME >0:18)
As somebody whistles a vague melody, George plays the introductory bass line of this Jackie Lomax song. Paul then suggests that they need to hear the words for his song 'When I'm Sixty-Four" and subsequently recites the first verse.

7.53   WHEN I'M SIXTY-FOUR (0:25)
Paul accentuates his recitation of the lyrics with a few dramatic chords on the piano.

"When I'm Sixty-Four" appeared on The Beatles' *Sgt. Pepper's Lonely Heart's Club Band* LP in 1967.

7.54   medley WHEN I'M SIXTY-FOUR / SPEAK TO ME (1:07)
George begins to play the "Speak To Me" bass riff again, and Paul wraps a Jamaican-flavoured piano improvisation around it, topped off with the lyrics to 'When I'm Sixty-Four." Ringo provides accompaniment. After the others stop, George continues to play a meandering series of bass guitar riffs. Michael jokingly mistakes the word 'valentine' in Paul's lyric for 'vaseline.'

7.55   SPEAK TO ME >0:11)
This fragment captures some more of George's fixation with the "Speak To Me" bass riff. Paul offers some seemingly unrelated vocalising, and then continues to read aloud, in this instance repeating someone's defence of transcendental meditation as Ringo thrashes about on his drums.

7.56   OH! DARLING (2:59)
Paul's gospel chords remind him of "Oh! Darling" and he begins to play that number as Ringo joins in on drums. After a rough start things improve as John and George join in, and the band turns in an excellent performance of the song. Once again Paul drops in a small bit of "One Night."

This fine performance is the musical highlight of the day. Given its compositional quality and the degree of work that had obviously been put into the song at some point, it seems odd that it was not more seriously rehearsed during these sessions.

7.57   MAXWELL'S SILVER HAMMER >1:19)
The available tape begins during the second verse, and as the whistling verse approaches the performance breaks down. Paul is unhappy because John and

George's whistling cannot be heard because they are not miked properly. As this problem is rectified John plays some "Maxwell" riffs on guitar.

7.58   MAXWELL'S SILVER HAMMER   (3:48)

This is a complete run through that begins with a couple of false starts that occur during the introduction because no one except Paul is whistling. Mal now has his anvil set-up (as Paul had suggested earlier) and can be heard striking it during the chorus (he's also singing, though he's not miked).Despite the mix-up at the beginning, the whistling breaks have been fully integrated into the song, and Paul sings all three of the verses, although the words to the second are unfinished, and those to the third are almost non-existent.

Nevertheless, he sings with great enthusiasm, and is obviously having a good time.

A portion of this performance was used in the film *Let It Be*.

7.59   MAXWELL'S SILVER HAMMER   >13:34<

Another long excerpt of a stop-and-start rehearsal. The available tape begins during a sprightly instrumental rendition, after which Paul jokes about a beach hat which has been sitting next to his piano. George then requests that they rehearse the end for Mal's benefit, and Paul runs through an instrumental chorus and the song's conclusion in an attempt to teach Mal where to strike the anvil.

Paul continues to visualise how "Maxwell's Silver Hammer" could be staged, after which he and John have a curious little discussion that light-heartedly parodies the serious tone of the morning's discussions. As Paul speaks, George continues to run through the song with Mal, unsure of whether to have him hit the anvil once or twice at the end. After a while, Paul joins in and mentions that he hasn't written the third verse yet. He then illustrates the verse/chorus structure, with emphasis on the placement of the whistling. This gradually evolves into a performance. As he had earlier, Paul praises the others' performance after the whistling verse (perhaps he considered his comment a part of the song) and pauses at one point to run over the chords and structure for John (whose playing has been noticeably discordant). When they reach the third verse Paul improvises some lyrics and as the performance concludes they once again try to work out how many times they want Mal to strike the anvil at the end of the song. George then offers a candid appraisal of his bass playing abilities, explaining that he can play the correct notes, but has little idea how to get a particular sound out of the instrument, and says that will have to be up to Glyn. Taking the song from the top, John and Paul offer mock stage introductions.

During the performance George suggests having a lot of people singing on the chorus, but Paul's too busy singing to respond. George and Paul harmonise nicely on the vocal chorus, but when they reach the whistling chorus the performance falls apart.

George then repeats his idea that a group of people be brought in to sing the chorus (as had been done for the "Hey Jude" promotional film) but John prefers to have the group learn the song themselves first. George elaborates, however, and suggests that the lyrics could be projected onto a large white screen behind the area where the band is rehearsing. Once again no one responds. The band then resumes the rehearsal where they left off (at the whistling chorus). As he had during the morning's rehearsal, Paul admonishes the others when their whistling gets a bit too fancy, and tells George to learn the basic tune first. He then counts down for a full performance, but it barely survives the introduction before he stops them. The available tape runs out at this point.

The "Maxwell's Silver Hammer" session concludes. Overall, they've been relatively successful, with a decided improvement between the first perform-ances and the last, and several important elements added to the song (foremost among them the hammer and anvil part). Despite all the attention given to the whistling breaks and chorus, when "Maxwell's Silver Hammer" is eventually recorded for *Abbey Road* all of the whistling parts will be dropped. Taking ad-vantage of the few moments between rehearsals, the crew prepares The Beatles' microphone set-up to record on Glyn's mono outfit. which is finally complete and operational. To this end they remove one of John's floor micro-phones and replace it with a boom mike, prompting a comment from Paul.

7.60   (IMPROVISATION) (0:09)
A brief, simple rock and roll guitar riff from John, who sings a couple of words, possibly to the sound technician.

7.61   A SHOT OF RHYTHM AND BLUES (1:55)
John leads the band through this very enjoyable performance. He has a sur-prisingly good recollection of the words and even offers a slight alteration of the original lyric to incorporate a mention of Zen Buddhism. Ringo starts to play half way through.

"A Shot of Rhythm and Blues" was recorded by Arthur Alexander in 1961 and was performed by The Beatles on BBC radio in 1963.

7.62   (YOU'RE SO SQUARE) BABY I DON'T CARE (0:44)
Another loose oldie while the technicians prepare the mikes. John starts sing-ing the song and George picks it up after everyone else loses interest. Ringo provides accompaniment on tom-tom.

This cover is another example of The Beatles' affinity for Elvis Presley hits. It was originally issued in 1951.

7.63   ACROSS THE UNIVERSE (0:31)
The Beatles play the song's instrumental introduction, but the performance breaks down before the first verse. John can't remember the first line of the song. George tries to help him out, but he doesn't know it either. John then expresses his dissatisfaction with the intro they used on their February 1968 recording.

7.64   ACROSS THE UNIVERSE (2:42)
The Beatles try the song again from the top, and after a struggle with the in-troduction they get underway. Ringo's drumming is a bit heavy-handed. John struggles with the lyrics, and eventually just compensates with vocalising. His frustration at not knowing the words eventually causes him to halt the per-formance.

It's tough to rehearse a song when no one, including its author, can remem-ber the words. Consequently, The Beatles are forced to wait until someone from Apple can arrive with the lyrics. Glyn performs some equipment checks as The Beatles wait.

7.65   ACROSS THE UNIVERSE >1:23)
Despite not knowing the lyrics John tries the song again anyway. As might be expected, it breaks down into a series of riffs.

John then complains that "Across The Universe" isn't up-tempo enough for him, and reasons that the band's mood would improve if they worked on more upbeat material. George caustically berates this attitude and suggests that they work on the songs, regardless of the tempo. John assumes they'll write some rock and roll numbers but bemoans the fact that he's too tired to do so. Paul sides with John, and agrees that the slower songs tend to put them in a lethargic mood. Yoko suggests "Give Me Some Truth," but John doesn't think that's fast enough either. He then sings a line from that song. Eric Brown arrives from Apple with the lyrics of "Across The Universe," and John is surprised to read some of the lyrics that he had forgotten.

7.66   GIVE ME SOME TRUTH (0:03)

A single line sung by John with guitar accompaniment.

7.67   (IMPROVISATIONS) (0:39)

George plays a wah-wah guitar piece derived from the chords of "Across The Universe." He vocalises near the end of the 'performance.'

John expresses his displeasure with The Beatles' February 1968 recording of "Across The Universe" while George indicates how much he likes it, including the two fans who had been recruited from the street to sing backup. That recording had not been issued by E.M.I., but had been donated to the World Wildlife Fund for release on a charity album. John has little faith that the charity record will come out, however, and prefers that the song be used in the current project rather than stay unheard.

7.68   ACROSS THE UNIVERSE >4:34<

Now that the lyrics have become available, rehearsals of "Across The Universe" begin in earnest. The available tape begins mid-verse but as The Beatles reach the chorus the performance falls apart because of the imbalance between Paul and John's mikes.

As Glyn adjusts the mike balance, someone fetches John a music stand to hold his lyric sheets. After John jokingly busks a bit of doubletime "Across The Universe," George returns to an earlier topic and says that he likes the slow tempo of the song. John replies that he couldn't speed it up if he wanted to because he wouldn't be able to sing all the words. He then asks for a record player, presumably to play an acetate of their '68 recording and suggests that George could play organ on the song. George is willing, but points out that he's not very good at that instrument. John indicates that the organ part is an uncomplicated drone, simply meant to replace the tamboura (an Indian instrument) which was used in the original recording. Throughout this discussion Paul and Ringo can be heard practising various elements of the song. The group takes the song from the top, then, but the miking is even worse than before. The available tape runs out after the first verse.

7.69   ACROSS THE UNIVERSE (0:44)

After the end of the previous performances George moves over to organ to test out John's idea of using it as a drone, and plays part of a verse as Paul sings. John immediately dislikes the effect, however, and drops the idea. George then wanders away for a few minutes while John attempts to achieve the drone effect on guitar and Paul tunes. For a few minutes there is no conversation.

7.70   (IMPROVISATION) (0:16)

While in the process of adjusting his guitar, John plays a string of brief rock and roll riffs, quickly reverting to tuning. This can barely be called a performance.

7.71   ACROSS THE UNIVERSE (3:47)
Continuing to experiment with his guitar, John plays several variations of "Across The Universe." The first is a very 'heavy' instrumental arrangement, which he quickly abandons. After some adjustments he begins playing a much lighter version which bears a very strong resemblance to his 1968 composition "Julia." He sneaks one line of vocal into this one. Paul follows on bass but the performance reverts to loose riffs before it gets going. John then takes the song from the top, but struggles with the introduction. When it finally gets underway, John and Paul play a single verse and chorus, with Paul offering staccato back-up vocals in falsetto, and John sounding sleepier than ever.

   Eric Brown dutifully informs the others that *Yellow Submarine* has won the 1968 New York Film Critic's Award for best animated feature. They are unimpressed. Paul scoffs, and both he and Ringo make fun of Al Brodax, the film's producer.

7.72   A CASE OF THE BLUES (0:35)
It would seem that John runs through a couple of verses of this song just to convince himself that it is too slow to use at this point. Paul follows along on bass.

7.73   "CUDDLE UP" (0:06)
A brief falsetto performance from Paul. This sounds like a line from an unidentified soul number. Despite having rejected the idea just a short time ago, John once again considers working on "Give Me Some Truth."

7.74   GIVE ME SOME TRUTH (0:09)
John offers a snippet of the song, with Paul joining in for a few words.

7.75   ACROSS THE UNIVERSE (0:07)
John laughingly starts to sing the first line of the song. Paul takes over and finishes it.

7.76   GIVE ME SOME TRUTH (0:52)
John and Paul try a bit harder during this performance, but John is unimpressed and work on the song is quickly abandoned.

7.77   FROM ME TO YOU (0:06)
Once again using a falsetto, Paul vocalises the first two lines to this 1963 Beatles single.

   John then complains that he has written too many chord changes into "Give Me Some Truth," making it hard to play. Obviously unhappy with the progress of the "Across The Universe" rehearsals, he wishes that the playback system was operational so that they could form a more objective opinion of their progress. With this said, he prepares the group for another performance, requesting that they shorten the chords.

7.78   ACROSS THE UNIVERSE (5:15)
A complete, if rather perfunctory run-through. John makes *his* displeasure with the performance clear as Paul looks on in a stupor. Following this, George asks if they want him to play a drone effect on his guitar. After Paul vocalises this he and John run through a single verse. As George practices the song's intro using his wah-wah pedal, Paul reads out the 1966 tour list which

is taped to his bass guitar, as he does so, John plays a brief riff from "Rock and Roll Music."

7.79　ACROSS THE UNIVERSE　(0:45)

George's rehearsal of the intro leads into another performance which quickly runs out of steam, with John offering only a single line of lyric. If each Beatle is to lead the rehearsals of their own songs, John is doing an awfully poor job. Perhaps aware of this, Paul warns him that he'd better take charge.

7.80　ROCK AND ROLL MUSIC　(1:50)

Obviously bored with "Across The Universe," John returns to "Rock and Roll Music." He delivers a very enthusiastic lead vocal (joined by Paul in spots), and does far better than one would expect at remembering the words.

"Rock and Roll Music" was written and recorded by Chuck Berry in 1957. The Beatles released a fine cover version on their *Beatles For Sale* album in 1964, and it's clear they are as fond of the song now as they were then.

7.81　LUCILLE　(1:12)

George, hoping to brighten things even further, leads the band into another oldie - this time Little Richard's 1957 hit. Paul takes the lead vocal and John joins in for the chorus.

7.82　LOTTA LOVIN'　(n/a - timed as part of 7.83)

Paul wants to do another oldie as he sings one line from this 1957 Gene Vincent song, but John is already playing the opening bars of "Across The Universe".

7.83　ACROSS THE UNIVERSE　(3:08)

Perhaps trying to capitalise on the improved atmosphere, John leads the band through another complete run-through. Unfortunately this one isn't even as good as the one that preceded the oldies (7.78), since it's entirely devoid of feeling. Once again Paul sings along, and the song almost breaks down as he forgets to shorten one of the choruses as John moves on into a verse. At the end of the song they play a short instrumental coda.

Since they can't seem to work up enthusiasm for "Across The Universe" they shelve it for the remainder of the day. Portions of this performance and 7.78 were edited together for use in the film *Let It Be*.

7.84　GONE, GONE, GONE　(1:50)

Having slogged through another performance of "Across The Universe," John heads into another oldie without hesitation. The performance is very upbeat, with John having fun on lead vocal and George playing a very nice guitar solo.

The original version of "Gone, Gone, Gone" was written and recorded by Carl Perkins in 1955.

Perhaps an indication of his state of boredom, Paul passes the time by reading out the various tradenames on his microphone.

7.85　DIG A PONY　(1:01)

Despite John's offer to teach this song to the other Beatles, it's clear from their performance that they've already played it at some point. Paul looks supremely uninterested (and even yawns at one point). By the song's end, even John sounds sick of it. The lyrics are either unfinished or (more likely) John can't remember them.

This performance can be seen in the film *Let it Be*. "Dig a Pony" wouldn't be fully worked up until the January 22nd Apple session.

"Dig a Pony" is the fourth original that John has considered for rehearsal in the past hour, and he has rejected them all since what he really wants to do is play a fast number. Paul consequently suggests the only appropriate original currently in the band's repertoire, "One After 909," and John agrees.

7.86   ONE AFTER 909 (0:47<

After a rough start The Beatles begin a loud, up-tempo performance, propelled by a solid backbeat from Ringo. The available tape runs out during the second verse.

7.87   ONE AFTER 909 >1:13)

This is the latter part of the performance started in 7.86. The Beatles' playing is sloppy but they *do* sound like they're enjoying themselves.

7.88   ONE AFTER 909 (1:08)

Paul starts vocalising the part of the song where the verse goes into the solo. As this quickly turns into a real performance, he starts to sing the lyrics. Brief as it is, this is the best available performance of the song from this day. Although John hardly sings, Paul's vocal is wonderfully spirited, as is his bass playing and Ringo's drumming. Their spirit here recalls the early Beatles.

7.89   ONE AFTER 909 (0:30)

As a response to Paul's frenzied rendition, John leads them into this short, careful and controlled performance. George then suggests they run through it again, but Paul expresses a concern that the simple charm of the song might be spoiled by overrehearsal. George had raised this point when "One After 909" was resurrected on the 3rd, but now he wants to rehearse it. At the prospect of routining "One After 909" Paul laughs and mock-screams in frustration, and Ringo rebels by bashing on his drums.

7.90   WHAT'D I SAY (0:16)

Following George's lead, the band jumps into the introduction to "What'd I Say." After a few bars they begin to improvise, but Paul stops them to play "One After 909."

7.91   ONE AFTER 909 (2:40)

The Beatles take it from the top (at the usual tempo), and deliver a complete performance. They do a credible job until John gets confused and starts singing halfway through George's guitar solo. The remainder of the performance is a bit ragged.

7.92   (IMPROVISATION) (1:05)

Immediately following "One After 909," John leads the band into this simplistic instrumental. Paul's bass line is nice, and Ringo bangs out the rhythm on tambourine. This is relatively good for what it is.

7.93   DON'T LET ME DOWN (1:29)

Paul, in an effort to avoid overrehearsing "One After 909," suggests moving on to "Don't Let Me Down." He sings the song's title, and this leads to a series of guitar riffs and stray lines of vocal as The Beatles prepare to rehearse the song. John is amazed because he's been thinking the same thing (which is hardly surprising, since he's run through almost his entire catalogue of unrecorded numbers in the past few hours). John then questions George about his use of wah-wah pedal, and George explains he'll use it in moderation, simply to have a phased effect.

7.94   DON'T LET ME DOWN (0:54<

Paul suggests that they try a complete run-through and they turn in an acceptable performance. The available tape cuts off during the second chorus.

7.95   DON'T LET ME DOWN   >0:43)

The Beatles are taking a bit of a break from serious rehearsals as Paul sings a slow, soulful variation of "Don't Let Me Down."

7.96   DON'T LET ME DOWN   >4:30)

The serious rehearsals continue as Paul wants to go over the verse a few times so he can get the phrasing right. After two passes at the second verse they continue on to the chorus and middle eight, which John and Paul sing in unison. The performance then breaks into an instrumental variation of the chorus. Finally, they return to the middle eight to work on the vocal inflections and bass line.

George's guitar playing reminds John of "Devil in Her Heart," a 1962 song by The Donays which The Beatles had covered on their second album *With The Beatles* (although he mistakenly thinks it's on their first album, *Please Please Me*).

7.97   medley DON'T LET ME DOWN / DEVIL IN HER HEART   (0:20)

After John's observation the band plays a hybrid of the two songs, featuring the lyrics to "Devil in Her Heart," the backing to "Don't Let Me Down" and George's guitar part common to both.

7.98   DEVIL IN HER HEART   (1:07)

John leads the group into a more proper version of the song, but he has great difficulty recalling the lyrics, and ends up vocalising half of them. Paul and George sing along.

7.99   DON'T LET ME DOWN   (3:22)

An excerpt from a stop-and-start rehearsal of the middle eight. Paul sings part of the middle eight and stops to remark that it doesn't sound light enough. Glyn, out from behind his recording console, agrees. They then try the middle eight 'lighter' but it barely hangs together. John remarks that he has to sing it the way he is because of the register required for the vocal and they try to lighten it up by playing it without Ringo. This succeeds, but John's too busy growling out the lyrics to notice. They then suggest a lighter part for Ringo, with more hi-hat and less drumming.

It's almost 5:00. John suggests listening to playbacks of "Across The Universe" before continuing on. George wants to eat.

7.100   DON'T LET ME DOWN   (0:20)

A brief a capella performance from Paul during conversation.

Besides being hungry, George is also suffering from a regularity problem, which he attributes to the change of hours necessitated by the film shoot. Evidently he heads off to the gent's lavatory, since he's not present for the next few performances.

7.101   THIRTY DAYS   (0:49)

John performs an enjoyable bit of this oldie. Paul offers a limited vocal backing.

"Thirty Days" was written and recorded by Chuck Berry in 1955.

7.102   REVOLUTION   (0:34)

A solo guitar instrumental from John. He plays the riff from his 1968 composition and follows up with variants of it. Paul sings the title of "Don't Let Me

Down." Michael informs them that rushes will be viewed in about half an hour.

7.103   A CASE OF THE BLUES   (0:07)
Another guitar variation from John.

7.104   BE-BOP-A-LULA   (1:42)
This one's a bit more substantial, as John sings this 1956 Gene Vincent classic, joined only by Ringo on drums. He attempts to play the guitar solo (which he obviously knows by heart), and clearly enjoys himself.

"Be-Bop-a-Lula" was a favourite of John's and was reportedly the first record Paul ever purchased.

7.105   medley LOTTA LOVIN' / SOMETHIN' ELSE   (1:09)
John and Ringo continue their trip through the Gene Vincent songbook with a stab at "Lotta Lovin'" (which Paul had sung a bit of earlier). The Gene Vincent/Eddie Cochran connection manifests itself as they break into Eddie's 1959 song "Somethin' Else," which is musically similar to "Lotta Lovin'."

7.106   (IMPROVISATION)   (0:21<
John and Ringo continue to play together on this simplistic instrumental jam. The available tape cuts off shortly into the performance.

More of this fragment has surfaced, but in the form of a playback (see 7.112).

7.107   (IMPROVISATION)   >0:59<
A continuation of the jam began in 7.106. As is his wont during this type of thing, John plays a repetitive riff as Ringo bashes out drums behind him.

7.108   (IMPROVISATION)   >1:13<
This tape fragment features more jamming from John and Ringo. George, returning from the bathroom, joins in near the end, and the jam peters out as the available tape cuts off.

7.109   SCHOOL DAY   (0:20)
This burst of guitar incorporates the beginning of Chuck Berry's 1956 "School Day." John sings a single line of garbled lyric. Everyone seems prepared to leave, but Paul wants to squeeze in a run-through of "She Came In Through The Bathroom Window" before they go, perhaps in order to give Glyn something listenable to record. As a response to Paul's suggestion, John plays a few bars from the song.

7.110   F.B.I.   (0:31)
John leads the band into this instrumental, which Paul whistles along to as he plays bass. This was originally recorded by The Shadows in 1961.

7.111   SHE CAME IN THROUGH THE BATHROOM WINDOW   (2:46)
Paul's claim that they know this song well enough is substantiated by this strong, serious performance. Since it was virtually finished the previous day, it's no surprise to find them turning in an adequate performance here. Paul's satisfied with the number but George questions the need to sing the same backing vocal as John, claiming that he can't sing the harmony part above him (a slot usually filled by Paul) because it is out of his vocal range.

7.112   (IMPROVISATIONS)   >1:44<
This is a portion of a playback of a jam session (see 7.106). As the tape is played back, someone (presumably Ringo) plays along on a set of conga drums.

It seems as if The Beatles spent the last few minutes of this day's rehearsal listening to playbacks, presumably of "Across The Universe," "She Came In Through The Bathroom Window," and this jam.

Wednesday, January 8th 1969

Despite the ominous discussions of the 7th, the group and the live show concept survive another day on the 8th. In the morning debates are held to a minimum as The Beatles run through their inventory of live show numbers. In the late afternoon, however, a lengthy exchange takes place, as Michael and Denis try to persuade The Beatles to continue their rehearsals aboard an ocean liner that will take them to Northern Africa where they will then perform at an amphitheatre. John is very enthusiastic about the idea, and Paul is quickly won over. Ringo and George are against the idea and while it seems Ringo is open to compromise, George is vehemently opposed to playing anywhere except Twickenham, describing the boat idea as costly and crazy. The Beatles eventually agree to sleep on the idea.

The session begins with the introduction of a new composition from George, "I Me Mine." The band subsequently spends a great deal of time working on the song, quickly bringing it up to the level of the other show numbers. Paul leads the group through "Let It Be," and also leads the first group rehearsal of "The Long And Winding Road." As The Beatles take stock of the show numbers, they offer relatively focused performances of "Two of Us," "Don't Let Me Down," "I've Got a Feeling," "One After 909," "Maxwell's Silver Hammer," "All Things Must Pass" and "She Came in Through The Bathroom Window." "All Things Must Pass" also undergoes more rehearsal. John is still unable to produce a new song for use in the show, offering only the uncompleted "Mean Mr. Mustard." Enthusiasm is hard to find throughout this session and all of them seem like they'd be happier somewhere else.

The session begins. For a change, it's George and Ringo who have arrived first. While they're sitting off to one side of the soundstage (still wearing their coats), George plays a new song that he's written. With no apparent provocation, he bitterly states that he doesn't care whether the song is used by the group or not and adds that he can use the song for his musical (two days earlier Apple had announced that George and Derek Taylor were collaborating on a stage musical about Apple. Although this never came about, George's comment indicates there was, at least, some germ of truth in the report). As he had expressed the previous day, George is very frustrated with presenting new compositions to the band only to have them rejected. This bit of dialogue was included in the film *Let it Be* with a stray guitar note inserted over George's profanity

8.1 I ME MINE (1:02<

George premieres his new song, accompanying himself on John's electric guitar (which isn't plugged in). At this stage the song features a flamenco guitar break. The available tape cuts off during the second verse.

One can reasonably assume that George was thinking of John and Paul when he wrote the lyrics to "I Me Mine," a song about self-absorption. Forty-one seconds of this performance were used in the film *Let It Be*.

George then begins to discuss the previous evening's television programs, but this immediately reminds him of a line from John's '1969 diary,' a comical little piece that had been written the previous year for *Aspen* magazine. George recites some of this from memory (amid much laughter) before returning to the original topic. The science fiction program that George and Ringo watched is *Immortality Inc.*, which aired on BBC-2's *Out of the Unknown* series at 9:05. It was based on a novel by Robert Sheckley. The program that followed that was *Europa - The Titled And The Untitled*, which was about how people regard honours and medals. It was the incidental music used in this program which musically inspired "I Me Mine."

As George begins another performance of his new song, Michael remarks that his high vocal register sounds like a castrato. Ringo seems to have no idea what this term means (it refers to the practice of castrating a singer in order to allow him to sing in a certain pitch).

8.2   I ME MINE (0:44<

This performance begins as George hums a bit of waltz, strums a few notes on the guitar, and launches into a more formal performance. As he begins the flamenco guitar break, the available tape cuts off.

8.3   I ME MINE >0:20<

This fragment is very likely a continuation of track 8.2. George sings the second verse, and Ringo joins along in the background.

George explains why he chose to use the flamenco guitar break in place of a more conventional bridge for "I Me Mine," quoting the Bob Dylan song "The Times They Are A-Changin'" in the process. He then starts talking about boots but Michael steers the conversation back towards the previous evening's TV programs. A lengthy and convoluted explanation of the plot of *Immortality Inc.* follows, as George and Ringo recount the story. As that conversation winds down, the discussion turns to *The Killing of Eagles*, a documentary which aired on Thames TV at 10:30. That program dealt with the strategic bombing of Germany during World War II and its effects.

George then asks Ringo if he's seen the film *Operation Cross-bow*. This dealt with the British intelligence program which kept track of German rocket activities during World War II. He also mentions the German's V-2 buzz bombs.

Finally, George describes a pair of boots that he wishes to own, and Paul, who has just arrived, offers to give George a pair that he has at home. George then offers to play his new song for Paul. Relations are surprisingly congenial, and George keeps his negative comment about John and Paul's acceptance of the song to himself this time around.

8.4   I ME MINE (1:47)

George runs through the entire song, once again accompanying himself on John's unamplified electric guitar. It's interesting to note that the lyrics to the verses, began only twelve hours before, are completely finished.

As George completes his performance, he wonders aloud if the lyrics to "I Me Mine" are grammatically correct.

As the next dialogue segment begins, Michael enthusiastically discusses the showmanship of singer James Brown. Consequently, Paul jokes that Ringo will do Brown's act during The Beatles' stage show, and the two of them briefly act this out. This reminds Paul of Jimmy Scott's stage announcements (Scott was the entertainer from whom Paul borrowed the phrase 'ob-la-di, ob-la-da') and he imitates a few lines from Scott's act.

A number of simultaneous discussions occur at this point. Ringo and Denis are talking about race horses, and the prices they command. Ringo mentions that he'd acquired a race horse at one point (presumably as a tax shelter), but never saw the thing. George and Michael discuss the morning's major news story - a report by the Advisory Committee on Drug Dependence that recommended that penalties be reduced for offenders who sold or used marijuana. George is pleased with the committee's findings, incredulously repeating the reports' assertion that marijuana is less harmful than alcohol even though the former carried a stiffer penalty for its use. John arrives and George, who is still fiddling around on John's guitar, explains that he's been warming it up for him. John dryly replies that he'd been dreaming about getting back to work (after the miserable session of the 7th, this seems far from likely). In response, Ringo and Paul team up for a bit of familiar schtick from *Laugh-In*. In the course of this, they mention Henry Gibson, a member of the *Laugh-In* cast, who would routinely recite poetry in the manner heard here. Evidence from throughout the sessions shows that all of The Beatles were avid *Laugh-In* fans. This is interspersed with a brief, almost indecipherable conversation about photographs - presumably those that Ethan Russell has been taking of the sessions.

8.5   medley (IMPROVISATIONS) / HONEY, HUSH   (3:48<

Now that everyone is present, The Beatles play this lethargic mish-mosh to warm up. This unusual performance combines bits of a number of songs - all but one too fleeting to be listed separately. It starts out as John sings a line from The Bar-Kays 1967 hit "Soul Finger" over some loose bass backing from Paul. George asks Kevin for another cushion to sit on (George habitually sat on a small cushion during these sessions). Paul starts playing a bass riff that resembles Little Richard's "Lucille" (obviously one of his favourites). Ringo joins in and Paul starts singing gibberish over it. Presumably thinking of food, he sings out the names of several different items. At George's instigation he bends 'french fries' into a parody of Marvin Gaye's "Hitch Hike." After a few more lines of nonsense, he and George launch into an improvised duet, with George offering response vocals that are, more often than not, too far off-mike to be deciphered. Paul sings a verse wrapped around some standard blues lyrics and George chimes in about footwear. When the song reaches the appropriate point, Paul lifts the chorus of "Honey, Hush" (originally recorded in 1953 by Big Joe Turner, but probably known to The Beatles through the Johnny Burnette Trio's recording from 1956). A second blues verse, and the "Honey, Hush" chorus follows.

8.6   HONEY, HUSH   >0:15)

This fragment captures the end of the previous performance, as Paul sings the chorus from the song several times.

8.7   STAND BY ME   (2:05)

Although George actually begins it, Paul sings most of this song in a mock-operatic voice. The refrain reminds him of "Figaro, Figaro, Figaro" from Rossini's 1816 comic-opera *The Barber of Seville*, and he breaks into this several times. The backing is primarily bass and drums with occasional guitar from George.

"Stand By Me" was a hit for Ben E. King in 1961.

As the performance limps to an end Paul asks them if they'd like to do a *real* number. John suggests they do "Shaking In The Sixties." This title is inexplicably tied to Dick James, the head of The Beatles' publishing company Northern Songs (in fact, John will improvise a brief song about it the next day). Paul seems to think this would make a good title for a cocktail book from Apple's chief financial advisor Harry Pinsker.

8.8   HARE KRISHNA MANTRA (0:58)

Having mentioned Harry Pinsker, Paul busks this off-beat parody, using Harry's name instead of "Hare Krishna." He attempts to call out other people with the first name of Harry, but can only seem to remember Harry Lauder, a popular Scottish entertainer from earlier in the century. The backing is plodding, led by Paul on bass. After the performance, John noodles a bit on guitar.

The "Hare Krishna Mantra," an ancient Hindu religious chant, had only recently been introduced to Western youth.

8.9   "WELL IF YOU'RE READY" (0:15)

Paul leads the band into this short up-tempo improvisation. Paul's vocal (what little there is of it) is rendered unintelligible by his heavy Elvis Presley impersonation. He excuses the poorness of his performance because he's standing.

8.10   HARE KRISHNA MANTRA (0:36)

Paul returns to the Harry Pinsker parody for another brief performance. He then suggests that they work on "Two Of Us" (which he refers to under its working title "On Our Way Back Home").

8.11   TWO OF US (3:22)

John stands up and joins Paul at a single mike as they begin a trial run for the live show, incorporating the most finished songs they've rehearsed thus far. Except for a botched beginning (John misses his cue to start singing) this performance is lively and fun, partially because it's played at a faster tempo than usual. In both middle eights Paul reverts to his Elvis impersonation, slurring the lyrics while John bends down and plays some strident rhythm guitar. Probably because they're working without lyric sheets, they both have occasional problems recalling the words.

An abridged version of this performance can be seen in the film *Let It Be*.

John and Paul are both pleased with the run-through. John, who on the 6th had wanted to vamp out the chords, proudly states that he's mastered the various guitar bits.

8.12   YOU GOT ME GOING (0:14)

This brief performance from Paul is most likely an improvisation. If it's not, he's certainly garbling the words. He introduces the 'song' and sings a couple of lines. There is only a very sparse backing behind him. George calls out for "Twist and Shout," presumably reminded of it by "You Got Me Going," which is part of its lyric.

8.13   TWIST AND SHOUT (0:03)

George plays the first few notes and stops.

The Isley Brothers' 1962 hit "Twist and Shout" had been covered by The Beatles on their first album and was often their concert opener. Back on the 3rd, George had suggested doing some oldies on the show. Now, during this 'dress rehearsal' this false start recalls that idea. Indeed, most of the following 'real' performances will be followed by a short teaser of an oldie. This is too consistent to have been anything other than intentional, and the idea will be continued when The Beatles eventually perform on Apple's rooftop on January 30th.

8.14   DON'T LET ME DOWN (3:00)

Paul requests "Don't Let Me Down" and John begins to count in for this number, but Paul reminds him that George's guitar introduction will serve that purpose. Undaunted, John counts in for George's introduction, and screams wildly after the first line. At one point John and Paul are singing different verses at the same time. Despite occasional lapses in John's recall of the lyrics, The Beatles turn in a fine performance, thanks in part to some excellent drumming from Ringo. After the performance, John offers a mock-stage announcement, and Paul calls out for "I've Got A Feeling."

8.15   I'VE GOT A FEELING (3:21<

A very strong, virtually complete performance. The Beatles' spirits are up, especially Paul, who exuberantly shouts after completing the middle eight. Although John and George seem to have some difficulty co-ordinating their lines, this doesn't detract from the quality of this performance.

This performance was intercut with a performance from the 9th for use in the film *Let it Be*.

8.16   ST. LOUIS BLUES >0:10)

A few instrumental guitar riffs of another 'oldie' as The Beatles contemplate what to play next.

"St. Louis Blues" is an early blues number written by W.C. Handy in 1914. It had been heavily covered, and by this time was certainly a standard.

Paul requests "One After 909." George, engaging in a mock interview of Paul, asks if they'll be doing any songs from their latest LP on the show. Paul drolly suggests Little Richard's "Lucille."

8.17   ONE AFTER 909 (3:24)

After two false starts, the performance kicks in. This is another strong, up-tempo performance. John and Paul share the lead vocal nicely, and John comically makes train sounds at one point. The song breaks down during the instrumental break, but is quickly restarted by John, and performed through to the end.

The Beatles often seemed to have difficulty knowing when to end "One After 909." Since the song is fast and only features two verses, The Beatles would repeat them and then lose track of their place in the song.

8.18   TOO BAD ABOUT SORROWS (0:14)

Another oldie from John - this time delving into the early Lennon/McCartney songbook. He sings little more than the title with some loose guitar playing behind him.

"Too Bad About Sorrows" was one of the earliest Lennon/McCartney compositions and was never formally recorded by the group. Paul will also sing part of this during the session of the 22nd.

Paul wants to know which song should be rehearsed next, which causes George to search for his clipboard. John facetiously refers to the morning's newspaper story concerning penalties for marijuana use. A comment from this dialogue about pot smoking members of the F.B.I. was included in both the *Let It Be* film and album.

8.19   JUST FUN (0:11)

John sings two lines from this song and backs himself on guitar.

"Just Fun" was another early Lennon/McCartney composition. Paul had briefly quoted from it on the 6th.

George has found his schedule, which contains the previous day's line-up ("Across The Universe," "Maxwell's Silver Hammer," "All Things Must Pass" and "She Came in Through The Bathroom Window"). George jokingly replaces the final title with "She Said, She Said," and John quickly responds with a performance.

8.20 SHE SAID, SHE SAID (0:20)

John begins this performance and the entire band comes in behind him. He sings one verse, scrambling the lyrics a bit.

"She Said, She Said," written by John, had been released by The Beatles on their 1966 LP *Revolver*.

Despite Ringo's desire to do "She Came in Through The Bathroom Window," Paul has decided that the band should run through "All Things Must Pass," possibly in fairness to George, who had none of his songs rehearsed the previous day.

8.21 ALL THINGS MUST PASS (1:58)

After a false start, The Beatles get through most of the song before it breaks down right before the middle eight. John has moved over to organ. The harmony vocals worked on during the 3rd are in place but they are not perfected. Paul's bass part is quite nice, and even John seems to be hitting most of the notes.

8.22 MACARTHUR PARK (1:23<

Paul and John play this nebulous instrumental between tries at "All Things Must Pass," barely hitting the notes.

"MacArthur Park" was a hit for Richard Harris in 1968.

8.23 ALL THINGS MUST PASS >0:14<

A fragmentary, lethargic performance. George sings a few lyrics as Paul plays bass.

Paul's bass is very prominent here, and he seems to have been in the habit of turning his amplifier up when working on a relatively unfamiliar song.

8.24 ALL THINGS MUST PASS >0:03<

A very brief instrumental fragment.

8.25 ALL THINGS MUST PASS >0:34)

Another fragment, which may possibly be the end of 8.24. George sings the last two lines of the song as Paul harmonises behind him.

George is unhappy with the way the rehearsals are progressing, but doesn't know what to do to improve the song. He and Paul consider the possibility of having George perform "All Things Must Pass" solo on acoustic guitar, but Paul feels that if the other Beatles are going to sing, they should play as well.

8.26 ALL THINGS MUST PASS (0:49)

In this fragment of rehearsal, George performs a bit of the song, perhaps to illustrate what he thinks is wrong with it. This is followed by a series of stray riffs, after which George sings two more lines.

Paul believes that a group arrangement can achieve the same feel as a solo performance if they can manage to bring out the song's light quality. He then asks George if he's willing to try a solo arrangement of the song, but seems to doubt George's ability to carry it off on his own. George isn't too keen on the idea, and John, in his own way, concurs that this would be quite an order.

8.27 ALL THINGS MUST PASS (1:54<

A very loose rehearsal, as George and Paul attempt to work out their vocal harmonies. John doesn't participate, but sits at the organ looking painfully bored.

8.28   ALL THINGS MUST PASS >0:01<

This briefest of fragments consists of nothing more than the word 'all.'

8.29   ALL THINGS MUST PASS >1:59<

The Beatles work on three part harmony, with John joining Paul and George to sing the title phrase in various vocal arrangements. As is customary, Paul takes the highest part while John sings the lowest.

8.30   ALL ALONG THE WATCHTOWER (0:15)

A brief performance of the first few lines, featuring George on guitar and vocal.

"All Along The Watchtower" was written and recorded by Bob Dylan in 1967. Jimi Hendrix had released a hit cover version of the song in late 1968. George would have been familiar with both.

George and Paul then discuss the work being done on their cars and Paul offers tangerines to everyone in sight. This exchange is unimportant except that it debunks another Beatles myth - Paul did not take public transportation to the Twickenham sessions, he drove.

8.31   MEAN MR. MUSTARD (3:15)

John plays piano and takes lead vocal on this performance. Although this is the earliest performance of this Lennon composition available from these sessions, a 1968 demo was released on *Anthology 3*. In any case, the song is unfinished, as John has written two verses but only a rudimentary chorus. John sings each verse twice and hums his vocal through another. Ringo does little more than pound out a beat.

There's a gap in the available material between "All Along The Watchtower" and "Mean Mr. Mustard." Despite their desire to go to lunch, the band decides to run through some songs which they hadn't played in the morning. Perhaps, having just wasted the last hour or so they felt that they wanted to get in some work before lunch. "Mean Mr. Mustard" would never be more fully realised than this. When it was eventually used in the medley on *Abbey Road*, the only major change was the name of Mr Mustard's sister from Shirley to Pam, in order to tie in with the song "Polythene Pam."

8.32   DON'T LET ME DOWN (0:34)

A brief attempt at the song, as John sings three lines of the middle eight. This performance is done at a slower tempo than usual and quickly dies out, perhaps because they realise that they don't really need to rehearse it.

8.33   ALL THINGS MUST PASS (3:15)

The earlier extensive "All Things Must Pass" rehearsals pay off with this complete performance, although John doesn't play piano much better than he plays organ. John and Paul sing harmony behind George, and John plays around with his vocal from time to time.

This is the only available performance of "All Things Must Pass" with John on piano.

8.34   FOOLS LIKE ME (2:01)

Probably because of the proximity of a piano, John is reminded of Jerry Lee Lewis, and breaks into this plaintive country number. The full band joins in one by one behind him, and George sings along and provides a well played guitar solo.

"Fools Like Me" was originally recorded by Jerry Lee Lewis in 1958. It was the b-side of "High School Confidential."

8.35   YOU WIN AGAIN   (1:18)

John follows "Fools Like Me" with another country song that Jerry Lee Lewis recorded, singing in a nasal twang reminiscent of the song's author, Hank Williams. John can only remember one verse, however, prompting George to join in briefly as the song breaks down, and Paul to tag on a few unrelated (and indecipherable) lines as a coda. George then suggests "She Came In Through The Bathroom Window" for the next number.

"You Win Again" was covered by Jerry Lee Lewis in 1957.

8.36   (IMPROVISATION)   (0:28)

John plays a simple repetitive piano riff while Ringo accompanies him with rimshots on his snare drum.

8.37   SHE CAME IN THROUGH THE BATHROOM WINDOW   (1:37<

Paul plays part of the song to illustrate the chord changes, and then (after a false start) begins a real performance. This is perfunctory, and taken a bit slower than usual. The available tape cuts off during the second verse.

8.38   MAXWELL'S SILVER HAMMER   (2:41)

This is the only available performance from this rehearsal session for "Maxwell's Silver Hammer." John has moved back to guitar, Paul is on piano and George is playing bass. It's clear that the song is almost finished as The Beatles attempt a complete run-through, prefacing the first verse with a whistled introduction. The rehearsal has been very long, or very unsuccessful, because Paul sounds disgusted and bored. Despite this, it's obvious that the whistling parts have been integrated, and that some work has been put into the unwritten second verse and Ringo's drumming. As they approach the third verse, Paul is distracted by George's attempt to test his microphone and the performance breaks down. Shortly before the available tape cuts off, Paul improvises two additional lines of lyric.

Almost an hour of tape is unavailable between this and 8.39, most of which is undoubtedly taken up with "All Things Must Pass" and "Maxwell's Silver Hammer" rehearsals.

8.39   I ME MINE   >0:34)

The tail end of another solo performance from George, who's running through the song for John's benefit. John sings along in spots, but his contributions are more mock-Spanish clowning than anything else.

8.40   I ME MINE   (1:27)

In response to John's comments, George plays the song again, apparently to show him that it isn't that hard. Paul and John sing along in spots.

John jokes that a collection of freaks can dance along with George's waltz. He then jokingly tells George to get lost - that The Beatles only play rock and roll and there's no place in the group's playlist for a Spanish waltz. Given George's defensive attitude about the band's rejection of his songs, it seems likely he would have been insulted and hurt by this reaction. Consequently, he offers no response.

John then jokes that he's ready to begin rehearsing "I Me Mine" by moving over to barrel organ. This is both a reference to his musical role in George's other song "All Things Must Pass," and a disparaging comment about the quality of the organ they have (barrel organ was a popular term for a cheap street organ used in the 19th century). After offering Paul some of what he's been snacking on, John unwraps a large painting that has been shipped to them anonymously and offers his interpretation of its meaning. A stray bit of feed-back reminds Paul of a January 6th conversation about sounds that can kill and he comments about the deadly bass frequencies. John, despite the fact that he's busy eating, is ready to press on with the "I Me Mine" rehearsal, and asks George what instruments he'd like them to play. As Mal prepares to makes copies of George's lyric sheet, John suggests Paul's accordion, but Mal informs him it's not present. It should be noted that George plays a number of brief, undistinguished guitar riffs during this conversation.

John takes Mal to task for not having all of their instruments on hand, and complains that they don't have a proper electric piano - the one at Abbey Road Studios never works. George explains that's because it's old and broken. Paul jokingly mentions Blossom Dearie, a female jazz singer with a baby-girl voice.

8.41   HOW DO YOU THINK I FEEL   (0:11)

George hums a bit of this tune, inspiring John to sing a few lines.

"How Do You Think I Feel" was recorded by Elvis Presley in 1956.

Denis has arrived since John's interpretation of the painting, so John repeats it for him and then holds a mock auction. Paul wins the painting, and immediately starts to auction it off himself.

8.42   THE BALLAD OF BONNIE AND CLYDE   (0:03)

Someone starts whistling this song. John picks up on it and sings a brief parody.

"The Ballad of Bonnie and Clyde" was a hit for Georgie Fame in 1968. It uses the same tune as an older song called "The Old Buck Dance."

The dialogue which follows is an excellent example of The Beatles' dysfunctional communication skills. John gives the painting he has received to Denis as The Beatles sit around bored, waiting for the technicians to complete installation of a new P.A. system. Yet they're unable to hold a straight conversation, even when one of them has something to say. It's not that relations between them are strained it's as if there *are* no relations between them. The previous day they had spent a good amount of time running through a series of John's songs which he had uniformly rejected out of disinterest. Now, with Paul and George having fulfilled their quota, Paul needs to know if John has come up with anything. However, this question, and the subsequent discussion is spoken flippantly. Paul can't inquire in a forthright manner, because John refuses to respond, and John won't answer in a forthright manner if there's any way he can avoid it. Nevertheless, the question does get asked, and John says he hopes to have a fast number written within a couple of days. He then joins Ringo in playing with the vocal effects achieved through the echo unit on the new P.A., reciting a butchered line from Little Richard's "Tutti Frutti."

8.43   HELLO MUDDUH, HELLO FADDUH! (A LETTER FROM CAMP)   (0:06)

John and Paul sing a bit of this Allan Sherman novelty while fooling around with the new echo unit.

"Hello Mudduh, Hello Fadduh!" was a popular novelty record issued in 1963. Its tune was taken from "Dance of the Hours" from Amilcare Ponchielli's 1876 opera "La Gioconda."

The new P.A. emits some horrendous high-pitched feedback. Michael jokingly suggests using this on a future Beatles album, evidently unaware that John and Yoko have already done so on their album *Two Virgins* and then asks if this is an example of the deadly feedback. John is restless and bored and wants to start performing. He announces he's going to play "Be-Bop-a-Lula," but accomplishes nothing more than stuttering into his microphone. Halfway through this, someone whistles a brief reprise of the "Ballad of Bonnie and Clyde."

8.44   I ME MINE (0:14)

A reasonably accurate snatch of performance from John, considering the fact that he had just heard the song for the first time a few minutes before. He plays a loose approximation of George's chords and sings an incorrect lyric. He then makes noises into his microphone, mutters some nonsense, and breaks into a fast guitar riff. This is a joke, not a performance.

Their new equipment seems to remind John of the Binson echo unit they had used at the Top Ten Club in Germany. He follows a mention of this with a number of further guitar riffs and some mock-Latin gibberish.

8.45   F.B.I. (0:06)

John has almost nothing but negative comments to make about "I Me Mine." He wonders how the band can perform such a song, complains about its shortness, and adds that he thinks it will be hard for George to sing.

This short instrumental (originally recorded by The Shadows) was also performed by John near the end of the session on the 7th.

Ringo, in very proper English, blurts out the title of Sir Edward Elgar's "Pomp and Circumstance." John is frustrated with having to wait. Perhaps as a critique of the technicians, he mentions that he's been playing an electric guitar at home while watching television and likens himself to Elvis Presley, who was known for his love of television.

8.46   "I'M GOING TO KNOCK HIM DOWN DEAD" (0:27)

Inspired by "I Me Mine," John breaks into this brief unidentified Spanish flavoured number, which breaks into an up-tempo boogie woogie a few seconds before it ends. Paul sings a couple of lines off-mike.

8.47   (UNKNOWN) (0:19)

As John fumbles his way through an instrumental waltz on guitar, Paul sings a single line from "Mr. Bass Man" (which we have not considered substantial enough to be logged as a performance).

The waltz is unidentified. "Mr. Bass Man" was originally recorded by Johnny Cymbal in 1963.

John then offers an oblique criticism of his role in George's new number by asking for an accordion and bagpipes and impatiently eggs the others on in attempt to get the rehearsals moving again. George is too busy trying to secure an acoustic guitar from Mal to pay attention.

8.48   OH! DARLING (1:51<

Though the equipment set-up is far from finished, Paul begins to play this sluggish rendition of "Oh! Darling," perhaps to placate John. John stops his aimless guitar noodling and joins in, as does Ringo on drums. Paul's piano is not miked and can barely be heard. George is still trying to get an acoustic guitar and does not participate in this loose performance. John then offers a few lines of sing-song, the lyric of which suggests that he needs to attend the lavatory.

8.49   I ME MINE (0:03)
A brief a capella performance by John, who sings the first line of the song.

Even though the lyric is from "I Me Mine," John sings it to the familiar tune of "Over The Waves," which was written in 1888 by Jonventino Rosas.

8.50   LET IT BE (7:48)
Although the equipment set-up is still not complete, Paul plays piano on an extended run-through of this composition. John, who's still munching, attempts to follow along on guitar but offers only unrelated riffs most of the time. After Paul vocalises the drum part for him, Ringo joins in. Only the first verse and chorus have been written, but Paul plays them again and again, either to refine them or simply to pass the time. With the exception already noted, there is no attempt to teach the song to the other Beatles or to formally rehearse it. At one point, Paul stops playing but Ringo continues on, refining his drum fills. No one's playing bass, and, once again, George does not participate.

It's clear from this performance that the other Beatles had little previous exposure to "Let It Be" (Paul had played the song on January 3rd, but George and John hadn't arrived yet). It's revealing to note that the group, only ten days away from the live show, allows nearly an hour to be wasted on an equipment changeover that could have been achieved while they had lunch.

Having had less-than-complimentary words for "I Me Mine," John doesn't spare Paul's new song either, suggesting that they change the song's Mother Mary character to Brother Malcolm.

The equipment setup is still not complete, so Paul suggests going off for a drink. George points out that it's nearly lunchtime anyway, and Paul is delighted.

Having wasted much of the morning, The Beatles get down to serious rehearsal right after lunch, choosing George's new song as a vehicle. The following series of "I Me Mine" performances are all fragments of this rehearsal session.

As we begin the afternoon session, George looks to get a cigarette (he smokes Kents) from Kevin and then returns to the topic of the grammatical correctness of a certain line from "I Me Mine," laughing as he recalls Paul's comical discussion of this subject from earlier in the morning.

8.51   I ME MINE >0:52<
This fragment of a rehearsal session consists of little more than a loose series of guitar riffs from George.

8.52   I ME MINE >1:01)
A disjointed, instrumental performance of the flamenco break. George stops to discuss the drum part with Ringo, leaving Paul playing by himself on bass.

George would like castanets as well as drums on "I Me Mine," and he tries to recruit someone (George Martin, one would guess) but is informed that this person will he otherwise occupied in the control booth during the live show.

8.53   medley I ME MINE / DOMINO (1:25)

Another "I Me Mine" performance begins, but Paul sings the lyrics to "Domino" instead. George stops playing guitar to engage in a generally indecipherable conversation about the stage set-up while Paul and Ringo continue on. Paul has forgotten all of the lyrics (except for the word "Domino"), and vocalises his way through the performance.

"Domino" was a popular waltz from the early '50's, originally sung in French.

8.54   I ME MINE (1:15<

The Beatles play another instrumental version, but this one is much more focused. John, who had been contributing little earlier, plays sustained notes on his guitar. This unique effect was apparently dropped shortly after this experimental run through.

8.55   I ME MINE >0:21<

This instrumental fragment is a continuation of 8.54.

8.56   I ME MINE >2:18<

This portion of rehearsal begins as another instrumental. George makes a few unsuccessful attempts to begin the song, but it doesn't get off the ground. Eventually Paul vocalises in a mock Spanish accent, indicating that John isn't the only one having trouble taking George's song seriously.

George calls again for castanets on the song, and somewhat surprisingly agrees with Paul that "I Me Mine" would be a good candidate for the live show.

8.57   I ME MINE >0:17<

This fragment features two attempts to rehearse the end of the song.

8.58   I ME MINE >0:51<

Another instrumental - but at a slightly different tempo this time. Paul vocalises a guitar part over the melody (similar to the one John was playing earlier), as John makes funny noises. Ringo loses his place and plays a drum fill at the wrong time.

8.59   THE LONG AND WINDING ROAD (0:47)

Paul plays a stately, solo rendition of his song on piano and sings a few lines as John jokes around.

Having already made fun of "I Me Mine" and "Let It Be," John could hardly let "The Long and Winding Road" pass without comment.. Nevertheless, he s ready to rehearse it, and asks (in his inimitable fashion) what the chords are and what key the song is played in. Despite his desire the "I Me Mine" rehearsals continue.

No one (except, perhaps, George) seems pleased to be rehearsing "I Me Mine." Ringo expresses his opinion that no matter how many times they run through the song he won't remember how to play it. George is surprised because he considers "I Me Mine" to be a simple song. Paul makes the interesting observation that the band has begun to mistake being sick of a song for actually knowing how to play it quite clearly implying that *he's* sick of "I Me Mine." George doesn't want a discussion, however, and signals the rehearsals to resume.

8.60   ADAGIO FOR STRINGS (0:11)

Paul plays the first few bars of a piece that he had also performed on January 3rd (see 3.1)

John jokingly instructs the other three Beatles to work on "I Me Mine" until they've perfected it while he excuses himself from the rehearsal to waltz with Yoko in an open area alongside the soundstage.

8.61   I ME MINE (0:27)

George begins playing the flamenco guitar break and counts in for a complete run-through before Ringo stops him.

George wonders if the flamenco guitar break he's playing breaks someone's copyright. He then counts down to perform the song, but Ringo stops him because he's oiling his bass drum pedal. George and Paul then discuss the new echo unit, after which each sings the title from George's 1963 composition "Don't Bother Me." This causes George to reminisce about writing the song while sick in bed in Bournemouth, England in 1963.

8.62   "TELL ALL THE FOLKS BACK HOME" (1:30)

This is primarily a solo performance from Paul, who returns to his bass and mumbles the song's brief, repetitive lyrics as Ringo tests out his bass drum pedal.

This seems to be an improvisation, although it may be a mangled cover version which has yet to be identified

8.63   I ME MINE (1:25)

The band (minus John, who waltzes with Yoko) runs through a complete performance. The musicianship here is exceptionally tight for a brand new song. George's vocal is quite well done, and Paul shouts out encouragement from time to time. After the performance George suggests that they run through it again, and then offers some dance tips to John and Yoko. Somehow, one is not surprised to find that John and Yoko don't quite know how to waltz.

8.64   I ME MINE (1:24)

The three Beatles play another tight, complete run-through, quite similar to the previous performance.

Michael likes the idea of John and Yoko's dance, and wants to do something theatrical like that for every song. He suggests closing the show with a sentimental number similar to "Good Night" (which was the closer for The Beatles' previous album). This causes John to ask the others' opinions on Vera Lynn's recently released cover version (which he has not yet heard). The Beatles are clearly tired of Michael's ideas, and jokingly answer in the affirmative to all of his suggestions. Despite this, Michael presses on, describing signs marked January 20th, 1969 (now apparently the date of the live broadcast) that he wants to hang on the set. John shouts out an agreement (perhaps hoping that it will get Michael to stop) and Paul once again raises the question of who will comprise the audience (this had been thoroughly discussed on the 6th). Michael suggests that anything human will do (as opposed to the empty chairs that Yoko had suggested) and wants to let the first thousand people on line into the show. John jokes. Paul agrees. Michael then offers the ghastly suggestion of having someone introduce each song through voice-overs.

8.65   TRUE LOVE (0:24)

In response to Michael's comment that "True Love" is his favourite song, Paul plays a few bars as John offers *his* warped idea of a love song. Paul follows with a few lines of "True Love"'s actual lyric.

"True Love" was written in 1956 by Cole Porter, and recorded the following year by Elvis Presley.

"True Love" reminds Michael of another standard ("A Pretty Girl is Like a Melody"). When Paul answers him in a patronising tone of voice, Michael whines about being put down. Paul hastens to assure him he's not doing that and jumps into the topic of stage design. Both Paul and Michael like the idea of building a circular arena at Twickenham, and Michael's comments indicate that he plans to use both film and video cameras to record the event. Denis mentions that they could still have the show at night, but Michael is unpleasantly reminded that his ideas along these lines were rejected the previous day and replies they'll do that for the next concert.

8.66   (UNKNOWN) (2:21)

Oblivious to the ongoing discussions, George begins playing a few simple chords on piano far in the background, and continues to play through the following two performances. He repeats the same few bars over and over, as if he's trying to work out a piano part for something, so this is certainly more than simple noodling.

In the meantime, Paul equates the proposed stage set-up with the one used on their 1964 television special *Around The Beatles*. Michael, still in favour of his theatrical approach, points out that the type of stage set-up that Paul favours had recently been used on Elvis Presley's comeback TV special, and argues that he doesn't want to see them repeating the set-ups they'd used in their prior TV shows. John and Paul reply that they haven't had that many shows. John can only think of *Magical Mystery Tour* and *Around The Beatles*, and Michael adds *The Beatles at Shea Stadium* to the list. But, to Paul, *Magical Mystery Tour* was a concept film and *The Beatles at Shea Stadium* was simply a filmed concert, and he's surprised to realise that *Around The Beatles* was their only true TV show. Michael mentions that Glyn had recorded The Beatles' performances for *Around The Beatles*. Paul had totally forgotten this, and now realises why Glyn has been making references to IBC, the independent recording studio where the basic tracks for *Around The Beatles* had been taped.

8.67   SHOUT! (0:13)

A short performance from John who sings and plays guitar.

John, who generally can't recall which Beatles song came from which album, obviously remembers that The Beatles performed "Shout!" on the *Around The Beatles* program.

Paul agrees that he doesn't want to recreate past glories, and Michael replies that there's a down side to any idea. John plays a fast guitar riff and Michael makes the astute observation that John is likely to break into song whenever serious topics are raised. He claims that John's guitar riff scares him (!) and refers to Paul as 'darling.' Paul's reply (he sarcastically calls Michael 'lovey') clearly indicates that he feels that Michael's gone a bit past the acceptable boundaries. Michael's mannerisms will annoy The Beatles occasionally during these sessions, and they'll suggest that they consider him a homosexual.

8.68   SWEET LITTLE SIXTEEN (0:46)

After Paul mockingly repeats Michael's assertion that he's scared by John's guitar playing, John performs this humorous parody of "Sweet Little Sixteen," altering the lyrics to reflect British rather than American cities. There's general laughter, and George finally stops playing piano to listen.

As Michael has said, John would rather play rock and roll than engage in the current discussion. "Sweet Little Sixteen" was recorded by Chuck Berry in 1958.

Once again, Michael indicates that he wants them to find a gimmick for each of the songs, and decide what order they'll be played in during the show. John reasonably points out that they might want to learn how to play the songs first, but Michael ignores him and returns to the subject of the show's finale.

8.69   MALAGUENA   (0:15)

A brief Spanish guitar instrumental from John.

"Malaguena" is a traditional slower flamenco tune. It was originally recorded as early as 1930, and laid down by Ritchie Valens in 1958.

Michael then expresses his opinion that they should end the show with a sad number but Ringo disagrees and wants to send them off on an upbeat note.

8.70   ALMOST GROWN   (0:54)

John sings the lead vocal and Paul sings backup on this lively Chuck Berry song. Musically, this isn't much because Ringo isn't playing, but the vocals make it fun.

"Almost Grown" had been a hit for Chuck Berry in 1959.

Despite the extensive rehearsals that have already occurred, Paul wants to return to "I Me Mine." He also wants something from Mal or Kevin, who have both disappeared. George explains that Mal is probably skiving (slacking off). This comment amuses Paul. John continues to play Spanish flavoured guitar riffs during this conversation, one of which resembles the 1965 Lennon/McCartney tune "Norwegian Wood."

8.71   WHAT AM I LIVING FOR?   (1:08)

John starts this performance and George takes over the vocal when John can't recall any more lyrics. Ringo plays drums and the three Beatles come together for a pleasant performance. Paul is busy having a conversation with Glyn, and sings a line from "Two of Us" during his conversation.

"What Am I Living For?" was recorded in 1958 by Chuck Willis.

Glyn then recalls The Beatles having performed an original rocker during the session of January 2nd and the others try in vain to help him remember the title of the song. Michael suggests "Route 66" and the others offer various suggestions as well. Paul asks for the name of the song that had preceded their performance of "Lucille." Jolson, thinking of the day before, answers "Rock and Roll Music" and begins to play it as Glyn and George continue to brainstorm over the identity of the missing rocker.

8.72   ROCK AND ROLL MUSIC   (1:13)

This is basically John's performance. George and Ringo back him but Paul's still talking with Glyn and doesn't contribute. The performance here is comparatively sloppy and John ends the song early. As the other Beatles perform Paul sings a line from "Get Back" in an attempt to identify Glyn's mystery song. "Get Back," however, is not the song Glyn is trying to recall. Paul finally settles the question by suggesting that Glyn search through the film tapes (of which over 100 had already accumulated) to find the song. Glyn, one would assume, let the matter drop.

8.73   I ME MINE   (0:50)

Ringo pounds out a waltz rhythm to lead the band back into the "I Me Mine" rehearsals. George's notices that his P.A. mike isn't working, but sings the first few lines of the song anyway. John sticks around and plays rhythm guitar. The performance breaks down after the first verse.

8.74   I ME MINE (1:02)

The Beatles try to pick up the performance at the break, but it quickly degenerates into a series of riffs and stray vocal lines. George is unhappy with Ringo's drum part (which reminds him of Richard Harris's "MacArthur Park") and tells him what he would like the cymbal part to sound like. After Ringo plays this Paul suggests it would be a good lead into a heavier bit even though they wouldn't be able to do that in waltz tempo.

8.75   I ME MINE >0:45<

Paul leads the band in an improvised example of the rock and roll break he envisions for the song, but George complains that any addition to the song means he'll have to do more work on it as well. Paul leads them into the flamenco part just before the available tape cuts off.

8.76   I ME MINE >1:18)

Led by Paul, The Beatles continue to rehearse the song's newly-written chorus, with George and Paul harmonising together. The new echo unit is used to full effect here, and Paul has his bass amp turned up full, perhaps in an attempt to monitor his own playing more easily. After a successful run-through of the chorus George stops the song at the beginning of the verse. George and Paul then debate the merits of singing 'I' or 'my' in the chorus. Paul explains that 'my' is easier to sing, but George insists on his own lyric. Paul is interpreting George's lyric as 'aye-aye' (a stock element of Latin-flavoured numbers) and (despite half a day's exposure to it) doesn't realise until now that the title of George's new song is "I Me Mine." Finally, George tells Paul to sing whatever he wants.

8.77   I ME MINE (3:14<

Paul begins another rehearsal of the chorus, testing out 'I' instead of 'my.' The rehearsal stumbles along as they attempt to find a satisfactory tempo. George stops one attempt to politely correct Ringo's cymbal part. At one point Paul leads them in a brief up-tempo demonstration. George then complains about the echo unit, which has been going on and off indiscriminately.

8.78   I ME MINE >1:10)

Picking up the song at the chorus, the band continues into the flamenco bridge and second verse. George begins to sing the words to the first verse by mistake, but quickly corrects himself.

  Despite the various tempo changes, the band has been unusually quick in learning this song. Consequently, this is a more than passable performance.

8.79   I ME MINE (0:55)

With the chorus rehearsed to satisfaction, The Beatles attempt the song from the top. The performance breaks down as they reach the flamenco guitar part.

0.80   I ME MINE >0:21)

Amid loose riffs, Paul loudly sings a few words from the song. George then tries to start another run-through of the chorus, but Paul stops him and says he doesn't need to rehearse it.

8.81   I ME MINE (1:33)

Once again, The Beatles take the song from the top. Although George's singing is perfunctory during the first verse, it becomes spirited as they reach the chorus. The performance of the chorus and flamenco break is very strong on everyone's part, and George sings an impassioned second verse.

An edited version of this performance can be heard in the film *Let It Be*.

8.82   I ME MINE   >0:07<

The Spanish guitar break, edited into 8.81 from an otherwise unavailable performance in the film *Let It Be*.

8.83   THE LONG AND WINDING ROAD   (3:04)

Paul plays the song on piano as he teaches it to George and Ringo, alternating between singing, vocalising, and calling out chords. Only the lyrics to the first verse and chorus have been written. John does not participate.

8.84   THE LONG AND WINDING ROAD   >0:04<

This and the following fragment are inadvertently captured on tape as the soundman announces a new sound roll and film slate.

8.85   THE LONG AND WINDING ROAD   >0:04<

See above.

8.86   THE LONG AND WINDING ROAD   >4:03)

The rehearsal continues as George makes a more concerted effort to play along on guitar. Paul concludes the song, but then begins playing it again at the chorus through to the end.

Instead of playing, John is off to the side of the stage talking to Denis, Glyn and Michael. As the available tape begins, Michael is candidly discussing his concern about the fate of the live show and once again raises his idea of a torchlit concert in a desert. He then pumps John for information about what Paul thinks. Although he receives no reply, the rest of the dialogue suggests a conspiracy between the filmmakers and John to convince the other Beatles to hold the show abroad. Michael insists that the show cannot be special if it's filmed in a studio environment.

8.87   LET IT BE   (2:54<

Paul calls out a few chords for George's benefit. and begins to play another piano based song, with Ringo offering sporadic support on drums. At one point John diverts his attention from his conversation with Michael and Glyn (above) and sings part of the chorus.

The stageside conversation continues. Michael remarks upon the tensions within the group. He believes that a live performance will bring the group together, and John agrees. He then notes that the documentary is out of steam and suggests that the boat show would revive it. Michael and John then have a brief exchange about the stage setup for the show's final number. John thinks it should be a singalong, and Michael wonders if they should lower the stage as the show progresses.

8.88   TO KINGDOM COME   >2:12)

George plays guitar and sings a relatively complete version of this song from The Band's *Music From Big Pink* album. Paul harmonises with him briefly, and John claps along at one point. This is the last performance of the day as The Beatles begin a long conversation about plans for a boat show.

Originally content to stage their live comeback in a London theatre or in Twickenham Studios, The Beatles are now entertaining the idea of performing in Africa or Saudi Arabia. Denis is obviously very excited about the idea, and is trying to sell it to Paul, George and Ringo (John already knows, and is agreeable). Surprisingly, Paul comes out in favour of it under the condition that they bring their British audience with them. Although Michael mentions this was one of Ringo's stipulations, Ringo obviously doesn't want to go at all. Throughout this dialogue (and that which follows) Michael will refer to the Beatles under various code names (Ringo's is Russia, George is France, and we never learn what Paul or John's is, nor any possible reason for this kind of thing). John is very excited about the prospect of a voyage. He's equally excited about the proposition of going to Russia, until he's informed that it's only Ringo's code name. George makes it quite clear that he sees no merit at all in the idea of taking a boat, suggesting that they do the show in England and then take a vacation.

After talking about the various shots which might be achieved in an outdoor setting, Paul and Denis reiterate their positive opinions about the voyage and seemingly win Ringo over, leaving George as the only holdout. After Michael refers to him as France, George exclaims that he's forbidden to visit that country. This is a reference to an assault charge pending there (see January 22nd for further details), although Paul seems to think it's for a drug charge. Michael and John continue to mention the advantages of playing outdoors, and Paul kids that it could all be achieved by back projection. After John muses a bit about the pleasures of playing rock and roll as the sun sets, the conversation returns to the subject of the English audience they plan to take with them. Denis points out that giving away tickets for the boat trip and show would be the charity angle that the group had discussed the previous day. This conjures up images in John's head of a boat full of idiots accompanying the group - but Denis and Glyn rush to assure him this isn't what they intend. George, adamantly against the idea, questions Denis, no doubt hoping to find a fatal flaw in the plan.

Paul and John agree that part of the reason the group is in a bind is because they take the easy way out and don't follow through on adventurous ideas which might stimulate their creativity. Having said this, they come out directly against doing the show at Twickenham, placing themselves in direct opposition to George and Ringo (who, although he wants to do the show in England, assures them that he's not refusing to go).

John, uncharacteristically direct, demands that Ringo give him one reason for the show to be held in England. Ringo responds that they should do it for their fans. This point of view is quickly met with arguments from John, Paul and Michael, who maintain that those people could be brought along with them. Clarifying this point, Paul explains that the first thousand people in line would still get show tickets, but they also would get a free boat trip. George asks if the film crew will be on the boat, and Paul describes how rehearsals and filming could continue in the ship's ballroom. Michael tries to get the matter put to a vote, and Ringo points out that Michael is the one who really wants to go away. John votes yes, as Paul apparently abstains in the hope that the idea will be accepted by group acclamation. Denis once again tries to talk George into going to Africa, telling him that he'll love it, but George caustically responds that he'd rather do the show in England and then go somewhere else and love it.

George and Ringo are horrified at the idea of being stuck with a boatload of fans, but Paul has moved on to thinking about whether to preserve their performance on film or videotape (he points out that the British television programs *Crossroads* and *Coronation Street* are done on video). George continues to complain bitterly, pointing out the impracticality of bringing the entire film crew and equipment on the boat. Denis reminds him that The Beatles can get whatever they want, and John seems irritated by George's nit-picking, claiming that the logistics are someone else's problem. He then likens the situation to occasions where E.M.I. denied The Beatles use of the A.D.T. machine (an automatic double-tracking tape recorder) and eight-track recorder. The Beatles got use of the equipment in question by just taking it (as Paul says). John wants to simply tell E.M.I. what they have planned and rely on them to take care of the details. Despite the pressuring from the others Ringo still feels very strongly that the show should be held in England.

Paul reminds Ringo that they are filming a television show and not just putting on a concert. Ringo agrees that a good location would look nice but still opposes the idea. Denis tells him that their public expects something spectacular and John explains that he considers the African location to be the most fantastic set on Earth. Ringo counters by saying that very few people will even *notice* the set, but John disagrees and Michael adds that the set would be very noticeable indeed after the audience had been satisfied with a certain number of close-ups of the banal. Ringo doubts this, given the current trends in musical documentaries, but Michael pompously informs him that he intends to make art. John remembers the pleasure he'd had playing outdoors on the rooftops in India the previous year, and equates the live show to that experience. Michael presses them again for a decision, but everyone demurs - even those who are in favour of going away. George, undoubtedly disgusted that the topic is even being discussed, sits for the moment in silence. Ringo sarcastically tells them that he won't be thinking about it, he'll be home watching television. Finally, George expresses his displeasure with the idea in the strongest terms yet, characterising it as insane and expensive. He and Denis discuss the financial situation, but John counters with an idea that the boat could be gotten for free in exchange for the publicity the band's performance would generate. George argues that they couldn't even get free amps in exchange for publicity, and that they took a loss on their film *Magical Mystery Tour*. Ringo tries another angle to dissuade them, and doubts that a boat could be secured quickly enough. Denis takes a 'you never know until you try' attitude, and John points out that when he acted in the film *How I Won The War* director Richard Lester was able to borrow a number of ships from the American Navy. Ringo correctly notes that there's a difference between using some passing ships for a little while and taking over an entire ocean liner for a week. George doesn't argue anymore, but is obviously disgusted that they're even discussing this. Despite this (and Michael's insistence that Twickenham simply won't do for the show) the others decide to sleep on it and head off.

Thursday, January 9th, 1969

As they had done on the 5th, The Beatles run through songs that are planned for inclusion in the show. Their performances on the new songs are growing better and better, and the band has very nearly perfected at least five of the songs, "Don't Let Me Down," "Two of Us," "I've Got a Feeling," "One After 909" and "She Came in Through the Bathroom Window." "Across the Universe" is also worked on extensively.

Two new McCartney songs are also rehearsed during this session. "Let It Be," given its first full scale workout, and "Get Back," which is still a work-in-progress. The lyrics of "Get Back" at this point, satirise a movement within the British government that called for the repatriation of non-white immigrants from the other member countries of the British Commonwealth. This theme also runs through three improvised songs done during the session, "Commonwealth," "Enoch Powell" and "Get Off!"

In addition to Paul's numbers, The Beatles play an early version of "For You Blue," which George had been briefly premiered on the 7th. John has not yet written the new number that Paul had asked for, and "Don't Let Me Down" and the revived "Across The Universe" are his only live show contenders at this time. The rehearsals of the 'show' numbers during this day are uniformly excellent and enjoyable. The Beatles are surprisingly focused on perfecting the songs, and for one day at least they all seem to be enjoying themselves.

The first available tape comes within a few minutes of the start of recording for the day. Once again, Paul and Ringo are the first Beatles to arrive, and Paul heads off to the piano to get in some early morning rehearsal. Unlike the previous sessions, however, he's brought his girlfriend Linda Eastman with him. Paul must have appreciated Linda's practical approach as she suggests that The Beatles could do the show at Twickenham, and asks Michael how he would manage the sound equipment should the show be held on a boat. Michael refers the problem to Apple and proceeds to tell Paul about a homosexual-oriented novel he's been reading. Understandably, Paul's not very interested and proceeds to the piano to play.

9.1   ANOTHER DAY (3:16)
After an instrumental intro, Paul sings a few verses of this song. Although the first two verses are substantially complete, the middle eight hasn't been written yet, and he fumbles around for a few moments searching for something suitable to play. When he doesn't find it, he simply runs through the same few verses again. The performance stops as someone begins playing castanets, which have been brought in by Mal for use on "I Me Mine."

"Another Day" was never recorded by The Beatles, but was used by Paul as his first post-Beatle single in 1971.

9.2   (UNKNOWN) (0:27)
Paul plays bits of two unidentified Spanish dances in response to someone playing the castanets.

9.3   (INSTRUMENTAL) >0:26)
The available tape captures the last few moments of this gentle unidentified piano instrumental. Since Paul's running through his piano songbook (as usual) it's likely this is a McCartney composition, or perhaps even an im-

provisation. Paul is singing very softly at the beginning of this, but no words are decipherable.

9.4   (INSTRUMENTAL) (0:29)
Paul launches into this semi-classical piano instrumental which he had also played on the 7th (see 7.4).

9.5   LET IT BE (0:42)
Next in line in Paul's piano repertoire is "Let It Be." Paul sings the first verse and a single chorus before moving on to the next song. Someone provides harmony on the chorus, and it's obvious that this is a song with a future.

9.6   THE LONG AND WINDING ROAD (0:47<
Predictably, Paul follows "Let It Be" with "The Long and Winding Road" as he continues to play abridged versions of these tunes simply to show them off.

9.7   LET IT BE >3:09)
It's 10:40. Paul plays the intro to the song and sings only a portion of the first verse before he sings the chorus. He explains that the song should get quieter on the word 'whisper' and runs through the chorus again, playing softer when he reaches that spot. He then vocalises his way through the second verse, explaining that he hasn't written it yet. He stops for a few moments to ask Kevin for a cup of tea, but resumes playing the songs introduction, which he repeats in a slow tempo.

As one would expect, the conversation quickly turns to the topic of a shipboard voyage to Africa which had been raised at the end of the previous day's session. Ringo comes out against the idea more firmly than he had at the end of the previous discussions, and is met with the argument that if they're going to have the show in England, they should simply build a set and perform at Twickenham. Despite this, several other British locations are mentioned, an airport, the Houses of Parliament and Liverpool Cathedral (all of which had been suggested previously).

9.8   HER MAJESTY (0:59)
Perhaps inspired by the talk about the Houses of Parliament, Paul begins to perform this playful ode to the Queen. The piano part has the same music hall feel as the earlier rehearsals of "Maxwell's Silver Hammer."

Although "Her Majesty" will pop up again during these sessions, it wouldn't be properly recorded until later in the year on *Abbey Road*.

Possibly inspired by the previous evening's radio program *Jazz Club* (which had aired at 8:15 on BBC's Radio 1) Paul, Ringo and company hold a discussion of dance jazz bands, mentioning Sid Phillips (a British jazz clarinet player) and songs recorded by 1950's musical humorists ("Chloe" by Spike Jones and "The Yellow Rose of Texas" by Stan Freberg). In addition, we learn that Ringo has won his battle to have his tea out of a mug rather than plastic cups.

9.9   GOLDEN SLUMBERS (3:55)
Continuing his journey through the McCartney songbook, Paul offers this rendition of a traditional nursery rhyme, stopping for a few moments to explain the genesis of the lyrics.

Having performed a series of piano ballads, Paul jokingly suggests he's ready for a *Songs For Swinging Lovers* type LP (*Songs For Swinging Lovers* is a Frank Sinatra record). Paul admits to having lifted the lyrics of "Golden Slumbers" from an old English folk song, but can't remember any more of the original melody than the tag line (In 1970 he'd state that he wrote his own music for "Golden Slumbers" because he couldn't read the sheet music for the original tune)

9.10   CARRY THAT WEIGHT (3:07)

As he had on the 7th, Paul ties "Carry That Weight" to "Golden Slumbers." It's clear from the following conversation, however, that "Carry That Weight" was considered an unfinished song unto itself, and was not simply a chorus grafted on to "Golden Slumbers." Paul extemporises several verses and sings the chorus several times in unison with Ringo.

Paul compares his conception of "Carry That Weight" to "Act Naturally," a song that Ringo had sung on the LP *Help!* Ringo's mention of the Maharishi suggests that the song was conceived the previous year in India and Paul indicates that the song was humorous when he originally thought of it. He and Ringo harmonise quite charmingly on several choruses in-between Paul's working out a storyline for the verses. Ringo's vocal part would be retained when the song was eventually recorded for *Abbey Road*.

9.11   THE LONG AND WINDING ROAD (1:09)

Paul plays a brief bit of "The Long and Winding Road" and works on some of the lyric. Despite his tinkering with "Carry That Weight" it's obvious that Paul doesn't care to seriously rehearse anything until the rest of The Beatles arrive.

Paul and one of the soundmen then engage in a discussion. When the project began on the 2nd, the sound was recorded by the film crew on one, then two Nagra tape recorders using the sound feed from a single mono console. On January 6th Glyn arranged for mono equipment to be brought from IBC Studios in order to record selected performances for the purposes of playback (this required utilisation of IBC's Console). This setup became operational on the 7th, and was used on the 8th as well. Back on the 6th, George Martin had ordered two four-track consoles and an eight-track recorder to be installed in order to professionally record the live show (or, presumably, to be at hand to cart to an off-site location). Now, on the morning of the 9th one of Michael's crew has taken an hour off to patch the film's sound recorders into the console Glyn had gotten from IBC. This allows the filmmakers to set microphone levels and equalise the sound (the ability to isolate certain microphones will be tested later in this session, as Michael tries to capture candid conversations). Despite these modifications to the set up, all is not well, since they still need to integrate George Martin's eight-track equipment.

Glyn joins the conversation and reports that the film crew's recorders are now patched into his IBC console. He's hesitant to go further, however, because multi-track recording would require setting up too many mikes, and because working with E.M.I.'s equipment would take him away from the mono console and leave the film sound, now set up for more professional mixing, with no professional to mix it. In the end, he decides to leave things as they are, not only because the venue for the live show is undecided, but perhaps because The Beatles' performances have hardly been worthy of preservation. Ringo suggests that the rehearsals be preserved on multi-track, but quickly realises what a waste this would be. Glyn assures him that mono tapes are still being recorded for playback purposes.

Paul then talks about the theme of "The Long and Winding Road." When Mal suggests working an obstacle into the song's storyline, Paul jokes that he has enough problems with the group, and doesn't need them in his songs as well. Michael then asks about a happy ending - a question which could be applied both to The Beatles and the song.

9.12   THE LONG AND WINDING ROAD (1:13)
In response to a question from Michael, Paul plays the conclusion of this song. He follows this up with a few off-key measures from "Taps" and tries in vain to play "First Call" before breaking into "Oh! Darling."

9.13   OH! DARLING (1:40)
It's surprising how strong a vocal performance Paul puts in every time he plays this song, even here where he hardly seems to be trying. This performance breaks down during the second chorus, as Paul starts hitting the wrong notes on his piano.

The echo unit becomes functional during this performance and can be heard on Paul's vocal.

It's now 11:15 a.m.. George arrives and half-apologises for being over an hour late to the rehearsal. Of course, no one minds because John hasn't shown up yet either.

9.14   (INSTRUMENTAL) (0:14<
Paul plays this ponderous, airy piano instrumental over the dialogue above.

9.15   (INSTRUMENTAL) >1:19<
Another instrumental improvisation. Ringo thrashes along on drums, unsuccessfully trying to find a beat.

9.16   FOR YOU BLUE (1:29)
George plays a pleasant solo version of his new song. Every now and then Paul provides harmony vocal.

This performance comes five to ten minutes after the previous one. Unfortunately, the available tapes lack the material which bridges them, during which George has retrieved his guitar, tuned it, and introduced Paul to the work he'd done on "For You Blue" the previous evening (a far less finished version of the song was performed two days earlier). As one might expect, the topic of the live show has once again been brought up and Paul, apparently referring to Yoko's constant presence at John's side, suggests a box be built to put her in during the concert.

George fondly recalls the feel of playing acoustically, comparing it both to skiffle (a British mixture of jazz and American folk songs popular in the 1950's) and traditional country blues (he uses Son House as an example). Although it works quite well in this style, "For You Blue" will eventually be reworked into a more urban blues style, perhaps to instrumentally accommodate the other Beatles. In the few minutes between this dialogue and the last performance, John and Yoko have arrived. John appears to ask for the results of the morning's vote on the live show ideas presented at the end of the previous day's session. George doesn't answer, but launches into a Lennonesque series of puns and nonsense. Paul refers to "For You Blue" as a number that George wrote the previous night, evidently having forgotten the earlier performances of the song.

9.17   FOR YOU BLUE (0:04)

George begins playing "For You Blue" again, evidently for John's benefit, but stops to engage in conversation. He then presents his less-than-flattering opinions of the daily newspapers, and certain columnists who write for them. He admits he reads them just to follow the stories about drugs (referring to the previous day's headlines).

9.18   FOR YOU BLUE >1:11)

George offers another solo performance, despite the fact that no one's listening. Since there's currently no part in the song for Ringo, he's off on the side holding a conversation with Michael and Linda. George stops playing after the second verse in order to allow John and Paul to tune.

It's 11:35. Before running through "For You Blue," John and Paul hold a brief discussion centred around vegetarianism. Separately, Ringo, Michael and Linda discuss the live show. The conversations fade in and out as the sound technicians experiment with the new console which is controlling the level of the individual mikes. Ringo, realising that the audience will be primarily composed of English and Americans, argues that the show should be held in England so that their television audience can identify with the people attending the concert. Michael, however, feels that The Beatles belong to the world, and cites the multi-cultural audience seen in their promo film for "Hey Jude."

9.19   FOR YOU BLUE (2:30)

After an extended instrumental introduction (during which John tunes his guitar) George leads the others into a complete performance. Paul provides a series of bubbly piano trills as the three Beatles run through George's number. John plays an exceptionally poor guitar solo because his instrument is badly out of tune. Despite the additional instrumentation, this performance still retains the light, acoustic feel George had spoken of earlier.

While this is going on Michael, Linda and Ringo talk about dancers.

9.20   FOR YOU BLUE (2:48)

After Paul plays around on piano for a few moments, they jump back into "For You Blue." After a false start, they play a fruity, disjointed version in which George extemporises lyrics. A few moments into the song Paul stops playing piano, presumably to move over to his bass.

As this occurs, Linda, John and Michael talk. After a brief mention of television personalities Frankie Howerd and Benny Hill, the subject turns to house hunting. John wants a quiet country place, and mentions British politician Lloyd George's old estate with its extravagant security features. Linda and Paul want to find a farm. John and George sing a few lines about Lloyd George to the tune of "For You Blue."

After Ringo heads off to his drums in order to join the rehearsal, Michael and Linda trade touching little compliments about him. Michael then takes his soundman off to one side and asks him if he's taping their conversations to which he receives an affirmative answer.

With more than an hour of the session already spent, The Beatles finally begin to settle in for group rehearsal. Paul requests a guitar pick.

9.21   (IMPROVISATION) (2:11)

The group's individual tuning efforts eventually gel into this repetitive blues instrumental. John offers a brief scat vocal at one point.

After wondering what day of the week it is, John suggests that George teach the group "For You Blue." George is, of course, agreeable to this, but Paul would rather follow the same format as the previous day (where the familiar songs are performed in the morning and new songs are worked on later in the day. John suggests "Across The Universe" as an alternative, but the band begins a performance of "Two Of Us" in a medium tempo instead (they'll rehearse "Across The Universe" in the afternoon). With rehearsals underway, Michael seeks the help of a technician in turning off his spy mike.

9.22   TWO OF US (1:15<

The Beatles attempt to play the song from the top, but things quickly break down. Three more tries ensue, but they're unable to make it through the first verse, first because John can't remember how many measures introduce the song, then because the tempo's off, and then because John can't remember the words. Paul suggests that everyone turn their amps down so they can hear themselves better.

9.23   TWO OF US >2:15<

This performance is joined during the chorus, and quickly breaks down as it reaches the middle eight. John can't remember how to play the bridge. Paul optimistically believes the middle eight will fall into place by itself. They begin another performance, which Paul stops because John is not singing into his microphone. John testily replies that he'll get around to it and they begin the song again. However, this performance is also marred by John. who begins singing too early. Despite this mistake, it continues through at least to the second verse, where the available tape runs out.

Despite Paul's desire, it's obvious that The Beatles are unable to run through the familiar numbers one after the other. Although they had played "Two Of Us" the previous morning, they hadn't rehearsed the song since the 6th, and John in particular has pretty much forgotten how to play it. One of the false starts, Paul's admonishment to John to sing into the mike and John's rejoinder were included in the film *Let it Be* with an additional line of dialogue from Paul grafted in from elsewhere in the sessions. It might also be noted that Paul, perhaps trying to get into the spirit of a live performance, stands up through this set of rehearsals. The others, however, remain seated.

9.24   TWO OF US >0:13)

As the available tape begins, the group is finishing up a loose run through of the bridge as Paul vocalises a percussion part.

9.25   TWO OF US (2:49)

A complete, up-tempo performance which features an unusual guitar accentuation of the galloping riff. It's obvious from his singing that John has gotten a copy of the words. George provides a pleasant harmony vocal, and this performance is enjoyable despite the sloppy guitar work.

The Beatles discuss how the backing vocals for "Two Of Us" can be done live. George facetiously suggests getting in a few female backing vocalists from Ray Charles' band. John wants to get in three men. Paul would like Glyn to set it up so that the sound is phased to give a double-tracked effect. Glyn responds that they would do this after the fact, but Paul wants it for the show.

The group can't seem to decide whether they want to discuss the live show or rehearse "Two Of Us."

9.26   TWO OF US (0:08)

Paul sings a line of the song in order to illustrate a point he's making about the middle eight. The others pick up on this, and play a few bars before the performance falls apart.

9.27   medley (UNKNOWN) / TWO OF US (0:16<

Another fragment. Over the galloping riff which introduces "Two of Us" John sings a few lines from an unknown number. The available tape cuts off just as Paul begins to sing "Two Of Us."

9.28   TWO OF US >2:01)

The available tape begins during the second verse. Once again, The Beatles are trying for a complete run-through and this is similar in quality, to the earlier performances, although John and Paul mistakenly sing the third verse twice. This may be a continuation of 9.27.

Glyn offers a playback, but The Beatles opt for a tea break. As the next discussion begins, they discuss the physical placement of their amplifiers for the live performance. Paul raises the valid point that the band should be situated in rehearsal the way they will be during the live performance. George jokes that they still have to learn how to dance for the show, prompting Paul's response that they should make up some between-song jokes as well.

9.29   BAA, BAA, BLACK SHEEP (0:21)

A two line performance from John with a loose guitar backing.

As The Beatles tune up for a go at "Don't Let Me Down" George notices the large Bluthner insignia on the side of the grand piano. He asks who this is, and compares the brand name on the piano to large oil company logos that adorn race cars.

9.30   DON'T LET ME DOWN (3:30)

After two false starts, The Beatles turn in a complete performance. George is now using his wah-wah pedal. Once again John has trouble with the lyrics, but is corrected by Paul. Despite this, the band turns in a credible performance, although John's vocal edges on self-parody at times. John then offers a meek stage announcement for the next song, and introduces it as "Suzy's Parlour."

9.31   SUZY'S PARLOUR (2:27)

John takes a nasal lead vocal as he kicks off this slightly off-color, up-tempo song. George and Paul provide backing vocals, and appear to be having a fine time. The chorus, an echo of '50's rock and roll if ever there was one, has John shouting out encouragement while George and Paul provide him with staccato 'rat-tat-tat' backing. The performance is followed by a brief reprise. John's having a fine time, and suggests that they make up a song on the spot.

An edited version of this performance can be seen in the film *Let it Be*. It *was* copyrighted in 1971 as a band composition under the title "Suzy Parker" (the name of a contemporary fashion model), but copyright registration is hardly reliable, particularly in this instance where it served simply to protect the soundtrack of *Let It Be*. The simplistic and slightly risqué lyrics, as well as John's post-song comments, suggest that this is an on-the-spot rock and roll improvisation, drawing heavily from 1950's prototypes ("Little Suzie" also appears in The Everly Brothers' "Wake Up Little Susie" and Ritchie Valens' "That's My Little Suzie." The chorus and backing vocals also reflect the music of that era). One wonders why this number was not considered for use in the live show, given The Beatles' oft-stated desire for more rock and roll type songs.

9.32   I'VE GOT A FEELING   (3:53)
The Beatles continue with another complete run-through. Once again, the performance is quite good. John twice sings a variant lyric about getting a facelift, but is confused where to come in with his vocal.

This performance was butchered for use in the *Let It Be* film.

9.33   I'VE GOT A FEELING   (0:43)
Paul offers this brief performance during conversation.

The descending guitar riff that Paul envisions for the end of the middle eight is a recurring topic of discussion from this point forward. Paul wants John to play smoothly enough that no jumps can be distinguished between the notes. John makes a few attempts during the conversation, but he's obviously not playing to Paul's satisfaction. Although the tapes have not become available, the Beatles undoubtedly spent the next ten minutes or so rehearsing the middle eight.

9.34   I'VE GOT A FEELING   >0:23)
Having gone over the middle eight, the band tries another full performance. Unfortunately, the available tape joins in only near the very end, as John and Paul trade vocals to wind up the song.

9.35   I'VE GOT A FEELING   (0:40)
John, Paul and George play various "I've Got a Feeling" riffs as John mutters about the tone setting on his amplifier.

9.36   ONE AFTER 909   (0:57<
After two false starts, The Beatles finally launch into the song. As he was on "Suzy's Parlour" John is singing in a nasal tone and mock echoes the song's lyrics. George's guitar has a heavy wah-wah effect.

A portion of this performance appears in the *Let It Be* film. The next two fragments, also from the film, are most likely continuations of this performance.

9.37   ONE AFTER 909   >0:22<
This fragment consists of the instrumental break and middle eight.

9.38   ONE AFTER 909   >0:16)
This fragment contains the end of a performance.

9.39   ONE AFTER 909   >0:11)
This is nothing more than a series of riffs which followed a performance which has not become available.

A couple of run-throughs are sufficient for "One After 909" and The Beatles are ready to move on to the next song. George recalls the previous day's schedule, which concentrated on "Maxwell's Silver Hammer," "I Me Mine" and "All Things Must Pass" and suggests Paul's number "She Came In Through the Bathroom Window." Paul is agreeable to this, and as John moves over to piano, the two trade mock stage announcements for the show.

9.40   NORWEGIAN WOOD (THIS BIRD HAS FLOWN)   (0:35)
A few extraordinarily loose bars of this song are played while John gets situated at the piano. Paul starts it off on bass and George follows along on guitar. As the song dies out they sing one line of the lyrics together.

Out of nowhere, Michael asks John if he has any tattoos. John replies that he has "God Save The Queen" tattooed on his arse and Michael bemoans the fact that they won't be able to use it in the show.

9.41   SHE CAME IN THROUGH THE BATHROOM WINDOW (0:14<

The "Bathroom Window" rehearsals begin. Unfortunately, the available tape of this performance cuts off during the second line.

9.42   SHE CAME IN THROUGH THE BATHROOM WINDOW >1:54)

This performance, which edits in on the available tape during the second verse, may very likely be a continuation of 9.41. The Beatles continue to perform competently, but without any particular enthusiasm.

John then makes fun of Michael as he complains about the microphone set up on the piano.

9.43   SHE CAME IN THROUGH THE BATHROOM WINDOW (0:08)

A brief instrumental performance from John, perhaps to illustrate the problem with the piano's miking.

9.44   BE-BOP-A-LULA (0:31)

Paul sings the first two lines from Gene Vincent's "Be-Bop-A-Lula" and tags his performance with a line from Vincent's other major U.K. hit "Baby Blue." This short, knock-off performance takes place while a member of the crew tries to rearrange the microphones to John's satisfaction. The entire band contributes, including John on piano.

9.45   SHE CAME IN THROUGH THE BATHROOM WINDOW (0:10<

This amusing fragment starts off with John singing the lyrics of "She Came in Through the Bathroom Window" in a cockney accent, similarly answered by Paul.

Tragically, this unique performance is abbreviated by the filmmaker's sound roll running out. The missing moments should be contained on a tape for the second camera, but this has not yet surfaced.

9.46   SHE CAME IN THROUGH THE BATHROOM WINDOW >2:00)

This performance edits in during the second verse. John and Paul are still having fun with the song. Paul has resumed his lead vocal role, while John is now ad-libbing. The performance has little else to recommend it. Following the performance John and Paul clown around with each other. This may be entertaining, but it also suggests that the group is not very interested in perfecting the song. Granted, approximately a half hour of "Bathroom Window" rehearsal has not become available to us, so it's possible they're simply bored with it at this point.

9.47   SHE CAME IN THROUGH THE BATHROOM WINDOW (2:10)

This performance is much looser and is done at a slower tempo. Paul makes fun of his own lyrics, and improvises an almost entirely new second verse, which mentions Dan LaRue (at this time in 1969 Danny LaRue was at the peak of his career as a female impersonator. LaRue appeared in the theatres of London's West End as a variety of British female singers, including Dusty Springfield, Lulu and Julie Felix). The musicianship is even worse than the earlier performances, and John takes a moment out to introduce Ringo to their imaginary audience. Paul suggests that they perform "Bathroom Window" once more "..With Felix" ("Once More With Felix" was the name of a current British TV program starring folk singer Julie Felix).

9.48   SHE CAME IN THROUGH THE BATHROOM WINDOW (0:18<

The Beatles are apparently ready to slog through another rendition. This performance cuts off on the available tape after two lines.

9.49   SHE CAME IN THROUGH THE BATHROOM WINDOW   (2:52)

George has become more adventurous in his guitar playing and is improvising embellishments around the melody.

9.50   RIGHT STRING, WRONG YO-YO   (0:05)

A brief a capella parody from John who renames the song "Right String, Wrong Yoko." The Beatles had done a proper performance of this Carl Perkins number on the 6th. Paul once again suggests that they break for lunch.

9.51   BOOGIE WOOGIE   (0:07)

A short piano performance from John, who sings the title.

"Boogie Woogie" is a piano style which first arose in the United States in the late 1920's. Although Pinetop Smith recorded "Boogie Woogie" in 1928, the form quickly became generic enough so that it's probable John is simply offering a few bars of music in that idiom rather than referencing any specific song.

9.52   BAA, BAA, BLACK SHEEP   (0:25)

John starts to sing something, but almost immediately stops and breaks into this children's tune. Ringo helps out on vocal, and someone taps out the rhythm on some bottles.

"Baa, Baa, Black Sheep" is one of the oldest songs in the "Get Back" sessions canon. This familiar nursery tune comes from *Mother Goose's Melodies*, first published in 1765. It might also be noted that The Beach Boys jokingly broke into this song on their 1965 album *Beach Boys Party!* In response to Paul's mention of it a few moments earlier, Michael asks about the song "Mr. Bass Man."

9.53   MR. BASS MAN   (0:05)

In response to Michael, John sings a few seconds from "Mr. Bass Man" as the group gets up to leave for lunch. George sings along for a few moments, and someone whistles the tune as well.

It might be noted that Paul's bass guitar carried a large sticker which read 'bassman.'

It's a few minutes after 1:00. The Beatles wind up the "Bathroom Window" rehearsal and head off for lunch.

9.54   GET BACK   (0:47)

An embryonic version of "Get Back" had been performed back on the 7th. This particular performance is hardly more refined. Their energy level restored by the lunch break, The Beatles bash out a hard rock jam, wrapped entirely around the "Get Back" chorus, with Paul shouting out the title. George then verifies the words of the chorus with Paul. The chorus should sound familiar to George - it's a paraphrase from "Sour Milk Sea," which George wrote and produced for Jackie Lomax in 1968. Despite Paul's claim that he's content just to leave it as a jam it's obvious that he's thinking about lyrics.

9.55   GET BACK   (3:10<

The jam starts up again, even looser than before. Ringo stops for a few moments as if he doesn't quite know what to play. Finally he bangs his drumsticks together and offers a series of rim shots on his snare. Half way through. Paul begins to sing. Certain familiar phrases are already present in the lyrics including various references to Arizona and California and drag, but many of the words are unfinished and Jo-Jo and Loretta haven't been conceived yet.

Paul laughs and calls "Get Back"'s lyrics meaningless. George reiterates his belief (previously expressed on the 3rd) that meaningful lyrics aren't necessary for a successful song, citing The Band's "Caledonia Mission" as an example.

9.56   GET BACK (4:57<

Paul improvises various place-names to go along with Arizona. This leads him to Puerto Ricans, and finally to Pakistanis, two minority groups in the United States and England. He then begins to improvise lyrics about discrimination.

Paul's discrimination theme was drawn from the morning's newspapers, which were occupied with stories about Prime Minister Wilson's public comments on this subject. These were in response to statements made by Member of Parliament Enoch Powell to the effect that too many non-white citizens of the greater British Empire were living on visas in England and competing for limited job opportunities.

9.57   GET BACK (3:39)

The jams continue. This is much the same as 9.56, only harder and louder. Pakistanis and Puerto Ricans have been joined in the lyrics by Mohicans (American Indians). Towards the end of this, Paul amuses himself by shouting out the title and groaning as loudly as possible into his microphone for several minutes.

9.58   GET BACK (1:03<

Another step forward in the evolution of the song. As The Beatles rehearse the song, JoJo makes his first appearance (as Joe) and the song's heroine develops a name, too - Teresa.

9.59   (INSTRUMENTAL) (0:40)

A slow bluesy jam between John, Paul and Ringo which fizzles out as Paul begins to speak about having a headache and the morning paper. He then relates the history of his song "La Penina," a substandard number which would never be recorded by The Beatles, but would appear later in the year (as "Penina") on a Portuguese single by Carlos Mendes. In relating the story, Paul reminds himself of a newspaper column which claimed that he lifted the "Ob-La-Di, Ob-La-Da" riff from Jimmy Scott. Paul denies this, and emphatically states his belief that borrowing the phrase 'ob-la-di, ob-la-da' from Scott does not constitute any sort of musical thievery.

9.60   LA PENINA (1:03)

A tentative, lacklustre performance in vehicle Paul is joined by John and Ringo, who are no doubt playing the song for the first (and possibly only) time.

9.61   (INSTRUMENTAL) (0:31)

Another brief, simplistic blues instrumental, after which John and George toss out a few lines from Gary U.S. Bonds' 1961 song "New Orleans."

9.62   ACROSS THE UNIVERSE (0:30)

Having introduced the song, John starts the intro. Ringo joins in on the second beat, and John stops and asks him if he's supposed to be playing. They begin again (without Ringo) but this performance quietly breaks down as John laughs about the sluggish tempo.

At this point The Beatles rehearsed "Across the Universe," the tapes of which are not available for study. In fact, though they spent nearly a half hour rehearsing it, only fragments and two sluggish performances have surfaced.

We come to an interesting exchange now. George has been questioning the harmony on "Across The Universe," and John and Paul caustically berate him for picking on details. As background for this bizarre exchange, it might be worth a moment to think about what we *haven't* heard during this session. At the end of the 8th discussions took place regarding the possibility of holding the live shoot overseas, or on board an ocean liner. John and Paul were in favour of the idea. Ringo and George were not, and they all agreed to sleep on it. Despite some early morning comments from Paul and Ringo, it seems that The Beatles have purposely avoided discussing the issue. If this is the case, perhaps they wished to conduct their discussions out of the range of Michael's roving cameras and spy mikes. The tone of John and Paul's comments suggests that both of them are angry with George. In fact, although it's all hypothetical, these lines sound very much like they're throwing George's own statements back in his face. It would not be improbable to assume that The Beatles discussed the idea of a foreign excursion during lunch, and that George flatly refused to participate. Also of note is a comment that Paul makes about an undesirable oriental influence, possibly an oblique reference to Yoko.

9.63   ACROSS THE UNIVERSE (1:01)
The Beatles play a double-time version of the first verse, with John and Paul offering tight pop harmonies. As the song reaches the chorus, John gives up while Paul continues on for a line or two, gradually slowing the song down to the original tempo.
  Following this, George seems to suggest that, given the spiritual elements of the song, John complete the lyrics in a traditional fashion by travelling out into the desert. John takes him seriously, and isn't too taken with the idea.
9.64   ACROSS THE UNIVERSE >0:06<
A few seconds of Paul and George attempting to work out their backing harmonies on the chorus.
9.65   ACROSS THE UNIVERSE >0:04<
This one's an even briefer fragment. Paul sings the first line of the song in falsetto, accompanying himself on bass as John recites the first line of Little Richard's "Tutti Frutti."
9.66   ACROSS THE UNIVERSE >0:01<
This fragment contains nothing more than a partial line sung by Paul.
9.67   TEDDY BOY >0:14)
The band puts "Across The Universe" aside for the moment, and busks this brief, up-tempo version of a McCartney composition from the previous year. After the first few lines, Paul stops the performance to talk about the song. He reminisces about "Teddy Boy" and "Junk," both songs he'd written in India the previous year. George isn't listening, but making dinner plans with someone who's off mike (indeed, the day's session will wind up right about 5:30, as George suggests here).
9.68   JUNK (0:16)

Paul and John sing a few lines in mock-French, simply to recall how the song goes.

It's interesting to note the mock-French lyrics, which include a smattering of multi-syllable English words sung in a heavy French accent. This type of linguistic word-play will show up again later in the year when The Beatles record "Sun King" for *Abbey Road*.

"Junk" would never be professionally recorded by The Beatles, but their 1968 demo would appear on *Anthology 3*, and the song would be recorded by Paul for his first solo LP *McCartney* in 1970.

9.69   ACROSS THE UNIVERSE (3:42)
It's hard to believe The Beatles could make it all the way through a performance as bad as this. John and Paul kick off the song singing the first verse in unison, after which George joins in for the chorus. Ringo's drumming plods along, and everyone sounds bored. John stops the performance to instruct Ringo to pause after each verse, but Paul starts the ball rolling again by picking up at the second verse, and John quickly joins in. Despite the fact that Ringo corrects his drumming, the latter half of the performance is no better than the rest.

9.70   ACROSS THE UNIVERSE (3:29)
Another complete performance, more workmanlike than the previous one. John and Paul harmonise well, although Ringo's overbearing drums are hardly appropriate to the contemplative nature of the song. Paul and John issue a Yoko-like bleat at the end of one of the lines. Paul thinks that they're improving.

9.71   "SHAKIN' IN THE SIXTIES" (0:37)
John's impromptu 'tribute' to Beatles' music publisher Dick James. As he sings the others come in behind him and play an "Ob-La-Di, Ob-La-Da" type rhythm. George picks up on this and parodies the tag to that song.

9.72   MOVE IT (0:55)
Inspired by "Shakin'" John decides to do "Move It" and takes the lead vocal on this cover of a Cliff Richard rocker, though his recollection of the lyrics is spotty. This performance runs directly into the next.

At the beginning of the song George asks the others if they're tired, and suggests they lay off the wine. "Move It" was one of the earliest British rock and roll hits which, despite their general disdain for Cliff Richard, would have been well known to all of them.

9.73   GOOD ROCKIN' TONIGHT (0:50)
John takes lead on another oldie, with occasional help from Paul. The musicianship is fine, but John and Paul's recollection of the lyrics is sporadic.

"Good Rockin' Tonight," written and originally recorded by Roy Brown, had been Elvis Presley's second single in 1954.

The Beatles then amuse themselves by recalling routines from *Laugh-In*. John's mention of actor John Wayne reminds George of a story about Wayne's son. Not to be beat John pretends he's Robert Mitchum's son, and breaks into gibberish. Paul begins to sing about Chris Mitchum, which he mutates into the name of British television personality Cliff Michelmore. As the band begins to play an instrumental (once again reminiscent of "Ob-La-Di, Ob-La-Da") Paul sings the title of "Oh, Donna," but John steers the performance into a cover version of Carl Perkins' "Tennessee."

9.74   TENNESSEE (1:59)

A pleasant cover of this oldie. John, George and Paul all share the vocals, with George having the best recollection of the lyrics. During the instrumental break Paul begins to vocalise Carl Perkins' guitar part, but George is on top of the situation and plays it instead. A complete performance, featuring three verses with occasional garbled lyrics.

"Tennessee" is one of the more charming cover versions from these sessions, with its lyrics about hillbilly music and atomic bombs. It was originally released in 1956 by Carl Perkins (although the vocal on the song was by his brother, Jay) and was on Carl's first album. Following the performance, John asks if they have any new songs to work on.

9.75   ACROSS THE UNIVERSE (0:10)

Perhaps as a suggestion that they resume the "Across the Universe" rehearsal, Paul sings the first line of that song, spurring John to shout a few garbled lines into his microphone and exclaim that he doesn't want to do that song anymore. He flips through his schedule of songs, and cries out in despair when he reaches "I Me Mine," no doubt remembering the extensive rehearsals from the day before.

9.76   HOUSE OF THE RISING SUN (2:32)

The band plays the first few bars of "I Me Mine," but John starts singing this traditional blues number instead. Paul joins in, and they have a fine time moaning and shouting their way through the song. From the few lyrics that can be deciphered, we can hear that John has given the song a local flavour singing about a house in Woolton town - the part of Liverpool in which he grew up.

"House of the Rising Sun" had been a hit for The Animals in 1965.

With another few minutes wasted, John calls out for them to play "Boadicea." Boadicea was a tribal Queen of the ancient British Celts around 61 AD. John expressed his admiration of her in his famous 1966 interview with Maureen Cleave. It was also the name of the state-of-the-art computer that British Airways was using at this time. John's use of it here, though, apparently as a song title, remains a mystery. John is still looking to move on to something new, having already gone through "Don't Let Me Down" and "Across the Universe." "Dig a Pony" seems to be out of consideration at the moment.

Paul begins to suggest "I Me Mine." George prefers "For You Blue," but runs into the problem of feedback from Glyn's P.A. setup and the lack of a setup for his acoustic guitar.

9.77   "COMMONWEALTH" (3:33)

As George and Glyn discuss the equipment problems, Paul begins to improvise this enjoyable rock and roll song. A hyperactive John offers response vocals, and even helps with the words at one point. The improvised lyrics refer to the hotly debated topic of the repatriation of immigrants to the British Commonwealth countries from which they came. Paul continues to sing in this vein, clearly satirising Powell's pro-repatriation movement, as he covers the situation in England and offers a travelog through the British Empire. The chorus consists of nothing more than Paul's shouting "Commonwealth," and John's affirmative response. As the song continues, John and Paul touch on

Britain's entry into the European Common Market, which had been denied in late 1968, making a pun out of the phrase "common market."

The issue Paul tackles in "Commonwealth" started to come into focus in early 1968 when the Kenyan government voted to deny non-Kenyans jobs, causing thousands of people of Indian and Pakistani ancestry living in Kenya to come to England. On February 27th The House of Commons passed legislation to limit this flow of people. This didn't satisfy Enoch Powell, a conservative member of Parliament, who started a repatriation movement soon afterwards. He responded to a race relations bill which was before The House of Commons in April by stating that it "would make coloured people a privileged class." Powell's outspokenness resulted in Conservative Party leader Edward Heath removing him from the Shadow Cabinet, calling his statements "racist in tone and liable to exacerbate racial tensions." The bill was passed in July, but the issue remained unsettled and was made the primary topic of debate when the leaders of the 28 Commonwealth nations met in London for a conference from January 7th through the 15th. That conference filled the headlines when this session took place and provided the subject matter not only for "Commonwealth" but for early versions of "Get Back" as well.

9.78   "ENOCH POWELL" (0:22)
Paul sings this short follow-up to "Commonwealth," performing it with a slow blues backing. He ends the song with another political comment, mentioning that Mr. Powell is now powerless.

9.79   "GET OFF!" (5:49<
George leads the band into a standard twelve bar blues (presumably "For You Blue") that the others quickly and easily pick up on. George doesn't sing any lyrics, however, and John and Paul soon turn the song into another political improvisation. Paul mutters about 'white power' (a continuation of the political commentary heard in the previous two songs) and calls out the names of some prominent blacks, but soon he and John start to call out any name that comes into their minds, offering a fascinating stream-of-consciousness glimpse into their collective memories (this foreshadows the "Dig It" improvisations which will occur later in the month). Consult the who's who which follows for details.

They stop for a moment and John offers a brief parody of Paul's song "Why Don't We Do It In The Road?" from the previous year's double album. They start up again as George requests time to play a solo acoustic number (perhaps "Ramblin' Woman" which he'll play in about 20 minutes). John pointedly ignores this request and resumes the improvisation.

9.80   FOR YOU BLUE (0:23<
Stuck in the middle of the "Get Off!" jams, George plays a few lines, perhaps hoping to lead them back into rehearsals.

9.81   "GET OFF!" >1:13)
The jam continues as John and Paul toss out some more names.

In the order in which they're called, here's the cast of "Get Off!" Unless otherwise specified, the name is called out by Paul.

MALCOLM EV.
Needless to says this refers to Mal Evans, The Beatles roadie. It's undoubtedly a play on the name of black activist Malcolm X.

JAMES BROWN

American soul singer. The Beatles spoke about him the day before, and will briefly cover "Papa's Got a Brand New Bag" during these sessions.

CASSIUS CLEAVAGE
Paul combines Cassius Clay (i.e., boxer Muhammad Ali), with a play on Eldridge Cleaver (another black activist).

DEIRDRE McSHARRY
Called by John, Deirdre McSharry was a magazine editor.

HUMPHREY LESTOUQ
An early TV personality from the U.K.. Lestouq presented a children's program called "Whirligig" which featured a string puppet named "Mr. Turnip."

JUDY GARLAND
U.S. actress who starred in many musicals including *The Wizard of Oz*.

JEREMY BANKS
Apple's photographic coordinator.

WILSON PICKETT
Another black U.S. soul singer.

JIMMY BROWN
Most likely James Brown again, although it's possibly a reference to the popular number "The Jimmy Brown Song," the Lonnie Donegan track "Jimmy Brown the Newsboy" or the American football player.

MALCOLM EVANS
Mal is honoured twice. Following this, Paul calls out the name of their home town (Liverpool).

BILLY TURNER
An early member of The Quarrymen, John and Paul's first group.

ERIC GRIFFITHS
Another Quarrymen member.

IVAN VAUGHN
Another Quarrymen member, and longtime friend of John's.

DUSTY SPRINGFIELD
A popular British singer.

RUSS CONWAY
Popular British pianist from the '50's and '60's. Conway had several #1 hits on the U.K. charts.

PETER BROWN
Apple employee and ex-assistant of Brian Epstein.

JOAN LITTLEWOOD
Innovative British theater director, most famous for *Oh, What a Lovely War!* (1963).

JOHN LENNON
At a complete loss to keep up with Paul's string of personages, John calls out his own name.

MARY WHITEHOUSE
Paul mentions the name of this British anti-pornography crusader, then suggests that Britain have a religious political party.

RICHARD NIXON
At the time, President-elect of the United States.

RONNIE CORBETT
An English television comedian who hosted the contemporary program *The Corbett Follies*.

DAVID FROST
An English television talk show host.

BETTY GRABLE
U.S. actress most famous for her World War II pin-up.

CLARK KENT
Continuing the thread of mid-century Americana. The mild-mannered Mr. Kent is, of course, Superman's alter-ego. This call very much amuses John. He repeats this name and he and Paul laugh.

SUPER AJAX
Suggested by Superman, no doubt, this is the name of a popular cleaning product.

SEAN O'MAHONY
John calls the name of the publisher of *Beatles Monthly*, a British publication for Beatles fans which was published throughout the 1960's.

JACK MacGOWRAN
Irish character actor. He appeared in *Wonderwall* (for which George did the score) and *How I Won The War* (which co-starred John).

ENID BLYTON
Well known children's author whose books would have been read by The Beatles as children.

MIKE ISSACSON
College acquaintance of John.

GEOFF MOHAMMED
Another crony from John's college years.

TONY CARRICKER
Another college pal. John calls this one, as well as the next.

BILL HARRY
Another college friend. Harry went on to found *Mersey Beat*, a pop-music newspaper from the early 1960's.

EMPEROR ROSCO
Popular disc jockey for Radio Luxembourg.

JUNE HARRY
John's still going through his college class list. June was another friend.

VIRGINIA HARRY
Paul chimes in with another Harry, in this case Bill's wife. John is greatly amused.

NORMAN ROSSINGTON
British character actor who played 'Norm' in *A Hard Day's Night*.

JOHN JUNKIN
British character actor who played 'Shake' in *A Hard Day's Night*.

TONY SHERIDAN
British singer who The Beatles met in Hamburg. Sheridan has a place in Beatles history as the vocalist on The Beatles' earliest recordings.

WINSTON CHURCHILL
British Prime Minister during the Second World War.

LESTER ACKERLEY
Controversial Merseyside promoter.

GERALD NABARRO
Equally controversial British member of Parliament. Nabarro was famous for his handlebar moustache and collection of cars with personalised number-

plates. A gap in the available tape follows this call, but there's not much missing.

Stuck in the middle of this light-hearted jam is a very interesting little moment. Paul complains about the volume of their amps, and John, chuckling, tells him to quit the group if he doesn't like it. Like the odd exchange which follows 9.62, the outright nasty tone in John's voice suggests that this might be an oblique reference to discussions revolving around the live show in which George threatened to leave the band. The Beatles may be under a self-imposed rule not to discuss these conflicts openly, but one gets the impression that John is quite annoyed (if not out-and-out angry) and can't restrain himself from an occasional swipe at George and his position on things.

ERIC CARGO
Presumably a play on Eric Clapton. At this point there's a small break in the available tape. As it resumes, the free-association jam is still going on.

Riled, perhaps, by John's mocking comment about quitting the group, George asserts himself by forcefully singing a line from "For You Blue," the song which he began playing a few minutes earlier which the others hijacked and turned into "Get Off!" He now tries to reclaim it, but fails, as John and Paul begin calling out English place-names. John, obviously quite pleased with this jam, suggests to Glyn that he tape it. It might be noted that, except for his instrumental backing, George has not contributed to this jam at all.

THE ST. BUTTERSFIELD CARGO
Presumably a play on the Paul Butterfield Blues Band. After this call the jam once again peters out and Paul's amp begins to feed back.

THE ELECTRIC STRING BACK, THE INCREDIBLE STRING VEST
These group names, called out by Paul and John respectively, are derived from The Incredible String Band, a '60's group. Paul then attempts to amuse John by making an allusion to John and Yoko's practice of showing up in public hidden in white bags.

9.82   HONEY, HUSH   (2:08)
John and Paul share lead vocals on a fine performance, much tighter and more energetic than the version done on the 8th. Unfortunately, they only seem to know one verse.

9.83   FOR YOU BLUE   (0:46)
The Beatles roll directly into "For You Blue." This performance swings nicely, but Paul stops it after the first verse because he can't hear George. He asks for George's vocal mike to be turned up, but George seems to prefer that the others play more quietly.

9.84   FOR YOU BLUE   (2:05)
A fairly tight run-through, with George singing the first verse and part of another. Although the lyrics aren't finished, the musicianship is quite passable. This is attributable to The Beatles having jammed on many 12-bar blues through the years. John correctly notes that the song is very brief. One may

detect a pattern in George's compositions from these sessions. They invariably start out as solo arrangements and are modified to accommodate roles for the others. In addition, it's obvious that George is trying to keep them short, perhaps to spare them all the drudgery of drawn out rehearsal.

There's a 10 minute gap in the available tape at this point, which undoubtedly contains further attempts at "For You Blue."

The Beatles then try to decide what instruments to play. George has switched to acoustic but desires a different guitar. It's just past 4 p.m..

9.85   "RAMBLIN' WOMAN"   (2:00)
As the others prepare to move on to "Let It Be," George begins a string of solo acoustic performances. As he plays, they stop tuning and talking, presumably to listen. George slightly alters the lyrics each time he sings the song's only verse. He's enjoying himself and laughing as he plays the guitar.

9.86   I THREW IT ALL AWAY   (2:03)
George moves right into this Dylan song as someone taps along in the background. While he knows the song's middle eight very well, he struggles with the verses. The performance is memorable in spite of this.

"I Threw It All Away" had to have been learned directly from the song's author during George's late 1968 trip to America. Dylan wouldn't even record the song himself until mid-February, 1969, for release on his *Nashville Skyline* LP.

9.87   MAMA, YOU BEEN ON MY MIND   (1:55)
George continues his solo acoustic medley with a fine performance of another Bob Dylan song. George perfectly captures the low-key emotion of the song as he runs through three of the song's five verses.

"Mama, You Been on My Mind" may also have been learned directly from Dylan. Bob chose not to release his own 1964 recording, but gave the song to Joan Baez.

The Beatles are aware of the general disarray of their rehearsal, and engagingly make fun of themselves as George finishes his solo set. Paul is more than ready to begin "Let It Be" (in fact, he starts to play it on piano as they talk) and John is impatient to get a bass guitar and join him.

9.88   LET IT BE   (8:05<
A stop and go rehearsal where Paul formally introduces this tune to the schedule. As the others aren't ready, he begins teaching the drum part to Ringo. A minute later John gets his bass and begins to play as Paul teaches him the chords, assuring him that the song will be very simple to learn. Paul takes it from the top at one point, but stops during the first verse to vocalise the cymbal part for Ringo. As this continues he vocalises the unwritten verses. John offers some awfully out of key harmonies on the chorus, and Paul tells him to vocalise rather than sing the words. This leads into some work on the vocal harmonies. George is chosen for the higher part, and Paul instructs John how to sing the lower harmony. They're still working on this as the available tape runs out.

In the next available tape, Ringo and Denis discuss Peter Sellers' part in *The Magic Christian*.

9.89   LET IT BE (1:34)

Although the tapes have not become available, the "Let It Be" rehearsal has been going on for nearly an hour, and George and Ringo have wandered off as John and Paul clown around with the song. Paul begins this loose performance with a mock sermon and, picking up on John's pun from the previous day, uses the name Brother Malcolm instead of Mother Mary. John sneaks in rock and roll riffs throughout, and as the song peters out seems to be attempting a single-handed jam.

Meanwhile, Michael and Glyn discuss the bugging device that Michael has placed on the set to better capture the conversation. Ringo seems annoyed that the device is there, and jokes that he would rather leave than continue being taped.

9.90   LET IT BE (0:58)

John continues to play riffs as Paul starts up "Let It Be" again. Paul performs the song solo on piano, fighting off John's intrusive guitarwork.

Ringo, Denis and Glyn continue to talk, and George wanders over to check out the bugging device, which Denis wrongly claims isn't functioning. Denis and Ringo then resume their conversation about filming *The Magic Christian*. Ringo expresses some concern about his character in the film, who does not appear in the novel, but Denis would rather discuss his idea for one of the film's sequences which he'd like to film on Wall Street in New York. Ringo is unimpressed with this idea, and feels that it's a waste of time to go all the way to America just to film one scene. Despite this, he's quick to add that he's not refusing to co-operate.

9.91   LET IT BE (1:27)

Paul starts another performance, as John tries to play along. After one verse and an instrumental passage the uninspired performance ends.

The discussion of *Magic Christian* continues, as Denis tries to convince Ringo that shooting on Wall Street is a wonderful idea. The conversation then turns to *The One-Eyed Wasp*, a book that Ringo feels can be made into a good film.

9.92   THAT'LL BE THE DAY (2:04)

Paul picks up on some riffs from John and begins a laid back performance of this song. Ringo and George don't participate. John keeps playing the bass riff after Paul has stopped, but quickly starts improvising rock and roll riffs again.

"That'll Be The Day," released in 1957, was Buddy Holly's first hit. An acetate of The Quarrymen's 1958 cover version (finally released on *Anthology I*) is the oldest known "Beatles'" recording.

Meanwhile, Ringo and Denis are still talking, and discuss taking off for a few hours to go see a new film. Although this tape is continuous, we're missing parts of the conversation because the soundman keeps cutting in and out from the feed of the spy mike. Because of this, we've missed the portion of dialogue where Denis tells Ringo what film he's talking about. Denis then explains why he feels that films take too long to make, and points out that *A Hard Day's Night* is the only picture he knows of that managed to avoid that problem. He then asks Ringo if rehearsals and filming will continue through the weekend, and Ringo wearily replies that he doesn't feel like coming in then. An assistant arrives and provides Denis with some information regarding flights to Tripoli. Mal plans to fly there to scout locations for the live show.

9.93   I'VE GOT A FEELING (0:16)
A short, off-key guitar instrumental from John, who then shouts for the others to pick up their instruments. John has finally grown bored playing riffs, and wants to resume the rehearsals.

9.94   medley JENNY, JENNY / SLIPPIN' AND SLIDIN' (2:22)
Once again John's guitar riffs lead Paul into a performance. Paul sings an indecipherable line of something before he begins "Jenny, Jenny." As the song progresses, first Ringo and then George join back in. Paul takes the song into "Slippin' and Slidin'" and then back into "Jenny, Jenny," and John even has a brief solo. At one point the song almost breaks down, but John calls out for them to keep going and the rest of the band comes back in. Paul plays the first few measures of "Let it Be," attempting to restart rehearsals of that song.

The original versions of "Jenny, Jenny" and "Slippin' and Slidin'" were recorded by Little Richard in 1956.

9.95   LET IT BE (3:43<
With all the band members now ready to play, Paul leads them back into "Let It Be." He sings the first verse (breaking up in laughter as John mocks the song's religious overtones) and the chorus, and vocalises through the other verses. John and George make a sincere attempt at the backing vocal, which consists of sustained vocalising. Paul makes a passing reference to one of the song's gospel sources as he mentions Aretha Franklin. Shortly thereafter he stops the performance to try to work on a brief instrumental break, and they take a few moments to discuss the song's arrangement with Glyn who assumes a position which would normally have been filled by George Martin.

9.96   LET IT BE >2:41)
In this rehearsal segment, the band works on an ending for the song. Once again, John mocks the song's religious overtones. As things wind down, George starts playing variations of the "Let It Be" guitar part, but the others do not participate.

It's already past five o'clock and Paul wants to take a five minute break. George, perhaps sensing a long evening of rehearsal, quickly asks to be excused. Paul agrees to call it a day, but wants to get in one good pass at "Let It Be" before they go.

9.97   LET IT BE (2:33)
The Beatles turn in a competent performance of the song considering their limited experience with it. Once again Paul vocalises his way through most of the later verses, singing whatever comes into his head (i.e., a lyric about the *Record Mirror*).

Paul is satisfied and, after a final few words about "Let It Be" The Beatles prepare to head home. As they do so, Yoko half-apologises to Paul for arriving late with John, and Paul facetiously replies that he's used to it. Michael then raises the topic of the live show which (at least as far as he's concerned) seems to have been avoided throughout the day. John is very keen on the idea of having the show in America and doesn't understand that his 1968 drug conviction would make getting a visa difficult. Assistant Neil Aspinall has apparently been dispatched to consult with E.M.I. head Sir Joseph Lockwood to

discuss this problem. Finally, Paul and Linda try to decide whether or not to
go out for a drink with the others.

Friday, January 10th, 1969

The tensions of the past week come to a head on the 10th. After another morning piano session from Paul (none of which has become available) and a rehearsal for "Get Back," George has a conflict with John during lunch. He then returns to the soundstage and casually states that he's quitting the group and walks out. Consequently, John, Paul and Ringo spend much of the afternoon jamming and engaging in trivial chat.

Needless to say, January 10th marks the dramatic highlight of the "Get Back" sessions. Unfortunately, little has surfaced from this day, making our sequencing difficult in spots. Our ability to interpret the dialogue also suffers, because many important exchanges have been fragmented.

The earliest material available to us from this day consists of lengthy dialogue segments. Paul is the first Beatle to arrive and is chatting with publisher Dick James about purchasing the publishing rights of someone's song catalogue. Ringo arrives, and the conversation turns to the previous evening's television viewing. Paul recounts Zsa Zsa Gabor's appearance on a BBC talk show hosted by Eamonn Andrews, and goes on to describe an incident that occurred when Zsa Zsa and her daughter were visiting Abbey Road Studios the previous year.

Paul, Ringo, Dick, Michael and Glyn then engage in trivial conversation regarding the disciplining of children, fear of flying and appendix removal. Dick makes sure that Paul and his family have received the telegrams he sent congratulating them on the birth of Paul's niece, Benna, which had occurred the previous month.

Although tapes are not currently available, we know that Paul performed another series of solo piano pieces on the morning of the 10th, including "The Long and Winding Road," "Let It Be," "Don't Let Me Down," "Maxwell's Silver Hammer," "I've Got A Feeling," "Get Back'' and "Lady Madonna."

10.1   ALL TOGETHER NOW >0:08<
A brief performance from John, who sings a few garbled lyrics while accompanying himself on unamplified guitar.

"All Together Now" was a McCartney number recorded in 1967 for the soundtrack of the *Yellow Submarine* film.

10.2   TWO OF US (2:00)
An energetic, if incomplete performance. The Beatles seem to have the song pretty much down, but during the second middle eight the performance breaks down.

Approximately an hour has passed since the earlier discussions. George has arrived, rehearsals have begun, and it's clear that a number of performances from this period of time have not become available.

As the next available tape begins, Paul wants the three of them to come crashing into "Get Back" the way they did on their song "Help!" In the following performance, they oblige him.

10.3   GET BACK (2:00)

The Beatles turn in this rollicking performance. Paul has done some work on the lyrics, and this is noticeably tighter than the previous day's efforts. The only major mistake is John's, as he starts to sing the verse about JoJo instead of the new third verse. However, this hardly detracts from the fun of this enjoyable run-through.

10.4   HI HEEL SNEAKERS   (1:56<
John and Paul share the lead vocal on a lively performance of this oldie. George provides capable guitar backing, and the whole band is clearly familiar with the song. The available tape runs out.

"Hi Heel Sneakers" was first released in 1964 by Tommy Tucker.

10.5   HI HEEL SNEAKERS   >0:44)
This instrumental fragment is the end of 10.4.

Whatever tensions had been building over the last several days between members of the band came to a head at lunch on the 10th, which came at this point.

10.6   I'M TALKING ABOUT YOU   (0:05)
John plays the guitar introduction to the song and stops.

"I'm Talking About You" was first recorded by Chuck Berry in 1961.

At this point, we are sadly reminded of the incomplete nature of the available source material. George is speaking to John and calmly announces he's quitting The Beatles *immediately*. The available tape cuts. Tapes of the events that led up to this moment are not available, and perhaps don't exist.

Almost as frustrating is the next fragment. George coldly suggests that the other Beatles write to the *New Musical Express* (one of Britain's music publications) in order to get a replacement for him, and seems to suggest that Apple's publicity department should deal with the change in personnel. The sarcastic tone of George and John's comments shows just how incapable they are of honest, rational communication even when faced with the disintegration of the group. As George would later note, when The Beatles fought they didn't yell at each other, but simply stopped communicating. And it's more than obvious that John and George have had a falling out.

Despite the fact that all four Beatles have since declared that George quit the band because of a musical conflict with Paul, evidence on subsequent tapes strongly suggests otherwise. So, what *really* occurred to make George leave? By the end of the following week it was widely reported in the contemporary media that a row had occurred between George and *John*. Sources reported a "personal tiff," but denied that the two came to blows. George was interviewed about it by the *Daily Express* on January 16th, and said: "There was no punch-up. We just fell out." This same report presumes that the conflict came over remarks John had made in an interview in the January 17th edition of *Disc and Music Echo* (obviously reported in the newspapers before the cover date) where he had claimed that "Apple is losing money. If it carries on like this we'll be broke in six months." Certainly, neither George nor Paul would have liked seeing The Beatles' business affairs made public. Although this, or the disputed location of the live show may have been a topic of discussion, these matters simply served to exacerbate an underlying conflict between the two.

Judging by evidence which we will examine more thoroughly in our commentary for the 13th, George had finally had enough of John's unwillingness (or inability) to engage in rational communication. His resentment was heightened by Yoko's habitual and presumptuous tendency to speak in John's place which, if accepted, would give her a voice in the future of the group equal to or overshadowing his own. Paul has similar misgivings, but chooses not to express them for fear of John leaving the group if confronted.

A history of problems between George and John certainly contributed towards a breakdown in communication between the two. Unquestionably, George felt slighted by a lack of musical respect. Throughout these sessions there have been instances where he's offered a new number to the others and been ignored ("Hear Me Lord" and "For You Blue") or derided ("I Me Mine"). George's bitterness about this comes up throughout the sessions, and John is probably resentful himself, since he sees George contributing a presentable new number every day or two while he himself is unable to write a decent new song.

In any case, George walked out of the sessions, quit The Beatles and drove home, presumably awaiting the weekend's business meeting to discuss the differences between them.

10.7   A QUICK ONE WHILE HE'S AWAY (1:22)
John sings and backs himself on distorted electric guitar. Only Paul's brief backing vocal stops this from being a solo performance. John doesn't seem to know any more than the song's refrain.

"A Quick One While He's Away" was originally recorded by The Who in 1967. John's performance of this may very well have been inspired by the relevance of the title to George's departure.

In the next brief tape fragment, John, clearly not broken up over George's absence, sarcastically calls for him to take the solo.

10.8   A QUICK ONE WHILE HE'S AWAY (0:51<
John begins the song again, though he's mutated the lyric. Ringo starts bashing away on drums behind him, and the performance turns into a jam.

10.9   (IMPROVISATION) >2:36<
This is clearly a continuation of the jam started at the end of 10.8. John plays a repetitive heavy blues riff while Ringo continues to attack his drum kit. Yoko joins in by screaming at the top of her lungs, basically just yelling out John's name. Paul runs his bass up and down in front of his amplifier, adding feedback to the cacophony.

It's interesting to note that Yoko, who has generally been seated next to or behind John up to this point, moves to the center of the soundstage for this performance. In a subsequent interview, Michael described this jam as "weird, angry," "brutal" and "passionate." Certainly it's the loudest, rawest performance to have become available from these sessions. Shots of this may be glimpsed in the documentary *Yoko Ono, Then and Now*.

10.10   (IMPROVISATION) >0:27<
Obviously the concluding moments of 10.9. John and Ringo have calmed down, and Yoko offers a few plaintive wails backed by feedback guitar.

10.11   TILL THERE WAS YOU   (0:18)

An off-the-cuff, three line performance by Paul, who accompanies himself on bass. Ringo lazily taps along on drums, and John even joins in for a few notes.

  "Till There Was You" had been covered by The Beatles on their 1963 album *With The Beatles*. It was a hit in 1961 for Peggy Lee and originally appeared in "The Music Man." In this and the following two performances Paul and John's vocals take on decidedly inebriated characteristics.

10.12   MAXWELL'S SILVER HAMMER   >0:06)

A short while earlier John had asked Paul what song they should tackle.

  Paul picked this title, ignoring the fact that George's absence would totally preclude any worthwhile rehearsal of it. This fragment captures Paul playing a bit of the song on bass.

10.13   MACK THE KNIFE   (0:11)

Ringo taps out a rhythm as John sings three half-remembered lines from this song. Originally titled "Moritat" in Kurt Weill's 1928 "Three Penny Opera," "Mack the Knife" was a hit in the '50's for many artists, including Marty Wilde and American Bobby Darin (who took it to number one in 1959).

10.14   MAXWELL'S SILVER HAMMER   (0:53<

Paul tries to get down to business by counting in over John's performance, but a loose, messy version ensues. John seizes the opportunity to offer a parody vocal.

10.15   MAXWELL'S SILVER HAMMER   >1:08)

A continuation of 10.14, featuring John singing in a very high falsetto. Paul chimes in with a Tiny Tim imitation. Even the instrumentation has taken on the form of a parody.

10.16   DON'T BE CRUEL   (2:26)

As John riffs, Paul begins to play "Don't Be Cruel"'s bass line. John picks up on this and begins singing the song with a distinctly nasal intonation as Ringo joins in on drums. Paul adds slurred backing vocals and John, with a chuckle, starts to sing "In The Middle of An Island," but can only remember two lines, improvising several others. He and Paul then turn back to "Don't Be Cruel" for a few bars, before the performance mutates into a jam.

  Tony Bennett popularised "In The Middle of An Island" in 1957. "Don't Be Cruel" was a hit for Elvis Presley in 1956. Certain lines in the song can be taken as references to George's departure.

10.17   medley "ON A SUNNY ISLAND" / THE PEANUT VENDOR / GROOVIN' / I GOT STUNG   (3:33)

The three Beatles break into this good-natured bossa nova medley with Ringo providing a consistent rhythm. After a bit of introductory vocalising Paul sings about being on a sunny island in the middle of a sea, which may be from an unidentified number or may just as likely be a mutated lyric from "In The Middle of an Island." John repeatedly responds by mentioning Costa del Sol (Spain) before he and Paul enjoy a brief whistling duet, at the end of which Paul begins offering birdcalls. This prompts the two to initiate a series of animal imitations. John begins calling out names (recalling the previous day's improvisation "Get Off!"), specifically, the Duke of Edinburgh (British Royalty), Sophie Tucker (popular singer), Manfred Mann (contemporary performer/group,), Robert Stigwood (ex-manager of Cream who started out with Brian Epstein's NEMS Enterprises) and "Besame Mucho" (the title of a song which The Beatles had performed in their early days and which they will resurrect later in these sessions). Paul begins to sing "In The Middle of an Island" once again, but stops himself and (with John's help) begins vocalising "The Peanut Vendor," raising his voice octave by octave in the manner of famed South American singer Yma Sumac. Perhaps mixing up his songs, Paul sings out the title of the '40's instrumental "Brazil" while the birdcalls remind John of the beginning of the Young Rascals' song "Groovin'," and he chimes in with the first line of the song. Paul chuckles and turns this potpourri in another direction by singing the first line of Elvis Presley's "I Got Stung." As he chirps the title in extremely high falsetto, John repeats the line from "Groovin'" and, as the number closes, recites a few words in mock-Spanish.

"The Peanut Vendor" was a hit in 1931 for Louis Armstrong, although many other artists performed it. "Groovin'" was a hit for The Young Rascals in 1967, and "I Got Stung" was recorded by Elvis Presley in 1958. The Beatles generally reserved this type of performance for the very beginning or very end of sessions, but George's absence has left them in no position to attempt any serious rehearsal.

10.18   THE PEANUT VENDOR   (0:12)
John offers this brief reprise as he begins to play the same rhythm in a different key. Paul and Ringo join in as John croons "Brazil," (again, mixing up the songs) but very quickly stops the performance and jokingly warns the others to leave before this all gets out of hand.

10.19   IT'S ONLY MAKE BELIEVE   (2:33)
Paul and Ringo begin playing anything that comes to mind, and John leads them into this 1958 Conway Twitty hit. Despite his obvious desire to clown around, John manages to do quite well for the first verse. As Paul chimes in and takes over the lead vocal the performance degenerates into buffoonery.

For much of this performance the crew's microphones aren't focused on the band, but rather on a stageside conversation between Michael, Neil and George Martin. Michael fears that George's having left in the fashion that he did will make it difficult for him to return to the group. Neil disagrees, noting that the Sunday meeting that is already planned will give George the opportunity to rejoin. Neil and George Martin then go on to describe the problems that George faces within the group. Their perception is that John and Paul consistently team up against George, and that they don't offer him enough freedom within their compositions. Neil is quite sympathetic to George's problem, pointing out that even a few months in such a position would annoy anyone.

10.20   "THROUGH A LONDON WINDOW"   (1:30)
Paul continues the frivolity with a falsetto rendition of this as-yet-unidentified song. John and Ringo back him with simple instrumentation, and the performance stops and restarts as Paul calls out the name Jeanina Ferris.

A further portion of the stageside conversation was captured during this performance. George Martin mentions that he had co-ordinated a string overdubbing session for George that evening as producer of Jackie Lomax's album, and wonders if George will show up.

The Beatles then abandon their instruments, move to another part of the set and socialise for a while. Neil Aspinall, George Martin and (eventually) Ringo's wife Maureen join the party, but very little meaningful dialogue occurs, about the matter of George leaving the band or anything else. In fact, George's departure doesn't even seem to disturb their plans for the live show (which are as nebulous as ever), at least as far as the other Beatles are concerned.

The dialogue begins with a discussion of the possibility of John getting a visa to play in the United States. The visa problems of Donovan, Mick Jagger and Keith Richard (all of whom had also been arrested for drug possession) are used as a point of reference, but it seems clear to everyone except John that he has little chance of being allowed to enter the United States to perform. Alternative sites close to the U.S. are considered, including Mexico, Bermuda. Barbados, and the Virgin Islands. This is followed by the appearance of two people from E.M.I. who head right for Paul, ask him something, and leave. One would presume from subsequent events that they're asking his permission to admit an interviewer from CBC (the Canadian Broadcasting Corporation). Michael tries to get a discussion going by asking what they want to do next and John jokingly answers that they split up George's guitars between them. A business meeting between the four Beatles has been planned for the weekend, and Ringo offers the deadpan remark that by that time the group may be down to *two*.

Michael then expresses great concern about the unidentified persons (most likely the people from CBC) who are wandering around the soundstage.

Neither John nor Paul care to help him out. Paul makes a few quips before joking with Michael that the newcomers are here to make their *own* film. This reminds John of Orson Welles, leading to an extended discussion of the famous actor. Ringo is bored enough to ask Michael about his career which causes him to give a long description of an incident that happened to him while acting in a play in Belfast. According to a later interview with Michael, one of George's parting lines to the others had been "see you around the clubs." The end of Michael's story (the star quitting the play) reminds Glyn of this, and he and Michael have a laugh at George's expense.

Michael starts to raise the topic of playing in America, but backs off for the moment when he notices that John isn't present. Paul and Ringo remark that he's probably off making art somewhere, with Paul going so far as to joke that he's probably in a bag with Yoko. Paul has already seen George walk out. Now he's wryly remarking on John's desire to play around with Yoko rather than sit with the others and possibly address the group's problems. Indeed, one gets the impression that Glyn and Michael would like to see John put Yoko in a bag and zip it shut, but perhaps Michael realises the impolitic nature of this train of thought, since he quickly changes the subject back to the live show and the people who are planning to go to Africa to scout locations. He tries to suggest Ethiopia as a possibility but serious discussion is out of the question as Paul and Ringo crack jokes at Michael's expense. At this point the intellectual content of the conversations reaches a new low as the fellows sit around telling knock-knock jokes, of which only George Martin's shows the least bit of creativity.

John and Yoko return having been with someone from CBC and Paul promptly nominates them for the 'irritant of the year' award. This refers to the British satirical publication *Private Eye*, which offered this award in its current issue in response to a question from George Martin, Ringo confirms that a nice vacation spot is not their main concern in picking a location for the live show Paul, obviously bored with the subject, suggests performing on the mouth of a volcano. Maureen advocates performing the show in England because they wouldn't be able to bring their British fans along if the went out of the country. As Paul continues to throw out unsupported ideas for the show's location (The Cavern Club, The Tower Ballroom) the film crew shifts from the CBC, who asks John if he'll participate in an interview they have scheduled with Yoko the following week. Michael has once again taken up using spy mikes to pick up stray conversations.

The CBC interviewer sets up a Tuesday interview with Yoko (and, he hopes, John) and mentions that he'd heard part of Yoko's improvisation with the band when he phoned earlier in the day. John and Yoko are both very pleased by this, but their pleasure is short lived when he mentions that he didn't like their album *Two Virgins*. However, in the fact of Yoko's insistence on its quality, he relents and suggests that maybe he wasn't in the right mood when listening to it. Continuing the thread of avant-garde recordings, he mentions John Cage's piece "Indeterminacy." Yoko, who worked for Cage in the early '60's, replies that she knows the piece only too well because she was responsible for translating it into Japanese. John's suggestive comment to Yoko about her relationship with Cage causes her to rebuke him as crude and nasty. He doesn't contradict her. The conversation then turns to the distribution of *Two Virgins* in Canada and the reaction to its infamous nude cover. The CBC man asks about Apple, and John readily admits it's not working out very well, but he doesn't sound too concerned.

The others then continue their discussion of the live show. Mal has been chosen to fly to Tripoli on Monday to check out possible locations. This doesn't sit too well with Neil, who implies that he doesn't trust Mal's judgement.

10.21   THE LONG AND WINDING ROAD   (3:54)
Paul, apparently weary of the live show discussion, retires to the piano as the conversation continues. He plays a fine instrumental version of the song, accompanying himself only with a brief bit of whistling.

Michael agrees that someone with the authority to make a decision (obviously not Mal) should scout out a location for the show, but everyone ignores the fact that since The Beatles *themselves* are not in agreement about the show they're hardly likely to invest this authority in anyone *else*. John introduces the gentlemen from CBC.

Michael then asks Mal about his experiences as a Beatle bodyguard, but the anecdotes he tells are surprisingly few (and quite uninteresting). Ringo recalls the scariest incident was when a member of the audience grabbed him by the head.

10.22   ADAGIO FOR STRINGS   (2:09)
Paul takes another pass at this, which he had also performed on the 3rd (3.1) and the 8th (8.60). He still can't get the piece to flow, and falters in his playing now and then. The conversation in the foreground continues unabated as Ringo and John share some of their bad memories of The Beatles' tour years while Glyn and Michael discuss some further incidents involving The Rolling Stones.

10.23   MARTHA MY DEAR   (5:27<

Paul performs a pleasant, instrumental version of his song from the previous year's double album, improvising now and then. Ringo vocalises and taps along. Unfortunately, Yoko intrudes by repeatedly screaming John's name (see below), but Paul is unfazed, and continues to play.

The tour discussion finishes up with a mention of Jimmy Nicol (who filled in for Ringo on tour for a brief period in 1964). The CBC interviewer departs and Yoko ominously requests a microphone. John flatly states that if George doesn't return by Tuesday he's prepared to have Eric Clapton fill his spot in the band. This is the first real indication that one of the Beatles is prepared to discuss this matter, and John states that he desires to carry on The Beatles regardless of George's actions, although he doesn't mind starting his own group if The Beatles break up. Michael hesitantly suggests that they lie and say that George is sick in order to explain his absence in the show. John shrugs him off, reaffirms his commitment to the project, and once again suggests that they get Clapton to join the band. At this point, judging by his tone of voice, he either doesn't care at *all* if George ever returns, or is doing an extremely good job of pretending otherwise if he *does* care. Unfortunately, Yoko, apparently sensing competition for John's attention, begins to call, then shout, then scream John's name repeatedly. The serious conversation then gives way to joking around, as Yoko's shrieks are met with a variety of comical answers from John and Ringo. John and Michael attempt to continue the conversation, but their efforts are futile in the wake of Yoko's obnoxious barrage.

As this session draws to a close, Michael timidly asks if they're planning another session for Monday. John kids that he'll bring Eric (Clapton), Jimi (Hendrix) and Tommy (?) along to replace George, and Paul kids with Maureen, telling her that *she* can join if she can learn three chords over the weekend. As Michael explains Paul's joke to a film crew member, John, Paul, Ringo and Yoko gather around a mike, and make fun of Michael (obviously considering him a homosexual). Michael returns to the conversation, oblivious to the whispered insults, and wonders aloud about what to do with the end of the project. John helpfully suggests that he stick it up his ass. A fitting end to a trying afternoon.

Monday, January 13th, 1969

On the morning of January 13th The Beatles are nearer to breaking up than they had ever been before. A meeting had been held at Ringo's house the previous day which had only served to make the situation between George and John worse. Since George refuses to appear for this day's session, John has evidently decided that *he* won't show up either. No one is able to contact him until the early afternoon, and he doesn't show up until approximately 3:00. While the others wait they engage in amazingly revealing conversations regarding John's relationship with Yoko and the future of the group. The anti-Yoko sentiment, which had been unexpressed to this point, comes through strongly here. Interestingly enough, there are no hard words directed at George, who had gone to the meeting in good faith, but had walked out in disgust when Yoko spoke on John's behalf and John offered little or no input. With the status of the band in doubt, Paul eventually agrees to push the date of the live show back one week.

Once John arrives, the three Beatles spend some time working on the lyrics to "Get Back," replacing the politically-tinged lyrics with the story of a transvestite and a loner but, understandably, little is accomplished and the session breaks up early, shortly before five o'clock. John, Paul and Ringo agree to return again the following day, although they can hardly hope to accomplish much without George.

The earliest available tape picks up around 11:00 a.m. Paul, Ringo, Linda, Michael, Glyn and Mal are seated in a circle chatting as Ethan Russell takes pictures. Someone has brought in an American 45 of Arthur Conley's recent cover version of "Ob-La-Di, Ob-La-Da." Since neither Ringo nor Paul has heard it, Michael offers to play it for them. Ringo remarks that the cover versions invariably leave out the word bra, and Paul mentions Marmalade's performance, which ends with a line about jam.

13.1 OB-LA-DI, OB-LA-DA (0:13)
A brief a capella performance from Paul, who's reminded of the song and sings a few lines.

As Paul and Linda look through some of Ethan Russell's photos the subject of John's physical appearance at the previous day's meeting is brought up. Michael asks *who* he was wearing, an obvious reference to John and Yoko's symbiotic relationship. This amuses Paul, who caustically refers to her as a famous oriental actress. Yoko *had* appeared in a low budget exploitation film entitled *Satan's Bed*, but Paul is more likely making fun of the news media's efforts to pin an occupation on John's unconventional girlfriend. A stray comment from Ringo then leads to a discussion of various terms and trade names used for sneakers.

13.2 OB-LA-DI, OB-LA-DA (2:00)
As Arthur Conley's cover version is played, Paul and Ringo occasionally sing along.

Paul echoes Ringo's observation that none of the "Ob-La-Di, Ob-La-Da" cover versions use the correct lyric. Of the current batch of covers, both Paul and Linda like The Bedrocks' record best. After a brief discussion on the perils of being photographed, the flip side of "Ob-La-Di, Ob-La-Da" is cued up.

"Sleep On, Otis" meets with a more positive response, but they quickly lose interest in it as the song progresses.

13.3   SLEEP ON, OTIS (2:00)

Paul and Ringo occasionally sing along to Arthur Conley's performance, improvising as they see fit. At one point, Ringo ad-libs a recitation about Otis and Big Bill Broonzy in heaven.

As might be expected, "Sleep On, Otis" spurs a discussion of Otis Redding's music (and Linda's photo session with him). The conversation moves on to the disintegration of Motown Records. A mention of the Holland-Dozier-Holland song-writing team's defection from that label reminds Paul of the current situation among The Beatles, as he points out the absence of half of the group.

As he had on the 3rd and the 9th, Paul talks about the 'ob-la-di, ob-la-da' man Jimmy Scott. After Paul weaves an amusing fantasy about how he came to acquire the phrase from Scott, the discussion moves on to other black musicians. Michael's mention of a trumpet player who he mistakenly believes played on "Penny Lane" raises the topic of session players in general, and Paul disparagingly remarks that most of them are more concerned with getting a gig than playing their instrument well. The rest of the conversation is given over to Michael expressing his great admiration for "Penny Lane."

13.4   BABY, COME BACK (0:04)

A one line a capella performance from Paul, complete with hand claps.

"Baby, Come Back" charted for The Equals in September, 1968. Ringo then asks who recorded the song "Build Me Up, Buttercup" causing Michael and Paul to express their admiration for that song.

13.5   BUILD ME UP, BUTTERCUP (0:18)

A brief a capella duet from Paul and Linda, which Paul fills out with some vocalising.

The Foundations' "Build Me up, Buttercup" was currently on the British charts.

The discussion of "Build Me Up, Buttercup" leads to a mention of other contemporary releases by The Grass Roots and Raymond Froggatt. The rest of this exchange concerns the personalities from the early rock and roll era. Paul asks if anyone still collects singles like they used to when they were teenagers. Denis does not, and Ringo claims that he never cared for LPs and only had 78's (at least until Capitol began sending him free product). As Linda reminisces about buying record albums in the '50's, Paul mentions that the first record *he* bought was Gene Vincent's "Be-Bop-A-Lula" in mid-1956. Glyn and Denis contribute the fact that *their* first purchase was Lonnie Donegan's "Rock Island Line" in late 1955. That recording introduced British audiences to skiffle, a precursor to rock and roll which (as Denis correctly observes) brought about a revolution in the musical styles of its time. Despite Paul's claim that the early skiffle records didn't excite him later sessions show that he is extremely familiar with Donegan's early work. Michael chimes in that *his* first record was Gary U.S. Bonds' "Quarter to Three," and Paul laughs because that was years later than the records they're talking about ("Quarter to Three" came out in 1960). He then tries to remember if "Be-Bop-A-Lula" predated Bill Haley and His Comets' "A.B.C. Boogie" (It didn't. "A.B.C. Boogie" came out in 1954), and Linda attempts to impress them all by rattling off the names of rock and roll stars she'd seen play at the Brooklyn Paramount

Theatre. Two other early singles are then briefly discussed (Lonnie Donegan's "The Battle of New Orleans" and Elvis Presley's "Heartbreak Hotel") before the conversation turns to Alan Freed, an American disc jockey and concert M.C. (he presented the Brooklyn Paramount shows) whose career was ruined in the payola scandal that rocked American radio in 1960. Also brought up is Moondog, a blind street singer who dressed like a Viking. Ringo adds to the conversation by saying a number of good things about Freed, who was instrumental in introducing many early rock and roll acts. Michael compares Freed to D.J. Murray 'the K' Kaufman (who followed), but this only causes Ringo and Glyn to make fun of Murray, who had self-servingly attached himself to The Beatles during their early tours of America. An anecdote about Murray's diminishing role in 1964's *Around The Beatles* program inspires Glyn (who had worked on the show) to ask Paul if he has seen producer Jack Good lately. Paul replies in the affirmative, but explains that they did nothing more than exchange greetings.

Neil Aspinall arrives and, aware that half of The Beatles are absent, asks what's going on. Paul, obviously expecting John to show up, explains that he has planned to work on the lyrics for songs that they haven't quite finished. Ringo, presumably with George's absence in mind, dejectedly wonders what the point is. Subsequent comments then suggest the focus and tone of the previous evening's business meeting, where The Beatles had come very near to agreeing to break up at least on an informal basis. However, like many other serious discussions between the four, the meeting broke up with matters unresolved. We learn that it is Paul's initiative that has brought them back to Twickenham (they are, after all, paying for Michael and his crew), and Ringo appreciates this because it's obvious that nothing can be settled with the four of them in different places. Paul feels that if they're going to break up playing together an extra week won't do any harm and confesses that he hadn't anything else planned for this day anyway

13.6 BUILD ME UP, BUTTERCUP (0:11)

Another brief a capella performance from Paul, who sounds bored.

The conversation continues and, if we read between the lines, more of the previous night's business meeting emerges. It seems that George had expressed his view that the future of The Beatles was a matter that should be discussed privately between the four members of the group. This would have implicitly excluded Yoko, but rather than having to choose between her and The Beatles, John appears to have pretended not to understand George's request. This childish behaviour angered George, who then walked out of the meeting. Paul and Neil don't believe John either, but are more tolerant of him. Soon after this observation Paul's voice is completely drowned out on the tape by the sound of a phone call that Michael is making. It seems likely that Michael is experimenting with surreptitiously recording phone conversations so that they, too, can be captured for posterity.

When we can hear Paul again he seems to go out of his way to justify John and Yoko's behaviour, pointing out that, whatever else it may be, it's at least sincere. This is a bit too much for Neil and Linda, who make *their* opinions obvious by a series of rude comments and noises. Paul understands, and adds that he doesn't always have the best opinion of John and Yoko either. Before he can go further, Neil reminds him that the conversation is being recorded.

It's to Paul's credit that he doesn't seem to mind, and he forges ahead, admitting that he'd rather compose songs without Yoko around and that he tries to please John *through* her. He realises this is silly, but places the blame solely upon himself, naively (and perhaps disingenuously) claiming that John and Yoko are actually very honest. Ringo and Michael ask Neil if John has been reached and told about the day's session, and Neil informs them that nobody's picking up the phone at John's house. Linda restates the opinion that the meeting would have been more successful had the four Beatles been left to discuss matters on their own, and tells the others that she regrets having attended. Sincere or not, this merely serves as a lead-in to her *real* point, that *Yoko* should not have attended since she did the lion's share of the talking. Paul agrees with her, but attempts to soothe any possible hurt feelings by pointing out that no one could pass up the chance to spend an afternoon at Ringo's house. Ringo jokes to Linda that if she had kept her mouth shut there would have been no problem and she good-naturedly plays along by adding that she just *had* to butt in every two minutes. They're obviously being sarcastic. In actuality, it seems likely that Linda sat by quietly while Yoko intruded upon the meeting, talking in place of John. Neil complains that John and Yoko's actions effectively turned the board meeting into a party and Paul agrees, but once more sticks up for Yoko, wondering if her presence isn't simply being used to excuse away the deteriorating Lennon/McCartney partnership. Paul then touches upon the power structure within The Beatles, and how John had evidently attempted to justify Yoko's involvement by pointing out how The Beatles tend to keep people out of their inner circle. Mal temporarily lightens the atmosphere by arriving with some toast for a snack.

13.7   BUILD ME UP, BUTTERCUP (0:16)
The mention of butter in the course of conversation spurs on yet another brief a capella rendition from Paul.

A remarkably candid conversation follows in which the dissatisfaction with Yoko and her effect upon John is finally addressed. Linda, Neil and Paul all see Yoko working her will through John, but don't wish to confront him about it until they have no doubt as to what's going on. Paul further criticises John and Yoko's belief in a 'heightened awareness' whereby people needn't verbally communicate with each other. He realises that this leads to a situation where they can't communicate at *all*. He bitterly complains about John's unwillingness to communicate, and offers an example by remembering an occurrence from a few days earlier where he had asked John for his opinion and received no response (this type of one-sided communication is supported by tapes from the sessions of the 3rd and 7th).

Michael, sensing Paul's desire to talk, tries to provoke him by asking how long John's been involved with Yoko. Linda tries to divert the topic by claiming that the real problem is a lack of communication between the four Beatles, but Paul insists that Yoko is part of the problem because she's so much a part of John's life. He then explains that they have two options, to oppose Yoko and get The Beatles back to four or to put up with her.

Finally, we have one of the Beatles directly addressing the problem that Yoko's relationship with John has caused. Although Paul's comments suggest otherwise, Yoko is *not* their primary concern (although she's certainly part of it), but John's refusal to live up to his own responsibilities within the group.

Paul is faced with a dilemma. If he confronts John, he's sure that John will simply quit The Beatles and devote himself to Yoko (which, of course, is what ultimately occurs), but he sees the group disintegrating *anyway*, both because of the vacuum caused by John's creative withdrawal, and George's unwillingness to tolerate John's behaviour.

Paul compares the current situation to someone striking because of unsatisfactory working conditions. This conversation is the first clear indication of *why* George is striking.

The question is, who is he striking *against*? If there had been conflict between George and *Paul*, one would expect to find *some* evidence of ill-will between the two. In fact, there are *no* negative feelings expressed, or even implied. Instead, it's very clear from the events of the previous day's meeting that George's discontent was directed at John.

Paul's attitude throughout these conversations not only indicates that his relationship with George is cordial, but tells us that Paul *sides* with George in his conflict with John - at least silently.

But why would Paul remain silent? The answer lies in his desire to preserve The Beatles, as he indicates that it wouldn't take much to push John out of the group since they've been together for so long. Michael recalls a discussion from the 10th where John clearly expresses his desire to carry on the group (even without George). Linda's response indicates that this topic had also been brought up at the previous day's meeting, and she tells how John had turned to Yoko and quipped 'I told you so' when the subject was raised. With obvious distaste towards the other woman, she goes so far as to express her belief that John had instructed Yoko to leave he and Paul alone when they're busy writing songs, but that Yoko had talked her way in anyway. Paul wearily responds that he doesn't know whether that's true or not.

Paul and Neil's final comments here sum up their frustration. Not only do they see Yoko talking for John, but they feel that when they talk to John they're *really* talking to Yoko, since John's only saying what Yoko *wants* him to say. Paul applies this to his efforts to write songs with John, and admits his embarrassment at having to address them both in order to get the work accomplished.

It should be noted that as Paul and Neil continue to discuss Yoko and the break-up of The Beatles, Ringo and Linda share a cosy little discussion about domestic animals.

Once again, Paul worries that they're not being fair to Yoko, arguing that she's not as bad as they think. But Neil strongly feels that she talks too much, and worries about her intruding while John and Paul write. Paul agrees that it would be great if she'd keep her mouth shut, but goes out of his way to explain how she *didn't* interfere when he and John were struggling with the lyrics for "I Will" the previous year. He realises that the problem is not so much with Yoko as John's reliance upon her, although he admits that he doesn't like her presence if only because she's a distraction to *him*. He then goes a step further and sticks up for *John*, claiming that when the two get *really* serious about something John won't allow Yoko to interfere and will actually participate in conversations (if this is true, it is not supported by the available tapes). He admits that John and Yoko go too far in their relationship, but tolerates it because it's always been characteristic of John to go overboard on things. He then explains that it's really not their business to tell John that Yoko can't attend their business meetings and that all they can really do is to express their displeasure to him. He tells Michael that he has done this, to some extent, by letting John know his displeasure in writing songs with Yoko present.

Michael asks Paul about the gradual decline of the Lennon/McCartney songwriting partnership, and Paul explains that it was waning even before Yoko's appearance, primarily because they no longer shared the physical closeness that they had in their early years. He still thinks, however, that The Beatles have the ability to play well (which doesn't mean they *are* playing well) and that the real problem is with their lack of communication, patronising each other and (as Michael points out) not speaking their hearts. Finally, Paul touches once more upon his desire not to be overly assertive towards controlling the future of the band, and claims that whatever he has to say is only one man's opinion.

Paul then reveals that the underlying motive behind the "Get Back" sessions was to force the group into the discipline of a 9 to 5 situation, claiming that even if it's a grind at times, at least they'd be able to reap the rewards of their work. Michael recalls John's comment that the act of working itself inspires one to work and Linda remembers George coming to the sessions for the previous year's double album and exclaiming how good it was to be back at work again. Ringo joins in, and adds that that if you just stay at home you're not inspired to do anything. These observations not withstanding, the sessions thus far have been *anything* but inspired.

Neil returns to the subject of John and Yoko and mentions how jarring it is to have Yoko constantly present, complaining that she intrudes to the point of sitting on their amplifiers. As Paul agrees, Linda brings up the interesting point that The Beatles might be underestimating their value, and that she can't envision a world without their music. Paul simply reiterates his feeling that it's not appropriate for him to confront John and Yoko about their behaviour, likening them to two children who are being naughty and would only act worse if chastised.

Paul continues to explain his understanding of John's psychology and implies the difficulty of dealing with someone who, for example, feels that no justification is needed for the nude *Two Virgins* sleeve beyond the fact that they felt like doing it. He explains that his tolerance for Yoko is a compromise to John's wishes and hopes that this will cause John to return the favour in some way. Michael (of all people) points out that with all the trouble she's caused within the group Paul has compromised *enough*, but Paul repeats his fear that if they attempt to restrict Yoko's involvement John will simply leave the group. Since the band obviously cannot discipline themselves, and Paul feels that it would be inappropriate to discipline each other, he wishes that they had an authority figure who could instruct them to show up on time and leave the girlfriends at home. George had expressed a similar opinion back on the 7th, when he had pointed out how things had gone downhill since their manager died. Neil, evidently aware that John is beyond the reach of authority, feels that authority wouldn't work in John's case. Finally, Paul remarks upon the absurdity of the current situation, and forecasts how silly they will appear to history if they break up simply because John insisted on bringing his girlfriend to the sessions (confirming that this was the root cause of the conflict). Paul's comments cause Michael, Neil and Linda to lament over the end of The Beatles.

Continuing to discuss the break-up, Paul offers an idea that he and Neil had come up with for the live show where the Beatles' performances would be intercut with news reports from around the world, with the final report announcing the break-up of the band. They all think this is a good idea, but Linda realistically points out no one really *wants* that kind of end. Their discussion of live satellite linkups invariably reminds them of the June 25, 1967 performance of "All You Need Is Love" on the *Our World* program. Linda points out that, because of the diversity of such a broadcast, The Beatles part could be straightforward, but teases Michael that this would mean he wouldn't get the shots of a sunset that he wants.

Michael attempts to resume the conversation about John, but Paul has little to add to what he's already said. Once again Linda expresses her opinion that the four Beatles need to be left alone to solve their problems, and Paul bluntly tells Michael that John wouldn't communicate at the previous day's meeting, but allotted Yoko to speak on his behalf, causing George to walk out halfway through. Linda then becomes a bit more specific - when she says the four Beatles need to be left alone, she really means that the four Beatles need to be left alone *without Yoko*. Neil sullenly informs her that he doesn't think this will ever be possible and mildly suggests that if the question is brought to John at least he'd have to make a decision to quit or stay, and the problem would be solved. Michael realises, however, that John needs to be given some way to save face in such a situation, or he's almost sure to quit. He then jokingly suggests that they drug Yoko's tea just to get a minute or two alone with John. He goes on to use several racial slurs against her - a dangerous thing to do had these comments been passed on to John. Linda joins in and expresses her feeling that Yoko would refuse to allow John to meet with the others alone. Once again, Paul defends John and Yoko's togetherness, claiming that it's not an entirely unnatural thing and repeating his feeling that it's not his place to tell John to leave Yoko at home. Michael understands this, but draws the line at the point where it's disrupting everyone else's life. Paul claims that trying to keep them apart would be seen by John and Yoko as an attempt to disrupt *their* life.

Neil then reports that Mal has been trying to phone John, but that his line is always busy, suggesting he's taken his phone off the hook. This annoys *everyone*, and as Ringo and Linda offer sarcastic comments, Michael suggests that Yoko be put in a black bag where she can't talk. Paul simply mutters that The Beatles seem to be down to two - realising for the first time that *John* seems to be on strike as well.

In response to a question from Michael, Paul then says they'll see out the week, and if things aren't settled by then they'll end the band. When Michael brings up the live show, Paul firmly tells him that everything's on hold until the situation with the two missing Beatles works itself out. Understandably, with the group on the verge of disintegrating, Paul isn't too concerned about sending people to Africa to scout out locations, but nevertheless instructs Michael to push back the date of the show by one day to compensate for the day's work they're in the process of losing. Neil points out that a change in the schedule will mean they'll probably have to look outside of England in or-

der to rent the necessary video equipment, but everyone except Michael is
now against that idea, with Paul admitting that he doesn't see why they should
bother.

The topic then shifts from where the show should be staged to how it should
be filmed. Paul sharply criticises Michael's *Rock And Roll Circus* project because it dealt more with the event than the music. Paul prefers that The
Beatles' performances be filmed more as a study, where the camera would
stay on each subject for an extended period of time, and reminds Michael of
an observation he had made on the 2nd citing a documentary they had seen
about Picasso (this is referenced on the 3rd as well). Michael defends *Rock
And Roll Circus*, and points out that it was never intended to be a documentary, but a family variety show.

Once again, Paul expresses his distaste for quick cutting and continues to
criticise *Rock And Roll Circus*. Michael accuses Paul of wanting to be like
Andy Warhol, referring to Warhol's practice of setting up a static camera and
simply letting it run. Paul disagrees, and explains that he simply means that
Michael should not focus on things like the background in an effort to be artistic. He says that what he'd *really* like to see for the live show is simply
straight reporting like a news program but Michael points out that it's part of
the film-makers job to make the act as interesting as they can and that the
film-making has got to be as exciting as the performers to prevent them from
looking foolish on stage.

Paul is not satisfied with Michael's justification for quick cutting, and
bluntly tells him so. Ringo mentions a clip he'd seen for Arthur Brown's song
"Fire" and complains he couldn't get anything out of it because of the camera-
work. Paul says that in real life you only have one viewpoint of an event but
Ringo reminds him that close ups are okay. Michael attempts to explain that
one *can't* view a film as one views a live event because the relationship between the audience and performer is different, but the others continue to argue
for a simplistic approach, and Paul warns Michael not to get caught up in his
Ready, Steady, Go image (Michael had worked as a director on that television
program, which featured quick cutting in its musical sequences). Neil mentions the promo film which had been made for 1967's "A Day in the Life,"
and this brings up the previous year's promo for "Hey Jude" which Michael
had directed. Paul, using this as an example, points out that Michael was so
busy capturing shots of the audience that he missed important shots of Paul
and the orchestra.

Paul then mentions a clip he'd seen on the previous night's BBC2 *Late
Night Line-up* and suggests that Michael track his cameras to allow for more
elaborate shots, while admonishing him not to leave out anything important.
As they return to a discussion of the approach used by Andy Warhol in *Empire State* (a 24 hour film documenting a day in the life of the famous building), Mal asks Paul if he wants to talk to John on the phone. Paul agrees and
continues to make his point that the live show should focus exclusively on
The Beatles, to the point of zooming in on John rather than focus on the scen-
ery. John's call is transferred through to the soundstage, and Paul heads off to
talk to him.

While he's gone, Michael and Linda engage in a catty little argument about
the way to film a musical event. Michael strongly resents having the others

question his style, defends his directorial abilities, and goes so far as to claim that he's more of a fan of the group than Linda is. Linda explains how, as a professional still photographer, she attempts to capture her subject by taking their picture at just the right moment - clearly suggesting her belief that Michael needs to learn a thing or two in this direction.

Unfortunately, even though Michael had evidently bugged the line, tapes of John and Paul's phone conversation have not surfaced. Paul returns, however, and we learn through him that John has agreed to come in.

Michael continues his discussion with Paul, and explains that if he compromises his artistic opinion, he wouldn't be doing his duty as a fan because he wants to do what he feels is best for the group. This causes Paul to joke that *another* member of their party is about to go on strike. Continuing in this vein, he laughingly tells the others that *he'll* quit the group if he doesn't get *his* way. Just as Michael seems to be getting unbearably self-important, he self-effacingly wonders if anyone would notice if he *did* quit the project. Finally, the discussion returns yet again to potential locations for the live show. Linda is surprisingly forthright in expressing her opposition to Michael's idea of holding the show abroad. They're still trying to argue Michael out of this idea as the available tape comes to an end.

Having failed with every other approach to get Paul and Ringo to agree to perform abroad, Michael tries to charm them by mentioning their unparalleled popularity and claims that the only reason he wants to do it abroad is because of the weather. Paul and Ringo are unimpressed and don't alter their stance. Paul suggests instead that Michael concern himself with how they can make the show visually interesting *without* going away. He proposes a honky tonk piano for "Maxwell's Silver Hammer," and then envisions a stage full of instruments. The topic then returns to how long Michael should focus on any one subject. Paul illustrates his point about limited camera cuts by discussing an interlude (a time filler between programs) from British television that slowed a piece of pottery being made from scratch. He then offers the idea that they should cut from The Beatles to Glyn, working the mixing board. Michael is opposed to this, and feels it would work better in the documentary. Paul disagrees by picking up on Mal's point that Glyn is also performing in a way when he is recording The Beatles and that Glyn's work is much more relevant to the project than Michael getting a shot of a camel.

Paul then tries to convince Michael that the variety of technical facilities available in England would overshadow the scenic advantages of taping abroad, although he admits that he would like to have both. As he continues to fantasise about the show, Michael asks him what he thinks is The Beatles' most successful television appearance. Paul (and everyone else) gives the edge to 1964's *Around The Beatles*, and Michael quizzes Paul on what filmmaking technique *he* would use for a rock and roll event (an exasperating question, since Paul has just been explaining it to him!). Paul and Ringo then extol the virtues of a stationary camera, and mention a country music program they had seen that had been staged that way. Paul then equates minimalist filmmaking technique with eastern medicine, explaining that both have the same goals as their more common counterparts, but approach their objectives from different angles. The discussion in interrupted by a member of the film crew who tells Michael that they're ready to show rushes. With John's arrival still an hour away. Paul agrees, and everyone heads off to Twickenham's small theatre to view the rushes before they go to lunch. It is almost 1:00.

13.8   DIG A PONY   >0:03)

This tail end of a performance (or perhaps just a stray reference) catches John almost inaudibly singing the song's title as he backs himself on electric guitar.

It's a little after 3:00. Having watched rushes and taken lunch, the group reconvenes John has finally arrived, and he and Paul engage in a discussion that relates back to the earlier dialogue where Linda had spoken as a Beatles fan. Paul points out that although the band members may not be happy with what they're producing, fans might still enjoy it.

13.9   GET BACK   (0:26)

Paul sings two lines. accompanying himself on bass. He stops to tell Mal to have his pencil ready and follows with a further bass riff.

It was standard operating procedure for Mal to write down a song's lyrics as John and Paul worked on them. "Get Back" was clearly one of two songs Paul had in mind when he told Neil earlier that he had hoped the three Beatles could work on unfinished lyrics.

Earlier that morning, Paul had disparagingly referred to John and Yoko's concept of heightened awareness. Now, perhaps only to create *some* common ground between them, he embraces this concept, remarking that he and John think alike on certain levels.

13.10   GET BACK   (0.09<

The Beatles attempt an up-tempo arrangement, similar to that played on the ninth. They take the song from the top, but the available tape cuts off during the second line. The vocals are slightly distant, and the heroine's name is Loretta Marsh at this point.

13.11   GET BACK   (1:45)

The rehearsals begin in earnest. Paul searches for a second name for Loretta, trying out Marsh and Mary. The Loretta verse is otherwise complete at this point. The Beatles take the song from the top but it quickly breaks down and they return to lyric problem. John suggests Loretta Marvin, and, jokingly, Loretta Meatball. Ringo works on his drum breaks.

13.12   GET BACK   (2:44)

Having temporarily solved the name problem in favour of Marvin, the group attempts to play the song straight through. Despite their best efforts, the performance is a disaster. John isn't quite sure what to sing, or when, and Ringo doesn't know when to sneak in his drum fills. At one point Paul yells out for a solo and John obliges with one of his worst guitar parts yet. George is sorely missed.

This performance contains the first available appearance of the third (and ultimately discarded) verse (which dealt with crowded living conditions for Pakistanis) which draws heavily from the politically oriented improvisations on the 9th.

13.13   GET BACK   >0:31<

This performance is fragmented on the available tape, so only the instrumental break and chorus are heard. It is similar in feel to 13.12.

13.14   GET BACK   (0:32<

Paul, playing bass, sings a single line and stops. After discussing the lyrics briefly he starts to play again, and John takes the first line. Paul then gives it a try, but the available tape cuts cuff again during the 2nd line.

13.15 GET BACK >0:10<
A portion of the JoJo verse.

13.16 GET BACK >0:48<
Another rehearsal fragment focusing on the JoJo verse. The name Marvin has reverted to Marsh and Paul has amended the place name to be Tucson, Arizona (another element which would retained in the final version). Paul mentions that Arizona is the location for *High Chaparral* an American television western which was currently being aired on British TV as well. After a few bars of intro, John leads them into another try at the song. Once again, the available tape cuts off shortly after they begin to sing.

13.17 GET BACK >0:03<
A fragment of the chorus.

13.18 (IMPROVISATION) (2:09<
An improvised swing instrumental to fill in some time between tries at "Get Back." John and Paul play their usual instruments, and Ringo taps along triplets on his cymbals before changing to drums.

13.19 GET BACK (2:05)
Apparently satisfied with the Loretta verse, they turn to the doomed political verse, which Paul claims sounds better than the JoJo verse. They work on the latter and Paul taps out the song's rhythm on his bass as he tries out various lyrics. They are still stuck on the second line of the verse.

13.20 GET BACK (0:44)
John plays an out of tune variant of "Get Back" on guitar, and Paul joins in with the bass line and starts singing the JoJo verse. They experiment some more with minor changes in the lyrics.

13.21 GET BACK (0:22)
A loose performance from Paul as he continues to work on the JoJo verse. John then plays some stray guitar riffs.

With less than two hours of work completed Paul then decides to call it a day. He discusses plans for the next session, hoping to avoid the confusion that occurred that morning. Michael announces that Denis has cancelled the arrangements for the show.

13.22 ON THE ROAD AGAIN (0:25)
A comment Paul makes about wrapping up the session inspires this brief instrumental from John, which develops into a brief, staccato "Get Back" riff.

Paul attempts to stick by his plan to push the show back one day for each rehearsal day missed, but he is easily convinced to take the more logical approach of delaying it a full week. It's very interesting to note that final decisions regarding the show come exclusively from Paul, with no consultation with John or Ringo. This includes the authorisation to pay the film crew even if they stand by while waiting for George's return.

13.23 IMPROVISATIONS (0:41)
As the above conversation occurs, John improvises on guitar in the background. Although he seems to sing a couple of lines at one point, the words are completely indecipherable. Once again, this is tagged with a ragged "Get Back" riff, after which John puts down his guitar for the day.

Since they've cancelled the video equipment, Mal asks Paul if he's ruled out using film. Paul responds that he hasn't ruled out anything and he and John joke with Michael about his repeated requests for flexibility. John jokes that he's leaving his favourite instrument behind as a guarantee to Michael that he will indeed show up the next day, and Paul offers to leave his previous Hofner bass, again drawing attention to the set list that is taped to it. He then offers another recitation of the famed list, and is so proud of this artefact that he offers to leave the bass out so that the camera crew can get a close-up of it.

It's a little before five. On their way out of the studio, John and Paul gather around one of the crew, who is reading the current edition of *Disc And Music Echo*. Paul looks over his shoulder and jokingly reads out a letter to the editor which appeared under the headline "grow up, Lennon!" He also spots a mention of the group Thunderclap Newsman in the magazine, and engages in a brief discussion of their guitarist Jimmy McCulloch (who would join Paul's group Wings as guitarist in the 1970's). When Michael continues to press him on the topic of the live show, Denis laughingly tells him to be quiet. After an elaborate series of goodbyes, Paul heads out, looking for John.

Tuesday, January 14th, 1969

The strike continues. After another morning's session at the piano, Paul sits around and chats idly with Ringo and the crew. John, who had spent the previous night taking drugs and watching TV with Yoko shows up late again and, despite being sick, immediately sits for an interview rather than join his two band-mates. Paul, bored and dispirited, suggests making detective movies or filming the auditions for *The Magic Christian* (occurring elsewhere on the lot) to pass the time. He eventually takes to climbing the chains hanging on the soundstage. Peter Sellers drops in for a few uncomfortable minutes, after which John and Paul trade one liners until they fall into a stupor. John decides to premiere a new song, but the session quickly ends as John and Paul begin to discuss George. Unfortunately Paul asks for the cameras to be turned off, after the day's session ends.

Paul, the first Beatle to arrive, has taken his usual early morning spot at the piano. He discusses the virtues of composing on that instrument with Tony Richmond, and compares Indian classical, modern classical and pop music

14.1   (IMPROVISATION) (0:41)
Paul improvises a piano instrumental and vocalises along with it.

14.2   (IMPROVISATION) (0:52)
Paul plays a piano boogie reminiscent of Jerry Lee Lewis's "Whole Lotta Shakin' Goin' On." He follows this up with a three chord blues workout and explains the limitless songwriting possibilities presented by the piano to Tony who apparently has no knowledge whatsoever.

14.3   MARTHA MY DEAR (1:14)
Paul performs this song from the previous year's double album, singing a few lines near the end of the performance.

14.4   SAN FRANCISCO BAY BLUES (1:12)
Paul plays this tune to illustrate how most older tunes fit a conventional chord pattern. Near the end he sings a few lines, evidently improvised, and mentions that his father (who was a jazz band musician) would know better than he. He encourages Tony to try playing, and laughingly vocalises a passage fit for a beginner (these few seconds were used in the *Let It Be* film before 14.10). Michael enters the discussion and mentions a CBS TV documentary on contemporary music which had been hosted by conductor Leonard Bernstein. He then confesses that he doesn't know very much about music either.

14.5   (IMPROVISATION) (1:07)
Paul improvises another piano piece, this time gospel-influenced. He and Glyn then reminisce about Lee Hazlewood's girlfriend Suzy Jane. Hazlewood, in addition to his work with Duane Eddy, was known for his recordings with Nancy Sinatra.

14.6   (IMPROVISATION) (0:56)
Another rambling piano improvisation from Paul.

14.7   (IMPROVISATION) (0:54)
Continuing his series of improvisations, Paul croons a few lines simply to illustrate another type of song.

14.8   "THE DAY I WENT BACK TO SCHOOL" (2:55)

To show just how easy songwriting is, Paul plays one that he made up earlier that morning. Although quite rudimentary (the lyrics consist of a single verse), this number is a fine example of Paul's incredible gift for melody.

This song was apparently forgotten by Paul as quickly as it was composed. No other performances or references to it are known to exist.

14.9   LADY JANE >0:14)

Paul half-heartedly sings three lines of the song while backing himself on piano.

"Lady Jane," a Rolling Stones number from 1966, is an ironic song for Paul to be playing, considering the fact that he had only recently ended his long relationship with Jane Asher. At the song's conclusion Paul doodles or the piano as someone plays some stray guitar in the background.

Ringo arrives, and is met by forced cheerfulness from all. This exchange can be seen in the film *Let It Be*.

14.10   (IMPROVISATION) (1:11)

As the unknown guitarist picks out a song, Paul and Ringo begin a boogie-woogie piano duet. Paul borrows some of the lyrics from Ringo's song "Picasso" and improvises others.

An edited version of this performance ended up in the *Let It Be* film. It was subsequently titled and copyrighted by Apple as "Jazz Piano Song," who list it as a McCartney/Starkey composition.

14.11   (IMPROVISATION) (0:27)

Paul lets his fingers wander aimlessly in a slow tune. Someone asks if he remembers how to play "I'll Follow The Sun."

14.12   WOMAN (0:10)

Paul offers a brief rendition of the 1966 Peter and Gordon hit that he wrote under the pseudonym Bernard E. Webb. Michael jokes that since George and John are both absent that *he'll* have to be the guitarist. Paul then talks about "Woman" and mentions that he preferred an earlier (unreleased) take of the song that Peter and Gordon had performed.

14.13   WOMAN >0:38)

Another performance from Paul, who shows his fondness for the song by refraining from the clowning that usually accompanies performances of this type. He then wonders if Peter Asher has kept the acetate of The Beatles original demo.

14.14   WOMAN (0:26)

After his anecdote about the "Woman" recording sessions, Paul does another performance to illustrate the original simpler arrangement of the song. He then offers an exaggerated impersonation of Gordon Waller's Scottish accent. The current careers of Peter and Gordon are then discussed. Gordon's latest solo release brings Johnny Cash to mind, and they talk about Johnny's *Live From Folsom Prison* album. Not surprisingly, we learn that Ringo is a big fan.

14.15   COCAINE BLUES (0:09)

Paul sings a flew lines from this Johnny Cash song, and imitates the crowd's response.

14.16   FLUSHED FROM THE BATHROOM OF YOUR HEART (0:04)

Ringo sings a single misremembered line of another song from Johnny Cash's *Live at Folsom Prison* LP. Ringo then relates a humorous story of his meeting with Johnny.

14.17   ON A CLEAR DAY YOU CAN SEE FOREVER   (0:02)

Inspired by some whistling in the background, Paul sings a few words from the song. That's all there is to this 'performance.'

"On a Clear Day You Can See Forever," the title song from a 1966 play, was popularised by Barbra Streisand.

14.18   (IMPROVISATION)   (0:50)

A slow, stately piano improvisation from Paul with vocalising over it.

14.19   THE BACK SEAT OF MY CAR   >2:25<

Paul unveils another work-in-progress. The lyrics are unfinished, but the tune is pretty and shows obvious promise.

"The Back Seat of My Car" was never recorded by The Beatles, and would not appear until Paul's second solo album *Ram* in 1971.

Paul and Ringo then discuss their television viewing from the night before. They were both unimpressed with the film *The Man Who Could Cheat Death*, an uncharacteristically sedate horror film from Britain's Hammer Studios. They go on to discuss other programs. and Ringo reveals that he watches television with the sound turned down.

14.20   THE BACK SEAT OF MY CAR   >0:41<

This fragment is primarily instrumental. Paul plays piano and mumbles a few lyrics.

Paul, undoubtedly aware that this session is shaping up to be another waste of a day, gladly takes a phone call rather than continue to entertain himself on piano. The available tape ends here. Presumably the soundman turned the tape recorder off while awaiting Paul's return.

14.21   (IMPROVISATION)   >0:17<

Paul plays another rambling piano instrumental, briefly considers a pass at "Lady Madonna," but stops.

14.22   "SONG OF LOVE"   (2:24)

Having completed his phone call, Paul plays a complete version of this sentimental love ballad, once again accompanying himself on piano. He sings most of the song in falsetto.

This appears to be a vocal improvisation around Brahms' "Hungarian Dance No. 4" as heard in the 1947 film *Song of Love* (the story of composer Robert Schumann and his wife). Evidently, Paul is remembering the tune and drawing upon the film's title for his inspiration for his lyrics.

14.23   "SONG OF LOVE"   (3:06)

Stumped, perhaps, for anything better to play, Paul treats Ringo and the crew to four more abbreviated renditions of "Song of Love." From the second 'take' on he uses various affected voices, including his Latin crooner imitation. On the final run-through he offers an exaggerated Elvis impersonation, slurring the words until they're unrecognisable. After this, the conversation turns to the publicity that accompanied the 1960 release of Elvis's "It's Now Or Never" single. In the course of this discussion Paul mentions La Scala, a famous opera house in Italy.

14.24   "AS CLEAR AS A BELL SAYS LA SCALA, MILAN"   (0:21)

Paul improvises a bit of light opera around his mention of La Scala, backing himself on piano and filling out the lyric with a bit of vocalising.

14.25   HELLO, DOLLY   (1:20)

Paul delivers a surprisingly straight version of this famous show tune. Ringo taps out the song's rhythm on his tea cup and saucer as Paul plays piano. Paul introduces himself as Frank during the songs indicating that Frank Sinatra's 1964 performance is the influential one here.

It is now past lunchtime. John and Yoko will soon arrive, but rather than join the group they will give an interview to the Canadian crew set up in a far corner of the studio. Paul jokes that he and Ringo are still together, at least, and, in order to have *something* to do, half-seriously suggests making a short film. Ringo is keen on the idea, and seems prepared to send Mal off in search of a script. As everyone jokes about the various roles they might assume, Michael interrupts to ask if the Canadian crew can share the soundstage. Paul and Ringo are completely indifferent. Michael then joins the 'let's make a film' conversation and, referring to John's absence, jokes that he can make a film about two dead Beatles. Paul, poking fun at early Fabian/Cliff Richard type film scripts, wants to have Glyn play the part of a drug peddler, Tony a fence and Ringo a school teacher. Ringo engagingly suggests that Michael play a traffic sign. Michael then points out that there are some girls around that they could use for sex interest, and Ringo jokingly points out that there are some boys around who are interested in the same thing.

They then bat around more half-baked ideas on how to spend the rest of their day, interspersing their conversation with the ubiquitous one-liners. One of Ringo's jokes reminds Michael of the first time they had met in Chiswick Park during the making of The Beatles' "Paperback Writer" and "Rain" promo films in 1966. Tony points out that a train is arriving - the train being an unfinished prop to be used in another film being shot at Twickenham. This causes Michael to propose making a movie about a train, and Paul excitedly suggests creating characters and improvising all the dialogue. Paul's attention drifts to John and Yoko's interview (which can be faintly heard in the background) and he suggests filming the Canadian crew as they work. Michael would rather shoot John shooting Yoko, and imitates the sound of a gunshot just to make sure his point is clear. Paul (obviously joking) finds this an agreeable idea. The ideas for the afternoon's film continue to flow. Mal wants a spy movie; Ringo, a silent. Michael suggests shooting a promotional film for the band's next single, but no one takes his suggestion seriously, doubtless because they have no idea what the next single will *be*.

Michael wants to get an actress for the impromptu spy film he wants to make, and remembers that casting for *The Magic Christian* is occurring at Twickenham. This is news to Paul and Ringo. Paul suggests taking the cameras and filming the auditions, while Tony jokes that he could play the feminine lead in drag. Ringo decides to find the auditions, saying that he wants to check out the women. Paul and Mal joke that they'd like to be present to see Ringo in bed with one of the girls, and Paul jokes that Ringo should get five girls for aesthetic interests. At this point, there's a gap in the available tape.

When we return to the sessions. Paul has been climbing the chains that are hanging along the back of the soundstage (an indication of just how bored he is). Michael tries to get a shot of this, but fails. Paul then invites Ringo or Mal to try, and vows to master it some other time.

John and Yoko have finished their interview and rejoin the others. Paul incites John to have a go at climbing the chains. John agrees, but quickly abandons his effort and explains that he's too old. John sits down and begins to parody the interview he'd just given, directing the questions at Paul. Paul plays along and, taking on a working man's accent, answers with obscenities when asked about religion and the Maharishi. The questions then turn to Ringo, who's asked about shithouses in Weybridge (a reference to John's previous residence) .

Things get even worse and, except for one fascinating passage, the dialogue degenerates into a series of in-jokes. Despite Ringo's warning that there are spy mikes around, Yoko asks John if he's gotten anything from Mal. By the furtive tone of the subsequent exchange, we can only assume that part of Mal's duties included purchasing drugs for the two. John explains that he has already given her everything Mal had given to him earlier in the day) but Yoko wants more. John suggests she ring someone named Tony, but she wants John to call instead. Also of interest is Paul's response to John's query about the future of the sessions. Obviously dispirited, he replies that they plan to sit around and do nothing for the next three weeks - just what they're doing now.

John and Paul briefly toss around the idea of spending the afternoon making a film but the conversation reverts to one-liners. Then they decide to construct a sculpture. Michael jokes that the documentary will certainly be Picasso-like if this happens. Mal tries to restore sanity by suggesting that they finish the words to the incomplete songs and Ringo thinks that John and Paul might make use of the free time by writing a new song together. Unfortunately, neither is inclined to do this, although John is prompted to sing a bit of nonsense which he introduces as a song he started the previous evening.

14.26 "YOU ARE DEFINITELY INCLINED TOWARDS IT" (0:09)
John improvises this newest Lennon creation, and although he readies his guitar for backing he doesn't use it.

Yoko asks John why he's wasting time. This skirts a serious issue - John's inability to produce acceptable new material for the group, and Paul's frustration (soon to turn to annoyance) over the situation. Instead of answering her, John makes a quip about masturbation, causing Yoko to call out for a censor. This leads into a brief discussion of what can and cannot be publically presented in the documentary. Certainly one of the things that *cannot* be included is a certain anecdote that John and Yoko both wish to relate (but won't) to Paul about their experiences in Coventry. Michael wants to film them sitting about talking about ideas for the film, justifying the waste of film that's gone into recording this day. As Michael and Paul trade drug jokes, Denis drops in with Peter Sellers. Michael jokes with the cameraman not to let Denis know they're wasting footage.

Here we get a few moments break from the unrelenting monotony as Peter is invited to join the festivities. He is accompanied by Joe McGrath, director and co-author of *The Magic Christian*. Peter is understandably perplexed by the sight of a film crew shooting The Beatles sitting around doing nothing and asks what they're doing. As Michael is called to the phone, Peter admits that he doesn't like meeting new people this way. Paul tries to put him at ease by claiming that they feel the same, but Peter seems *very* uncomfortable and doesn't sit down. The forced conversation causes John to remark on Eamonn Andrews talent for such situations. This reminds Paul of Andrews' demeaning comment to Zsa Zsa Gabor which they had talked about on the morning of the 10th. While they're on the subject of insults, John reminds them of the "grow up, Lennon" letter which appeared in the current issue of *Disc and Music Echo* (see also dialogue near the end of the 13th). Peter refers to Ringo as Youngman, the name of Ringo's character in *The Magic Christian*.

One of Peter's colleagues wonders why The Beatles are evidently making a film with no music in it. Paul dodges the question by first claiming they're in conference and then explaining that they're allowing themselves to be embarrassed. John continues to verbally regurgitate small pieces of his subconscious by dredging up the introduction he'd used for "Suzy's Parlour" on the 9th, and, a bit later, a snatch of song he'd sung on the 8th. Peter and Denis ask John if he'd like to contribute a minute and a half sound collage to "*The Magic Christian*" (something along the lines of "Revolution 9" which had appeared on the previous year's double album). John is willing, if the price is right, but Paul bitterly reminds them that John isn't too good about coming through on his promises to write new material. John would never create a piece for the film, and ironically it would be Paul's song "Come and Get it" (performed by Badfinger) which would be played over the credits. In the process of joking about his wardrobe, John mentions singer Tom Jones. Peter reacts violently to Jones' name and recalls his appearance on Jones' television program. John talks about celebrities who have had to do embarrassing television appearances to pay their taxes (such as actor Mickey Rooney and boxing champion Joe Louis) and Paul jokes that The Beatles will still have their trade when they go bankrupt. As Peter prepares to leave, Michael remarks that the documentary is running out of steam.

Yoko responds to Michael's concerns about the disintegration of the project by joking about how wonderful it is for everyone to be sitting around doing nothing. John asks to see Ringo and Peter run through some lines from *The Magic Christian*, but Ringo explains that he still hasn't received a copy of the script. As John and Paul trade one-liners drawn from the current press, Peter once again prepares to leave, but is stopped by John who jokes about giving him marijuana in Piccadilly. Of course, John isn't serious, and only aims to make Peter, who's already fidgety, even *more* uncomfortable. What he doesn't realise is that he's dealing with someone whose mind wanders similar uncharted paths, and Peter gleefully plays along, turning the tables by apologising to John for arriving without drugs because he knows how fond John is of them. John mock-protests that they've given up drugs, and makes reference to a sanitised statement to that effect in Hunter Davies' authorised biography *The Beatles*. John feels the need to one-up Peter by engaging in forbidden topics of discussion and warns Peter not to leave needles in the men's lavatory.

He mentions his October, 1968 arrest on drug charges and explains that he understands that people in show business need to take drugs to relax. Although spoken in a joking fashion, this is probably not very far from John's personal justification for his own drug abuse. Oblivious to the rolling cameras, John goes a step further, and flatly states that drug-taking is better than exercise. Yoko, in an attempt to add to the fun, jokes that shooting up heroin is exercise. Although expressed jokingly, it's obvious that these statements reflect her true opinions. Sadly, such irresponsible, self-destructive attitudes have allowed John's self-confessed heroin dependency, which has obviously impaired his ability to function.

Peter finally departs and John spits out a line from Little Richard's "Long Tall Sally." Paul and Ringo derail the drug discussion by bantering about pheasant hunting. Paul, perhaps envisioning the day's highlights being beamed to a worldwide television audience in Michael's documentary sarcastically asks if Michael's getting all this on film. Michael assures him that he is, and Paul compares the project to a horror movie where the hero is followed everywhere by a prying cameraman. John's reply reminds him that this perfectly describes John and Yoko's soon-to-be-completed film *Rape*.

George Martin visits the Twickenham asylum. This sobers up John long enough to admit that they should address their problems while they're together, but Paul refuses to take the cue, and returns to pondering the possibilities of making a short film about drug taking rather than waste the footage on them sitting around talking. As Paul attempts to recreate the morning's dialogue about the short, Mal, in a fine example of bad timing, asks about the number of songs the band will have ready for the show. This meets with nothing but sarcasm from the others, including Ringo who offers to play a ninety minute drum solo. As talk about the-film-that-will-never-be continues, George Martin tunes out the three Beatles and starts discussing microphones with Glyn.

Everyone (with the exception of George Martin and Glyn, who are continuing their own discussion, is profoundly bored. John continues to quote songs ("Help!" and "Tutti Frutti," to be precise), rattles off bits of poetry, and interviews Paul, but even *he* seems annoyed at this sad state of affairs and bitterly suggests that they boycott George whom he obviously blames for their inactivity. After discussions of John's visit from some hippies and conjectures about Glyn's ancestry (Augustus John, whom they mention, was a famed painter), Michael suggests they leave early and come back the following day. This reminds John that he was late for the present session, and he explains that he was busy taking drugs and watching TV the night before. Paul, in an interesting (and perhaps intentional) role reversal, refuses to let John speak seriously, and rattles off a couple more one-liners. Yoko tries to sidetrack John's obvious guilt about his lack of responsibility by reminding him of the pleasant aspects of their nightlong party. There's an interesting quality in the tone of John's comments here, as if, wanting to say something serious for a change, he's forgotten quite *how*.

They then engage in more idle chatter about the train sets being worked on in the background, homosexuals on television, and contemporary musicians. John also makes an indirect reference to the doomed Apple boutique and its demise (and free distribution of its stock) by stating that it was a plan from the beginning to give everything away.

Michael once again tries to discuss the fate of the documentary, but unknowingly offers John another straight line, and is answered with a quote from George's song "Within You. Without You." John goes on to talk about Lord Baden-Powell, a British Boy Scout leader who discouraged masturbation, and offers the best joke of the day by self-deprecatingly claiming that masturbation doesn't make one go blind, but short sighted. The mail arrives, and John reads a letter to Paul suggesting Mary Hopkin's next single. Paul turns the tables. and tries to egg on John by asking about his *Two Virgins* LP. John offers a surprisingly straight answer, presumably echoing his standard interview response. At this point, they finally run out of steam, and we are treated to nearly a minute of dead silence, punctuated only by the sound of their chairs squeaking.

Mal suggests a bit of rehearsing, but Ringo flatly rejects this idea because he feels sick. Michael claims to be ill as well, but he wants everyone to continue to get together each day because he fears they might otherwise never get together again. Ringo and John share a snatch of sentimental song, and Yoko once again jokes how wonderful it is that all this is occurring. No one laughs, and John and Paul revert to trading one-liners inspired by *Laugh-In*.

Ringo's illness inspires John to relate how he interrupted his interview with the CBC earlier in the day to throw up. He blames this on self-abuse rather than any real illness, and Paul begins to lecture him with a further stream of nonsense. John joins in, and he and Paul quote (in a roundabout way) from The Bonzo Dog Band's "Canyons of Your Mind," Bob Dylan's "Mr. Tambourine Man" and The Beatles' own "I Want to Hold Your Hand" and "Ask Me Why." John and Paul then engage in a duel of witticisms, and Ringo jumps in with a couple of lame jokes of his own. Finally, Paul wearily proclaims that this can't go on forever and John agrees, offering to perform the incomplete song he had started the previous night. Michael, hoping to salvage something out of the day's footage, suggests that he and The Beatles engage in some staged conversation as they preview John's new song. It is nearly 3:45.

14.27   "MADMAN"   >7:19)
John abandons his guitar and plays electric piano. Because George is absent Paul is forced to take offer on guitar. After a breakdown and false start, John leads Paul and Ringo through seven (mostly identical) verses. Since a chorus has yet to be written, they simply engage in some weak jamming in its place.

"Madman" was never released in any form.

14.28   medley MEAN MR. MUSTARD / "MADMAN"   (3:49)
With a paucity of new compositions, John returns to "Mean Mr. Mustard" which had been given an almost identical run-through on the 8th. He switches back to "Madman" about three minutes in and improvises a chorus, playing the same simple piano part for both songs.

14.29   "WATCHING RAINBOWS"   (5:30)
Paul begins to play the guitar part for "I've Got a Feeling," and John joins in and improvises three verses based upon one of the lines in his song "I Am The Walrus." This leads into a chorus, of sorts, then evolves into a jam.

This is the only available performance of "Watching Rainbows."

14.30 (IMPROVISATION) (1:22)

Since they can't effectively rehearse, the three Beatles turn to some late-session jamming. This generic bit of rock and roll is up-tempo, but not particularly energetic.

14.31 (IMPROVISATION) >5:58)

This jam is in progress as the available tape begins. Its riff reminds one of Chuck Berry's 1955 song "You Can't Catch Me," while the single lyric cannot be attributed to any particular song.

14.32 TAKE THIS HAMMER (2:51)

John leads the three Beatles into this traditional American folk song. Although the musicianship is pretty shoddy, John seems to be having fun.

"Take This Hammer" (also known as "Prisoner's Work Song") had been covered in the late '50's by Lonnie Donegan.

14.33 JOHNNY B. GOODE (1:42<

After a bit of riffing and noodling on the electric piano, John begins playing the "Madman"/ "Mean Mr. Mustard" groove. This mutates into another Chuck Berry type jam which becomes "Johnny B. Goode" when John begins to sing. The available tape runs out just as John finishes the first chorus.

This Chuck Berry composition originally appeared in 1958.

14.34 "MADMAN" (0:40)

This is virtually a solo performance from John, who accompanies himself on electric piano as things wind down. He sings half a verse as Paul offers a bit of background vocalising, apparently bored with the song, John goes directly into the next performance.

14.35 YOU KNOW MY NAME (LOOK UP THE NUMBER) (0:18)

John sings nothing more than the title of this song and backs himself on electric piano. Once again, Paul chimes in with a brief backing vocal.

"You Know My Name (Look up The Number)" had been written by John in 1967. The Beatles had attempted a recording of it that year, but it was left unfinished. The group did not work on the song further during these sessions, but the 1967 recording was eventually completed and released as the flipside of "Let It Be."

Michael, in an attempt to prod John and Paul into discussion, asks if the filming should be moved to E.M.I., and if the live show should be abandoned. John begins to explain that anything they do rests on George's actions, but Paul interrupts him and suggests another day at Twickenham with the cameras off but ready. He explains that George is in Liverpool and will be returning to London the next day, and John suggests going to see him. As they begin to discuss George, Paul indicates that he wants filming to stop. A few seconds after Paul's statement the available tape ends.

Wednesday, January 15th, 1969

This aborted session brings an end to the dismal Twickenham rehearsals. Paul, the first (and possibly only) Beatle to arrive, runs through "Oh! Darling" for the benefit of the film crew.

George had been contacted the previous evening (or perhaps even that morning) and a meeting of the four Beatles was set for that afternoon.

15.1   OH! DARLING (0:19)

A solo piano performance from Paul, who takes the song from the top. It is interrupted by Glyn, who asks him to start over.

15.2   OH! DARLING (3:24)

Paul begins another solo performance. He is playing around with the vocals and has abandoned any attempt to perform the song seriously.

15.3   OB-LA-DI, OB-LA-DA (0:12)

After "Oh! Darling" Paul jokes around by breaking into a few lines from this earlier song.

Following the afternoon's meeting, differences between the four Beatles were apparently put aside, and the group agreed to reconvene in front of the cameras at Apple's new basement studio a week later (January 22nd). Although the idea of a live show was still alive, it had been reduced to, at best, a 'live for the cameras' performance. The ten days spent at Twickenham, while not entirely unproductive, probably represented a new low in The Beatles career.

Wednesday, January 22nd, 1969

This day marked the first group sessions at Apple. Although the idea of going abroad to perform has been abandoned, a live performance for the cameras still appears to be the goal.

Despite a good number of jam sessions and oldies, there is a serious attempt to rehearse some of the new songs, and, for the first time, professionally record them for reference purposes. That no serious takes were intended this first day is substantiated by Paul's comment "Beatles - rehearsal" on the box that contains the second multi-track tape recorded by Glyn. A good assessment of the quality of this day's performances can also be found on that tape box, where Paul has written "only good for conversation (if anything)." The rehearsals centred around four songs: "Dig A Pony," "Don't Let Me Down," "I've Got a Feeling" and "She Came In Through The Bathroom Window." "Don't Let Me Down" and "I've Got A Feeling" are inferior to some of the Twickenham takes, but progress on "Dig A Pony" is apparent.

If Paul's psychological withdrawal on the 14th signified the collapse of The Beatles' spiritual centre, the morning of the 22nd represents a new musical low. The performances are so bad that the tapes are barely listenable. During the afternoon, things greatly improve as Billy Preston makes his first appearance at the sessions. He plays keyboards on "Don't Let Me Down" and "She Came In Through the Bathroom Window" and impresses The Beatles enough to be invited for the rest of the sessions.

It should be mentioned that many of the available tapes from this day are in extremely fragmentary condition, which accounts for the short running time of many of the performances listed, and for the scarcity of dialogue.

22.1   DAYDREAM   (0:49)

As this tape begins, John and George are sitting around discussing music - an unremarkable activity for anyone else, but quite noteworthy for them. George, John and Ringo then break into "Daydream," (a hit for the Lovin' Spoonful in 1966) with George calling out the chords for John's benefit, and both of them harmonising on the vocal. During this performance Paul arrives and we suddenly find the four Beatles back together again. John asks Denis O'Dell if they can sue over an article written by Michael Housego which had appeared in the previous day's edition of *The Daily Sketch*. Titled "The End of a Beautiful Friendship?," this publicly reported the fight between John and George that had occurred on the 10th (unfortunately, without details), and suggested that the two Beatles might have even thrown some punches at each other. It's this detail that offends John (although none of them are quite sure what Housego actually said), and he explains that The Beatles have never come to physical blows except for one instance in Hamburg (which he and George laugh about). John then says how much he likes the photo of George which illustrates Housego's article, and pokes fun at Housego's representation of The Beatles (John, it should be noted, doesn't come off too well in Housego's report). George disdainfully dismisses the press, and he and John break into "You Are My Sunshine."

22.2   YOU ARE MY SUNSHINE   (1:58)

A loose and breezy rendition, not very much musically, but quite touching to hear as the two Beatles musically mend fences. Both of them harmonise on what they can remember from the lyrics, and Ringo offers some peppy drumming. Characteristically, toward the end, John starts singing about how he's his own sunshine, and George a few caustic lyrics about Michael Housego.

"You Are My Sunshine" was a hit in 1941 for Bing Crosby, although the song was obviously a standard by the time 1969 rolled around.

22.3   WHISPERING (0:14<

As "You Are My Sunshine" winds down, John plays the introduction to "Twenty Flight Rock" but instead the band breaks into the 20's standard "Whispering." Unfortunately, the available tape fades after only a few seconds.

"Whispering" was a hit both in 1920 and 1954 for Paul Whiteman. Widely covered, The Beatles might have known it from Les Paul's 1951 recording.

22.4   I SHALL BE RELEASED (1:47)

A lazy, off-key rendition, held together solely by Ringo's drumming. George, who plays Leslie'd guitar, only sings the first verse, and that's off-mike. A far better performance of this was done on the 2nd.

22.5   (IMPROVISATION) (1:07)

John holds a generally inaudible discussion with the crew as George and Ringo engage in a simplistic jam.

As John recites a line from the 1963 Crystals hit "Da Doo Ron Ron," Paul interrupts to lead the group into one of the few meaningful conversations from this session as they reminisce about their previous year's sojourn in India, during which they studied transcendental meditation under Maharishi Mahesh Yogi. Evidently Paul has had his home movies of their trip edited together into a proper film, presumably for his own amusement. Their egos, which had been suppressed during the studies with the Maharishi, have rebounded with a vengeance and they now find it incredible that they could have *ever* placed themselves under someone's spiritual guidance. The fact that this dialogue appears in the film *Let It Be* is of importance in itself, as it indicates that The Beatles felt so negatively about their time in India that they did not mind their criticism being presented to the public.

John suggests that Paul's film be called "What We Did On Our Holidays," equating it to a schoolboy's term paper and implying that he perceives the whole Maharishi episode as nothing more than a juvenile misadventure.

22.6   ACT NATURALLY (0:13)

John (on electric guitar) and Paul (on acoustic) sing this brief duet.

"Act Naturally," a 1963 hit for Buck Owens, had been covered by The Beatles on their 1965 *Help!* LP.

With the entire group together for the first time in nearly two weeks, they launch into a light-hearted rehearsal of John's song "Don't Let Me Down." Unfortunately, the available tape consists of little more than extremely brief fragments of music and dialogue.

22.7   DON'T LET ME DOWN (0:06)

Nothing more than a false start. George begins to sing the first line, but John forgets to join in and the performance breaks down.

John introduces this performance as the second take. This does not refer to the multi-track recordings which have yet to commence, but simply means it's the second performance of the day (the first has not come to light).

22.8   DON'T LET ME DOWN >0:36<

This fragment consists only of two tries at the middle eight. John laughs his way through his vocals.

22.9   DON'T LET ME DOWN >0:24<

Another fragment of the middle eight. Instead of the proper lyric, John sings out the names of Dickie Murdoch (a British radio personality from the 1950's) and Dickey Doo (a popular recording artist).

22.10   DON'T LET ME DOWN (3:06)

A complete performance. John is playing guitar and George's guitar is being processed through a Leslie speaker. The band sounds as if they're trying for a perfect run-through. They very nearly succeed, except at the start of the second verse where John briefly forgets the lyrics, and is led back on track by Paul.

The Beatles then discuss the technical problems involved in using a Leslie speaker in place of George's standard guitar amp. Leslie speakers, generally used with organs, rotate internally to give the sound a swirling effect. John wants George to play without the Leslie effect during the middle eight, but George points out that this would be impossible and also complains of the lack of volume he's getting from the equipment.

22.11   I'VE GOT A FEELING >6:07<

The available tape joins this rehearsal in progress as a loose instrumental 'swing' variation of one of the "I've Got A Feeling" guitar riffs and then turns into a series of repeated riffs during a discussion of how George's guitar part should sound. After Paul and John each toss out a few lines of lyric, a more or less complete performance begins. John mumbles some of the lyrics, and twice uses an impromptu line about soft drinks - presumably a topical reference. After the run-through, the riffs start again as Paul tries to relate to George exactly what he's looking for in terms of the guitar lead.

These performances are noticeably weaker than the ones done during the sessions of the 8th and 9th, but this is not unusual - the band is attempting here to *perfect* the song, rather than learn it. John obviously prefers the softer quality here, both in terms of 'lightness' and the country and western arrangement. Because of their plan to record without overdubs, however, Paul finds it impossible to sing the song as he would prefer, and, consequently "I've Got A Feeling" retains its hard edge.

22.12   I'VE GOT A FEELING >2:05)

An uncoordinated performance in which The Beatles run through the song, playing it with a hard edge but maintaining some of the country feel. John urges Paul to keep singing during the duelling verse when Paul evidently forgets to join in. During the course of this performance John and Paul misquote Martin Luther King Jr.'s famous "I have a dream" speech which he gave on August 28, 1963 during a civil rights march on Washington D.C.. This was brought to mind by a television program which had aired on ITV the previous night entitled *Deep South* which examined American race relations in Mississippi, and included excerpts from King's speech. Neither John nor Paul seems too clear how much time took place between the speech and King's assassina-

tion, but this is hardly surprising since they'd only first heard the man the previous evening. It's interesting to note how their discussion of the speech reflects their training as musicians, as they're more interested in the tremolo in
King's voice and the poetic nature of his words rather than the issues he'd
been discussing.

22.13   I'VE GOT A FEELING (3:39)
The Beatles return to a loose rehearsal of "I've Got A Feeling," discussing
George's guitar part and trying out a number of different variations. Amazingly, Paul is *still* not happy with the way the descending guitar piece at the
end of the bridge is being played. A number of attempts at perfecting the
bridge follow, the final one featuring vocals. John tries to remember a black
singer who did a song called "I Had A Dream," and tells Paul that they could
make that the last Beatles single. The identity of the real song Called "I Had A
Dream" that John half-remembers is open to question. It's possibly a 1966
R&B hit by black Stax artist Johnnie Taylor, but Ray Charles also recorded a
song by this name in the late '50's.

22.14   I'VE GOT A FEELING >0:17)
A fragmentary performance of the bridge. Following this, John uses an announcer's voice to broadcast a news report about George being brought up
under assault charges in France. This refers to an incident from May of 1968
where George allegedly tripped a photographer named M. Charles Bebert
while attending the Cannes Film Festival. This resulted in an assault charge
and civil suit, which John makes fun of by joking that he hopes their public
never finds out about *his* beating up the Maharishi. He then reads a newspaper
article regarding the outcome of George's trial which had taken place (without
George present) on January 20th. Needless to say, George was not jailed
(which he could have been under French law), but fined 1,000 francs.

22.15   (IMPROVISATION) (0:57<
As John reads the newspaper article about George, the band jams loudly behind him. As the music winds clowns John improvises a bit of lyric. Paul then
jokes that, with all the publicity they'd been getting The Beatles don't need a
press department. John offers the playful suggestion that Apple initiate a silent
press department that simply responds to everything by refusing to comment.

22.16   EVERY NIGHT >1:13)
This track, and the two that follow are marred by feedback and excessive reverb. Paul unenthusiastically runs through this unfinished number while John
and George offer discordant accompaniment. The end result is a loud, messy
performance that grates on one's ears.

"Every Night" was never professionally recorded by The Beatles and would
not appear until Paul's 1970 solo album *McCartney*.

As on the 5th, John makes noises into the microphone simply to hear his
voice reverberate.

22.17   DIG A PONY (0:20)
As "Every Night" dies out, The Beatles quickly get down to serious business
as John counts into this performance. They successfully finish the song's instrumental introduction, but it breaks down before John starts to sing.

22.18   DIG A PONY (2:01<

The Beatles unenthusiastically attempt the song again. John still hasn't settled on the final lyrics. The performance is passable, but is marred by technical problems.

22.19   DIG A PONY   >0:04)

The very end of a performance, possibly 22.18.

22.20   WATCH YOUR STEP   (0:19)

As "Dig A Pony" ends the band rolls into an instrumental performance of this song which was written and recorded by Bobby Parker in 1961.

22.21   NEW ORLEANS   (3:34)

An energetic cover version marred by reverb, distortion and feedback. John takes the lead vocal, although it's George who gets the performance moving again after it almost breaks down. Both of them sound like they're having fun, and this is the first available performance of the day in which George really participates.

Part of the reason the sound is so bad is that The Beatles have their amplifiers turned up very loud, and fed through echo units. Oddly enough, this sound very likely inspired the choice of "New Orleans," since the hit 1961 Gary U.S. Bonds recording has a similar recording quality, known at the time as 'The Norfolk Sound.'

After a brief 'oldie' break, John wants to get back to work on "Dig A Pony," and offers some instructions. He then ignores his own suggestion and plays "Madman" instead.

22.22   "MADMAN"   (1:56)

In a brief break from the "Dig a Pony" rehearsals, John has another try at "Madman" (which he had premiered on the 14th). This may have been suggested by the musical similarity between "Madman" and "New Orleans" which is quite apparent. The performance lapses very briefly into "New Orleans," reverts to "Madman" and begins to fall apart as Paul tries to improvise a middle eight. John tries to end the performance several times, evidently intending to lead the rehearsals back into "Dig A Pony," but Paul ignores him.

"Madman" seems to have been briefly in competition with "Dig A Pony" for John's composition of choice. As "Dig A Pony" progresses, however, "Madman" is abandoned, and this is the last known performance.

22.23   DIG A PONY   (1:03<

The "Dig A Pony" rehearsals continue with this unexceptional run-through. As usual, John plays havoc with the lyrics.

22.24   HI HEEL SNEAKERS   >2:00)

In this atrocious performance, John literally screams out the lyrics to the song, as Paul joins in with his own off-key wailing. George plays a poor guitar solo, and another instrumental jam ensues.

22.25   MILK COW BLUES   (0:44<

John takes lead vocal and trades guitar riffs with George. Ringo has apparently lost interest and offers no percussion at all. This is almost as bad as "Hi Heel Sneakers."

"Milk Cow Blues" was written and first recorded by Kokomo Arnold. John's inspiration is the 1960 recording by Eddie Cochran rather than the 1955 boogie arrangement by Elvis Presley.

22.26   MILK COW BLUES   >0:03<

A few seconds more of the performance started in 22 25.

22.27   medley / MY BABY LEFT ME / THAT'S ALL RIGHT   >3:01)

John sings this frenetic Elvis tribute consisting of two songs written by Arthur Crudup. This performance is quite rough, but it has more life than anything else attempted at this session.

"That's All Right," Elvis's first single in 1954, had been performed by The Beatles on BBC Radio in 1963. "My Baby Left Me" was released by Elvis in 1956.

22.28   HALLELUJAH I LOVE HER SO   (1:12)

A loose vocal from John inspired by Eddie Cochran's 1960 recording. John changes one of the lines to work in a mention of the name Doris (presumably Doris Day, who's mentioned during "Dig It" on the 26th), just one in a long series of Doris references which dot the Apple sessions. John's recollection of the song's guitar part is very poor, and George's post-song compliment of John's solo is obviously facetious.

The Beatles had been covering this Ray Charles composition as far back as 1960.

Following this performance, we have a light-hearted conversation which apparently refers to Alex Mardas, head of Apple's dormant electronics division and his plans to create a neckless guitar. Mardas was responsible for building an unusable recording console in the Apple studio. Consequently, it's not surprising to hear The Beatles trading jokes at his expense.

22.29   LITTLE QUEENIE   (0:55)

This is still another loose, substandard performance. John takes the lead vocal. Ringo is not playing and George's guitar is distorting horribly. With the day nearly half over, The Beatles are *still* hopelessly attempting to tune their guitars.

Chuck Berry is the victim this time, having written and recorded "Little Queenie" in 1959.

22.30   WHEN IRISH EYES ARE SMILING   (0:16)

John offers this one and a half line performance as he and George continue to tune.

"When Irish Eyes Are Smiling" was written by Chauncey Olcott, George Graff Jr. and Ernest R. Ball in 1912.

22.31   QUEEN OF THE HOP   (0:45)

Paul and John team up for another horribly off-key performance on this cover version. Neither of them can remember the words.

"Queen of the Hop" was a hit for Bobby Darin in 1958.

Paul wants to return to the "Dig A Pony" rehearsal. John doesn't seem to be too interested.

22.32   "ALL I WANT IS YOU"   (0:47<

Based upon Paul's referring to "Dig a Pony" under the title "All I Want Is You," John quickly improvises an entirely new number based upon that line, borrowing a few lines from "Madman." The backing also seems to be improvised.

22.33   medley IN THE MIDDLE OF AN ISLAND / GILLY GILLY / OSSENFEFFER KATZENELLEN BOGEN BY THE SEA   >0:52)

In the midst of tuning, John sings the first couple of lines from "In the Middle Of An Island." The tempo reminds Paul of another song from the '50's, and he and John harmonise nicely on "Gilly Gilly...." Paul continues to sing the song by himself, as John makes arrangements to get home after the session.

A brief but pleasant return to the mid-1950's, with cover versions of Tony Bennett's "In The Middle Of An Island" and The Four Lads' "Gilly Gilly Ossenfeffer Katzenellen Bogen By The Sea," neither of which can be considered rock and roll by *any* stretch of the imagination.

22.34   medley (IMPROVISATION) / GOOD ROCKIN' TONIGHT   (4:43)

Much like "All I Want Is You," which he had improvised from a line in "Dig A Pony," John takes a phrase from Chuck Berry's "Roll Over Beethoven" and wraps a song around it. George adds to the hodge-podge by singing a bit of "Hully Gully" after which the song mutates into a jam. This peters out into disjointed guitar riffs which eventually build back into a performance. During the lull, Paul has begun to read aloud from a newspaper article about the group. John resumes his "Roll Over Beethoven" spin-off as Ringo pounds out a rhythm on tom-tom. After John tosses in a half-remembered verse from "Good Rockin' Tonight," George wraps up this mess with a line from Bob Dylan's "Down In The Flood."

Musically, this is little more than a loose jam which incorporates parts of other songs. The Beatles had covered Chuck Berry's 1956 "Roll Over Beethoven" on their second album and "Down In The Flood" originally appeared on Bob Dylan's "Basement Tapes" demos.

Taking on an announcer's voice, Paul recites more than half of the article written by Michael Housego which appeared in the January 21st edition of *The Daily Sketch*. This recalls the earlier jam where John read out a negative article about George. Despite his jeering tone and laughter, Paul must realise that the bad press is, in this case, mostly on target, and he purposefully avoids certain lines in the article which would displease the others. George obviously sees the irony in it, and sums up the current status of their personal interrelationships with a line about losing friends lifted from Dylan's "Down in The Flood." This prompts John and George to engage in a brief conversation about Dylan's "Basement Tapes," but this doesn't get very far because John has apparently lost his copy of the tape without having listened to it.

22.35   FORTY DAYS   (1:23)

Paul leads the band into this oldie and attempts to amuse them with his Elvis voice. Eventually John begins singing some more lines from "Forty Days," but this is followed shortly by George leading the band into a brief rock and roll jam.

"Forty Days" was a variant of Chuck Berry's "Thirty Days," which The Beatles had already covered during the Twickenham sessions. It appeared under this title in versions by Cliff Richard and Ronnie Hawkins.

Continuing the Elvis theme, Paul recalls the spoken introduction to Elvis's recording of "Milk Cow Blues Boogie." John and Paul then attempt a pun based on the similarity of "All I Want Is You" to the name of Al Aronowitz, a newspaper reporter.

22.36   TOO BAD ABOUT SORROWS   (0:57)

Paul spontaneously begins belting out this early Lennon/McCartney song. The others follow, although their backing is ragged and off-key. Paul can't remember the words very well, and George evidently gets bored and begins to jam in a faster tempo.

John had offered a short performance of this song during the session of the 8th.

22.37   DIG A PONY   (1:52<

This performance is tighter than the previous ones. Apparently on the spur of the moment, Paul introduces a falsetto line to cap off the song's introduction. This will remain part of subsequent performances, although it was edited out of the official release on the album *Let It Be*.

22.38   DIG A PONY   >1:00)

An edit separates this from 22.39, which may very well be part of the same performance. George's lead guitar is quite spotty throughout. John follows the song with a few seconds of improvisation.

22.39   I'M READY   (0:08)

A brief bass riff from Paul, who sings one line from this 1959 Fats Domino tune. This is done merely to convey the fact that he's prepared to give "Dig A Pony" another try.

22.40   DIG A PONY   >0:28)

As the available tape edits in John and Paul are singing a loose warm-up of the song. This quickly falls apart and turns into a series of riffs. As they're about to begin another take the available tape cuts off.

22.41   YOU'VE GOT ME THINKING   >1:07)

George, Paul and Ringo all played on Jackie Lomax's recording of this song, which would appear on his *Is This What You Want?* album later in the year. Paul takes the lead vocal here, turning in an excellent imitation of Lomax's style. George sings along in spots and, a few moments after the performance, returns to it with a brief guitar riff. John and Paul comment on a "Dig A Pony" rehearsal (which is not yet available), and poke fun at its nonsense lyrics.

22.42   PAPA'S GOT A BRAND NEW BAG   (0:03)

A two line a capella rendition from Paul.

"Papa's Got a Brand New Bag," a 1965 James Brown hit, had recently been covered by Otis Redding.

22.43   DIG A PONY   (0:03<

As a performance begins the available tape abruptly edits.

22.44   DIG A PONY   >1:19)

This is the last half of a performance. Although his singing is fine, John is still tinkering with the lyrics. As the performance ends Paul tags on the word 'girl' which inspires the next two 'performances.'

22.45   SHOUT!   (0:12)

John sings a single line from The Beatles' own song "You're Gonna Lose That Girl" replacing the word 'lose' with 'shag' (a British synonym for 'fuck'). The mindlessness continues as John and Paul sing a brief portion of "Shout!" replacing "Shout!" with 'shag' as well. Following the performance, George sings a snatch of an old English folk song called "Oh, No John, No."

We are then treated to more of the type of wordplay which dominated the 14th, as John utters his deathless comment about Charles Hawtrey and 'deaf aids' which was ultimately used to lead off the *Let It Be* album. For the record, Charles Hawtrey was a famous British comedy actor (a cast member of the popular "Carry On..." films) and 'deaf aids' was a term for hearing aids that The Beatles used to describe their amplifiers.

22.46 DIG A PONY (0:07<

This begins as a loose performance under the conversation above. John begins to sing, but a few seconds later the available tape cuts off.

22.47 medley DIG A PONY / "WILLIAM SMITH BOOGIE" (0:46<

Over some guitar riffs, John intones a few lines about William Smith and his crisps. As George and John begin another attempt at "Dig A Pony," Paul makes noises into his microphone and, in a demented falsetto, gurgles further improvised lyrics as he continues to improvise the "William Smith Boogie" on bass. This is all done under very heavy reverb.

22.48 "YOU GOTTA GIVE BACK" >0:22)

A fragment of another improvisation. Paul yells out some improvised lyrics. John then calls for them to resume "Dig A Pony," offering a mock stage announcement in the process.

22.49 DIG A PONY (0:06<

The very start of another performance which has been severely truncated on the available tape.

22.50 DIG A PONY >3:52)

A complete run-through. Rather than just rehearsing, the group is attempting to lay down a releaseable performance. John's vocal is particularly strong. On both this and the following performance Ringo experiments with drum fills at the beginning of the song.

22.51 DIG A PONY (4:03)

Despite an occasional vocal slip-up from John, this is the best available performance of the song to have come from this session. It's complete, and everyone is obviously giving their all to capture a strong performance on tape. Shortly after the performance ends, Paul light-heartedly points out how their playing has improved, a comment on the quality of the earlier takes

This track was released in 1996 on *Anthology 3*.

Upcoming performances indicate that a series of "Don't Let Me Down" rehearsals occurred at this point which have not become available.

22.52 medley I'M READY / (IMPROVISATION) >0:34)

This brief jam was listed on the multi-track tape box by Paul as "Rocker" but in reality it's nothing more than another improvisation, sandwiched between a couple of lines from Fats Domino's "I'm Ready." The musicians seem to be moving in different directions as the electric piano plays something like Chuck Berry's "Down the Road Apiece," and the guitar (something like) Les Cooper's 'Wiggle Wobble."

Some time has passed since the "Dig A Pony" rehearsals. It's now mid-afternoon, and we are given the first indication that keyboardist Billy Preston has joined the session.

22.53 medley SAVE THE LAST DANCE FOR ME / DON'T LET ME DOWN (0:38)

Once again, The Beatles postpone one of their own songs in favour of an oldie. John and Paul share the lead vocal. After one verse, the band crashes into the chorus of "Don't Let Me Down" for two lines

"Save The Last Dance For Me" was a 1960 hit for The Drifters.

22.54 DON'T LET ME DOWN (3:49)

After a false start, The Beatles and Billy make it through a fine, if slightly lacklustre performance. During the instrumental break John yells for Billy to take the solo and Billy obliges. John is happy with this, and calls for a reprise.

Once again, aware that Glyn is taping, the band tries a little harder to turn in a credible performance. John has cause to be happy with Billy's contribution. Since the early Twickenham rehearsals he's been wishing for a keyboard break in the song, but there weren't enough Beatles to allow it. Now, the problem is solved. This performance and the two that preceded it were chosen for inclusion on the aborted *Get Back* album

22.55 I'VE GOT A FEELING >0:31<

A portion of the bridge, followed by part of a verse. Despite the fragmentary nature of the available tape, this is clearly part of a full performance. The descending guitar part is temporarily replaced here by a few sustained notes.

22.56 I'VE GOT A FEELING >0:11<

Another fragment featuring part of the chorus. Once again, this is obviously part of a longer take.

22.57 I'VE GOT A FEELING >0:27<

This starts out with very quick guitar runs which gradually evolve into a loose rehearsal of one of Ringo's drum fills.

22.58 DIG A PONY >0:19)

The Beatles rehearse "Dig A Pony" into "I've Got A Feeling." This fragment captures the very end of a performance, and runs into the next song.

22.59 I'VE GOT A FEELING (3:18)

A complete performance. Although John and Paul are playing around with their vocals, this actually puts a bit of spirit into the song rather than detracting from the performance. After sitting out "Dig A Pony," Billy once again plays keyboards.

The Beatles then discuss the descending riff that comes at the end of the bridge which is still a problem. John claims to have a mental block and Paul counts through it in an attempt to straighten them out.

22.60 I'VE GOT A FEELING (1:23)

This is a loose rehearsal of riffs beneath much of the dialogue mentioned

22.61 I'VE GOT A FEELING (3:30)

Another rehearsal take. John still can't play the descending guitar riff.

Paul suggests that they call it a day, but John has enough energy left to want to try "Get Back." Glyn asks if they want to hear playbacks of their rehearsals. If not, he intends just to erase them. John is unhappy at the prospect of erasing a Beatles performance (no matter how much it deserves it), but Paul realises there's nothing worth keeping. Nonetheless, John wants to retain the day's takes so they can hear how they've progressed, and Glyn admits that the reason he suggested erasing some of the earlier takes is that he's out of recording tape. They settle this by agreeing not to record any more and offer an inventory of what they've recorded thus far ("Don't Let Me Down," "I've Got A Feeling" and "Dig A Pony").

22.62 I'VE GOT A FEELING (3:10)

The rehearsal of an ascending guitar riff for "I've Got A Feeling" leads the band into a repetitive three chord jam incorporating several lines from Bo Diddley's "Road Runner." The two quote from that song by singing "beep

beep!" in harmony. This inspires Paul's post-performance comment that he misses singing in harmony as they did on their early single "Please Please Me."

22.63 I'VE GOT A FEELING (3:11<

They begin this performance at the second verse. Paul stops and recalls how they had performed the song before he began yelling out his lines, and the performance breaks down into another loose rehearsal. John and Paul attempt to sing harmony vocals, but the available tape runs out.

22.64 DON'T LET ME DOWN >0:06<

A fragment of an obviously longer performance. The distant quality of the sound suggests that this is a playback, but it is too brief for us to be certain.

22.65 SHE CAME IN THROUGH THE BATHROOM WINDOW >5:03<

Rather than "Get Back" (which was John's suggestion) The Beatles turn to this McCartney number. One wonders why they bothered, since they all sound rather uninterested. Perhaps they're simply running through the song to introduce it to Billy Preston. After an initial sluggish run-through, Paul offers various suggestions and instructions. He requests a big cymbal crash at one point in the song, and discusses the feel he wants for the backing. The vocals are also discussed. Paul wants it to be a tight three part harmony, with a rolling background such as they had used on their song "I Am The Walrus." George plays a very brief riff from "I've Got A Feeling."

John informally invites Billy Preston to join the group for the remainder of the project. He suggests that Billy be provided with copies of the performances taped during the day, but Paul and George feel he can learn the songs better by just coming in and playing them. John's comments imply that a live show (even one strictly for the cameras) is still intended, and that an album will result from it.

22.66 SHE CAME IN THROUGH THE BATHROOM WINDOW (3:05)

Paul leads The Beatles through a slow, perfunctory performance, with John on keyboards as Billy sits out. Paul's vocal is devoid of the energy that could be heard on many of the Twickenham performances of this song.

Faced with the problem of having run out of recording tape, Glyn flips the multi-track reel over and records in the other direction (possible because he was only using 4 of the tape's 8 tracks to record on). This performance was thus preserved on multi-track and eventually released on *Anthology 3*.

This is the last available performance of the song from the "Get Back" sessions, and it apparently wouldn't be revisited until a July 25th, 1969 session for *Abbey Road*.

Thursday, January 23rd, 1969

This day's session was dominated by rehearsals of "Get Back." The group ran through that number extensively, with and without Billy Preston, eventually committing a number of takes to multi-track tape.

This session was quite brief, running little more than four hours. There are no serious rehearsals except for "Get Back," although we're treated to a performance of Ringo's "Octopus's Garden." At one point, The Beatles must have planned to rehearse "Maxwell's Silver Hammer," since an anvil is situated prominently in the middle of the studio, but probably abandoned this plan once the rehearsals began.

This session is also unusual because of its mood. The Beatles are happy, smiling, laughing, and obviously having a blast rehearsing "Get Back" - a far cry from their mood at Twickenham.

This day was also unique because two separate sessions took place. The Beatles would return that evening (without the film crew) and record versions of "I've Got A Feeling" and "Dig A Pony."

In the first available tape fragment, Paul and Apple publicist Derek Taylor discuss Mary Hopkin's upcoming LP on Apple. Paul wants to enclose a Valentine brand postcard with each copy of the album, but worries that Capitol Records in America will compromise the quality. He then disdainfully recalls working with Mary on cover ideas for the album. George tosses out a few jokes. If John and Ringo are present, they're silent.

23.1 (DRUM SOLO) (0:24)
As the previous conversation winds down, Paul borrows Ringo's drum kit and begins to play a rudimentary drum solo. George jokes that they can call Mary Hopkin's next album "Next of Hopkin."

23.2 OCTOPUS'S GARDEN >0:13<
Ringo plays a new song on the piano, while John and Yoko share a snack. Someone calls out for "Across The Universe," but John tells them that song has been abandoned in favour of "Dig A Pony.' Although a break in the available tape separates this fragment from 23.3, they are undoubtedly part of the same performance

"Octopus's Garden" had not been written when Ringo played his songs-in-progress to the others on the morning of the 3rd. It would not be properly recorded until the *Abbey Road* sessions later in the year.

23.3 OCTOPUS'S GARDEN >0:22<
Ringo only sings the first verse, which is all that is written at this point. As one would expect, "Octopus's Garden" is a very simple number, not dissimilar to "Taking A Trip to Carolina" and "Picasso," which he had performed on the 3rd. John asks Ringo if George hasn't written a song for him. Ringo replies that George has written a number for *both* of them, and sings a couple lines representative of the song.

23.4 "HEY, HEY GEORGIE" (0:09)
Ringo's brief performance of George's 'song' from above. He accompanies himself with a simple piano backing.

It was a tradition in The Beatles to let Ringo sing lead at least once per album. To this end, Paul and George had each checked on Ringo's songwriting progress earlier in the sessions, and now John does the same. As it finally turned out, however, Ringo would not record a song at these sessions.

John then discusses his July 1968 art exhibit, "You Are Here" with cameraman Tony Richmond.

23.5 GET BACK (0:57<

Although John and George join in tentatively, this performance really belongs to Paul and Ringo. Ringo has forgotten his drum part, and taps out a simple 4/4 rhythm, which gets more complicated as the performance progresses. The available tape cuts off during the second verse.

23.6 GET BACK >1:21<

This performance is very probably a continuation of 23.5. George offers a guitar embellishment which will be dropped as the day progresses. Paul sings a chorus and second verse and is just beginning another chorus as the available tape cuts off. It's obvious the song needs work.

As George and Paul work out the chord progression for "Get Back," Paul insists that nothing be done to make the song lose its rock and roll feel.

23.7 GET BACK (2:03<

George begins this performance with a guitar riff during the above conversation. The others follow and play an extended introduction John and Paul begin to call out the title to one another and Paul sings a chorus before beginning the Loretta verse.

23.8 GET BACK >3:09)

The rehearsals continue. Ringo has reverted to a simple beat. Paul improvises some lyrics about Loretta's attire (this idea will remain with the song in the coda to the released single). He then starts the song from the beginning. When he runs out of lyrics he begins to improvise again.

Paul then takes a moment to explain the words of "Get Back," but sheds little light on the trite lyrics.

23.9 GET BACK (1:02<

Paul sings a few illustrative lines, with sparse accompaniment. This evolves into a full group performance, but the available tape cuts off soon thereafter.

23.10 medley GET BACK / REACH OUT I'LL BE THERE >2:07<

This is a continuation of 23.9. George compares "Get Back" to "Reach Out, I'll Be There" and starts singing that song as the others continue to play "Get Back." The two songs intertwine. Finally, the performance turns into "Get Back," but soon after the first verse the available tape cuts off.

"Reach Out, I'll Be There" was a hit for the Four Tops in 1966.

23.11 GET BACK >0:16<

This fragment cuts in during the guitar solo. It's a continuation of 23.10.

23.12 GET BACK >1:09<

Only a second or two of tape is missing between this and 23.11. After an instrumental break, John and Paul rehearse the chorus.

23.13 GET BACK >1:07)

John and Paul rehearse their harmonies, trying out a lower register. They pause briefly as Paul tells George to play strident chords.

23.14 GET BACK (1:40<

George and Paul's discussion leads into another performance. Following Paul's suggestion, George experiments with playing simpler chords.

23.15   GET BACK >0:19)

A few instrumental measures, and the tail end of the chorus lead into the following conversation.

Paul describes the genesis of "Get Back" and says that he dropped the protest lyrics because he wasn't happy with them. George is more concerned with arranging the song's verses, choruses and guitar solos than he is with its lyrical content, and compares one of the song's elements to their 1965 recording "I'm Down." John suggests that one of his solos be given to Billy.

23.16   GET BACK (0:39)

This performance is nothing more than a series of riffs heard during the conversation above.

At this point The Beatles break for hunch. John and Paul return to the studio before Ringo and George and are joined by Billy.

23.17   (IMPROVISATION) >0:53<

Since half of the group is not present, The Beatles are unable to resume rehearsals and use this time to indulge in an avant-garde jam session featuring Yoko. John pounds out a beat on the back of his guitar. Paul thrashes about on drums, and Yoko contentedly shrieks into the microphone. Billy doesn't participate. John begins to play slide guitar just before the available tape cuts.

This and the next four fragments are obviously part of the same improvisation. These horrible few minutes are even worse than Yoko's contribution from the 10th.

23.18   (IMPROVISATION) >1:35<

John has abandoned any attempt to *play* his guitar and tries to create feedback by waving it in front of his microphone. He continues to bang on the instrument, wave it over his head, and even pokes it into Yoko's face at one point. Paul keeps drumming and Yoko keeps wailing.

23.19   (IMPROVISATION) >0:38<

Paul's drumming has subsided. John is now drawing high-pitched feedback from his guitar and Yoko whimpers in sympathy. Paul's drumming picks up, and Yoko begins to shriek again.

23.20   (IMPROVISATION) >0:14<

A continuation of 23.19.

23.21   (IMPROVISATION) >1:11<

John has now stood up, and is waving his guitar in front of his amplifier in order to create feedback. Yoko's vocals begin to evolve into obnoxious bleating

23.22   (IMPROVISATION) >0:28<

Billy has moved to organ for this sluggish blues instrumental. John and Yoko do not participate.

This bears some resemblance to Howlin'Wolf's "Sittin' on Top of The World" (which had recently been covered by Cream), but is too loose to definitively identify.

23.23   GET BACK >2:22)

The available tape edits in just as a performance is breaking down. Paul calls out for a solo and John makes a decent attempt to play one. They start over,

but once again the performance breaks down, as Paul jokingly apologises.
They start again from the solo and get through the chorus and second verse
before another breakdown during the chorus.

  Although this performance of "Get Back" is still rough, The Beatles have
clearly progressed since the performances earlier in the day. Billy is now contributing on electric piano.

  Following this, they discuss John's guitar solo. John, who rarely solos, is
straying a bit too much from the song for George's taste. Paul wants to make
sure John doesn't play two identical solos.

23.24   GET BACK (0:45)
John makes repeated attempts at the guitar solo while Paul sings the song's
second verse

23.25   GET BACK (0:15)
John plays some brief' "Get Back" riffs, and follows them with some intentionally poor guitar solos. He then candidly remarks about his inability to perform solos, and this reminds George of their terrible musicianship on their
later tours. This amuses all of them, and Paul tells an anecdote about Jimmy
Nicol, the drummer who filled in for Ringo for part of the 1964 tour. The
band then prepares for another take of "Get Back," which Paul jokingly announces as "Begin The Beguine," a Cole Porter standard.

23.26   GET BACK (2:42)
The Beatles take the song from the top. John and Billy trade solos, but this
take is quite sloppy.

  John plays an awful final solo, and claims he played it well the first time
around but that his mike was off. Glyn apologises for this error, but no one's
really concerned. The available tapes of this and 23.27 derive from studio
play-backs later in the day. Consequently, occasional singing or percussion
from the control room can be heard. They have been listed here because no
"clean" tapes of these rehearsals have surfaced.

23.27   GET BACK (3:37)
This rehearsal fragment concentrates on the guitar solo and ensuing chorus.
The performance grows out of stray vocal lines and guitar riffs. Billy plays
electric piano for a while and then Paul begins a brief, very up-tempo rendition. They take the song from midway through the guitar solo, completing the
chorus but breaking down before the second verse. After everyone laughs they
attempt the solo and chorus once again, but they meet with similar results.

23.28   GET BACK (>2:00)
The available tape edits in before the first solo, which Billy once again carries
on keyboards. The song continues through the chorus and second verse, and
ends with an instrumental coda leading into some stray riffs.

23.29   I'LL GET YOU (0:11)
A brief send-up performance from Paul, who sings two lines with half-hearted
backing.

  "I'll Get You" had been the b-side of The Beatles' 1963 hit "She Loves
You." Perhaps the earlier mention of that song brought it to mind.

  Paul jokes about getting Hong Kong flu, but with a flu epidemic sweeping
England at the time, the joke falls flat. Much more amusing is John's enthusiastic solution - take drugs - which is possibly his standard solution to any
problem. With "Get Back" reasonably perfected, The Beatles attempt a dry

run-through of the anticipated live performance (even though their only audience is Yoko, who's reading a newspaper and ignoring them) and John and
Paul have a great time.

23.30   GET BACK (0:07)

The Beatles begin a performance, but it breaks down when Glyn interrupts to
inopportunely issue instructions to second engineer Alan Parsons. This causes
John and Paul to mercilessly rib him for interrupting their performance
(there's a good chance that George Martin never got called fuck face, even in
jest!). This exchange reminds John of their early live performances at the
Jacaranda, a nightclub where the group was reported to often swear at the
crowd from the stage.

23.31   GET BACK (2:38)

The long rehearsals bear fruit as the band turns in a fine performance.

At this stage this performance was marked 'best' and Glyn Johns went on to
mix it and prepare acetates for The Beatles to hear.

23.32   I'VE GOT A FEELING (0:18)

"Get Back" ends, John thanks everyone and The Beatles launch immediately
into a few seconds of this song. After the instrumental introduction Paul and
John decide to play it for laughs and offer some parody lyrics in silly voices.

23.33   HELP! (0:43)

As Paul collapses in laughter at "I've Got a Feeling," John hunches over his
mike and begins to sing "Help!." Paul joins in with comic harmony vocals as
they completely trash their 1965 single. This performance runs directly into
the next one.

During the session on January 7th John had said that he had been performing
this song well lately and suggested they rehearse it for inclusion in the live
show. This is certainly not an attempt at *that.*

23.34   PLEASE PLEASE ME (0:21)

John and Paul continue to make fun of themselves, this time destroying their
1963 hit. They never make it beyond the first line of the lyric. John then suggests that they sit down.

Having capped off their attempts to record "Get Back" with some light-
hearted throwaways, The Beatles retire to the control room to listen to playbacks. Following this, they dismiss the film crew and take the rest of the
afternoon off. This was because they would return to the studio that evening
for a more typical recording session, without the presence of the film crew.
There, along with Billy, they would record takes of "Dig A Pony" and "I've
Got A Feeling." Glyn would mix several of these (along with "Get Back") the
following night, and present acetates to The Beatles on the 25th. We believe
that a mix-up in documentation between recording and mix dates resulted in
an incorrect attribution of these performances to the 24th in Mark Lewisohn's
book *The Beatles Recording Sessions.*

23.35   DIG A PONY (3:45)

This performance is marred by Ringo's rather plodding drum part, and ragged
falsetto harmonies from Paul.

This take was chosen by Glyn for the aborted *Get Back* LP.

23.36   I'VE GOT A FEELING (2:41)

An acceptable performance which breaks down as John and Paul reach the duelling verse because John's playing is too loud. Unfortunately, George's guitar is badly out of tune.

The Beatles will discuss this particular breakdown of "I've Got A Feeling"
on the 26th (following 26.13). It was inexplicably chosen for inclusion on the
unreleased "Get Back" LP, and (27 years later) on *Anthology 3*.

Friday, January 24th, 1969

Had Billy Preston been present at the start of this session, The Beatles would probably have continued to perfect "Get Back." Since he was not, "Two Of Us" became the session's focal point. The band first attempted to perform the song electrically (as they had during most of the Twickenham sessions) and then opted to try it acoustically instead. Even though this new arrangement was clearly still in the rehearsal stage, Glyn Johns preserved a number of takes on multi-track tape.

This day also saw the professional recording debut of two other songs. The first of these was Paul's "Teddy Boy," a song which he had written the previous year in India and which he had performed briefly on January 9th. The second was John's composition/improvisation "Dig It."

After Billy Preston's arrival late in the afternoon all of the remaining serious rehearsals centred around "Get Back," which had become the consensus choice for the next Beatles single. George Martin joined Glyn Johns and Geoff Emerick in the crowded control room as the group made a half-hearted attempt to record a releaseable performance of the song. Having failed at that, they packed up and went home for the evening.

Apart from the songs mentioned above, The Beatles also devoted a fair amount of time to other performances. In addition to at least seven Chuck Berry songs, they covered various numbers popularised by Lonnie Donegan, Guy Mitchell and Arthur Alexander and revived a number of early Lennon/McCartney compositions, such as "Hot As Sun" and "I Lost My Little Girl." Paul also ran through an inventory of his works-in-progress, offering up "Her Majesty," "There You Are, Eddie" and "Every Night."

The beginning of the session featured a protracted discussion about Billy Preston's involvement in the project The Beatles had all agreed to have Billy play keyboards on the sessions, but John's suggestion that they permanently add him to the group is met with Paul's objection that four Beatles are enough. John and Paul do agree though, that a book should be released to coincide with the film/television show.

Most of the tape recorded on this day has become available. This, together with extrapolation based on song fragments and performances which are obviously part of longer rehearsal sessions, has enabled us to get an unusually clear picture of January 24th.

The earliest material available from this day's session comes before Paul, Ringo and Billy have arrived. John is passing the time by talking about himself (and Yoko) to Michael and a tired-looking George. This particular exchange concerns *Rock and Roll Circus*, for which John had performed "Yer Blues" with an all-star band five weeks earlier. He's worried that he'll come out looking like some kind of rock and roll freak if Michael isn't careful. Unless he's being sarcastic, John's comment about his public image is severely inconsistent for someone who, if anything, revelled in his anti-establishment image.

John then offers an interesting *Rock And Roll Circus* anecdote as he remembers violinist Ivri Gitlis' negative reaction to Yoko's vocalisations during an extended improvisation which followed his performance of "Yer Blues." He continues to boast about how he was able to lead the band into this improvisation (based on a Bo Diddley riff from "Road Runner") without even having to stop for a count-off. John must have been particularly pleased by this accomplishment since The Beatles rarely improvised on stage.

The discussion of the *Rock and Roll Circus* jam session continues as John proudly discusses Yoko's involvement, dropping the names of several celebrity 'fans' in an attempt to add legitimacy to Yoko's unorthodox performances (The Who and Eric Clapton were also participants in the event). John also mentions the jam session with Yoko from the previous day's session. He then suggests that the jam might be used on John and Yoko's next LP.

As the next available tape begins, John is still talking about *Rock and Roll Circus*, although his point is a little more obscure. In addition to the professional film crew, John and Yoko had their own personal cameraman film their performances, and John's comments seem to centre around his delight at the rough sound quality which was a result of the off-line miking. He compares this to the less-than-perfect sound heard through a Philips Cassette player (cassette players were relatively new at the time, and Philips, as the inventor, had a virtual monopoly on their manufacture) and is so enthusiastic that he suggests The Beatles intentionally record a number on such equipment. Although the other Beatles never took him up on his idea, John didn't forget it, and used a rough cassette recording of the song "My Mummy's Dead" on his 1970 solo album *John Lennon / Plastic Ono Band*.

24.1   GET BACK   (0:24)
John plays a few instrumental bars, undoubtedly recalling the previous clay's lengthy rehearsals of this song. Michael asks if they're going to put out "Get Back." Both John and George's answers to him indicate they feel the rehearsals for "Get Back" are far from finished. Indeed, they will return to the song later in the day. John then quotes from an interview with Eric Clapton that appeared in the film *Cream - Farewell Concert from the Royal Albert Hall, London*. In that interviews Clapton explains his guitar's "man tone" and "woman tone" and gives a brief example of how these can be achieved.

24.2   GET BACK   (0:23)
John plays this riff to illustrate Clapton's "man tone''/ "woman tone" technique.

24.3   (I CANT GET NO) SATISFACTION   (0:25)
This guitar riff immediately follows the previous one. Both are played at half-tempo.

"(I Can't Get No) Satisfaction" was a hit for The Rolling Stones in 1960.

The next discussion is separated from 24.3 by an edit in the available tape. Some time has passed, and Paul has arrived. The discussion centres around the musical background and qualifications of Billy to play with the group. The Beatles originally met Billy in Germany in 1962 when he was acting as part of Little Richard's backup band. For the past several years, however, he'd been on the road as part of Ray Charles' Orchestra. Paul seems a bit concerned that Billy's current preoccupation with jazz (or big band, more accurately) might not fit The Beatles' style, but John makes the point (using Ray Charles as an example) that one style does not preclude performing in another.

24.4   WHAT'D I SAY (0:07)
Since the title of this song had been mentioned in the previous conversation, it is almost inevitable that one of the Beatles would perform a short riff.

The Beatles also performed a brief cover of this 1959 Ray Charles classic during the session of January 7th. They had also played it live as part of their set early in their career.

24.5   (BASS RIFF) / GET BACK / (IMPROVISATION) (3:34)
Throughout the conversation that follows, John, Paul and George each take turns playing indistinct riffs. The last of these seems to be a variation of "Two Of Us," although it also resembles George's early song "If I Needed Someone."

The discussion about Billy continues. Paul reiterates his position that Billy is primarily a jazz performer (comparing him to Ray Charles), but John insists this isn't necessarily indicative of Billy's desire, since he's not powerful enough to dictate the kind of music he'll play. George backs John. To him Billy's playing is much funkier. Both George and John then defend jazz in general, and John ends the discussion by proclaiming that having Billy play with the band would be great whatever his style is. The subject then turns to paying Billy for his work. Paul mentions that they would have been paying session musician rates (the industry minimum wage) if they had hired keyboardist Nicky Hopkins (evidently their original plan). John reminds Paul that Billy must also be compensated for appearing in their TV special. Obviously believing that it's not their place to discuss the subject with Billy directly Paul suggests they simply instruct Ron Kass (head of the music division of Apple) to talk to Billy and settle the matter. Suddenly, John indicates in no uncertain terms that he'd like to see Billy join The Beatles on a permanent basis. Rightly feeling that two days involvement is rather too short an apprenticeship for membership in the world's most influential pop combo, Paul is taken aback, and we get close to direct conflict between the two Beatles. Paul characteristically uses humour to defuse the situation by half-jokingly stating that it's bad enough with four Beatles, and then candidly admits how the subject is causing dissension. George chimes in with a story about having asked Bob Dylan to join The Beatles, although it's obvious he means to join The Beatles on their televised performance rather than become a member of the group. He makes the comment that he'd like to get a number of rock and roll luminaries into the project, which suggests that George, at least, would love to one-up the *Rock and Roll Circus* project. Paul pounces on George's comment to prove his point: one doesn't have to become a member of The Beatles in order to play with them. He then rushes to assure the other Beatles how much he really likes Billy, equating him to Nicky Hopkins and relating how he himself had gone overboard in his enthusiasm the previous day (when he had invited Billy to be on the show). This is a common method of argument for Paul: to point

out how he used to hold the other's point of view, but 'came around,' implying that the others should (and will) eventually 'come around' as well. This
time, however, John ignores Paul, and chortles in delight at the prospect of
adding so many new members to the band that the new members outnumber
the Fab Four. Paul makes a final attempt to dismiss John's idea of a fifth
Beatle, suggesting that Billy may be like Michael Brown, an early drummer
for the band (back in their days as The Quarrymen) who was kicked out of the
group when the other members grew tired of him. Paul agrees to have Billy on
the show, and to pay him his due, but he won't sit still for having him join
The Beatles.

Immediately following this pseudo-argument is an intriguing example of
psychological by-play between Paul and John. Paul attempts to continue the
discussion, but is cut off by John, who criticises Paul's business-like outlook.
John chooses to avoid confrontation (or even discussion), and answers by
spouting nonsense. Paul, perhaps sensing John's increasing hostility, backs
away from his argument and enthusiastically supports (some part of) John's
point of view. Again, this is typical for Paul: to argue to a certain point, and
then, if he doesn't appear to be winning the argument, make a 180 degree
turnaround (at least for the moment) as if to say 'if you can't lick 'em, join
'em .'

The next available dialogue segment appears to be a continuation of the discussion about Billy, with Paul's observation that The Beatles can use him as a
freelance session musician without necessarily putting him under contract to
Apple.

As part of the general discussion of signing Billy to The Beatles' label, John
begins to discuss having signed someone else (Trash? The Iveys?) simply because he'd felt embarrassed about the amount of money the group had spent
on multiple auditions. John's final comments illustrate his desire to turn Apple into a more businesslike enterprise. This attitude is reinforced by John's
contemporary comments about Apple's poor financial situation in an interview with Ray Coleman printed in the January 18th edition of *Disc and Music
Echo*.

24.6   (IMPROVISATION)   (4:01)
The first 1:11 of this consists of loose riffs, repeating the instrumental theme
found in 24.5. These finally develop into a full-fledged instrumental performance which comprises the first group performance of the day. Ringo joins in
on drums about half way through.

One of the technicians is rightly concerned that Ringo's bass drum is too
loud, and asks Mal to find someone who can place a towel in it to muffle the
sound.

24.7   (IMPROVISATION)   (0:02<
The instrumental performance from 24.6 starts up again at the end of the
above conversation only to be truncated after a few seconds by an edit in the
available tape.

The discussion about Billy continues. John gleefully comments that The
Beatles have gone from 3 to 4 to 5 members in the past few days. George's
comments indicate that he's fully aware of the prestige which would be ac-

corded someone who's performing with The Beatles. He worries that Billy's skin colour alone would cause undue attention, and wonders whether Billy can take it. Following up on this, John ponders whether Billy's presence might be seen as a race-relations statement on the part of the group - as *their* "I have a dream" proclamation.

24.8   GET BACK / (IMPROVISATION)   (0:20)
Several riffs, played during the following conversation. This is primarily a riff from "Get Back," but a few bars of the persistent instrumental sneak in at the end.

George follows up the above conversation with the observation that it wouldn't be fair to Billy to disqualify him because his presence would take focus off The Beatles.

24.9   (IMPROVISATION)   (0:11)
After a brief pause, another guitar riff resurfaces from the instrumental played during 24.5 - 8. This dissolves into tuning.

Ringo then asks the valid question of whether or not The Beatles are attempting to make a record now (as compared to rehearsing). John and Paul seem to indicate no, but Paul mentions that one performance from the previous day was worthy of being released, but wasn't properly recorded. Paul rightly states that "Get Back" is the first song (or, at least, the first non-acoustic song) that they've been able to really get into. John half-seriously rebuts this by mentioning the titles of two of his own songs.

24.10   GET BACK / OB-LA-DI, OB-LA-DA   (0:51)
This starts out as a half-baked version of "Get Back." Paul, however, interjects the bass riff from "Ob-La-Di, Ob-La-Da," which prompts the others to play that song. John sings the first verse (imitating Paul's voice), as Paul sings backup. This messy hybrid very quickly quits, and The Beatles move on to more serious rehearsal.

Though John isn't taking his singing any more seriously here than he did on January 3rd, this performance lacks the fun found in the earlier one. Unlike that rendition, the lyrics here basically match those of the legitimate release. The music here still has overtones of the instrumental they've been playing for the past couple of minutes.

24.11   GET BACK   (0:48<
As the previous performance ends, John indicates that, as far as he's concerned, it's time to get down to business. This particular performance is sluggish and heavy, giving little indication that The Beatles had thoroughly rehearsed this song the previous day. It is prefaced by a brief false start in which John begins in the wrong tempo, and is corrected by George. The available tape cuts off after the first verse.

24.12   GET BACK   >0:54
This is possibly a continuation of 24.11. John sings the first verse of the song at the wrong time (perhaps intentionally), and the performance quickly comes to an end.

Once John screws up the rehearsal of "Get Back" by singing off-beat, Paul calls a halt to the performance and jokingly compares him to Chuck Berry. This is likely a reference to one of Berry's occasional off-sync performances (such as "Vacation Time," which The Beatles perform later in these sessions). John explains his off-performance by indicating that he had been intentionally filling in Billy's part. In fact, Billy's absence causes the band to abandon serious attempts at "Get Back" until his late afternoon arrival. Paul then tries to remember the title of a song in which, as here, the musicians lose the beat. Both John and George recognise the song by Paul's description: a horrendous little tune called "Give Me Love" which was the b-side of "Angel Baby," a 1960 release by Rosie and the Originals. John manfully admits he's prone to missing beats.

The conversation then moves to the idea or a photo book from the sessions. It's important to note that, at this time, the book is simply a tie-in to the television broadcast rather than to a record album. John has designer John Kosh in mind to work with Ethan Russell's slides of The Beatles, which John gushes about, and which Paul admits he hasn't seen yet. John's indicates that he'll talk to John Kosh about it the following Monday - an indication that, at this point, John foresaw taking weekends off as they had at Twickenham. The conversation cuts off as John begins discussing Derek Taylor's role at Apple.

24.13 SOLDIER OF LOVE (0:30)
John takes the vocal lead on this ragged performance, with occasional help from Paul. John cannot remember *any* of the words beyond the first line.

24.14 medley CATHY'S CLOWN / SOLDIER OF LOVE /WHERE HAVE YOU BEEN >1:26)
The available tape begins with George vocalising the guitar part for "Cathy's Clown." Paul begins to sing that song, but is cut off by John who begins to sing "Soldier Of Love." George follows John's lead, but Paul turns the song back to "Cathy's Clown" as soon as he is able, with George singing back-up, although they seem to remember the words to "Cathy's Clown" only slightly better than "Soldier Of Love." After a single verse of this, John begins to sing the chorus of "Where Have You Been" (and remembers most of the words!). Paul concludes this mess by reprising a single line from "Soldier of Love."

"Soldier Of Love" was originally recorded by Arthur Alexander in 1962 and had been performed by The Beatles during a 1963 BBC radio broadcast. "Cathy's Clown" was a major hit for the Everly Brothers in 1960. "Where Have You Been" is another Arthur Alexander song from 1962. John will return to it later in the day. Both of these songs had been performed by The Beatles in their early live performances.

24.15 LOVE IS A SWINGIN' THING (0:10)
John is reminded of another song, but gets almost *all* of the words wrong this time.

It's interesting to follow The Beatles' stream of consciousness as they jump from oldie to oldie. In this case, they seemed to have even skipped a step. "Soldier Of Love" apparently brought the Shirelles' 1962 hit "Soldier Boy" to mind, but they've opted instead to play a cover of that song's *flipside*, "Love Is A Swingin' Thing."

24.16 medley WHAT'D I SAY / LOVE IS A SWINGIN' THING (0:40)
George is reminded of Ray Charles' "What'd I Say." He mentions the title of that song and proceeds to play it note for note behind John and Paul's "Love Is a Swingin' Thing" vocal.

24.17 ON THE ROAD TO MARRAKESH (1:44)
John gives a straightforward, unenthusiastic rendition of his 1968 composition. The band is horribly out of tune.

This is not a serious performance, since "On The Road to Marrakesh" was, at this point, no longer considered a contender for serious rehearsal. It differs little from the performance from the morning of the 2nd, except that John seems to have forgotten some of the lyrics.

24.18 TWO OF US (2:51)

This run-through is very likely part of the first attempt to rehearse the song at Apple. As with "I've Got A Feeling," The Beatles show little sign that they had nearly perfected the song at Twickenham. George has reverted to playing the slower tempo riff that he had played during the January 6th rehearsals, ignoring the advances the band had made during the sessions of the 8th and 9th. Paul experiments with various ways of playing the song and John leads the band through a disjointed rehearsal that is often interrupted for discussion about how the song should be performed.

John is concerned that the performances of "Two Of Us" are too stiff, and sings a few lines to show Paul how he would like the song to go. It's interesting to note that John has usurped Paul's role of band director for the moment, reshaping what is essentially one of Paul's compositions while Paul remains relatively silent. John evidently doesn't have the words in front of him, and has little idea what the correct words are. Halfway through this segment the group stops rehearsing the instrumental intro, and tries out a new ending for the song. After this brief diversion they return to rehearsing the first verse, and play this for a while before the available tape cuts off.

The next fragmentary dialogue exchange begins with Paul working out the lyrics for "Two Of Us." John jokes that the lyrics refer to drag queens and Paul kiddingly responds that perhaps Paul and Paula (an American male/ female singing duo) should perform the song instead of The Beatles. John and Paul each take a moment to kid each other with effeminate affectations before Paul once again begins to work on the lyrics for the song.

24.19 TWO OF US (0:03)

A few mangled guitar strums from the beginning of "Two Of Us," with a single line of parody lyric about being drag queens crammed into the music. This barely qualifies as a performance.

24.20 TWO OF US >0:03<

A brief fragment from what was very likely a long series of "Two Of Us" rehearsals.

This fragment is notable because it's the first available acoustic performance of "Two Of Us." The Beatles had discussed playing the song acoustically back on January 3rd, acting on a suggestion from Glyn. The idea was not implemented at that time because of the difficulty of staging acoustic performances in a live setting.

24.21 TEDDY BOY >3:52<

After a brief teaser during the session of January 9th, we have a full (perhaps too full) run-through of Paul's 1968 composition, performed virtually solo by him on acoustic guitar. The available tape begins in progress (although the lyrics are intact), and is only interrupted for a few seconds as Glyn breaks in over a loudspeaker and asks Paul to keep playing so that he can record the performance for posterity on multi-track tape. Paul obliges by starting over again from the first verse. The song cuts off on the available tape as the filmmaker's sound roll runs out, although the multi-track recording undoubtedly still resides somewhere in the E.M.I. archives.

"Teddy Boy" was written by Paul in India the previous year, and would never be officially released by The Beatles, although it would eventually appear on Paul's 1970 solo album *McCartney*. The title is a pun which refers both to the name of the song's lead character and to a style of tight pants and slicked back hair affected by some British teenagers in the early 1960's (including John and Paul).

24.22   TEDDY BOY   >7:30)
This lengthy performance begins with a brief instrumental fragment that may be the end of 24.21. This is followed immediately by a stop and start rehearsal, as Paul teaches the chords to George and John. It then flows into a full-fledged performance, with the other Beatles following along as best they can. As Paul goes through verse after verse, John begins to lose interest and breaks into a series of bogus square dance calls during the second instrumental break. As the performance finally winds down Paul offers the song for inclusion on their schedule.

Through Glyn's poor judgement this run-through (which has three of the four band members not even knowing how to play the song!) was mixed, edited and slated to appear on The Beatles aborted *Get Back* LP. A butchered version of it was finally released in 1996 on *Anthology 3*.

24.23   TEDDY BOY   (0:05)
Just seconds after the monumental performance above has ended Paul begins to play the song again. Everyone is spared another performance as Glyn interrupts to ask Paul if he wants to hear the tape played back. Paul wants to rehearse more first.

24.24   TEDDY BOY   (0:10)
Paul plays a brief skiffle arrangement and sings a few lines, obviously as a joke. He then recalls the genesis of "Teddy Boy," which was written in India the previous year. John is barely listening.

24.25   TEDDY BOY   (0:49)
A loose, basically instrumental rehearsal which allows Paul to (once again) show John the chords for the song. This ends with a brief reprise of Paul's skiffle riff.

24.26   "BALLS TO YOUR PARTNER"   (0:03)
Mal serves liquid refreshment too the group, undoubtedly alcoholic in nature. This inspires Paul to break into a traditional Liverpool drinking rhyme. From this point, the mood gets noticeably lighter for a while, as the performances loosen up and The Beatles have more fun.

24.27   ACH DU LIEBER AUGUSTIN   (0:03)
"Ach Du Lieber Augustin" is a traditional German folk song, whose tune is appropriated by Paul for use with another rude little rhyme about a certain Mister Bangelstein. "Bangelstein's Boys" was a television program about a rugby team which had aired on ITV the previous Saturday evening.

24.28   TEDDY BOY   (0:05)
Another short instrumental performance from Paul which quickly disintegrates into tuning. Paul suggests that they rehearse "Two Of Us" (and note that the title is "Two of us" here, not the original "On Our Way Home"). The

rest of the conversation is obscure, although one of John's comments concerns 'Magic Alex' Mardas.

24.29   TWO OF US   (0:18<

After a minute or so of tuning, Paul begins to play the introductory guitar part for the song. After a moment he stops, counts off and begins to play a proper take, but the available tape cuts off soon after.

Again, just a bit of a much lengthier series of "Two Of Us" rehearsals.

The next available tape features a discussion about the contents of a meal which the Beatles (and company) are considering ordering, presumably from Apple's own kitchen. In the middle of this Paul chimes in with an interesting anecdote about his career as a young carpenter. He mentions "Mother o'Mine," an English standard from 1903 with lyrics by Rudyard Kipling (although there have been a number of songs with similar titles).

24.30   TWO OF US   (0:40)

Paul sings several lines from the song while accompanying himself on acoustic guitar. He then vocalises a bit as he plays, and the tune begins to wander away from "Two Of Us" into aimless improvisation.

Meanwhile, the lunch discussion continues and we are given a rare opportunity to glimpse The Beatles' taste buds at work. In an interview with Ray Coleman (printed in the January 18th edition of *Disc and Music Echo*) John had talked about his current macro-biotic eating habits. It's not surprising there that he's interested in brown rice and vegetables for his meal. A few moments later, when it's (somehow) indicated to him that (despite Mal's assurances) the desired rice dish is not available, he suggests they just get some brown rice (he doesn't want white), and settles for Yoko's suggestion of a mushroom omelette with vegetables. George wants cheese sauce with his cauliflower. Ringo suggests mashed potatoes, and is jokingly castigated by John not to order them. Paul seems more concerned with the mechanics of being fed than with the content of the meal.

24.31   POLYTHENE PAM   (1:37)

As George completes the arrangements for lunch, John breaks into this performance of his own composition. He accompanies himself on acoustic guitar, and Paul joins in after a bit. Although he remembers the words, John keeps stopping and restarting the songs as if he can't quite remember how to play it. At the end, he meanders off into various unidentifiable riffs.

Like "On The Road to Marrakesh," "Give Me Some Truth" and "Mean Mr. Mustard," this is a relatively advanced Lennon composition that was not considered a serious candidate for rehearsal at these sessions (in this case, it seems, because John intended to give the song away to another group). Consequently, this is the only "Get Back" era performance of this number which has come down to us, although a '68 demo was released on *Anthology 3* and the song was, of course, recorded later in 1969 for *Abbey Road*.

John then refers to the futility of rehearsing with acoustic guitars with the knowledge that these instruments cannot be used in concert. In spite of this, Paul suggests that they continue the "Two Of Us" rehearsal, seemingly only worried that the others might be getting tired of it.

24.32   TWO OF US   (3:16)

The Beatles get down to business and attempt to record a releaseable take. Sadly, they fail miserably. No one seems quite sure of what tempo to play the song at, and George's bassline and Ringo's drumming fail to mesh.

Although this is a complete run-through, The Beatles could not have been pleased with this early attempt.

Despite the availability of superior takes, this performance was chosen for 1996's *Anthology 3* release.

24.33 (IMPROVISATION) / TWO OF US (1:14)

The other Beatles ignore Paul's suggestion, and begin playing a simple, repetitive improvisation, broken up here and there by some indecipherable falsetto vocals from George. Paul interjects the introductory guitar part for "Two Of Us," as if to remind the others to perform that song.

24.34 TWO OF US (3:30)

No one except Paul seems to be particularly concerned with the quality of their performance here. John messes up the words (as usual) and shows little effort to harmonise. Ringo stops playing altogether for about twenty seconds. Despite that, this is a complete performance, taken at a slightly slower tempo than usual. This also marks the first available appearance of the song's distinctive whistling outro.

Despite instructions that Paul gives to Glyn, the second of this day's attempts to 'take' the song have not yet begun. This was probably a last run-through before the official recordings began.

24.35 MAGGIE MAE (0:10)

John and Paul perform this number with the same sense of fun as "Balls to Your Partner" (24.26). This performance breaks down after a few lines. as John shouts something in response to one of the song's lyrics.

"Maggie Mae" derives from "Darling Nellie Gray," an 1856 minstrel song by American Benjamin Russell Hanby. The English corruption was recorded by The Vipers Skiffle Group in 1957.

Glyn advises the group that he's ready to begin serious taping. John jokingly (and correctly) refers to his vocal style during the latter part of "Two Of Us" as a mixture of Phil Ochs and Bob Dylan.

24.36 THE TWO OF US >2:11)

Another fun performance. John and Paul trade verses in over-enunciated British, Scottish, and Jamaican accents. John also manages to sneak in a reference to his infamous nude appearance on the "Two Virgins" record sleeve at one point.

24.37 MAGGIE MAE (0:58)

A charming performance. John and Paul are obviously having more fun performing "Maggie Mae" than "Two Of Us."

This was probably the tag to a performance of "Two Of Us" Which is not available (in fact, a significant amount of this particular "Two Of Us" session is missing). "Maggie Mae" is longer here than in any other available performance.

24.38 "I FANCY ME CHANCES' (0:27)

Without missing a beat, John and Paul go from "Maggie Mae" into this number. They remember very few of the lyrics beyond the title.

"I Fancy Me Chances" has not been identified. It may be a Lennon/McCartney composition, or even an improvisation.

The group still hasn't eaten. When Mal reminds them of this fact, John and Paul jokingly order a series of repulsive dishes (such as boiled testicle).

24.39   TWO OF US (3:23)
This take uses a less elaborate guitar intro than following performances. Although it's complete, this is a particularly lifeless attempt. John bemoans the fact that he keeps forgetting how to play the song and refers to Paul's comments about singing in a stiff manner (see entry 24.18).

24.40   TWO OF US (3:29)
After a brief false start, The Beatles offer a complete performance. This one is adequate (if again uninspired except for John's errors in the lyrics).

This take was presumably the last for the moment and marked 'best' on the multi-track tape box (even though they would return to the song later in the day). It was subsequently chosen by Glyn for inclusion on the unreleased "Get Back" LP.

24.41   MAGGIE MAE (0:36)
Another duet from John and Paul. Although it's lacking some of the energy of their earlier attempts, multiple tries have allowed them to agree on the lyrics.

This take was chosen by Glyn for *Get Back*, and included on the album *Let It Be*. It might be noted that despite the arrangers' credit they give themselves, there's no real difference between this and the 'traditional' skiffle arrangement.

Paul wonders whether they should stop and listen to playbacks of "Two Of Us," and then expresses his pleasure that the group is getting familiar enough with the songs that they can simply call out a title and play the song straight through.

It's very likely that at this point, The Beatles decided to pack it in and have lunch. Quite a long lunch, it seems, since they're away for the next two and a half to three hours. While we can only offer conjecture, it's possible that an Apple business meeting was held after the meal, which would explain their absence from the recording studio, and offer an opportunity for the contractual situation regarding Billy Preston to be resolved. When they finally *do* return, the first thing they do is spend some time reviewing their earlier recordings .

24.42   TEDDYBOY (playbacks) (0:41<
The Beatles are squeezed into the tiny Apple control room listening to a playback of 24.22. Paul is humming and singing along to the playback in spots while John and George both seem to be ignoring it completely.

This and the following listing are only considered as individual performances because Paul is 'performing' along with the playback.

24.43   TEDDY BOY (playback) >2:38)
A continuation of the playback, separated on the available tape by an edit. Paul continues to sing along in spots, apparently quite happy with his song.

John then asks Glyn why the multitrack recordings can't be mixed at the same time as they're recorded. When Glyn balks at this idea, John seems to suggest that they could use a second tape recorder to capture the feed from the live mix. However, we have no evidence this was actually ever attempted. In the middle of this discussion George offers his critique of the film-in-progress (probably continuing a topic he'd begun underneath the "Teddy Boy" playback), pointing out the monotony of the material they've filmed thus far. George is careful to explain that he's not suggesting having the film crew intrude *too* much, and points out that he doesn't want to be filmed eating. John completely ignores George's aversion to lunch being filmed, and enthusiastically embraces the idea of having the film crew record them not only eating, but waking up in the morning and even visiting the bathroom (Yoko helpfully points out that people are animals, too). John also makes the important observation that he's become used to the presence of the film crew. John and George then brainstorm for ideas to make Michael's film more interesting (Paul uncharacteristically has no suggestions to offer). George suggests that the filmmakers capture some wild angles in their shots. John wants them to film The Beatles leaving their homes in the morning - an idea which, in modified form, was taken up when footage was eventually shot (and used in "Let It Be") of each Beatle arriving at Apple studios. Once again, John's comments indicate that he had planned to take the weekend off (or at least assumed that the film crew would be doing so).

24.44   TWO OF US (playback)   (0:05<

A fragmentary tape of the first few seconds of the song. This is listed because it's a playback of a take which has not otherwise become available.

24.45   TWO OF US   >0:39)

The Beatles are back in the studio in the process of warming up. Paul sings a few lines of "Two Of Us" over a guitar backing John fumbles around on slide guitar, trying to get himself in tune. As he does so, Paul keeps playing the instrumental guitar intro to "Two Of Us" over and over, seemingly just to keep his fingers busy.

24.46   GET BACK   (0:13)

Spurred on by Ringo's drumming, Paul plays the instrumental introduction to "Get Back." The performance breaks down before the lyrics begin, and Paul moves immediately into the next tune.

24.47   (IMPROVISATION)   (0:12<

An instrumental improvisation with John fumbling along on guitar behind Paul. This appears to be a variant of "Two Of Us" and is similar to the early arrangement of that song played on January 2nd.

24.48   HER MAJESTY   >2:11)

Paul once again backs himself on acoustic guitar. Halfway through the song Ringo joins in on drums and John makes a very poor effort to follow along on slide guitar. Paul is singing in a falsetto sing-song voice, apparently feeling that his number is extremely cute.

When "Her Majesty" was eventually released on *Abbey Road* it ran only 23 seconds. There's no element here that isn't in that short performance. It's longer simply because Paul repeats the same single verse over and over.

During this, George asks Mal to help someone retrieve some quarter inch recording tape from storage. Our best guess is that George wants tape in order to make personal copies of the multi-track recordings. This type of recording tape was also used for the Nagra which was being used to record the film soundtrack, but the fact that he only needs one reel would be inconsistent with that use.

John and George also discuss some obscure implement that fits (or doesn't fit) on their respective fingers. This probably relates to the implement that John's using to play slide guitar.

24.49   "THERE YOU ARE, EDDIE"   (4:03)

As the previous performance ends. Paul offers up another of his own compositions for acoustic guitar, this time a gentle folk tune. The lyrics to this song are deceptively simple as Paul sings about a dog named Eddie. John laughs and exclaims that Paul has written another song about his dog (Paul had written "Martha My Dear" the previous year). He and Paul then sing a few choruses, replacing the name Eddie with Tiger, Bernard, Nigel, and finally Mimi (who's a cat).

"There You Are, Eddie" has a simple structure that has more in common with some of Donovan's songs than anything The Beatles ever recorded. This would hardly be surprising, since The Beatles and Donovan had visited India together the previous year, and Paul had attended Donovan's sessions at Trident studios the previous November. Influences aside, the song is not that different structurally from Paul's earlier performances of "Teddy Boy" and "Her Majesty." In each of these performances he takes a very simple lyric and repeats it over and over. Yet the lyric may not be as simple as it appears, as it seems to revolve around an actual person (unnamed) that Paul has ill feelings toward. One of the names that John suggests, Nigel, is a reference to the poem "Good Dog Nigel," which appeared in his 1964 book *In His Own Write*. 'Mimi' (introduced to the song by Paul is a reference to John's Aunt Mimi Smith who raised him. This song was never released and, except for a brief reprise later in the day, was never again performed, to our knowledge.

24.50   EVERY NIGHT (2:15)
Paul continues to run through the McCartney songbook. John asks what key the song is in, and once again proceeds to offer extremely poor accompaniment on slide guitar. Although the song has potential, the lyrics and tune are unfinished at this point, and the performance is unfocused. Paul segues this song directly into the next.

"Every Night" was recorded the following year for Paul's first solo LP, *McCartney*. It had already been given a brief workout at the session of the 22nd.

24.51   "PILLOW FOR YOUR HEAD" (2:28<
Paul sings a clearly unfinished lyric, very little of which is decipherable beyond the title, which he repeats a number of times. John, having given up trying to follow along, is simply playing whatever comes into his head.

It's unclear whether this embryonic love song was to have been part of "Every Night," or a separate song. In any case, it was never commercially released, and (except for the following fragment) no other unreleased performances have come to light.

24.52   "PILLOW FOR YOUR HEAD" >0:54<
This is obviously a continuation of the loose rehearsal begun in 24.51. It is separated from that track by a break in the available tape.

24.53   HOT AS SUN >1:23)
Having apparently exhausted his arsenal of new songs, Paul reaches back to this very early composition which he had written in the late 1950's. It's basically an instrumental, although Paul mumbles some nonsensical lyrics throughout. The other Beatles are familiar with the song and offer a reasonably good performance.

It should be remembered that a rage for exotic music existed in the 1950s (when this song was written). This tune is very much a part of that tradition, in this instance Polynesian in inspiration. This song would be revived once again in 1970 as an instrumental for Paul's first solo album *McCartney*.

24.54   CATSWALK (0:01<

Only the first five notes of the guitar intro.

"Hot As Sun" has reminded Paul of other early Lennon/McCartney compositions, and he asks John how one of them ("Looking Glass") went. John says that he doesn't remember, and Paul makes the point that all of the early numbers sounded the same anyway. This said, he demonstrates by playing the first few notes of the early Lennon/McCartney composition "Catswalk." Unfortunately, the available tape cuts off almost immediately after he begins to play. Although The Beatles never properly recorded or released this composition, it was given by Paul to Chris Barber's Jazz Band, who released it in 1968 under the title "Catcall."

24.55   I LOST MY LITTLE GIRL >5:03<

The nostalgia trip through the prehistoric Lennon/McCartney catalogue continues with a performance of this song, which Paul has repeatedly claimed was the first one he ever wrote. Surprisingly enough, it's John who takes the lead vocal here, with Paul occasionally prompting him on the lyrics or singing backup. The effect is completely charming, and John's sense of fun is contagious. George provides the rhythm on electric guitar and offers a brief solo. Towards the end of the available tape (which is fragmentary on both ends), the performance edges towards an instrumental. The tune here reminds one of Donovan's "Season Of The Witch."

24.56   TWO OF US (0:02)

This fragment consists of only a few notes from the instrumental introduction.

After having given it extensive rehearsal earlier in the day, The Beatles return to "Two Of Us." This series of "Two Of Us" rehearsals was neither lengthy nor (as far as we can tell) preserved on multi-track tape.

24.57   TWO OF US (3:28)

With the after-lunch frivolity out of the way, The Beatles attempt a serious take. Unfortunately John and Paul's vocals are poorly miked, making John distant and Paul virtually inaudible. They run through a complete version of the song, but the performance is a bit too restrained to be very good and more polishing is clearly needed.

24:58   TWO OF US (0:03)

Once again, we hear only the first few notes of the song before the available tape cuts off. During the course of this John jokes about smoking marijuana.

24.59   medley TAKE THIS HAMMER / LOST JOHN / FIVE FEET HIGH AND RISING / "BEAR CAT" / BLACK DOG BLUES / RIGHT STRING, WRONG YO-YO / RUN FOR YOUR LIFE >8:49)

The Beatles take a break from "Two Of Us" rehearsals and have a little fun with this hodge-podge of oldies. To begin with, John takes the band into a slow version of Lonnie Donegan's 1959 "Take This Hammer" (he had also led an electric performance of the song on the 14th). Paul and George sing along (although George characteristically neglects to sing into his mike). This gives way to Donegan's 1956 "Lost John," with John again taking the vocal lead. George then steps forward vocally and steers the band into Johnny Cash's 1959 "Five Feet High and Rising." They all remember the song (though not much of it), so John moves them onto the traditional "Black Dog Blues" with almost no difference in the instrumental backing. George, with

John's help, offers a few lines from "Right String, Wrong Yo-Yo" (which they had covered more substantially on the 6th) before John takes a decided left turn and sings the entire first verse of his 1965 composition "Run For Your Life" in a duet with Paul. After a brief reprise of "Black Dog Blues" the medley finally winds down.

24.60   medley TWO OF US / HELLO, GOODBYE   >0:21)

As they finish playing the concluding bars of "Two Of Us " Paul breaks into the coda of his 1967 composition, incorporating some of the "Two Of Us" tune.

24.61   DIGGING MY POTATOES   (0:50)

Instead of capping off "Two of Us" with "Maggie Mae," as they had earlier, the group follows it with a different skiffle tune. This flows into the next performance without pause.

Paul and John share lead vocals as they gleefully rip through a trilogy of skiffle classics (this and the following two songs are performed in tandem). Like many skiffle songs, "Diggin' My Potatoes" was based on an American folk tune. Lonnie Donegan recorded a version in 1956, from which The Beatles undoubtedly learned it.

24.62   HEY LILEY, LILEY LO   (0:09)

Paul breaks into a few lines from this catchy skiffle tune, before John leads him into the next performance.

"Hey Liley, Liley Lo" was originally released by The Vipers Skiffle Group in 1957.

24.63   ROCK ISLAND LINE   (1:06)

Obviously delighted to be playing old skiffle songs, the band breaks into a joyful cover of Lonnie Donegan's arrangement of this American folk standard. John's slide guitar finally meshes with Paul's acoustic, making this performance very enjoyable.

Lonnie Donegan's 1956 recording of "Rock Island Line" energised a generation of British youth and got the proto-rock n' roll ball rolling, at least as far as Great Britain was concerned. The influence of this number cannot be over-emphasised. It popularised skiffle in the U. K., and directly led to the formation of hundreds of amateur skiffle bands, among them John's first group, The Quarrymen.

24.64   (IMPROVISATION) / (UNKNOWN)   (0:20<

The first part of this consists of a wordless lullaby, vocalised by Paul as he accompanies himself on acoustic guitar. This develops into an unidentifiable number which quickly cuts off on the available tape.

24.65   MICHAEL ROW THE BOAT   (1:00)

After a brief pause, The Beatles return to Lonnie Donegan, in this case covering his 1961 interpretation of this traditional spiritual. Paul begins singing, but only remembers one line, and mumbles his way through the forgotten verses. This performance runs right into "Rock-A-Bye Baby (which in turn runs into "Singing The Blues").

24.66   ROCK-A-BYE BABY   (0:17)

One of the oldest cover versions of the 'Get Back' session canon. Spurred on by some slide guitar licks from John, Paul vocalises a few bars of this lullaby as "Michael Row The Boat" concludes.

"Rock-a-Bye Baby" dates from 1884 from the pen of one Effie I. Canning, with lyrics adapted from 1765's book *Mother Goose's Melodies.*

24.67   SINGING THE BLUES (2:38)

Paul takes the lead vocal on this fine performance and Billy makes his presence known for the first time this day, playing keyboards. Paul obviously knows this song by heart and this performance is marred only by John's sloppy work on the slide guitar.

Written by Arkansas song-writer Melvin Endsley, "Singing The Blues" was an American hit for Marty Robbins in 1956. It was almost immediately covered by Guy Mitchell, whose version of the song was *also* a hit, both in the U.S. and U.K, making Mitchell's version the influential one.

24.68   KNEE DEEP IN THE BLUES (0:07)

"Knee Deep in The Blues" was the follow up single to "Singing The Blues" for both Marty Robbins and Guy Mitchell. Like that tune, it was written by Melvin Endsley. Unfortunately, Glyn interrupts Paul's performance after only one line.

24.69   DIG IT (0:45<

At this point, "Dig It" is little more than a loose improvisation with the musicianship being something less than impressive. The jam has barely started before this fragment cuts off.

"Dig It" was, at this point, a far different song than the version heard on The Beatles' "Let It Be" album, sounding more like a cross between the traditional "Sailor's Hornpipe" and a slowed down rendition of Neal Hefti's "Batman," as played on slide guitar. Two days later The Beatles would record a radically different version of this song. Despite John's announcement of the song as "Can You Dig It," we've chosen to use the more familiar title.

24.70   DIG IT >0:12<

This fragment is probably part of the same performance as 24.69, captured on tape as the sound technicians changed reels. Paul has now joined in on vocals, singing very close to the mike in order to distort his voice. Neither Paul nor John is singing anything more profound than the title, or variants thereof.

24.71   DIG IT (0:17)

After a *Laugh-In* style spoken intro, this performance breaks down shortly after it begins for unknown reasons.

John's slide playing reminds Paul of American blues.

24.72   DIG IT (4:07)

John adds a few more phrases to the lyric and Paul interjects a light-hearted mock-radio announcement that the performance is coming straight from Chicago, featuring the famous blues musician Blind Lame Lennon. The performance isn't too bad, even though (as Paul remarks at one point) John is out of tune. John wraps up the improvisation, chuckles, and compliments the others for a job well done.

24.73   DIG IT (4:56)

Slightly less cohesive than the last performance, this one is distinguished by Billy's participation. It is more of an instrumental than the earlier takes, and the band seems to be making a conscious effort to induce seasickness upon the listener. Following the performance, John offers a mock-announcement of his own, as he introduces the previous song as "Can You Dig It" by Georgie Wood and the next song as "Hark, The Angels Come." This line was grafted to the January 26th performance of "Dig It" and released on the album "Let it Be" Little Georgie Wood was a British novelty singer. "Hark The Angels Come" is presumably a corruption of Mendelssohn's "Hark The Herald Angels Sing."

The Beatles then direct the rearrangement of their equipment. John suggests they do "Get Back" as Billy noodles on the keyboard.

24.74   GET BACK (0:59<

This is essentially an instrumental performance, which Billy edges towards improvisation. It features only one line of lyric (the wrong lyric, we might add) sung off-mike by John.

This is the only available performance of "Get Back" which features slide guitar, and it's also very likely the last slide guitar performance of the day. As we can hear on the next available series of tapes, The Beatles are setting up their equipment in a different playing arrangement in preparation for rehearsing "Get Back" (to which they can turn now that Billy has arrived). As usual, this is not accomplished without the problems of loose patch chords, unacceptable microphone levels and undesirable feedback.

A few hours earlier, The Beatles had discussed paying Billy for his work on the sessions (see entry 24.5). Now that Billy has arrived, Paul addresses the subject directly. Unfortunately, Billy's response is not picked up on the tape.

John seems more concerned about getting his guitar to function.

24.75   GET BACK (2:50)

A complete performance which is workmanlike at best and embarrassing at worst. Billy sounds unsure of his solo, John's guitar solo is wretched, and even Paul doesn't seem to be putting much into this one.

24.76   "THERE YOU ARE, EDDIE" (0:14)

A brief a capella performance from Paul. Ringo begins playing the introduction to "Get Back" near the end of this, but no one joins in.

The dialogue continues. As he had at Twickenham, Paul worries about the images that are being captured. He's probably noticed that the cameramen have been taking very brief shots, and fears that a rather disjointed film will result. Michael, however, not only assures Paul that they're filming master shots (which they can dub any-old-dialogue over, since you can't see The Beatles' lips move), but are recording long shots of each of the four Beatles equally. This doesn't seem to impress Paul, and he indicates that he'd prefer a static film that doesn't jump around from subject to subject. Characteristically Michael rushes to agree, even though those properties are the antithesis of "Let It Be" as it was finally assembled.

24.77   GET BACK (0:06)

There are various "Get Back" riffs going on underneath the previous exchange which have not been included in the timing here. "Get Back" is sung by Paul with an appropriate instrumental flourish (complete with cymbal crash from Ringo) as a lead-in to a series of more proper rehearsals. Mal checks John's equipment as technical problems continue to plague them.

24.78   GET BACK (0:36)

Another pseudo-performance. A series of "Get Back" guitar riffs punctuated by Paul testing his vocal mike level. As soon as Paul's satisfied that the mike's performing properly, he stops fooling around and counts down for a proper performance. Various other brief riffs surface here as well, including "Ticket to Ride" and "(I Can't Get No) Satisfaction."

24.79 GET BACK (2:49)

A complete run-through of the song. John continues to have problems with his guitar, and neglects to play most of the first solo. Billy seems to be struggling a bit with the song. There is noise from a loose patch chord heard throughout. Half way through this lackadaisical performance, Paul starts whooping, much as he had in the earlier performances of "Get Back" on January 9th. As a serious take, this one was dead on arrival.

John remarks that he slept through the solo (i.e., he forgot to play). John and Paul are both dissatisfied with their mike levels.

24.80   medley GET BACK / LITTLE DEMON /MAYBELLENE / YOU CAN'T CATCH ME / BROWN EYED HANDSOME MAN (2:14)

This is truly a medley. It starts out as "Get Back," which continues (in instrumental form, with variations) for the rest of the performance, as lyrics from various other songs are grafted on. Paul starts out singing a few lines of up-tempo a capella "Get Back" lyric from the first verse of the song. As the other Beatles join in, this develops into an exaggerated double-time arrangement, as Paul whoops out some nonsense syllables. This reminds him of Screamin' Jay Hawkins' "Little Demon". He sings a single verse, but can barely remember any of the words.

The performance almost peters out, but Paul keeps the bass line running, and begins to sing Chuck Berry's "Maybellene." When he momentarily stumbles on the lyric, John picks up the slack with a few half-remembered lines from Berry's "You Can't Catch Me." Paul throws in another three lines from "Maybellene," before leading the band into a sloppy instrumental break, more like "Get Back" than anything else. After Paul sings a single further line from "Maybellene," John continues the Chuck Berry thread with "Brown Eyed Handsome Man," with Paul joining in on the chorus. This begins to develop into another instrumental break, which quickly breaks down.

As we indicated above, "Maybellene," "You Can't Catch Me" and "Brown Eyed Handsome Man" were all written and recorded by Chuck Berry. "Maybellene" was Berry's first single in 1955, while "You Can't Catch Me" followed later that year. "Brown Eyed Handsome Man," also briefly covered by The Beatles during the session of the 2nd, was originally released in 1956.

Following this performances John asks Glyn for another mike, and Paul asks for his to be turned up. Obviously, the equipment is *still* not operating to The Beatles' satisfaction.

24.81   SHORT FAT FANNIE (1:21)

John takes the lead vocal on this performance. After completing one verse he gives way to Paul and George, who whistles the rest of the song. The musicianship is quite competent here, but John's recollection of the lyrics is not nearly as strong as George's was during the performance of the 3rd. Near the end, someone is playing high pitched harmonies on his guitar, which reminds John of a piano. Paul calls out for "Get Back" and once again requests more volume on his mike.

24.82   GET BACK (0:05)

A brief a capella parody from John, who inserts the name Efrem B. Zimbalist into the song. Zimbalist was a renowned classical violinist. His son, Efrem

Zimbalist Jr. was a contemporary singer and actor, and starred in the American television program *The F.B.I.* John is probably referring to the latter.

Glyn tells Paul that he'll adjust the mike level once Paul starts singing.

24.83   GET BACK   (1:33<

A strong performance, unfortunately cut off on the available tape during the second verse. Billy seems to have composed himself and is playing better. John manages a fine solo during the first instrumental break.

The next group of performances are contained within an unusually intact segment of tape (nearly 32 minutes). Glyn has been joined by Geoff Emerick and George Martin, making one of their rare appearances. Much of the following is dedicated to setting the sound levels and preparing the instruments for a more serious attempt at recording. Wrapped around these events are the expected riffs, tuning, and oldies that The Beatles invariably played when not engaged in serious business.

24.84   GREEN ONIONS   (0:07)

Billy plays a brief riff from this instrumental which was a hit for Booker T. & The MGs in 1962.

24.85   GET BACK   (0:41)

This is more of an outgrowth of The Beatles' attempt at tuning than anything else. The 'performance' features Billy warming up with an assortment of riffs from "Get Back," punctuated by occasional guitar riffs and a steady hi-hat beat from Ringo, which leads into the next (more proper) performance of the song.

24.86   GET BACK   (3:19)

A complete performance which sounds close to the take The Beatles would ultimately release as a single, except that the tempo is slower, and the musicianship is a bit less tight than one would desire. This *does*, however, sound like a legitimate attempt by the group to record the song, particularly Paul who is singing here rather than simply filling in the words in their proper places. Oddly enough, the take is ruined by Billy's poor solo (which is usually quite competent). John's second guitar solo is also quite awful. As a coda, John leads Ringo and Billy into a jazz instrumental improvisation vehicle which draws to a close with a chuckle from John. Someone recalls the song's political overtones and applies them to Reykjavik, probably thinking of Great Britain's dispute with Iceland over territorial fishing rights (known at the time as "cod wars"). The discussion then turns to the matter of guitars (with a few notes from "Get Back" and a lot of aimless tuning thrown in). John asks Kevin Harrington for some new plects (i.e., plectrums, another term for guitar picks), and Paul describes a problem he has with one of his guitars - it's strung backwards (which enables the left-handed Paul to play it), but retains the right-hand oriented nut, a grooved, angled piece on the fretboard which keeps the strings spaced properly. Because of the inappropriate angle of this piece when the guitar is reversed (turned upside down), Paul has problems with the strings slipping off.

24.87   BAD BOY   (3:18)

Evidently growing bored with the guitar discussion, John begins playing "Bad Boy," and actually remembers most of the words. Along with Ringo's drumming, this performance features some uninspired accompaniment from Billy, and occasional vocal contributions from Paul. It breaks down for a few moments as Paul and the engineer have a discussion about setting the levels of Paul's bass, but picks up again, leading into an extended instrumental. John sings the last verse as Paul and the engineer continue their discussion about levels. John plays around with the lyrics (as usual) and the performance concludes with some extended tuneless riffs, not included in the timing above.

"Bad Boy" was originally recorded by Larry Williams in 1959. The Beatles covered the song on their 1965 U.S. LP "Beatles VI."

Paul continues to discuss the problem with the nut on his guitar. He wants a screwdriver to pry the offending piece off and turn it over, which would fix the problem.

24.88   SWEET LITTLE SIXTEEN   (1:47)

While Paul and George continue to discuss the technical problems with the engineer, John begins to sing this cover version of Chuck Berry's classic. Ringo and Billy join in at the second verse, and continue playing throughout the tune. Ringo does a fine job emulating the distinctive rifle cymbal heard in Berry's original. Without pause, this leads into the next performance. "Sweet Little Sixteen" was originally recorded by Chuck Berry in 1958. The Beatles performed the song during their early live career and on the BBC, but never professionally recorded it.

24.89   AROUND AND AROUND   (1:04)

Since "Around and Around" is essentially "Sweet Little Sixteen" with different lyrics, the transition between the two is exceptionally smooth. Except for one verse (in which he basically stops singing) John once again remembers most of the words. At one point, Paul vocalises the piano part for the song. Paul is finally satisfied with his mike.

"Around and Around" was recorded by Chuck Berry in 1958.

24.90   ALMOST GROWN   (1:45)

John's trip through the Chuck Berry catalogue continues. Paul and George offer spirited backing vocals supporting this fine performance. The whole band is finally involved. The final verse of the song is played as an instrumental - either John has remembered all of the words that he's able to, or he's tired of singing.

"Almost Grown" was recorded by Chuck Berry in 1959.

Paul has given up the idea of fixing his own guitar, but determines to have it fixed the next day. George Martin, temporarily taking over for Glyn as producer, is still unsatisfied with the levels (or concerned with Paul's satisfaction). The session is beginning to run longer than usual, and Martin comments upon this fact, assuring the crew that the rehearsal won't last much longer, and reminding them that the band has gone overtime before. In response to Martin's request, Paul begins repeating a single note on his bass guitar in order to set the levels. John picks up on the tempo of this for the introduction to the next song.

24.91   SCHOOL DAY   (1:30)

John leads the band into another Chuck Berry song. He makes it through the first verse without a hitch, but begins to stumble on the words when he reaches the second. Paul joins in on vocals, but neither of them can remember very much more than the final verse. Nevertheless, this is still an enjoyable, spirited performance.

"School Day" was originally recorded by Chuck Berry in 1956.

Paul then mentions that he's hungry - another indication that the rehearsal's run overtime - but wants to do "Get Back" once more so they can pretend they've accomplished something. Both he and John appear to realise that they haven't had the most productive of afternoons. George obviously wants to leave.

24.92   medley STAND BY ME / WHERE HAVE YOU BEEN (2:34)

Once again, John picks up on a bass riff from Paul and starts singing this oldie, accompanied instrumentally by Ringo and Billy. Although he's involved in conversation with the engineer during the early part of the song, Paul sings along during the first chorus, and the performance gels (however briefly). In response to a question about his phrasing, Paul keeps singing the word 'darling' over and over in an American accent as John leads them into the chorus for "Where Have You Been."

Loose as it is, this is still a much better rendition of "Stand By Me" than The Beatles gave on January 8th. "Where Have You Been" had been performed earlier in the day, also as part of a medley. This suggests that John has forgotten the verses.

John sings a single illustrative line from "Lady Madonna," evidently remembering another instance where Paul sang with an American accent. He then remembers that they've pledged to give "Get Back" one more try, and seems to want to spur the band on to that performance. Paul, however, responds with a couple of lines from "Lovely Rita."

24.93   LADY MADONNA (0:03)

A single line sung by John (with Paul joining in on the last word), accompanied by a few strums on the guitar. This tests the outer limits of our definition of performance.

"Lady Madonna" was a single for The Beatles in 1968.

24.94   medley LOVELY RITA / GET BACK (0:09)

Two lines from Paul, sang with an illustrative nasal twang to the accompaniment of several riffs from "Get Back."

"Lovely Rita" was, of course, one of Paul's compositions for The Beatles 1967 LP *Sgt. Pepper's Lonely Hearts Club Band."*

24.95   GET BACK (5:59)

This is really two performances rolled into one. In general, this take is relaxed, assured, and fun. The musicianship is fine, particularly during the first half, and particularly from Billy. Paul and John both seem to be having a great time. When the song reaches the point where Ringo's drum fill would normally introduce the coda, Ringo misses his cue entirely and John takes over on guitar, prompting Paul to begin the song from the top, without missing a beat. The second half here is sloppier than the first, but still fun, leading toward a brief instrumental improvisation (led by Billy), and concluding with various improvised exhortations from Paul, referring to the clock and telling the others that it's time to go home.

Although undocumented in Mark Lewisohn's *The Beatles Recording Sessions* book, several elements strongly indicate that this, the day's final version of "Get Back," was preserved on multi-track tape (for instance, a direct comment from John that Glyn is taping which follows 24.93). This performance of "Get Back" was broadcast on U.S. radio in 1969, which may suggest that someone walked off with the master tape.

John (never one for improvisation) complains about the extended performance of "Get Back" as Paul remarks upon the film crew's practice of wiping
the film slates blank at the end of each day (the film slates held such information as the slate number, date and a count of the number of days that filming
had taken place).

Everyone except John (and the sound crew) is evidently preparing to leave,
prompting Paul's pointed comment that it's seven o'clock and time to go
home. John chooses to sit around and play various instrumentals and riffs -
not an uncommon way for one of these sessions to end.

Obviously, by this time it's been decided to hold Saturday rehearsals.

24.96   LONELY SEA (1:34)
John plays this gentle number to himself as the others prepare to leave.

"Lonely Sea" was originally recorded by The Beach Boys in 1963. Surprisingly, this is the only Beach Boys cover to have surfaced from these sessions.
This is prefaced by a few seconds of aimless riffing, and followed by another
minute of riffs, none of which can properly be called a song.

24.97   (UNKNOWN) (0:59)
This is the only one of this particular series of solo guitar 'performances'
which can rightfully be considered a song. It's an up-tempo rock and roll tune,
which John seems to enjoy playing. After this, he returns to playing riffs, this
time from "All Things Must Pass," "Get Back" and "I've Got A Feeling."

Michael wishes them a good night and the session ends.

Saturday, January 25th, 1969

The session of the 25th centred around three songs, "Two of Us," "Let It Be" and "For You Blue." While work on the first two wavered uneasily between rehearsals and attempts at recording, The Beatles approached "For You Blue" with complete focus and recorded a number of releaseable takes.

With several exceptions, the available source tapes from this day are extremely fragmentary. This is because they generally come from work prints from the day's rushes, as opposed to after-the-fact edits derived from the raw Nagra reels. The rushes were fragmentary because the camera crew was still only attempting to capture shots, rather than record entire performances.

The availability of source material for this and the following four days is extremely limited, and the reconstructions of these days should be considered preliminary pending additional source material.

25.1   ON THE ROAD AGAIN >0:41<
George and John sing a few lines off-mike. This mess degenerates almost entirely into aimless riffing, except towards the very end of the fragment, where it veers back into the song.
   "On The Road Again" had been a hit for Canned Heat in 1968.

25.2   (UNKNOWN) >0:10)
A few seconds of instrumental blues which echoes both "I'm a Man" and "Mannish Boy." Unless a longer tape surfaces, this cannot be definitively identified.
   The next available tape comes approximately an hour into the session. Paul finds that his suggestion to work on the middle eight of "Two Of Us" is met by no response *whatsoever*, so he sarcastically answers himself. This suggests that although the band members aren't fighting, they're not communicating either.

25.3   (IMPROVISATION) (0:52)
John and Ringo fill time with this banal, off-key improvisation while the other band members change instruments to prepare for the "Two Of Us" rehearsal. John's electric guitar noodling is reminiscent of the chord sequences he'd used for "Julia" and "I've Got a Feeling." George sings faintly in the background as the performance winds down.

25.4   (IMPROVISATION) (0:30)
John and Ringo play another improvisation - this time a more up-beat instrumental. Paul has received his acoustic guitar and is in the process of tuning it when John stops playing.

25.5   ANOTHER DAY (0:35)
Paul offers a half-hearted performance of his song, as Ringo tries to follow him (in vain). Halfway through the second verse John interrupts to let Paul know he is ready to play 'Two Of Us."
   Paul had performed "Another Day" on the piano on the 9th, but uses an acoustic guitar here.

25.6   TWO OF US (13:09<

A lengthy (and quite loose) rehearsal of the song's middle eight. This segment begins as Glyn inquires about their plans, wondering, no doubt, if they're serious enough to want to commit some part of their performance to multi-track tape. John quickly says they're not and the rehearsal gets underway. Paul points out that the middle eight needs elaboration, and vocalises one to George. Paul and John acknowledge to George that the riff is best suited for bass, but neither suggests that George play it on the bass strings of his guitar (which is how the problem is eventually solved), although Paul suggests he could play it in a blues style. Because of John's request to continue they repeatedly go over the riff behind the first line of the middle eight, and over five minutes pass before they venture further into the song. After singing a verse badly out of key (perhaps in response to John's poorly tuned guitar), they run through the middle eight several more times. John punctuates their serious rehearsals of the middle eight by clowning with the verse, offering a histrionic vocal, a couple of verses of Dylan imitation, and a French accent (which prompts Paul to count in for the middle eight in German). There are also a number of instrumental tries during which neither John nor Paul cares to sing. Despite all of the kidding around, their playing grows progressively tighter.

25.7 TWO OF US >0:32<
The rehearsal continues. John and Paul harmonise nicely as they experiment with the song by singing in a higher octave than usual. John is obviously having a fine time, and drops two 'sock it to me's into the lyric, quoting the popular catch phrase from *Laugh-In*.

As The Beatles rehearse, Yoko moves behind one of Ringo's drum baffles, tacks up sheets of paper, and paints Japanese ideograms.

25.8 BYE BYE LOVE >0:02<
Unfortunately, the available tape is nothing more than a very brief snippet of a longer performance. John and Paul harmonise on one line of the song and the tape cuts off.

"Bye Bye Love," a 1957 hit for The Everly Brothers, was probably brought to mind because its vocal harmonies are similar to those that John and Paul are attempting to achieve on "Two of Us." This entire performance is reported to have been preserved on multi-track tape in the E.M.I. archives.

25.9 TWO OF US (0:22<
This begins with a 7 second false start which breaks down during the guitar introduction. They begin the song again from the top, but the available tape cuts off during the second line of the song.

The existence of a false start suggests that they're trying for a 'real' performance.

25.10 TWO OF US >0:51<
This excerpt picks up right before the middle eight. As on 25.9, the band has temporarily stopped clowning around, and is trying for a more serious take.

25.11 TWO OF US >0:16)
The available tape edits in at the song's conclusion, which suggests that this may be part of the previous performance. John whistles as the song draws to a close, an element which, of course, was kept in the final arrangement.

Paul then asks Glyn's opinion of The Beatles' performance, and despite his positive reaction Paul feels that they are not quite ready to record a finished version of the song. He opts instead for further rehearsal of the middle eight.

25.12   TWO OF US   (0:06<
Paul tries to start the song at the second middle eight but begins at the wrong place. He apologises and the available tape cuts off.

25.13   TWO OF US   >3:13<
The Beatles continue to rehearse the middle eight. John and Paul repeat a single line again and again, only once foraying beyond the middle eight.

25.14   TWO OF US   >2:00)
Five to ten minutes have passed since the precious rehearsal fragment, as we edit into a performance in progress. John calls out for them to play the chorus and end the song, but Paul interrupts to discuss his idea for a guitar fill. John and Paul agree that John should play short guitar fills while Paul continues to play the basic rhythm. Paul suggests that John co-ordinate his efforts with Ringo's drum fills. This concept was eventually assimilated into the song, but in a very toned-down manner. Following this brief discussion, they continue to play from the middle eight.

25.15   TWO OF US   >0:10<
Paul sings a few lines while John weakly chimes in, beginning to sound bored.

25.16   TWO OF US   >0:14<
Another brief excerpt severely truncated on the available tape. John and Paul sing a few lines of the chorus before the performance cuts off.

25.17   TWO OF US   >0:06<
This fragment of the song's ending is probably part of the previous performance, once again severely fragmented

25.18   TWO OF US   >0:33)
Another fragment. John fools around a bit with the lyrics and Paul mentions the connected themes of ("Get Back, "Two of Us," Don't Let Me Down" and "Oh! Darling." John agrees, and jokes that he and Paul need to be lovers for "Oh! Darling." Paul says he was planning to wear a skirt on the show in any ease.

Although there's a considerable gap in the available tapes at this point, it's a safe assumption that at least some of tile time was spent on preliminary attempts at "For You Blue." For that number, George has switched to acoustic guitar, Paul is on piano, and John plays slide guitar.

25.19   FOR YOU BLUE   (2:16)
It appears that this performance grows out of a loose rehearsal which has not otherwise become available. The band's less-than-precise playing actually adds a measure of charm to this performance, with the exception of John's poor slide guitar solo in the instrumental break.

This is a complete performance, and most likely the first take of "For You Blue" committed to multi-track tape. It was released in 1996 on *Anthology 3*.

25.20   FOR YOU BLUE   (2:31)
Although quite passable, this performance has the earmarks of an early take. Everyone sounds slightly unsure of their parts, and George's vocal is strained and uneasy. The piano is undermiked.

The middle eight was excised from this performance and grafted onto a different performance (25.23-24) in the film *Let It Be*.

25.21   FOR YOU BLUE   (0:26)

George plays the song's introduction and begins to sing. He messes up the words of the second line and the performance breaks down.

25.22 FOR YOU BLUE (2:36)

After a brief pause they start the song again from the top. As Paul plays during the instrumental break George calls out the name Bluthner, a reference to the brand of piano that's being played. John turns in a nice guitar solo, and George's vocal is more confident than in 25.20.

25.23 FOR YOU BLUE >1:31<

This performance is a bit more polished than 25.22, but there's still obviously room for improvement. Tile available tape cuts off at the beginning of the second verse, which was edited from the film *Let It Be*.

25.24 FOR YOU BLUE 0:23)

The final (third) verse of the song, used in the film *Let It Be* in lieu of the second verse. This is most likely from the same performance as 25.23, but there's no way to verify this unless an unedited source tape surfaces someday.

25.25 FOR YOU BLUE (2:52)

This take is prefaced by the sound of someone rattling the ice cubes in his glass, and a brief false start.

This performance is much tighter than the previous two. John in particular is more restrained on his slide guitar solo.

This take was used both for the unreleased *Get Back* LP, and (with a re-recorded vocal) for the *Let It Be* album. This would lead one to assume it was certainly the best (and probably last) take, instrumentally speaking.

Following the performance, John compares his slide playing to blues guitarist Jimmy Reed. The Beatles then head into the control room to hear playbacks. John picks up part of a mike holder and jokingly describes it as an invention of 'Magic' Alex Mardas. Glyn, in turn, jokes that it's a twenty-channel mixer (referring to Alex's failed attempt to build a mixing console). Shortly before the available tape cuts off, Glyn resumes playbacks of "For You Blue," starting the tape at Paul's piano break.

25.26 TAKE THIS HAMMER (0:08)

George offers this brief performance as The Beatles converse. He's backed by John banging on the side of the mixing console.

The Beatles head back into the studio. John sits cross-legged on the floor and takes up bass in order to rehearse "Let It Be." George plays standing up, as he had for "For You Blue." Yoko keeps interrupting John in order to kiss him.

25.27 EARLY IN THE MORNING (0:24)

This is nothing more than a short warm-up, with George taking the lead vocal.

"Early In The Morning" was performed and composed by Bobby Darin in 1958, and covered by Buddy Holly.

25.28 LET IT BE (1:33<

After a false start, Paul intentionally jokes with the lyrics. Obviously, this is not a serious performance.

We have audio for the first 15 seconds and last 38 seconds of this performance. Fortunately, silent film footage bridges the gap. Why the gap? When compiling the work print, the editor simply cued up consecutive sound reels from the same cameraman. Since this performance overlapped reels, the 41 missing seconds is the time it took the soundman to switch reels on the Nagra recorder.

Half way through this performance, John notices that he doesn't have a microphone for his harmony vocals. George Martin obligingly sets one up for him.

25.29   LET IT BE >1:13<

The performance is dragging along and almost stops altogether before it lurches into the instrumental break Paul sings an entire verse in mock-gospel gibberish.

25.30   LET IT BE >0:12)

The very end of a performance, probably 25.29.

25.31   LET IT BE (0:07)

Paul plays the opening bars. He then hesitates and chooses to play another song instead.

25.32   (INSTRUMENTAL) (0:16)

Perhaps having just noticed John lying on the floor, Paul plays him this brief lullaby. He stops after George asks if he knows how to play "Chopsticks" and plays a brief finger exercise.

25.33   (INSTRUMENTAL) (0:09)

As Paul plays this brief exercise, John follows along on bass.

25.34   LET IT BE (0:12<

Paul sings the first four lines of the song before the available tape cuts off.

25.35   LET IT BE >1:07<

The available tape edits into this performance during the instrumental bridges After the chorus Paul mumbles his way through a verse, obviously because he has not yet written the lyrics. John sits up in order to be on mike for his harmony vocals. This is probably a continuation of 25.34.

25.36   LET IT BE >0:11<

Once again, the group has gathered together in the Apple control room to hear playbacks. This and the following three fragments are playbacks of a performance which has not otherwise come to light.

25.37   LET IT BE >0:05<

A few words of lyric from the first verse, nothing more.

A continuation of 25.37. John points out something in a magazine to George, after which both of them join in to sing along with the playback.

25.38   LET IT BE >0:33<

A continuation of 25.37. John points out somerthing in a magazine to George, after which both of them join in to sing along with the playback.

25.39   LET IT BE >0:14<

Another brief fragment, obviously a continuation of 25.38. John is still singing along to the playback.

25.40   LET IT BE >0:49<

Now better able to judge the state of their performances. the group heads back into the studio and resumes rehearsal. The available tape edits in during the instrumental break. John is playing a single maraca, but quickly puts it down to continue his part on bass. The Beatles continue through the chorus before this fragment comes to an end.

25.41   LET IT BE >1:26)

The available tape cuts in as Paul talks his way through a verse. George's guitar playing is unfocused, and John stops entirely for about 15 seconds and stares ahead blankly. John and George have grown tired of rehearsing and want to attempt to record "Let It Be." Unfortunately, they need to work out the structure of the song. Despite his limited input on some topics, George always seems to steer the conversation when it covers the arrangement of verses and choruses.

25.42   LET IT BE   (0:44)

This loose collection of "Let It Be" riffs can be heard under the discussion above. Paul plays some generic piano trills near the end of the conversation, but this is far from a real performance.

25.43   LET IT BE   (1:02<

This performance, only 11 seconds of which is audible on the available tape, appears to be an attempt to record the song.

25.44   LET IT BE   (3:43)

A complete run-through, and clearly the best performance to have become available from this day. Still, the group is far away from recording a releaseable take. Obviously, Paul intends for the song to have three verses but has thus far only written lyrics for the first two. The band sounds tired, obviously aware that their performance here would not be suitable for release.

   This performance was released on 1996's *Anthology 3*.

25.45   "CRAZY FEET"   (0:05)

Paul tinkles with the piano keys and sings a few words. This 'song' has thus far eluded identification.

   After cursing his microphone for causing feedback, John bangs out a rhythm on it as George tries to organise the structure of "Let It Be."

25.46   PLEASE PLEASE ME   (0:32)

This brief performance is the only available indication of what an early, slow arrangement of "Please Please Me" might have sounded like. Paul sings a couple of lines, and George harmonises by singing a line from "Let It Be."

This is the last available performance from the 25th. It's likely that the session is near its end.

Sunday, January 26th, 1969

For the first time in almost a year, The Beatles spent both days of a week-end recording, inspired more by pragmatic than artistic reasons (Ringo's work on *The Magic Christian* would begin in eight days and only a handful of songs were up to par). Billy Preston rejoined the sessions, and their work was almost totally focused on the two McCartney ballads, "Let It Be" and "The Long And Winding Road." In between rehearsals and the recording of these two songs, a number of energetic oldies were recorded, as well as a unique pass at "Dig It." While little was accomplished in terms of finished takes, the two ballads were polished to the point of near completion.

George and Ringo are the first Beatles to arrive. After Mal assures Ringo that John and Paul are both expected, George provides some background to his song "Isn't It A Pity." He jokes and quotes the spoken introduction to Tiny Tim's recording of Jerry Lee Lewis' "Great Balls of Fire" in which Tiny introduces the number as one originally recorded "way back in the '50's" (The Beatles will cover "Great Balls of Fire" later in the day). He then recalls John's off-hand rejection of "Isn't It a Pity" three years earlier, but his pleasant demeanour can't hide the residual bitterness he feels over the incident. He explains how he had considered giving the song to Frank Sinatra to record, but had decided against it when he realised that Sinatra would record almost anything. A brief fragment of a playback of "Get Back" can be faintly heard during this conversation, but no one seems to be listening to it.

26.1   ISN'T IT A PITY   (I:42)
A lovely acoustic performance from George. He sings both of the song's verses, and is vocalising through a third when he stops to engage in conversation.

After praising "Isn't It A Pity," Mal reminds George of another folk number he'd written. Glyn arrives, and the others greet him.

26.2   WINDOW, WINDOW   (0:58)
George performs two verses and the chorus of this pleasant original. It certainly sounds like a folk tune, and it's clear that this is yet another of George's compositions that would have no place in the live show.

George recorded a demo of this song for his 1970 album *All Things Must Pass*, but it was never properly recorded or released

Ringo jokes about Glyn's lack of sleep. This leads to a discussion of the mixing facilities at Apple. Throughout the project Glyn would take the multitrack tapes to Olympic Studios (elsewhere in London) to mix them and prepare lacquer acetates for the band to hear. Mal and Ringo question why the equipment borrowed from E.M.I. can't be used for mixing, and Glyn delicately explains that while there is a mixer, they have none of the necessary ancillary equipment.

26.3   LET IT DOWN   (0:25)
George, still on acoustic guitar, plays the song's introduction but stops to make an observation that it would be nice if he could feel as happy coming into a session as he does leaving it. He then remarks that, with the heavy

schedule of sessions, the days all seem the same. His comments reveal that the previous day's session had ended with a performance of "Let It Down" (tapes of which have not become available).

26.4   LET IT DOWN (0:29)

Two short instrumental passages from George. Ringo moves over to the piano and begins playing.

The long days of recording during the afternoon and mixing at night have taken their toll on Glyn, and he and George joke about their various stages of exhaustion as Ringo slips in a reference to the live show. George then explains how he's had great difficulty envisioning a group arrangement for one of the acoustic numbers he's just played (perhaps "Isn't It a Pity" - certainly not "Let It Down"), and asks Ringo how he's coming along with his song-in-progress "Picasso". He then learns that Ringo has abandoned that tune in favour of "Octopus's Garden" (George had not been present when Ringo premiered the song on January 23rd).

26.5   OCTOPUS'S GARDEN (6:22<

Ringo performs one verse of the song, accompanying himself on piano, and then explains that :he hasn't written any more. George jokes that Ringo's learned another chord and, quickly picking up on the tune, joins in on acoustic guitar and tries to help Ringo finish composing it. Ringo makes a feeble attempt at creating a chorus, and George shows him some chords on the piano that he feels might be appropriate. George then returns to strumming his guitar, and the two are still brainstorming as the available tape runs out.

One should note that, officially, "Octopus's Garden" is credited to Ringo as sole composer. Obviously, a bit of charity took place since even these few minutes of rehearsal show George making a significant contribution to the song.

26.6   OCTOPUS'S GARDEN >0:05<

A brief fragment captured as the soundman changes reels.

26.7   OCTOPUS'S GARDEN (3:07)

George and Ringo continue their composing efforts. Together they work on a verse, but it fails to flow and they abandon it. George suggests that they start again, and George Martin (who has just arrived) vocalises along with their performance. The song breaks down, and George is demonstrating some further chords on the piano as John and Yoko arrive.

Portions of this (as well as 26.9 and much of the adjacent dialogue) were included in the film *Let It Be*.

26.8   OCTOPUS'S GARDEN (0:42)

Ringo begins playing the song again on piano and George sings some of the lyrics. John asks Ringo what instrument he'd like John to play on his number. He's willing to do anything except bass (he had been forced to play bass on "Let It Be" the previous day). Ringo laughs and suggests that John play the drums. John agrees, but wonders if Paul wouldn't prefer that spot. Paul will, in fact, get his turn at the drum kit later in this session.

26.9   OCTOPUS'S GARDEN (1:15)

Ringo and George attempt another run-through, as John joins in enthusiastically on drums. The performance breaks down and George and Ringo resume their composing effort as John continues to bash away on the drums, wrapping up his solo by singing a single line of the "Octopus's Garden" lyric. As he's doing this, Paul arrives with Linda and her five year old daughter Heather.

Even before he removes his coat, Paul begins enthusing about the dubs of various songs that Glyn had given each of them the previous day. Perhaps with a touch of sarcasm, he exclaims that The Beatles are obviously the best group of all time and jokes that they should release the dubs immediately as-is. Ringo, just a bit more down-to-earth, rightly dismisses their performances as awful, adding his opinion that "Get Back" (23.31) was the only good song, and he wasn't particularly keen on that either. George feels that most of the performances are unpolished owing to the fact that they haven't finished working on them, but adds that he liked "Get Back" (Paul assures him the songs will improve). John hasn't even bothered to listen to the dubs, having left them in his car. Everyone is very careful to greet Heather.

26.10   (UNKNOWN)   (0:31)
Ringo begins playing "Octopus's Garden" again, but quickly switches to this unidentified boogie. A very brief, faint vocal can be heard as the performance winds down.

John, certainly a believer in E.S.P., then tries to verify his suspicion that he and Paul had had simultaneous dreams the previous night. George sarcastically comments on this, and George Martin ends the discussion by requesting that Ringo play "Octopus's Garden" one more time.

26.11   OCTOPUS'S GARDEN   (3:11)
Ringo performs the song again, and John continues his amateurish drumming behind him. George, Paul and George Martin join in on the vocals, and George Martin comments that the song needs one more chord.

George composes the few bars that will link the "Octopus's Garden" verses but Ringo points out that they still need to compose a second verse and a middle eight. The conversation turns to the dubs of "Two Of Us" (24.40), and George comments that he would like to add his own voice to John and Paul's harmonies. Despite Paul's agreement, it appears that this idea was never acted upon.

26.12   "SHE'S A LITTLE PIECE OF LEATHER"   (0:38)
John sings this silly piece of doggerel possibly directed at Heather. This has only been accorded the status of performance because he accompanies himself on drums. John had also sung a bit of this during 26.8 (without accompaniment) .

26.13   TWO OF US   (0:12)
To illustrate a point, George plays and sings a few lines from this song.

Paul continues to enthuse about the acetates, and delightedly points out the humorous touches that John gave to his performances on "I've Got a Feeling" (23.36) and "Dig a Pony" (23.35). These off-the-cuff elements are what Paul enjoyed so much about the dubs, other aspects of the recordings being comparatively irrelevant. Ringo reiterates his view that "Get Back" was the best of the lot, and John and George agree, with George calling "Get Back" their next single.

26.14   DIG A PONY   (0:23)
A short performance from George on acoustic guitar to illustrate a point about the version on the dubs.

26.15   OCTOPUS'S GARDEN   (0:41)

Ringo performs a short bit of the song again as Paul vocalises along. John joins in again on drums, and continues bashing after the performance has ended. Ringo and George then talk about the origins of the song, and it's revealed that Ringo got the inspiration for "Octopus's Garden" by learning about the sea creatures (and their gardens) while vacationing in Sardinia in October of 1968.

26.16 OCTOPUS'S GARDEN (1:04)

Ringo makes the observation that the song's too fast, and jokingly plays an up-tempo rendition. George joins in on acoustic guitar and provides most of the vocals as John drums and Paul vocalises along with the song. Heather then relates an octopus story of her own as Paul jokingly suggests that the band abstain from Scotch, at least until after lunch (it might be noted that many empty liquor bottles can be spotted throughout the studio). John provides a bit of sing-song concerning Isadora Duncan and her employment at Telefunken (Duncan was a famed Parisian dancer from early in the century. Telefunken is a German company). This impromptu rhyme appeared in the film *Let It Be*.

A considerable amount of time is unaccounted for at this point. When the available tapes resume, it's afternoon, Billy has arrived, and the band is preparing to rehearse "Let It Be."

In a bizarre dialogue John and Paul have a mock argument. Despite the fact that they're obviously fooling around, there's an uncomfortable degree of truth bubbling just below the surface as John chastises Paul for a lack of discipline (which, of course, is John's great problem).

26.17   WINDOW, WINDOW (1:04)

George sings the first verse as the other band members try to play along. Paul takes over the vocal, effectively trashing the performance, and ends with a few chords from "Let it Be."

26.18   I'M TALKING ABOUT YOU (0:47)

The banter between Paul and John reminds George of this song from The Beatles' early 60's repertoire. He sings a bit of it in the background (still off-mike) and John takes over the vocal. The backing is quite loose, and a comment from Paul brings the performance to a close.

"I'm Talking About You" was written and recorded by Chuck Berry in 1961.

Paul stops the performance to suggest they get back to the "Let It Be" rehearsal. One is not quite sure whether John is joking when he shoots back that Paul's the one who's making everyone so miserable. John's bitter tone does a 180 degree turnaround as he breaks into a mock radio announcement thanking everyone for birthday presents. Paul chimes in with a remark about Christmas - presumably an echo of similar statements that appeared each Christmas on the flexidiscs distributed to members of the official Beatles fan club.

26.19   LET IT BE (0:05<

A brief fragment of the beginning, which is severely edited on the available tape.

26.20   PIECE OF MY HEART >0:1/)

As he had done twice on the 3rd, George sings a portion the song's chorus, accompanying himself on guitar. John comments that playing bass is like being forced to stay after school, and Paul adds that he must play "Let It Be" a hundred times as punishment. George calls in vain for Mal. With Mal not around, George asks someone else to get him some drugs.

26.21 LITTLE YELLOW PILLS (0:45)

George's desire for drugs brings this number to mind. He takes the lead vocal as the others join in, but his recollection of the song is sketchy at best.

Like "Speak to Me" and "You Got Me Thinking," "Little Yellow Pills" is from the Jackie Lomax album "Is This What You Want?" which George produced in late 1968.

26.22 HIGH SCHOOL CONFIDENTIAL >0:55)

Paul plays piano and takes lead vocal on this oldie, basically accompanied only by Ringo's drumming. He remembers little more than the chorus, which he repeats a few times before going directly into the next song.

"High School Confidential" was recorded by Jerry Lee Lewis in 1958 as the theme song for a film of the same name.

26.23 GREAT BALLS OF FIRE (2:18)

After a haphazard beginning, the band comes together for a lively performance. Paul begins to sing with Jerry Lee in mind, but remembers the recently released Tiny Tim cover version and modifies his vocal accordingly. George offers a comparatively competent guitar solo, and restarts the song at one point after Paul has given up. Following the performance Paul and Heather briefly mention Mr. Tim.

"Great Balls of Fire" was recorded by Jerry Lee Lewis in 1957. Tiny Tim's version had just been released as a single in the U.K.

26.24 DON'T LET THE SUN CATCH YOU CRYING (2:30)

Paul steers this band into this oldie as soon as "Great Balls of Fire' ends. After a rough beginning the song comes together rather nicely. Paul obviously knows the song by heart, and everyone else seems fairly familiar with it as well (although, as usual, John has difficulty recalling the lyrics). John interjects a single line from his 1968 number "Sexy Sadie."

"Don't Let The Sun Catch You Crying" is based on Ray Charles' 1960 performance. It's not to be confused with the Gerry And The Pacemakers' hit of the same name.

George is leafing through a men's magazine and pointing out the various women to Paul. It doesn't take much to follow John's train of thought as he's reminded of an American group called The Motherfuckers. This was not a singing group, as John obviously believes, but something of a militant political group who were in the news at this time as they tried to battle promoter Bill Graham for control of The Fillmore East.

26.25 (IMPROVISATION) (0:30)

A loose jam between Paul (on piano) and Billy (on organ) which takes place (during the conversation discussed above.

26.26 SUICIDE (0:44)

Paul brings the conversation about The Motherfuckers to a close by kicking into this song. He accompanies himself on piano and John interjects a few lines, obviously quite familiar with the number.

"Suicide," one of Paul's earliest compositions, has never been officially released in any form except for a very brief passage that was included on the *McCartney* album. Oblivious to young Heather's presence, John and George continue to peruse the girlie magazines giving John the idea to create their *own* magazine using Apple's female employees. Following this exchange, the magazine will find a place of honour on George's music stand.

26.27   DIG IT   >8:23)

With the band still on their "Let it Be" instruments, John leads them through this rollicking improvisation, extemporising lyrics around the title phrase. Heather bleats along as John and George engage in some call and response vocals. As the performance dies out, John exhorts everyone to continue, causing Paul to improvise a counter melody behind him. John then calls out the title of Bob Dylan's "Like a Rolling Stone" a number of times and, recalling the "Get Off!" jam (9.79, 9.80), begins tossing out names (The F.B.I., the C.I.A., the BBC, B.B. King, Doris Day and Matt Busby), finishing up by repeatedly shouting the title as the performance winds down.

Other than the title and the improvised nature of the performance, this bears little resemblance to the "Dig It'"s done on the 24th. Even though it is inferior to the earlier jams of this type, it was used, with different edits for each, on (the unreleased) *Get Back* album and the *Let It Be* album and film. For the record, B.B King was (and is) a legendary blues singer (whose name was also invoked on the 3rd), Doris Day a popular American actress and singer, and Matt Busby the manager of the Manchester United soccer team.

26.28   RIP IT UP   >0:33)

Most of "Rip It Up" has not become available. As we begin, John and Paul are winding down their performance with the end of a chorus. Paul then starts the song up again and (as John joins in) they sing one more verse a capella. The band joins in for one more chorus and George plays a brief guitar solo before they all move directly into "Shake, Rattle And Roll."

"Rip It Up" was originally recorded by Little Richard in 1956. The Beatles would have been intimately acquainted with both this and Elvis Presley's cover, done that same year. A portion of this was issued on *Anthology 3*.

26.29   SHAKE, RATTLE AND ROLL   (1:35)

Paul and John share lead vocal on this exciting performance. This is one of the better oldie performances from the entire project, and everyone has a wonderful time with it.

"Shake, Rattle and Roll" was recorded by R&B shouter Big Joe Turner in l9S4. This was quickly picked up by early rockers, and covered by Bill Haley and His Comets (also in 19.54), and Elvis Presley (in 1956). Once again, The Beatles were probably well acquainted with all of these. This (and the end of "Rip it Up') was included in the film "Let It Be" in a fairly undoctored state. It was also preserved on multi-track tape (along with the end of "Rip it Up" and the following three performances) and mixed by Glyn on March 13th. A terribly edited version was released on "Anthology 3."

26.30   medley MISS ANN / KANSAS CITY / LAWDY MISS CLAWDY   (3:40)

A fine rock and roll medley. As the song begins Paul starts singing the lyrics to "Miss Ann," but John and George choose to sing "Kansas City' instead. After less than a minute of "Kansas City," Paul steers the song back to Miss Ann," and John joins him on the vocals. After a brief instrumental break John begins singing "Lawdy Miss Clawdy." with Paul joining in. An excellent, lively performance all around, diminished only by everyone's inability to recall more than snatches of each song's lyrics.

"Miss Ann" was performed and co-authored by Little Richard in 1950. "Kansas City" was obviously brought to mind by the Little Richard connection (it was recorded by Richard at the same session as "Miss Ann"), but the arrangement here is the 1959 R&B original as performed by Wilbert Harrison (this is notable because the group had used Little Richard's arrangement on their 1964 album *Beatles For Sale*). "Lawdy Miss Clawdy," another R&B standard, had been initially recorded by Lloyd Price in 1952, but, again, it's probably Elvis they're thinking of here, who recorded the song in 1956. This medley was presented in an abridged form in the film *Let It Be*.

26.31   BLUE SUEDE SHOES   (2:09)

John leads the band into another oldie, and once again shares the lead vocal with Paul. This is one song they all know by heart, and the performance is very enjoyable. Paul calls for an organ solo from Billy, and John plays around with the song's lyrics as the performance draws to a close.

While The Beatles had also performed "Blue Suede Shoes" on the 3rd, here they do the song justice with a very nice performance. When Glyn mixed this song on March 13th, he severely mixed down Paul's vocal. Although "Blue Suede Shoes" had originally been recorded by Carl Perkins in 1955, it's Elvis' 1956 classic they're thinking of here. A butchered version of this was released in 1996 on *Anthology 3* with the entire first verse omitted.

26.32   YOU REALLY GOT A HOLD ON ME   (3:16)

George leads the band into yet another oldie, sharing lead vocals with John, whose inability to remember the song's lyrics or structure mars the performance. Ragged is the best way to describe this attempt, as they don't quite seem to remember how to play it.

"You Really Got a Hold on Me" was written by Smokey Robinson and recorded by him with his group The Miracles in 1962. The Beatles had previously covered it on their 1963 album *With The Beatles*. An edited version of this performance was included in the film *Let It Be*.

26.33   LET IT BE   >0:27)

John does a humorous parody on the song's title. The instrumental backing is half-hearted, as one might expect.

26.34   YOU REALLY GOT A HOLD ON ME   (0:08)

As "Let It Be" dies down, George tries to lead them back into this song. He plays the introductory notes, but no one picks up on it.

26.35   LET IT BE   (0:02<

Paul counts in and plays just a few notes before the available tape edits.

26.36   LET IT BE   (3:55)

This is a complete performance, with Paul singing an impromptu combination of the first and second verses in place of the as-yet-unwritten third. Also of note is the entire band's participation in the song's introduction, an idea which will be dropped when they return to the song on the 31st.

This was probably considered the best performance of the day. It was mixed by Glyn on March 10th but was not chosen for either *Get Back* or *Let It Be*.

26.37   LET IT BE   (0:14)

In this brief rehearsal fragment, John, Paul and George practice the backing vocals backed only by John's bass.

Paul says that he's had enough and, after a substantial rehearsal session (little of which is available), The Beatles put "Let It Be" aside and move on to "The Long And Winding Road."

26.38 THE LONG AND WINDING ROAD (1:48)

This performance grows out of tuning, as Paul leads the band through a loose cha-cha arrangement, singing at first in broken English and then in mock Spanish. The instrument assignments remain the same as they were on "Let it Be."

Portions of this performance and the one that follow were included in the film *Let it Be*.

26.39 THE LONG AND WINDING ROAD (3:21)

A complete run-through. The limited attention given to this song at Twickenham (and the complete lack of work on it at Apple to this point) shows (in fact, "The Long and Winding Road" will *never* be perfected and a flawed take from the January 31 session will serve as the official release. Paul initially attempts a straight performance, but quickly veers into self-parody, and makes a feeble attempt to teach backing harmonies to the others.

26.40 (IMPROVISATION) >1:53<

An instrumental boogie featuring John on slide guitar. Billy is playing piano while Paul plays drums as Ringo sits idly behind him. Yoko is trying to add her vocal talents but her microphone is not on. While the music is not particularly interesting or well done, everyone seems into playing it.

26.41 (IMPROVISATION) >0:28<

Obviously a continuation of 26.40. Yoko's microphone is now live and she is moaning into it.

26.42 "I TOLD YOU BEFORE" >8:18<

Another repetitive jam as The Beatles wrap up the session. Billy is playing keyboards and Paul continues on drums. John interjects some scat singing and Heather joins along (perhaps inspired by Yoko?). Finally, George begins singing more seriously and the jam grows more focused, but his lyrics are little more than an improvised couplet, repeated over and over. For what it is, this is relatively entertaining.

If previous sessions are any indication, the group called it a day after these end-of-the-session jams.

Monday, January 27th, 1969

Most of this day's session consisted of rehearsals for "Get Back" and "I've Got a Feeling." Indeed, the work on "Get Back" was so successful that one of the takes was eventually chosen as the a-side of The Beatles' next single. Work on "Don't Let Me Down" (the single's eventual b-side) was not quite as successful, and although a number of takes were recorded none were polished enough to consider work on the song complete. Unlike previous sessions, Billy Preston was present throughout the day.

27.1   (INSTRUMENTAL) (0:22<
Paul returns to a slow piano instrumental he had also played on the 25th (see 25.32).

27.2   STRAWBERRY FIELDS FOREVER (2:06)
Paul is still playing piano, and only an occasional guitar riff can be heard behind him. After humming a few lines, he softly sings the first verse. Glyn arrives and tells them about his bad luck in having had an automobile accident with a police car on the way into the studio. Paul, having softened his playing to listen to Glyn, comes back and sings a final verse of "Strawberry Fields," this time on mike.

"Strawberry Fields Forever" was, of course, written by John in 1966.

Mal assists George with a technical problem, as John and Paul punctuate the conversation with scat-calls from "Get Back." This conversation follows a number of takes of "Get Back," none of which have become available.

27.3   OH! DARLING (6:30)
Paul leads the band into this performance, which starts out slow and bluesy. John and Paul share the vocal, and Paul is playing bass after having played piano on all the available Twickenham performances (Billy replaces him on keyboards). They're all obviously having fun with this break from "Get Back." and extend the performance longer than usual. As the performance ends John announces that he's just learned that Yoko's divorce has come through. He sings about having been freed, and the performance restarts.

For the record, Yoko wasn't officially divorced from Tony Cox until February.

A portion of this performance was released in 1996 on *Anthology 3*.

27.4   GET BACK (0:19)
As Paul reprises a few lines from "Oh! Darling" Ringo plays "Get Back"'s drum introduction as the band heads back into rehearsals of that number. Although Paul sings a bit of the first verse, this is nothing more than a loose warm-up which quickly breaks down.

27.5   GET BACK 2:07)
This one is played strictly for laughs. Paul sings through the song in pseudo-German, switching to pseudo-French for the final verse. The vocal aside, the musicianship on this performance is quite good, and one can tell that a finished performance is right around the corner.

27.6   GET BACK (2:42)
The band delivers a superb performance, featuring strong solos from John and Billy. George provides a nice choppy rhythm guitar and Paul delivers the lyrics in his usual assured style.

This was the performance used for the single, as well as for the *Get Back* and *Let It Be* albums. In each case additional material was grafted on to the end (see 28.01 and 30.13).

On the album *Let It Be* the inconsequential dialogue preceding this perform-ance was padded with additional dialogue derived from some unknown point in this session. This includes John's memorable little rhyme parodying Paul's Loretta verse. Paul's reference to Rosetta (also in the pre-song dialogue) may have been suggested by a song called "Rosetta," which he had recently pro-duced for The Fourmost.

27.7   I'VE GOT A FEELING (0:33)
Glyn is preparing to record "I've Got a Feeling," but stops them during the song's intro because he's not ready yet. The performance then degenerates to loose riffing.

Paul is ready to forge ahead even though the guitars are out of tune. He jokes about speaking in French - presumably a reference to the accents that he and John had used earlier when fooling around with "Get Back" (see 27.5). John comments in French how filthy he thinks that language is.

27.8   I'VE GOT A FEELING (0:51)
Following up on his own suggestion, Paul offers a French count-in. He stops the performance during the second verse, though, pointing out that they are way out of tune.

27.9   I'VE GOT A FEELING (4:16)
In this rehearsal segment, Billy picks up on George's suggestion and repeat-edly plays one of the song's riffs as John and George tune their guitars. As they're doing this, Paul starts to sing. John joins him on the second verse, and the song teeters on the edge of breakdown until they reach the troublesome guitar part at the end of the bridge, at which point they pause to discuss it (see below). Paul starts again from the first verse but quickly stops the rehearsal in order to go for a real take.

The guitar riff that ends the bridge had been a major sticking point during re-hearsals on the 9th and the 2ind. Remembering this, Paul laughs, and avoids the problem by telling everyone to not discuss it and hope that it works itself out. Paul and George then refer to the riff as it appears on the acetate that Glyn had prepared of "I've Got a Feeling" (23.36).

27.10   I'VE GOT A FEELING (3:23)
John suggests once again that they speed up the tempo a bit. They're clearly uncomfortable with this, however, and Ringo consistently has trouble keeping the beat. Although Glyn is recording their performance, they must have real-ised this one wasn't working, and turn in a cursory performance.

27.11   I'VE GOT A FEELING (0:36)
Paul counts in for another attempt, but it breaks down almost immediately. Glyn announces that he has to change the tape, so the band plays a loose in-strumental version punctuated by "What'd I Say" riffs from George.

27.12   medley / "YOU WONT GET ME THAT WAY" / THE WALK (3:44)
With a few minutes of free time on their hands while Glyn changes tapes, Billy leads the band into a basic blues jam. Paul improvises some generic blues lyrics followed by what he can remember of Jimmy McCracklin's 1958 song "The Walk." John chimes in with a few misremembered lines as well and Paul returns to his improvised lyrics as "The Walk" winds down.

Despite their impromptu nature, these few minutes are quite entertaining. The concluding portion of "The Walk" was captured on multi-track tape, and was mixed by Glyn for acetates prepared on March 10th

27.13   I'VE GOT A FEELING   (3:59)

A conscious attempt to recapture the playfulness that they all liked about the acetate of their performance on the 23rd (23.36). As the song almost breaks down because of feedback from his guitar, John jokingly apologises for screwing up again (referencing a Peter Sellers' recording titled "I'm So Ashamed"). After this amusing moment they start again and turn in a spirited performance. Paul and John are not quite in sync with their call and response vocals but this doesn't detract from the performance. John sings in a gravel-voice for one of his verses.

Despite its rough edges, this performance was deemed the best take from this session and was mixed by Glyn on March 13th. It was not scheduled to appear on the *Get Back* album, however, being passed over in favour of the breakdown recorded on January 23rd (23.36).

27.14   I'VE GOT A FEELING   >0:46)

This fragment has much the same feel as 27.13, and consists of one of John's verses, in which he's playing around with his phrasing. Rather than moving on to the dual verse, however, he leads the band into a Bob Dylan song.

27.15   RAINY DAY WOMEN #'S 12 & 35   (0:43)

John remembers few of the song's lyrics, but is obviously having fun nonetheless. Despite the off-the-cuff nature of this performance, Ringo turns in an impressive drum part.

"Rainy Day Women #'s 12 & 35" is a Bob Dylan classic from 1966.

Ringo offers an opinion about "I've Got a Feeling"'s arrangement as he says the guitar shouldn't be played throughout.

27.16   I'VE GOT A FEELING   (3:51)

This performance is a good example of one of The Beatles' problems. Having delivered a fairly strong (but less than perfect) performance (27.13), they just can't go the next step and record a releaseable take. Instead, they deliver this half-hearted attempt, and by the time they reach John's solo verse they've given up any pretence of turning in a serious performance. As this winds down, John offers some awful guitar fills, then reprises two lines from "Rainy Day Women #'s 12 & 35."

27.17   I'VE GOT A FEELING   (2:52<

Another run-through from the top. Paul expresses his growing boredom with the rehearsal by changing the title to "I've Got Another Feeling." The descending guitar riff in the bridge is still rough, and John's response vocals sound forced. John also forgets the words during his verse.

27.18   I'VE GOT A FEELING   >0:13<

Various "I've Got a Feeling" riffs as Paul facetiously announces they'll meet the next morning at six.

27.19   DIG IT   >0:33<

John delivers another unique version of this song, different from both the slide guitar attempts of the 24th and the impromptu performance of the 26th. The instrumentation is strongly reminiscent of "I've Got A Feeling."

At this point The Beatles retired to the control room to hear some playbacks, presumably of the day's work on "Get Back" and "I've Got a Feeling." They also took a listen to a few performances from the 26th, including "Dig It" (26.27} and at least some of the subsequent oldies (26.28-26.32).

In the next available dialogue segment, Paul relates an anecdote revealing the perils of travelling by car when one is a Beatle.

27:20 THE LONG AND WINDING ROAD (0:09)

A very short instrumental bit with Paul playing piano and John on bass. Paul mentions that he needs to leave soon.

This short performance is the only representation available of the day's brief attempt at "The Long And Winding Road."

27.21 SAVE THE LAST DANCE FOR ME (0:36<

John plays a simple riff on bass which Paul picks up on piano. Paul sings, but his vocal is very faint.

27.22 (IMPROVISATION) >0:45<

John, Paul and George are all preparing to leave while Billy plays an up-tempo boogie with Ringo following along on drums. John grabs his collection of mounted clippings detailing his life with Yoko, and heads out of the studio as the session draws to a close. Paul wonders if they should go out to eat.

Tuesday, January 28th, 1969

Another productive day of recording sessions, centreing around "Get Back" and "Don't Let Me Down." The Beatles also recorded versions of "I've Got a Feeling" and "One After 909," and are reported to have recorded "Dig a Pony," "Love Me Do," and several instrumentals featuring Billy Preston. None of these have become available for study, although a 6:22 performance circulates which purports to be the Billy Preston jams (It should be explained that we are not satisfied that these recordings are authentic and have decided not to include them here).

28.1   GET BACK   >1:02<
Only a portion of the song's coda is currently available, as Paul tosses out some lines about Loretta's clothing. His vocal disintegrates into forced laughter as the available tape fades. The performance here is a bit slower than those recorded the previous day.

Part of this was excerpted for the coda on the "Get Back" single. The latter part of the performance was used as a tag to both the *Let It Be* film and *Get Back* LPs. This is the only available performance from of a series of "Get Back" takes that occurred here.

28.2   DON'T LET ME DOWN   (3:44)
With work on "Get Back" completed satisfactorily, the group turns to the song which will ultimately serve as that single's flipside. This complete performance bears a reasonable resemblance to the one that was eventually released, but some off-notes can be heard and Paul's bass playing is not quite up to his usual high standard. Still, it's obvious that the song is close to completion.

28.3   I'VE GOT A FEELING   (0:03)
John attempts to leap into another song just as "Don't Let Me Down" dies down, but George Martin interrupts him with a request that the band take a break to tune their instruments. John reacts to this with mock-violence and reminds everyone of the 1963 incident where he punched cavern deejay Bob Wooler.

28.4   DON'T LET ME DOWN   (3:33)
The band comes together perfectly for this take. John gives a strong vocal performance, finding a nice balance between singing and screaming the lyrics. Billy underscores the whole performance with a fine keyboard part.

This take was released as the b-side of the "Get Back" single, with additional vocals grafted on from another take to create a double-tracked effect in the song's finale. Once again, it's likely that this performance is only a small representation of multiple attempts at the song.

28.5   I'VE GOT A FEELING   >0:51<
This is more of a collection of riffs than a performance of the song. Billy plays short licks on the electric piano, Ringo taps along on cymbals and Paul thumps out the bass line as he sings a few lines and vocalises. John, preoccupied with Yoko, joins in with a few guitar riffs just before the available tape cuts off.

28.6   ONE AFTER 909   (0:58)

The band starts off with a very loose arrangement of "One After 909." John and Paul sing a couple of mangled lines from Chuck Berry's 1958 song "Jo Jo Gunne," and the performance turns into a jam.

With a paucity of new material. Paul suggests that the band returns to "One After 909," which they had last performed at Twickenham. After a number of (unavailable) performances, Paul is worried about overrehearsal, but wants to give it one more go so that Glyn can try to capture a usable performance on multi-track tape.

28.7 ONE AFTER 909 (3:11)

After a false start, Paul vocalises the guitar introduction and a complete performance follows. Billy provides a fine keyboard part, and the song moves along nicely until John completely forgets the lyrics during the second middle eight, causing him to engagingly make fun of his own error. Once again, there seems to be a conscious effort to capture a sense of spontaneity here.

With the exception of the January 30th rooftop performance, these are the only Apple performances of "One After 909" to have surfaced.

Following the performance, John mentions how he and Paul had given The Rolling Stones "I Wanna Be Your Man" in 1963 to record as their second single. John reveals here that he had tried to give them "One After 909" instead, but The Stones were not interested.

28.8 HAVA NEGEILAH (0:31<

The Beatles turn in brief, rock and roll arrangement of this traditional Jewish song, led by Paul on bass and Billy on keyboard. John sings the title shortly before the available tape cuts off.

28.9 (IMPROVISATION) (0:33)

The band's tuning efforts develop into this loose instrumental, as Paul repeatedly tests his microphone.

28.10 medley "THE RIVER RHINE" / THE LONG AND WINDING ROAD (4:10)

Billy leads the band into this blues improvisation. Paul extemporises some fitting lyrics, repeating them (with variations) a number of times. As the backing continues unaltered, he sings a blues arrangement of two verses of "The Long And Winding Road" before returning to the "River Rhine" lyrics. Instrumentally, the band turns in some fine performances, once again indicating their mastery of this musical form.

This is the only available performance of "The Long And Winding Road" featuring Paul on bass rather than piano, and is the only known blues arrangement.

28.11 THE INNER LIGHT (0:39)

The drone of a guitar note reminds John of Indian music, which in turn reminds him of this Indian-influenced Harrison composition. He offers a short performance, accompanied by George on guitar.

"The Inner Light" had been the flip side of The Beatles' "Lady Madonna" the previous year. It's interesting to note that John recalls the lyrics relatively well. This is unexpected considering his limited involvement in the original recording and the fact that he has trouble remembering the lyrics to his own number "Across the Universe" which had been recorded around the same time.

28.12 I GOT TO FIND MY BABY (0:26)

Paul shouts out a misremembered lyric. George and John pick up on it, and the band runs through a brief and ragged performance.

"I Got to Find My Baby," written and recorded by Chuck Berry in 1960, had been performed by The Beatles on BBC radio in 1963.

Paul then suggests returning to "One After 909." John is clearly not pleased with this idea, and points out that it would be wasting their time to work on a song they already know so well.

28.13   SOME OTHER GUY   (0:14)

Billy plays this solo, instrumental rendition on keyboard as John and Paul discuss "One After 909."

This 1962 Ritchie Barrett hit had been a part of The Beatles' early repertoire.

28.14   OLD BROWN SHOE   (7:07)

George introduces another of his compositions to the sessions. He leads the band on piano while everyone else assumes their regular instruments. They attempt the song from the top, and turn in a loose performance. Clearly the rehearsal has been going on for some time because the band members have a cursory knowledge of the tune. The performance breaks down midway through when George makes a number of mistakes on piano. They restart with the last verse (the lyrics, it should be noted, are complete) and play the song through to the end. Since they don't have an ending worked out, the performance moves into a jam led by Billy, and then back to the top of the song. They run through the song again, still quite loosely, and simply stop dead after completing the last verse.

"Old Brown Shoe" was recorded by the group the following April, and released as the b-side of "The Ballad of John And Yoko."

28.15   OLD BROWN SHOE   (3:02)

A few minutes are missing between the last rehearsal and this one. Billy is no longer playing. John and Paul offer only tentative efforts, and John's guitar playing bears little resemblance to the song, while Paul's bass is nearly inaudible. Despite its problems, this bouncy run-through is still enjoyable. Once again the lack of an ending causes the performance to break down at that point.

After the performance John complains about the abundance of chords in the song, and George responds that perhaps Billy should play piano so that George can replace John as the primary guitarist. John is slightly offended by this, and begins playing the song's main riff in order to demonstrate his ability.

28.16   OLD BROWN SHOE   (2:53)

John's riffing leads directly into this performance. George considers playing the song in the key of D, but John suggests A, and they give it a try. The change in key causes George's vocal to be stiff, and George's concern about John's guitar playing ability is proven to be justified, as John offers inept accompaniment. The performance slides into a jam shortly before it ends.

28.17   OLD BROWN SHOE   (2:22)

John begins jamming on guitar, but George steers it into "Old Brown Shoe." John turns up the volume on his guitar and tries punctuating the song with short, hard-edged licks. While this is an improvement over what he's been doing, it doesn't fit the tone of this song. The performance breaks down at the start of the second bridge.

28.18   OLD BROWN SHOE (6:46<

After a brief discussion of the desired tempo, The Beatles restart at the first bridge. The performance is loose, and George vocalises a few verses instead of singing. As the song teeters on the edge of breakdown John leads the band into a brief jam before George leads them back into the beginning of the song. They make it all the way through the song this time, with John making a first attempt at a guitar solo. With no ending for the song worked out yet, they simply go right back to the first verse and continue on. After the performance nearly breaks down (perhaps out of boredom), George leads them back to the first verse yet again as the available tape runs out.

28.19   OLD BROWN SHOE (2:55)

The rehearsals are paying off as The Beatles deliver a fairly strong run-through. John's guitar work is spotty and Billy still isn't contributing, but Ringo's fine drumming on the off-beat and George's assured vocal carry the performance.

28.20   SOMETHING (3:43<

George exhumes another song from his collection of unfinished numbers. This rehearsal segment, however, bears little resemblance to the superb performance which would be recorded for *Abbey Road* the following April. As it begins George is frustrated with his inability to complete the second line, and John suggests filling the spot with anything for the moment.

Although the melody is more-or-less complete, the words are unfinished and everyone's performance is unsure (George asks at one point if they know how the tune goes). The rehearsal breaks down when they reach the middle eight as George stops to teach them the chords.

"Something" was suggested by the title of "Something In The Way She Moves," a song recorded by James Taylor for his Apple album.

During the course of the rehearsal George had asked Glyn to mix his vocal microphone into the P.A. system. Glyn asks about this as Paul suggests some further lyrics.

28.21   SOMETHING (4:30)

The rehearsal continues as the band begins a more serious run-through. George turns in a comparatively sincere vocal, John supplies back-up vocals, and Paul provides his usual competent bass line. He and John try out the unfinished lyrics, and the full band runs through the backing before the available tape cuts off.

28.22   "HOW DO YOU TELL SOMEONE?" >1:59<

George leads the band in this ragged performance. John tries to follow along on guitar with little success and he and Paul ultimately take refuge in "Get Back" riffs.

Although it's unidentified, this is presumably a very rough original, slightly reminiscent of George's 1965 song "If I Needed Someone."

28.23   POSITIVELY 4TH STREET >1:02<

George takes lead vocal and plays guitar on this loose performance. The others, obviously not interested, offer discordant accompaniment

"Positively 4th Street" was recorded in 1965 by Bob Dylan.

The Beatles then finally get around to talking about exactly what they're doing. Despite having successfully recorded a number of performances, Paul isn't really sure if they are making an album or simply rehearsing for a live performance. The consensus is that they are making an album and preparing for a live show. Since they don't have an album's worth of songs ready, John suggests that they perform what they have on the following Thursday and then rehearse another batch of tunes which could be taped at a later date. The Thursday deadline for the live performance is due to Ringo's commitment to begin work on *The Magic Christian* the following week.

Since his compositions have been routinely rejected or ignored by John and Paul, George is thinking about releasing them as a solo album rather than giving them to other artists to record. John and Yoko are supportive of the idea, most likely because it would allow *them* to continue making albums together without causing friction within The Beatles. George's comments have a hint of bitterness to them, as he makes mention of the unspoken rule within the group that limited his contributions to one song per album side. Many of the songs that George has stockpiled were used on his first solo album *All Things Must Pass*.

28.24   GET BACK   (0 28<
This performance is being played back during the conversation above.

28.25   TEDDY BOY   >1:13<
Paul had formally introduced this composition on January 24th and had evidently set it aside after a deservedly lukewarm reception. Now he takes another stab at showing it to the group and, as before, John makes it obvious that he cannot take this trite composition seriously. Far from offended, Paul joins in the laughter himself.

It's unclear why this bit of silliness (not even *charming* silliness) was preserved on multi-track tape, and it's even less clear why this snippet was released on *Anthology 3* (where it was edited together with a run-through from the 24th).

28.26   GET BACK   >0:18<
More playback (this time of the guitar solo), which stops shortly after George begins to perform "Let It Down."

28.27   LET IT DOWN   (2:03<
George offers a solo run-through of one of the dozens of songs that he has in reserve. He accompanies himself on electric guitar, offering a nicely understated, quiet performance. This is quite similar to the version he played for John at the beginning of the sessions on the 2nd.

28.28   I WANT YOU (SHE'S SO HEAVY)   >0:47<
A loud, raucous performance whose jagged guitar and plodding drum-work suggest the usual end-of-the-session jam. John sings one line and the entire band joins in.

"I Want You" would ultimately be recorded for *Abbey Road*.

John then mentions that Allen Klein has shown up. This indicates that negotiations between the two for Klein to run John's business affairs had already begun. Klein would ultimately be another wedge driven into the already troubled group.

28.29   I WANT YOU (SHE'S SO HEAVY)   0:41)
John leads Ringo and Billy in a tentative attempt at the song. This is sparser than 28.28, but more worked out. John sings another two lines from this new song, literally as he's walking out the door.

Wednesday, January 29th, 1969

John had left the previous day's rehearsal singing snatches of "I Want You." Not surprisingly, that was the first number attempted at this rehearsal (although no tapes have become available). It's likely that much time was spent discussing the impending performance on the Apple rooftop (which had been considered since at least the 26th), although we don't get the formal rehearsal which one would expect (perhaps because Billy is absent, or perhaps because they didn't want to over-rehearse). Instead, the band spends their day running through some of George's numbers, playing Buddy Holly tunes, and rehearsing "One After 909" and "Teddy Boy" (again!). Unfortunately, tapes of the latter two numbers have not become available

The first available material from this day is a speech that Paul gives to John as several members of the crew look on. Ringo can be faintly heard engaged in another conversation in the background and George is apparently not yet present. Paul makes a sincere attempt to convince John that a live performance at this time is absolutely crucial if the group intends to keep in touch with their audience. He compares the band's nervousness about live performances to how they felt when they first played in public, and points out that once they overcome this, the show will be great. Unfortunately, it's *George* who is dead-set against the shows, and it is *he* and not John whom Paul must convince to return to the stage. This exchange appears in the film *Let it Be*.

29.1   ALL THINGS MUST PASS   >1:36<
The Beatles return to a song which had been extensively rehearsed at Twickenham, but virtually ignored to this point during the Apple sessions. George sings as Paul and Ringo follow along, but John ignores the performance completely as he sits tying his sneaker, whispering to Yoko and lighting a cigarette. George is playing a Leslie'd guitar, perhaps to compensate for the lack of organ.

29.2   ALL THINGS MUST PASS   (2:54)
A full performance on which everyone contributes (John plays organ in Billy's absence). This is nothing more than a cursory run-through, just to reacquaint themselves with the song

29.3   LET IT DOWN   (2:33)
The instrument assignments remain the same as they turn in an uninspired performance of another of George's songs. They make it all the way through, but the musicianship is far from impressive, despite the fact that George has been playing the song for them at various points throughout the sessions.

29.4   LET IT DOWN   (1:22)
The Beatles try the song again, and the resulting performance is a slight improvement over the previous try. Paul delivers an enthusiastic backing vocal during the chorus.

29.5   DIG IT   >0:54<
This performance is lyrically similar to the one from the 26th (see 26.21), but is performed at a much faster tempo. Paul contributes a scat backing vocal.

29.6   VACATION TIME   (0:46)

John takes the lead vocal on this loose cover of an obscure Chuck Berry number. This brief performance is not without charm, but falls apart, probably because of their trouble remembering the song.

"Vacation Time," written and recorded by Chuck Berry, was the b-side of his 1958 single "Beautiful Deliliah."

29.7   medley / CANNONBALL / NOT FADE AWAY / HEY LITTLE GIRL (IN THE HIGH SCHOOL SWEATER) / BO DIDDLEY (2:59<

This medley begins with Ringo pounding out the drum beat for "Cannonball" (an instrumental) as George plays along on guitar. After a few bars they segue into "Not Fade Away" and George provides a few lines of vocal. John joins in, and sings a bit of "Hey Little Girl." Apparently able to remember nothing more than the song's catch phrase, he switches to "Bo Diddley." All four numbers here share the 'Bo Diddley beat,' and flow together seamlessly.

"Cannonball," recorded in 1958, was one of many Duane Eddy instrumentals The Beatles were familiar with. "Not Fade Away" was released in 1957 by Buddy Holly and The Crickets. "Hey Little Girl (In The High School Sweater)" was recorded by Dee Clark in 1959 and "Bo Diddley" was, of course, written and performed by Bo Diddley in 1955. For some reason, Glyn preserved this mess on multi-track tape.

29.8   MAYBE BABY (2:27)

Buddy Holly was a great influence on The Beatles, and they pay tribute to him here with a series of entertaining cover versions. This particular performance is complete, with John taking the lead. For once, he has a good recollection of a song's lyrics, and all of them have fun recalling this tune.

"Maybe Baby" Was a 1958 hit for Buddy Holly and The Crickets.

29.9   medley PEGGY SUE GOT MARRIED / THINKING OF LINKING (1:43)

John leads the band into another Buddy Holly song, but he has almost no recollection of the lyrics except for the title. After letting the performance lapse to an instrumental, John begins singing what words he can remember from "Thinking of Linking," which was evidently a Holly-inspired original.

Buddy Holly's "Peggy Sue Got Married" was released posthumously in 1959. This is the only known performance of "Thinking of Linking," one of the earliest Lennon/McCartney collaborations. Unfortunately, everyone seems to have half-forgotten the tune.

29.10   CRYING, WAITING, HOPING (2:23)

George takes over from John on this one as The Beatles perform another Buddy Holly classic. John and Paul provide pleasant backing harmonies, and George plays a fine guitar solo (which draws a compliment from Paul). Again, they have a bit of difficulty recalling the lyrics. Nevertheless, John remarks on how much fun this is, and he's right.

"Crying, Waiting, Hoping" was posthumously released as the b-side of "Peggy Sue Got Married." The Beatles performed the song at their audition for Decca in 1962, and a year later for BBC radio.

29.11   MAILMAN, BRING ME NO MORE BLUES (1:47)

John takes the lead vocal on this one with support from George. Again, it's obvious the band knows this one by heart, and John tries his best to duplicate Holly's vocal mannerisms.

"Mailman, Bring Me No More Blues" was recorded by Buddy Holly in 1957. A severely edited and rearranged version of this performance was released on *Anthology 3*.

29.12 BESAME MUCHO (1:03<
29.13 BESAME MUCHO >0:12<
29.14 BESAME MUCHO >0:18<
29.15 BESAME MUCHO >0:20)

These four fragments all derive from the same performance. Paul does his best Desi Arnaz imitation and belts out the lyrics as well as he can remember them. John chimes in with an occasional background vocal, but this one is Paul's show.

These four fragments appear in the film *Let It Be* (an unedited tape has yet to surface). "Besame Mucho" was a regular in The Beatles' repertoire in the early 1960's, and had been performed at their auditions for Decca and E.M.I.. The Beatles undoubtedly picked the song up from The Coasters' 1960 performance.

29.16 ALL THINGS MUST PASS (2:56)

This ragged performance is notable for the vocals in the first verse. Paul sings the first line and John sings the second before giving way to George, who sings the rest of the song. It's a shame that this ad hoc arrangement wasn't pursued more seriously. As the performance continues, it's clear that George is the only one really showing interest in it.

29.17 ALL THINGS MUST PASS (0:10)

Paul initiates a very brief reprise.

In the next available tape segment, The Beatles and Michael discuss the following day's rooftop concert. Paul seems unconcerned about the state of the rehearsals, and George jokes about playing on a rooftop to a bunch of chimneys, but *does* seem enthusiastic about performing. Michael is worried about what songs they'll do, but, again, Paul is unconcerned. John mentions that the rooftop performances will be recorded for potential release, and they all seem in a relatively good mood, which will carry on into the next day. These few minutes of dialogue can be heard in the home video release of The Beatles' *Anthology*.

In the next brief fragment, John jokes that The Beatles will spend the night at George's house to prepare themselves for the show. Michael asks for a copy of the lyrics to study, and Paul responds that The Beatles will be happy to back him up if he cares to do the singing. Obviously, everyone is on the verge of departing for the evening.

Thursday, January 30th, 1969

As planned, The Beatles took to the roof around lunchtime. A makeshift stage had been constructed, and extra cameras were brought in to film The Beatles' performance and the reaction of bystanders on the street below. Glyn remained in the basement, monitoring the multi-track recordings and occasionally speaking to the band via intercom. George Martin, who had originally been expected to oversee the recording, apparently played the same role he had throughout much of the month - bystander. The Beatles ran through "Get Back" (three times), "Don't Let Me Down" (twice), "I've Got a Feeling" (twice), One After 909" and "Dig a Pony" with snatches of standards at the end of some of the songs. George held true to a decision he had made as far back as January 7th and none of his songs were performed. The impromptu concert was halted when the police arrived, but by then the group had more than exhausted their repertoire of new songs. Although these performances are a bit rough around the edges, they have a liveliness and focus that is missing from most of the January rehearsals. Sadly, this would be the last public performance The Beatles ever gave.

30.1   GET BACK   (2:58)
The group runs through this number as a warm-up (in fact, this take will be marked "rehearsal" on the multi-track tape box). John and George are noticeably sloppy in their guitar work, but Paul is simply overjoyed to be performing live again, and offers an impassioned lead vocal.

30.2   GET BACK   (2:57)
A much tighter performance, with fine musicianship from everyone. Paul improvises a bit on the lyrics. John reads a meek request for the next song.
   This performance appeared in the film *Let it Be*.

30.3   DON'T LET ME DOWN   (3:12)
John and Paul sing a very tight harmony on the song's opening chorus. The performance is quite good until John blows the first line of the second verse, singing gibberish because he can't recall the lyrics. This performance runs straight into the next.
   This take appeared in the film *Let It Be*.

30.4   I'VE GOT A FEELING   (3:24)
Easily the best performance of the song that has surfaced. George plays an intentionally distorted guitar and Paul delivers a superb vocal. John fiddles with the lyrics a bit, and sings the title of Little Richard's "Ooh! My Soul" as the song comes to an end.
   This performance appeared in the film and on the album *Let It Be*.
   John worries about being heard, and wisely ignores Michael's suggestion to lean over the edge of the roof so that people can see him.

30.5   ONE AFTER 909   >0:06)
The band, led by Billy, loosely rehearses the song as they wait for the crew to ready themselves.

30.6   ONE AFTER 909   (2:40)
Another exceptional performance, as the band rolls smoothly through this song. George inserts a number of fine guitar licks, and John and Paul team for a flawless vocal.

This performance, though live, was obviously considered best, and was used for the aborted *Get Back* album as well as the *Let It Be* album and film.

30.7   DANNY BOY (0:04)

John sings a single misremembered line as a tag to "One After 909."

"Londonderry Air" is a traditional Irish song which was revived under the title "Danny Boy" in 1913. It had been a hit for Conway Twitty in 1959.

The Beatles are unsure of what to play next. Glyn suggests "Dig A Pony" and John dispatches someone to get him the words. Michael suggests some oldies in the interim, but this proves unnecessary because John's clipboard is close at hand.

30.8   DIG A PONY (3:37)

George counts in for "Dig a Pony," but Ringo stops him in order to adjust his hi-hat. That accomplished, they turn in a credible if somewhat perfunctory performance, with John singing the lyrics from a clipboard which Kevin holds in front of him.

This performance was included in the film, and appeared on the *Let It Be* album, where a few seconds of lyric were edited out of both the intro and outro.

The January weather begins to take effect on John, who comments that he's getting cold and can't play his guitar properly.

30.9   I'VE GOT A FEELING (3:26)

The band opts for another pass at "I've Got A Feeling." The performance is inferior in nearly every way to the earlier one (30.4). George is a bit more experimental with his guitar part, and John sings the correct lyrics this time.

30.10   A PRETTY GIRL IS LIKE A MELODY (0:04)

Once again John sings a bit of a standard as a tag to a performance.

30.11   GET BACK (0:02)

The band begins to play "Get Back," but John interrupts the performance and asks to do "Don't Let Me Down." Paul sings out the title of that tune, and they launch into another performance.

30.12   DON'T LET ME DOWN (3:12)

It's probable that another pass at this song was requested because of John's lyric flub in the first attempt. John doesn't wait for the second verse this time, though, and ruins the take on the very first line of the first verse. The group, understandably, lets their musicianship get a bit sloppy the rest of the way.

30.13   GET BACK (2:56)

Without hesitation, George leads the group into the closing number. At the end of the first verse, John and George's amps go out and the performance almost breaks down. Paul and Ringo carry on, and George quickly rectifies the amplifier problem, allowing him and John to join back in. As might be expected, the performance is rough, but Paul's exuberance carries it along. When they reach the coda Paul improvises some lyrics in response to the presence of the police. This performance appeared in the film *Let It Be* and was released on *Anthology 3*.

The show is over. Paul thanks Ringo's wife Maureen for her ardent applause, as John utters a humorous aside comparing The Beatles' performance to an audition. These comments would be tagged onto the end of "Get Back" (27.6) when it appeared on the *Let It Be* album.

Friday, January 31st, 1969

The Beatles and Billy Preston returned to the basement of Apple to perform three songs that were not appropriate for presentation on the rooftop, "Two Of Us," "The Long And Winding Road" and "Let It Be." Unlike the earlier Apple sessions, these performances were very camera-conscious, and The Beatles were obviously attempting to record releaseable takes. "Two Of Us" was committed to tape easily, as only a breakdown and three complete takes were required. "The Long And Winding Road" and "Let It Be" required more time. The film crew had allotted a take number to each of the nine substantial performances done on the rooftop, so the first performance done on this day was dubbed take 10. Since new take numbers weren't assigned after breakdowns and false starts, many takes consisted of multiple performances (to avoid confusion, we have added a letter to the take number in such cases). It should be noted that the circulating tape of this session has been intentionally butchered, presenting only brief fragments of many of the complete takes.

The session begins with a bit of *Laugh-In* inspired nonsense as The Beatles prepare to record "Two Of Us."

31.1   TWO OF US   (0:13)
Take 10A. This performance breaks down during the introduction because the tempo is far too slow. John then tunes his guitar as Paul speaks to an unidentified Jim (the same person, perhaps, whom they had sung about on the 7th).

31.2   TWO OF US   (0:43<
The first verse of take 10B, fragmented on the available tape. John's attempts at tuning seem to have made the situation worse, since his acoustic guitar (and Paul's) are very much out of tune. George, in lieu of playing bass, picks out the song's bass line on the bass strings of his electric guitar.

31.3   medley / TWO OF US / FRIENDSHIP   >0:24)
The conclusion of take 10B. As the song winds down John sings a brief, obscene parody of "Friendship." Paul joins in and sings the tag-line to Marmalade's version of "Ob-La-Di, Ob-La-Da."

"Friendship" was written in 1940 by Cole Porter. It was a popular number for Ethel Merman.

31.4   TURKEY IN THE STRAW   (0:06)
John sings this parody to the familiar tune of "Turkey in The Straw."

"Turkey In The Straw" derives from "Old Zip Goon," a minstrel song from the early 1800's.

31.5   TWO OF US   (3:21)
Take 11. The Beatles attempt the song at a faster tempo and deliver a flawless performance. Since a fourth verse was never written, John and Paul sing the third verse twice. Ringo plays a number of interesting drum fills throughout.

It was this performance (not take 12, as stated in *The Beatles Recording Sessions*) that was chosen for the *Let It Be* album. It also appears in the film, where the whistling outro has been replaced by the one from take 12.

31.6   'DEED I DO   (0:07<
John and Paul sing this a capella duet. A few seconds into this performance Michael calls for the film crew to cut. Since there is no evidence that Glyn recorded this track either, the rest of this performance is probably lost forever.

"'Deed I Do" was written in 1927 by Walter Hirsch and Fred Rose.

31.7   TWO OF US (3:43)
Take 12. This performance is quite similar to take 11, although it's intentionally taken a bit slower. John makes flopping noises over the song's beginning and end, and Paul follows the performance with a brief a capella snatch of Elvis's "I Got Stung."

31.8   THE LONG AND WINDING ROAD (0:30)
Take 13A (miscalled on the available tape as take 14). This performance breaks down in the first verse as Glyn interrupts because of a technical problem. For the rest of the session, Paul has moved to piano, John plays bass and the others are on their usual instruments.

31.9   THE LONG AND WINDING ROAD (0:03<
The first line only of take 13B.

31.10   THE LONG AND WINDING ROAD >0:09)
The end of a complete performance, most likely 13B.

31.11   THE LONG AND WINDING ROAD (0:18)
A knockoff, not a take, performed as Paul waits for the crew.

31.12   THE LONG AND WINDING ROAD (0:03<
The first line only of take 14.

31.13   THE LONG AND WINDING ROAD (0:02)
Take 16A. A brief false start.

31.14   THE LONG AND WINDING ROAD (0:13)
Take 16B. A breakdown, as Paul hears a note he doesn't like.

31.15   THE LONG AND WINDING ROAD (0:03<
The first line of take 16C. Another obviously longer performance truncated on the circulating tape.

31.16   LADY MADONNA >0:12<
The band takes a break from "The Long And Winding Road" and performs a fairly well-played jam of their 1968 single. Once again this is a fragment representing a longer performance.

31.17   THE LONG AND WINDING ROAD >0:04)
The tail end of a loose run-through, obviously not a take.

31.18   THE LONG AND WINDING ROAD (0:03)
Take 17B? A performance quickly interrupted by Glyn.

31.19   THE LONG AND WINDING ROAD (0:01<
Take 17C? Only the very beginning of the song is heard before the available tape cuts off.

31.20   THE LONG AND WINDING ROAD (3:42)
Take 18? A complete performance of the song, and a keeper. Paul recites the middle eight lyric over the instrumental break, obscuring Billy's organ solo, and plays a brief coda on the piano at the song's conclusion.

This performance was chosen for inclusion on the *Let It Be* album, where Paul's voice has been mixed out of the instrumental break, and an overdubbed orchestra and choir added. The original undubbed take (which was to have been used on the unreleased *Get Back* LP) was ultimately released in 1996 on *Anthology 3. The Beatles Recording Sessions* identifies this performance as take 19, but it obviously differs from 31.22, which is clearly identified on the raw tape as take 19. The "take 18?" designation is an educated guess on our part. This performance may be any of the unaccounted for takes or simply a longer version of one of the severely truncated performances scattered throughout this session.

31.21 THE LONG AND WINDING ROAD >0:09)

A fragment of another brief rehearsal, or perhaps take 18B.

31.22 THE LONG AND WINDING ROAD (3:31)

Take 19. Another fine, complete performance. As might be expected, there is little that differentiates this take from 31.20, except for some minor lyric variations and the lack of the spoken lyric over the instrumental break. John remarks that he's satisfied, and Ringo agrees. It's probable that the group took a lunch break at this point.

This performance appeared in the film *Let It Be*.

31.23 LET IT BE >0:06

An instrumental fragment from a rehearsal.

31.24 LET IT BE (0:50)

Take 20A. The Beatles play the same instruments that they had for "The Long And Winding Road." The quality of this first take indicates that the band spent a considerable amount of time rehearsing the number before the cameras rolled. The performance goes along fine until Glyn notices that Paul is singing too close to his mike, causing distortion on his vocal. Glyn stops the take at the start of the chorus in order to correct this, much to John's annoyance.

31.25 LET IT BE (0:05)

Take 20B. A breakdown during the introduction.

31.26 LET IT BE >0:13)

This fragment represents the end of a full performance, perhaps take 20C.

31.27 LET IT BE (0:03<

The introduction to take 21. Severely edited on the available tape.

31.28 LET IT BE >0: 14)

Take 22? This performance is showing signs of breaking down when Paul begins singing drunkenly, effectively ending the take.

John requests a bathroom break in his own inimitable fashion, as George plays a riff that resembles Dylan's "All Along The Watchtower."

On the next available fragment, Paul discusses "Let It Be"'s tempo. Three lines of dialogue from this conversation were edited onto the beginning of "The Long And Winding Road" (31.20) on the unreleased *Get Back* album.

31.29 LET IT BE (0:11<

Take 23. Only the introduction is heard before the available tape edits.

31.30 LET IT BE >0:06)

The end of a performance, possibly take 23.

31.31 LET IT BE >0:21)

Take 24? This performance is falling apart when Paul and Billy turn it into a unique soul rendition.

George makes a passing reference to John Barham, an arranger who would provide the orchestral scores for his *All Things Must Pass* album the following year.

31.32 LET IT BE (0:44)

Take 25. This performance breaks down at the start of the chorus, causing John to issue a stream of light-hearted profanity. Paul and John then clown around in mock German, and Paul counts down in that language for the next take.

31.33   LET IT BE   (0:12<

Take 25B. Another performance severely abbreviated on the available tape.

31.34   LET IT BE   >0:27<

Take 25C? While the performance sounds passable, Paul has given up, once again using Brother Malcolm instead of Mother Mary in the song.

31.35   medley / LET IT BE / TWELFTH STREET RAG   (0:10)

Take 26A. Paul begins playing the song's introduction but quickly switches to "Twelfth Street Rag."

"Twelfth Street Rag" was composed in 1914 by Euday Bowman.

31.36   LET IT BE   (0:06<

Take 26B. This performance is truncated on the available tape, but it probably broke down anyway since a phone rings as Paul plays the introduction.

31.37   LET IT BE   >0:29<

This fragment represents a portion of the chorus of an unidentified take. It was edited into take 27B in the film *Let It Be* for unknown reasons.

31.38   LET IT BE   (3:49)

Take 27A. A virtually flawless performance, marred only by a mediocre guitar solo from George.

The Beatles would return to this track on April 30th, when George would overdub another guitar solo. That version was chosen for inclusion on the *Get Back* album. More overdubbing occurred on January 4, 1970, when another guitar solo was recorded and brass and cellos were added. A mix featuring these overdubs (but the April 30th guitar solo) was eventually released as a single. A further mix (done March 26, 1970 by Phil Spector and featuring the January 4th solo and a repetition of part of the final chorus) was included on the *Let It Be* album.

31.39   LET IT BE   (3:51)

Take 27B. George laughs over the song's introduction, but the band turns in another excellent performance nonetheless. Little differentiates this from take 27, except that Paul alters one of the lines.

George's laughter was mixed out when this performance was included in the film *Let It Be*. The performance is shown in its entirety, although extra material was edited into it (see 31.37)

This session brought the production side of the project to a close, although post-production would continue for more than a year.

Appendix 1: Post Production

When Michael Lindsay-Hogg's film crew packed up and left Apple on the evening of January 31st, it was clear that enough material had been shot to produce a television special or documentary film. But had enough worthwhile performances been recorded to produce The Beatles' next LP? The consensus opinion certainly must have been that it hadn't, since the tapes (apart from a February 5th mixing session of most of the rooftop performance) were left untouched until March. At this point, someone (one would assume Paul) directed Glyn to go through the tapes, choose a number of performances, mix them and present them to the group so that they might decide if anything could be done with them. Glyn set about doing this at Olympic Studios on March 10th, when he mixed the following tracks: "Get Back" (23.31), "Teddy Boy" (an edited version of 24.22), "Two of Us" (24.40), "Dig A Pony" (23.35), "I've Got A Feeling" (23.36), 'The Long And Winding Road" (31.20), "Let It Be" (26.36), "I'm Ready" (22.52), "Save The Last Dance For Me" (22.53), "Don't Let Me Down" (22.54), "For You Blue" (25.25), "Get Back" (27.6) and "The Walk" (a portion of 27.12). He had acetates made of his work, omitting "I'm Ready" and "Save The Last Dance For Me" and inadvertently including a brief snippet of "I've Got a Feeling" (23.32) in the process.

Glyn's choice of performances was strange to say the least, as he relied heavily on the tracks that he had already rough-mixed and presented to the band on lacquers while the sessions were still in progress. These included a performance aborted in the middle ("I've Got a Feeling"), a first-ever group attempt at a new number ("Teddy Boy") and rough, early performances of songs that would be polished as the sessions wore on ("Two Of Us, "Let it Be" and "Don't Let Me Down"). Perhaps Glyn had chosen these for the sake of convenience, but it's more likely that he had Paul's enthusiasm for them in mind (see dialogue following 26.9). Glyn spent three more days mixing at Olympic, producing the following tracks: "Two Of Us"(31.5), "The Long And Winding Road" (31.22), "Lady Madonna" (31.16), "Let It Be" (31.38), "I've Got A Feeling" (27.13), "Dig It" (24.3 and 26.27), "Maggie Mae" (24.41), "Rip It up" (26.28), "Shake, Rattle And Roll (26.29), "Miss Ann"/ "Kansas City" / "Lawdy Miss Clawdy" (26.30), "Blue Suede Shoes' (26.31) and "You Really Got a Hold on Me" (6.32).

It's likely that Glyn's work wasn't immediately heard by the band, as Paul was married March 12th and left for a honeymoon in America shortly thereafter, John was travelling with Yoko throughout Europe, and George was busy with a drug arrest. With the album on hold for the moment, the attention turned to the group's next single. "Get Back" (27.6, with a portion of 28.1 edited on) and "Don't Let Me Down"(28.2) were chosen as the a and b-side, respectively, and were mixed by Glyn and Paul at Olympic on April 7th (Glyn's March 10th mix and E.M.I.'s Jeff Jarratt's March 26th mix of "Get Back" being bypassed and released little more than a week later. It's interesting to note that the January 28th performance of "Don't Let Me Down" had been chosen over the January 22nd one included on the March 10th acetate. This would mark the last time the session tapes would be searched, as all subsequent work (both by Glyn and Phil Spector) would be limited to the performances already mixed by Glyn.

Later in April it was decided that an album could in fact be made out of this collection of tracks, but "Let It Be" would require overdubbing. This was accomplished on April 30th, as George added a new guitar solo to track 31.38 (the 26.36 performance being dropped from consideration). As Glyn worked through May to piece the album together, it was announced in the music press that the record, to be titled *Get Back*, would be delayed past the originally-announced June release date. Glyn completed work on the album on May 28th, with the following track listing: "One After 909" (30.6), "I'm Ready" (22.52), "Save The Last Dance For Me" (22.53), "Don't Let Me Down" (22.54), "Dig A Pony" (23.35), "I've Got a Feeling" (23.36), "Get Back" (the single edit), "For You Blue" (25.25), "Teddy Boy" (24.22), "Two Of Us" (24.40), "Maggie Mae" (24.41), "Dig It" (a 3:59 excerpt of 26.27), "Let It Be" (31.38 with the overdubbed guitar solo), "The Long And Winding Road" (31.20) and a short reprise of "Get Back" (a further fragment of 28.1). A rough edit of the album, featuring a much longer excerpt of "Dig It" as well as a few seconds of extra dialogue scattered throughout, was also prepared around this time. The June 7th edition of *New Musical Express* included a quote from John, who stated that the album, now titled *Get Back, Don't Let Me Down and 12 other songs*, would be released in July.

When July arrived, it was announced that the album would be released in September, in conjunction with the television special *and* a theatrical film (which would encompass the TV show and include further footage). A further album culled from the "Get Back" tapes, consisting of oldies, was also said to be on the drawing board (This proposal was little more than someone's fancy notion, as only four oldies had been mixed, and they were definitely not up to releaseable standard). When September arrived, it was announced that the album would be pushed back to December, ostensibly to avoid a clash with *Abbey Road*, the new album the band had produced in the interim and would release on September 26th. The September 20th issue of *Rolling Stone* featured a 'track by track' review of *Get Back*, and on September 22nd Boston radio station WBCN aired the entire acetate that Glyn had prepared on March 10th, (as a Buffalo radio station had done a short time before) mistakenly referring to it as the *Get Back* album. Glyn's rough edit of the album also slipped out and was aired, and by the end of the year bootlegs of these two broadcasts were circulating throughout America.

Michael had completed post-production work on the film by December, with the television special idea now completely dropped. The album was held back yet again, this time to add two songs ("I Me Mine" and "Across The Universe") which were featured in the film but not included on the record. Both songs had been extensively rehearsed at Twickenham, but neither had been recorded when the group moved to Apple. George, Paul and Ringo reconvened at Abbey Road Studios on January 3rd, 1970 and recorded "I Me Mine" with George Martin producing. The following day they added further overdubs to "Let It Be" (31.38), including another new guitar solo. "Across The Universe" proved to be something of a problem, as John was vacationing in Denmark and had no desire to return to England and participate in the session. Glyn simply returned to the February 1968 recording of the song (which had finally been released on December 12, 1969 on a World Wildlife Fund Charity album) and remixed it. On January 5th Glyn completed his new attempt at *Get Back*, which featured the same basic line-up as the previous one except for the inclusion of "I Me Mine" and "Across The Universe" and the deletion of "Teddy Boy" (which Paul had decided to re-record for his first solo album). Glyn ignored the new overdubs that had been done for "Let It Be," choosing the mix featuring the April 30, 1969 overdubs instead.

The second version of *Get Back* met with the same fate as the first, it was rejected by the group. They did agree to release "Let It Be" as their new single on March 6th, (using the April 30th guitar solo but some of the orchestral overdubs from January 4th) backing it with "You Know My Name (Look up The Number)," which had been started in May of 1967 and completed in April of 1969. At this point American producer Phil Spector was called in to try to make something commercially viable out of the "Get Back" tapes. From March 23rd to April 2nd Spector created fresh mixes for most of the songs, choosing to ignore all of the early, rough takes in favour the later, more polished ones. He also chose to add overdubs to "Across The Universe," "The Long And Winding Road" and "I Me Mine." The running order of Spector's album, now dubbed *Let It Be*, was "Two Of Us ' (31.5), "Dig A Pony" (30.8, with a few lines edited out of the intro and outro), "Across The Universe" (the February, 1968 recording with new overdubs), "I Me Mine" (the January, 1970 recording with overdubs, artificially lengthened by editing), "Dig it" (a 0:48 excerpt of 26.27), "Let It Be" (31.38 with the January 4th guitar solo and overdubs and also artificially lengthened), "Maggie Mae" (24.41), "I've Got A Feeling" (30.4), "One After 909" (30.6), "The Long And Winding Road" (31.20 with new overdubs), "For You Blue" (25.25, with a new lead vocal over-dubbed in January, 1970) and "Get Back" (27.6 crossfaded with dialogue from after 30.13). The album was released May 8th, virtually coinciding with the release of the film which was also christened *Let It Be*.

Spector's work on *Let It Be* has met with substantial criticism, much of it coming from Paul himself. But while Spector's production may have been very heavy-handed in some areas (especially "The Long And Winding Road"), the *Let It Be* album is at least a respectable collection of commercially viable music. By comparison, the *Get Back* album, its historical interest and occasional charm aside, is an abysmal mess. It serves its duty as a chronicle of January, 1969 too well, revealing a group of four unhappy musicians generally giving the worst performances of their otherwise illustrious career.

Appendix 2 : Recording and Filming

Audio recording of the "Get Back" sessions was conducted in three separate fashions. First, the film crew utilised two Nagra mono reel-to-reel tape recorders to capture nearly every moment of the sessions during which a Beatle was present. It should be noted that recording was sporadic on January 2nd, and that the recording equipment was shut off between takes on January 30th and 31st. Each recorder was assigned to a camera, and each time that camera began filming a beep would be heard on the tape to allow for synchronisation of the sound at a later time. Short reels running at a very fast speed were utilised, so only about 16 minutes were captured on each roll. Since two recorders were running, the minute or so that would be lost when reels were being changed on one machine would usually be captured on the other. At Twickenham, the rolls for each recorder were simply numbered consecutively, and these numbers were announced (when the soundmen remembered) at the start of the roll with the appropriate camera designation (A or B) added on. A total of 223 rolls were recorded in this fashion at Twickenham. When filming moved to Apple the recording process remained the same, but the numbering system differed slightly. The sound rolls that corresponded with each camera were still numbered consecutively, but the A rolls were arbitrarily restarted at #400, and the B rolls at #1014. 307 rolls were recorded at Apple, making for a total of approximately 530 rolls (about 141 hours, though only 80 or so of it is unique). A few additional rolls of non-Beatle material were also recorded, such as street interviews during the rooftop concert and chats with Apple's office help.

The second method of audio recording was the mono equipment brought into Twickenham by Glyn Johns for the purpose of playback. Glyn recorded performances on January 7th through 10th and 13th simply so The Beatles could assess their performances before they continued rehearsing. None of these tapes have surfaced, and it's possible that they no longer exist.

The final method of recording utilised was the professional multi-track facilities at Apple on E.M.I.'s mobile unit. More than ten hours of material were recorded in this fashion, almost all of which was also captured on the film crew's equipment (albeit in lesser quality). From these tapes the performances on the album *Let It Be* and some of the performances in the *Let It Be* film were culled (the multi-track tapes, mixed into mono, were utilised for the soundtrack for the majority of the Apple portion of the film). They were also used for the aborted *Get Back* album and on the 1996 archival release *Anthology 3*.

Two cameras were used for most of the sessions, although additional ones were employed for the rooftop concert. Standard film clapboards were used, but only when the film rolls were changed (rather than each time the camera was turned on). Each new film roll resulted in a fresh slate number, but unlike the sound rolls, the number were not exclusive to a particular camera. For example, while there exists both a 75A and 75B sound roll, there is only one slate 75. Although the slates were numbered consecutively throughout the sessions, it should be noted that there were some departures from this system. On January 2nd, take numbers were utilised (loosely), and on January 3rd a system using both slate and take numbers was tried (and abandoned). On January 30th and 31st, the slate numbers were set aside in favour of precise take numbers. In all, approximately 450 slate numbers and precisely 27 take numbers were utilised, indicating that nearly 500 rolls of film were used.

It should be remembered that during filming at Twickenham the intended end product was still a television documentary (to precede the live broadcast), which would probably have been only 25 to 55 minutes in length. With this in mind, filming was done in brief spurts, and rarely, if ever, was an entire performance filmed. The Twickenham portion of the film *Let It Be* shows this clearly, as every performance there is shown in abbreviated form (and very often not in proper sync, as film of multiple performances has been edited together in an attempt to provide enough footage to go with the available sound recording). For example, close examination of "Suzy's Parlour" reveals that no footage of John (the lead singer of the song) was shot, and that various other shots of him have been edited together with synched shots of Paul and George in an attempt to create the illusion that we see him singing it. Rather than being a Beatle scholar's dream, viewing the unedited Twickenham footage would more likely be a frustrating nightmare.

Song Index

Coming Soon From Helter Skelter

Waiting for the Man: The Story of Drugs and Popular Music
by Harry Shapiro
Due in April 320 pages, ISBN 1 900924 08 0 Price: £12.99
First published in 1988, this is the definitive study of the extravagant, if sombre, association between drugs and popular music. Shapiro tells in detail the stories of the most famous heroes - Charlie Parker, Jimi Hendrix, Jim Morrison, Keith Moon, Sid Vicious - and examines the relationship between two billion-dollar industries. Fully revised, and including over 100 pages of new material covering the rise of Ecstasy and dance music; rap music and "crack" cocaine, and the return of the wasted junky rock star that came with the Seattle grunge scene. Featured artists in these new sections include Shaun Ryder, Tupac Shakur and Kurt Cobain.

Solo: A Biography of Sandy Denny by Pamela Winters
Due in May. 256 pages, ISBN 1 900924 11 0 Price: £12.99
Sandy Denny became famous as the distinctive singer Fairport Convention, and later with Fotheringay, as well as releasing four highly acclaimed solo albums. Melody Maker voted her best female singer in 1970 and 1971. But like many of the great musical artists of the seventies, she took refuge in drink and drugs. Sandy Denny died 20 years ago in mysterious circumstances, and this is the first ever Biography. US music journalist Pam Winters has had unprecedented access to Sandy's personal papers. She has interviewed at length all those who were close to her, to produce an illuminating portrait of one of the great English singers.

Coming Soon From SAF Publishing

An American Band - The Story of Grand Funk Railroad by Billy James
ISBN: 0946 719 26 8 224 pages (illustrated) UK £12.95
Grand Funk Railroad were one of the biggest grossing US rock 'n' roll acts of the seventies - they sold millions of records and played to sold out arenas the world over and were often cited as the loudest rock and roll band in the world. An American Band charts Grand Funk's meteoric rise to fame. The mixture of management hype, rock 'n' rolling and political beliefs, might seem naïve by today's standards, but their mammoth success as the 'people's band' has rarely been equalled since. Recently reformed and playing arenas in the States, this is a fascinating look at one of the hardest rocking bands of the seventies.

TEDDY BOYS DON'T KNIT - The Story of Viv Stanshall and the Bonzo Dog Doo-Dah Band by Chris Welch ISBN: 09467119 27 6
Viv Stanshall was one of pop music's true eccentrics. During the sixties he fronted one of Britain's funniest and most surreal musical outfits, The Bonzo Dog Doo Dah Band. However, Stanshall's life was one of extreme highs and lows, varying from playing pranks with The Who's Keith Moon to depression, alcoholism, and his final sad demise in a house fire. Former Melody Maker editor Chris Welch is a long-time Stanshall afficianado and recounts his incredible life story - a man who on the one hand could write lyrics for Steve Winwood, whilst on the other accused of attempting to murder his wife.

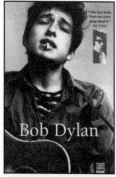
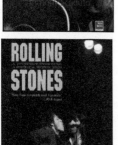

Available Now From Helter Skelter Publishing

Like The Night -
Bob Dylan and the Road to the Manchester Free Trade Hall.
ISBN: 1 900924 07 2   192 pages (illustrated). UK £12.00
The full history and background to the show that would become Bob Dylan's latest album, the most famous bootleg in history, now The Bootleg Series vols 4 and 5.
"When Dylan went electric, he both alienated the audience that had championed him and changed the face of rock music.
Lee's enjoyable and atmospheric reconstruction of this phase of Dylan's career is essential reading." **Uncut Magazine**
"CP Lee was there, but the point is that he can put you there too". **Greil Marcus**

XTC - The Exclusive Authorised Story Behind the Music
by XTC and Neville Farmer
ISBN: 1 900924 03 X   306 pages (illustrated). UK £12.00
Co-written by one of the most popular - and usually reclusive - cult bands of all time, this book is timed to coincide with their long-awaited new album.
"A cheerful celebration of the minutiae surrounding XTC's music with the band's musical passion intact. It's essentially a band-driven project for the fans, high in setting-the-record-straight anecdotes. The personality of Partridge dominates this book as it does XTC's music. Superbright, funny, commanding." **MOJO**

GET BACK: The Beatles' Let It Be Disaster
by Doug Sulphy and Ray Schweighhardt

A detailed document of the group's breakdown seen through the prism of the Get Back recording sessions. Instead of making the planned new album, the greatest band in the world were falling apart.

"Monumental... Fascinating and revealing" **Goldmine**

If you find difficulty obtaining any title, all Helter Skelter, Firefly and SAF books are stocked by, and are available mail order from:
Helter Skelter Bookshop, 4 Denmark Street, London WC2H 8LL Tel: 0171 836 1151 Fax: 0171 240 9880.

New Titles From SAF Publishing

Wish The World Away - Mark Eitzel and the American Music Club
by Sean Body   ISBN: 0 946719 20 9
192 pages (illustrated)   UK £11.95

Mark Eitzel's songs are poignant, highly personal tales, encapsulating a sense of loss and loathing, but often tinged with a bitter twist of drink-fuelled humour. Through his solo work and that of his former band American Music Club, Eitzel has been responsible for some of the most individual and memorable records of recent years. Through unrestricted access to Eitzel, former band members, associates and friends, Sean Body has written a fascinating biography which portrays an artist tortured by demons, yet redeemed by the aching beauty of his songs.

LUNAR NOTES - Zoot Horn Rollo's Captain Beefheart Experience
by Bill Harkleroad with Billy James   ISBN: 0 946719 217
160 pages (illustrated) - UK £11.95

Bill Harkleroad joined Captain Beefheart's Magic Band at a crucial time in their development. Beefheart rechristened Harkleroad as Zoot Horn Rollo and they embarked on recording one of the classic rock albums of all time - *Trout Mask Replica* - a work of unequalled daring and inventiveness. Further LPs, *Lick My Decals Off Baby* and *Clear Spot*, highlighted Zoot's skilled guitar playing and what a truly innovative band they were. For the first time we get the insider's story of what it was like to record, play and live with an eccentric genius such as Beefheart.

Meet The Residents - America's Most Eccentric Band! by Ian Shirley
ISBN: 0946 719 12 8   200 pages (illustrated) UK £11.95
Fully updated and now available again!

An outsider's view of The Residents' operations, exposing a world where nothing is as it seems. It is a fascinating tale of the musical anarchy and cartoon wackiness that has driven this unique bunch of artistic mavericks forward.

"This is the nearest to an official history you are ever likely to get, slyly abetted by the bug-eyed beans from Venus themselves". **Vox**

"Few enthusiasts will want to put this book down once they start reading". **Record Collector**

Digital Gothic - A Critical Discography Of Tangerine Dream
by Paul Stump   ISBN: 0946 719 18 7
160 pages (illustrated) UK £9.95

In this critical discography, music journalist Paul Stump picks his way through a veritable minefield of releases, determining both the explosive and those which fail to ignite. For the very first time Tangerine Dream's mammoth output is placed within an ordered perspective.

"It focuses fascinatingly on the pro soporific roots of the group and their place in a cool electronic lineage which traces right up to Detroit techno". **Mojo**

"A stimulating companion to the group's music". **The Wire**

Available Now From SAF Publishing

The One and Only: Peter Perrett - Homme Fatale by Nina Antonia
ISBN: 0946 719 16 0
224 pages (illustrated). UK £11.95
An extraordinary journey through crime, punishment and the decadent times of The Only Ones. Includes interviews with Perrett and all ex-band members.
"Antonia gets everyone's co-operation and never loses her perspective on Perrett". **Mojo**
"Antonia is the ideal chronicler of Perrett's rise and fall. From his time as drug dealer, to the smack sojourn in The Only Ones, Perrett's tale is one of self-abuse and staggering selfishness". **Select**

Plunderphonics, 'Pataphysics and Pop Mechanics by Andrew Jones
ISBN: 0946 719 15 2
256 pages (illustrated) UK £12.95
Chris Cutler, Fred Frith, Henry Threadgill, Ferdinand Richard, Amy Denio, Lindsay Cooper, John Oswald, John Zorn, The Residents and many more...
"The talent assembled between Jones's covers would be interesting under any rubric. Thought provoking and stimulating". **Mojo**
"Jones's book is perhaps the first study of the growth of these techniques within the avant-garde. Packed with fascinating interviews and written with wit and insight". **Q magazine**

Kraftwerk - Man, Machine and Music by Pascal Bussy
ISBN: 0946 719 09 8
200 pages (illustrated). UK £11.95
Uniquely definitive account of Kraftwerk's history, delving beyond their publicity shunning exterior to reveal the full story behind one of the most influential bands in the history of rock music. Based on interviews with Ralf Hutter, Florian Schneider, Karl Bartos, Emil Schult and many more.
"Bussy engagingly explains why they are one of the few groups who've actually changed how music sounds". **Q magazine**
"I doubt this book will ever be bettered". **Vox**

Wrong Movements - A Robert Wyatt History by Mike King
ISBN: 0946 719 10 1
160 pages (illustrated). UK £14.95
A sumptuous and detailed journey through Robert Wyatt's 30 year career with Soft Machine, Matching Mole and as a highly respected solo artist. Packed with previously unpublished archive material and rare photos. Commentary from Wyatt himself, Hugh Hopper, Mike Ratledge, Daevid Allen, Kevin Ayers & more.
"King's careful chronology and Wyatt's supreme modesty produce a marvellously unhysterical, oddly haunting book". **Q magazine**
"Low key, likeable and lefty. Like the man himself". **iD magazine**

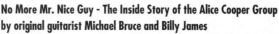

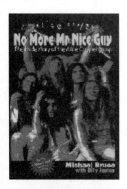

No More Mr. Nice Guy - The Inside Story of the Alice Cooper Group
by original guitarist Michael Bruce and Billy James
ISBN: 0946 719 17 9   160 pages (illustrated). UK £9.95

Michael Bruce opens the lid on his years with the platinum selling group, revealing the truth behind the publicity stunts, the dead babies, the drinking, the executions and, of course, the rock 'n' roll.

"I'm Eighteen changed Alice Cooper from the group that destroyed chickens to the group that destroyed stadiums". **Village Voice.**

"It might even be argued that the band defined what it meant to be a role ridden seventies teenager". **Rolling Stone**

Wire - Everybody Loves a History by Kevin Eden
ISBN: 0946 719 07 1
192 pages (illustrated). UK £9.95

A fascinating look at one of punk's most endearing and enduring bands, including interviews with all band members. A self-analysis of the complex motivations which have often seen the various members cross the boundaries between music and art.

"Any band or their fans could feel well served by a book like Eden's". **Vox**

"Eden delivers a sharp portrayal of the punk industry's behaviour, influence and morality". **Q magazine**

TAPE DELAY by Charles Neal
ISBN: 0946 719 02 0
256 pages (illustrated). UK £11.95

Marc Almond, Cabaret Voltaire, Nick Cave, Chris & Cosey, Coil, Foetus, Neubauten, Non, The Fall, The The, Lydia Lunch, New Order, Psychic TV, Rollins, Sonic Youth, Swans, Test Department and many more...

"A virtual Who's Who of people who've done the most to drag music out of commercial confinement". **NME**

"Intriguing and interesting". **Q magazine**

Dark Entries - Bauhaus and Beyond by Ian Shirley
ISBN: 0946 719 13 6
200 pages (illustrated). UK £11.95

The full gothic rise and fall of Bauhaus, including offshoot projects Love and Rockets, Tones on Tail, Daniel Ash, David J and Peter Murphy. Ian Shirley unravels the uncompromising story of four individuals who have consistently confounded their detractors by turning up the unexpected.

"A brilliant trench-to-toilet missive of who did what, where and when. It works brilliantly". **Alternative Press**

"Solidly researched account of goth-tinged glam". **Top Magazine**

Available From Firefly Publishing

an association between Helter Skelter and SAF Publishing

Poison Heart - Surviving The Ramones by Dee Dee Ramone and Veronica Kofman   ISBN: 0946 719 19 5
192 pages (illustrated). UK £11.95
A crushingly honest account of his life as a junkie and a Ramone.
"One of THE great rock and roll books...this is the true, awesome voice of The Ramones". **Q magazine** *****
"His story - knee deep in sex, drugs and rock and roll - is too incedent packed to be anything less than gripping". **Mojo**
"A powerful work that is both confessional and exorcising" **Time Out.**

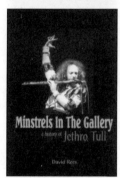

Minstrels In The Gallery - A History of Jethro Tull by David Rees
ISBN: 0 946719 22 5   224 pages (illustrated) - UK £12.99
At Last! To coincide with their 30th anniversary, a full history of one of the most popular and inventive bands of the past three decades. Born out of the British blues boom, Jethro Tull sped to worldwide success and superstardom - the band were one of the biggest grossing acts of the seventies. With LPs like *Aqualung, Thick As A Brick* and *Passion Play*, Anderson mutated from the wild-eyed tramp through flute wielding minstrel to the country squire of rock n' roll.
"Rees has interviewed all the key players and told the Tull tale with zest and candour. A fine read for Tull fans and non-believers alike." **MOJO**

DANCEMUSICSEXROMANCE - Prince: The First Decade
by Per Nilsen   ISBN: 0946 719 23 3
200 pages approx (illustrated). UK £tbc
For many years Per Nilsen has been a foremost authority on Prince. In this in-depth study of the man and his music, he assesses the years prior to the change of name to a symbol - a period which many consider to be the most productive and musically satisfying. Through interview material with many ex-band members and friends Nilsen paints a portrait of Prince's reign as the most exciting black performer to emerge since James Brown. In this behind the scenes documentary we get to the heart and soul of a funk maestro.

All Helter Skelter, Firefly and SAF titles can be ordered direct from the world famous Helter Skelter music bookstore which is situated at:

Helter Skelter,
4 Denmark Street, London WC2H 8LL
Tel: +44 (0) 171 836 1151   Fax: +44 (0) 171 240 9880.
Consult our website at: http://www.skelter.demon.co.uk

This store has the largest collection of music books anywhere in the world and can supply any in-print title by mail to any part of the globe. For a mail order catalogue or for wholesaling enquiries, please contact us.